Tolley's
Dictionary of Tax and Accountancy

D1351025

Tolley's
Dictionary of Tax
and Accountancy

David Collison FTII FCA
Tax Consultant, Cambridge

Members of the LexisNexis Group worldwide

United Kingdom	Butterworths Tolley, a Division of Reed Elsevier (UK) Ltd, Halsbury House, 35 Chancery Lane, LONDON WC2A 1EL, and 4 Hill Street, EDINBURGH EH2 3JZ
Argentina	Abeledo Perrot, Jurisprudencia Argentina and Depalma, BUENOS AIRES
Australia	Butterworths, a Division of Reed International Books Australia Pty Ltd, CHATSWOOD, New South Wales
Austria	ARD Betriebsdienst and Verlag Orac, VIENNA
Canada	Butterworths Canada Ltd, MARKHAM, Ontario
Chile	Publitecsa and Conosur Ltda, SANTIAGO DE CHILE
Czech Republic	Orac sro, PRAGUE
France	Editions du Juris-Classeur SA, PARIS
Hong Kong	Butterworths Asia (Hong Kong), HONG KONG
Hungary	Hvg Orac, BUDAPEST
India	Butterworths India, NEW DELHI
Ireland	Butterworths (Ireland) Ltd, DUBLIN
Italy	Giuffré, MILAN
Malaysia	Malayan Law Journal Sdn Bhd, KUALA LUMPUR
New Zealand	Butterworths of New Zealand, WELLINGTON
Poland	Wydawnictwa Prawnicze PWN, WARSAW
Singapore	Butterworths Asia, SINGAPORE
South Africa	Butterworths Publishers (Pty) Ltd, DURBAN
Switzerland	Stämpfli Verlag AG, BERNE
USA	LexisNexis, DAYTON, Ohio

© Reed Elsevier (UK) Ltd 2001

All rights reserved. No part of this publication may be reproduced in any material form (including photocopying or storing it in any medium by electronic means and whether or not transiently or incidentally to some other use of this publication) without the written permission of the copyright owner except in accordance with the provisions of the Copyright, Designs and Patents Act 1988 or under the terms of a licence issued by the Copyright Licensing Agency Ltd, 90 Tottenham Court Road, London, England W1P 0LP. Applications for the copyright owner's written permission to reproduce any part of this publication should be addressed to the publisher.

Warning: The doing of an unauthorised act in relation to a copyright work may result in both a civil claim for damages and criminal prosecution.

Any Crown copyright material is reproduced with the permission of the Controller of HMSO and the Queen's Printer for Scotland. Any European material in this work which has been reproduced from EUR-lex, the official European Communities legislation website, is European Communities copyright.

A CIP Catalogue record for this book is available from the British Library.

ISBN 0 75451 009-3

Typeset by M Rules, London
Printed and bound in Great Britain by William Clowes Limited, Beccles and London

Visit Butterworths LexisNexis *direct* at www.butterworths.com

Preface

My intention in constructing this dictionary is to provide a work of reference that puts words in their context and explains concepts in the two disciplines of taxation and of accountancy. I aim to provide a work that is useful for the practitioner and for the student.

For the accountant, tax matters have always been important and are often the aspect of accounting that is foremost in the client's mind. In constructing this dictionary, I aim to provide a ready reference for the practising accountant who can refer to definitions relating to his own discipline and also to the specific, and special, definitions used for taxation.

For those who specialise in tax, accounting concepts are important. In the past five years, the courts have demonstrated, again and again, that in interpreting tax matters they will consider the principles of accounting practice. Starting with Finance Act 1998, tax statutes have referred directly to accounting standards. I, therefore, in this volume, incorporate the definitions used by the bodies responsible for setting accounting standards, so these are readily accessible to the tax practitioner. Where a definition is taken from an accounting standard, the name of the accounting standard is given in square brackets.

Most definitions given in this volume carry a reference to a source. The reader who needs to consider a definition further can, thus, refer to the statute or the court decision or the accounting standard in which the term is defined. It must, of course, be remembered that a definition is given for a specified purpose. In tax legislation, in particular, a definition frequently applies solely to a particular tax charge.

This volume explains terms. It is not an explanation of how a tax charge or a tax relief operates. For that, the practitioner and student should refer to its sister volume *Simon's Tiley and Collison: UK Tax Guide*, published in September each year by Butterworths Tolley, which describes and explains the many aspects of the UK tax system.

For both taxation and accounting, principles of general law are important. I have, therefore, included definitions of those legal terms that I feel are most relevant to taxation and accountancy. For many legal terms, I am indebted to Dr James Penner of LSE Law Faculty who readily agreed to my using material he has written for Mozley and Whiteley's Law Dictionary, also published by Butterworths Tolley.

This is the first edition of this work. My intention is to update the text from time to time to reflect the continual development of concepts and principles, as well as to reflect the Government's enthusiasm for inventing at least one new term in each year's Finance Act. I would be very pleased to hear from any readers who would like to suggest further terms that could usefully be included or aspects of existing terms that could be developed.

David Collison
Cambridge, September 2001.

A

ACA. Associate of the Institute of Chartered Accountants in England and Wales.

ACCA. Associate of the Chartered Association of Certified Accountants.

AGM. Annual general meeting.

ATII. Associate of the Chartered Institute of Taxation. *(When established in 1930, the letters stood for Associate of the Taxation Institute Incorporated.)*

AVC. Additional voluntary contribution.

'A' list. A list of the present members of the company made out by the liquidator in the course of winding-up who are primarily liable to contribute to the assets of the company.
See CONTRIBUTORY.

Abandon. To cease to hold, use, or practice; to give up, renounce (OED).

(1) Expenditure on a project that is abandoned can be a tax 'nothing' (that is, there is no income tax or corporation tax relief), unless the expenditure can be shown to have been incurred as part of a continuing trade and is correctly shown in accordance with commercial accounting practice to be a deduction in computing the profits of that trade. Statute provides relief for certain categories of abandonment expenditure in the oil industry (FA 1991, ss 62–66).

(2) If a capital sum is received on the abandonment of a right, this is likely to be a disposal for CGT (TCGA 1992, s 22); applied to the abandonment or rights in an employee's contract in *O'Brien v Benson's Hosiery (Holdings) Limited [1978] STC 549, CA* but there is probably no CGT charge if the sum is received to the surrender of something which is not an asset (for example, the right to play amateur rugby – *Jarrold v Baustead (1964) 41 TC 701*).

(3) When an individual abandons his/her domicile of choice, the individual's domicile reverts to the domicile of origin. 'A person abandons a domicile of choice in a country by ceasing to reside there and by ceasing to intend to reside there permanently or indefinitely and not otherwise' (per North J – *IRC v Duchess of Portland [1992] STC 149 at 155a* quoting, with approval rule 13(1) in *Dicey & Morris* The Conflict of Laws 10th Edition 1980 page 128 paraphrasing *Udny v Udny 1869 LR1 SC & Div 441*).

(4) RIGHT(s) or CLAIM(s). The giving up or WAIVER of a legal right or claim by failing to pursue it or prosecute it in a timely fashion, often inferred from the right- or claim-holders acting inconsistently with it, eg inferring a LESSOR's abandonment of his right to evict a LESSEE following his giving a notice to his lessee to quit the leased property by thereafter accepting further rent under the LEASE.

Abatement. (1) *In commerce* it means a deduction made from payments due.

(2) *Abatement amongst creditors* takes place where the assets of a debtor are not sufficient to pay his creditors in full, so that they are compelled to share the assets in proportion to their debts.

(3) *Abatement amongst legatees* in like manner is enforced where there are not sufficient assets to pay the legacies in full. But pecuniary or general legacies abate proportionally before specific legacies and before demonstrative legacies until the fund out of which the latter are payable is exhausted; and 'in addition' a legacy may be expressly preferred to another of the same class.
See LEGACY.

Abbreviated accounts. A company that is within the definition of 'a small company' or 'a medium sized company' is entitled to file for public access with the Registrar of Companies a set of abbreviated accounts (Companies Act 1985, s 246). These accounts show a Balance Sheet (specified in Companies Act 1985, s 8A) but considerably fewer notes to the Balance Sheet than are required for full statutory accounts. A small company is not required to include in its abbreviated accounts a Profit and Loss Account, although this is necessary for a medium sized company (Companies Act 1985, s 256A).

Abnormal dividend. An abnormal dividend is one of the five circumstances that triggers the transaction in securities legislation (TA 1988, ss 703–709) to cancel a tax advantage. A dividend is regarded as abnormal if (*a*) it substantially exceeds a normal return on the consideration provided paid for securities or (*b*) it is a dividend at a fixed rate and substantially exceeds the amount which the recipient would have received if the dividend had accrued from day to day and he had been entitled only to so much of the dividend as accrued while he held the securities (TA 1988, s 709(4)). (For the Revenue view, see Inland Revenue *Tax Bulletin*, Issue 5, November 1992; see also *Cedar plc v Inspector of Taxes [1998] STC (SCD) 78.*) This special rule applies only if he sells or acquires a right to sell those or similar securities within six months. A charity or pension fund that receives an abnormally high dividend can be treated under these provisions as having obtained 'relief' from tax, even though it enjoys an exemption from tax in respect of ordinary dividends (*IRC v Universities Superannuation Scheme Ltd [1977] STC 1*).

Abode. A man's residence, where he lives with his family and sleeps at night. It may include a place where the person in question works and has his business. In *Cooper v Cadwalader (1904) TC 101*, an American was held to be resident in the UK for the fiscal year because he had an abode (a shooting lodge) in Scotland, which he visited during the year. Since the enactment of TA 1988, s 336(3) by FA 1993, s 208, the Inland Revenue have not treated an individual as resident in the UK solely on the basis of having a place of abode but the existence of a place of abode may undermine an argument that the taxpayer has left the UK permanently and it is also taken into account in deciding whether a person coming to the UK is treated as resident from the date of arrival. The existence of a place of abode in the foreign country is regarded by the Revenue as significant in judging a claim that a taxpayer has a foreign domicile.

Above the line. In accounting theory, there is a line drawn on the Profit and Loss Account separating the entries that compute the profit or loss from the entries that show how profit is distributed. The first set of entries is referred to as 'above the line'. FAS 3, introduced in October 1992, specifies that both exceptional and extraordinary items that arise from the activities of the business should be shown 'above the line'. The effect of this is that published earnings for share figures incorporate items such as sale of a headquarters building for a large profit (or at a loss). Since 1992, some companies have quoted the earnings per share figure on the basis specified in the accounting standard and also given an earnings per share calculated without the extraordinary and exceptional items in the year's Profit and Loss Account.

Absolute interest. The charge to income tax on income arising from a beneficiary's entitlement to an estate of a deceased person depends on whether the beneficiary's interest is absolute or limited (TA 1988, s 696 cf s 695). A beneficiary has an absolute interest in residue if, on the hypothesis that the administration were then complete, he would be entitled to the capital or a part of it in his own right (TA 1988, s 701(2)).
Contrast LIMITED INTEREST.

Abus de droit. A concept in French law, and the the law of other European civil law jurisdictions. There are two aspects of abus de droit. The first is a notion of the statutory French code and enables the administration to attack agreements freely intended and concluded by the party, by requalifying their nature and reconstituting the reality of the operations to reassess the tax due. The second has developed in a European context to consider the principles defining the manner and the extent to which a state, an institution or a person within the European union may use principles of community law to avoid rules of domestic legislation to which they may otherwise be subject. The principle of abus de droit is said to have been used by the VAT Tribunal in *Halifax plc* (1 March 2001) when the Tribunal defeated a scheme operated by Halifax Group to obtain 100% recovery of input VAT by putting into companies specially created for the purpose any supplies that were subject to partial exemption, thereby seeking to maximise the VAT recovery. However, in that case, Stephen Oliver QC, President of the VAT Tribunal, took steps to avoid the automatic assumption that the case was a direct application of the concept of abus de droit, by concluding his judgment with the words: '. . . it would be unnecessary, inconsistent and potentially misleading if we were to express views on the hypothetical application of that principle to the present circumstances'.

Acceptable distribution policy. Profits of a controlled foreign company are subjected to UK corporation tax by an assessment on its UK parent company. These rules do not apply if the foreign company follows an acceptable distribution policy. The conditions which must be met to satisfy this test are: (*a*) a dividend is paid by the foreign company for the accounting period in question; (*b*) it is paid during or within 18 months after that period (the Revenue may extend the time allowed for this); (*c*) the company distributes by way of dividend an amount not less than 90% of its available profits for the accounting period to UK residents and (*d*) the dividend is subject to UK tax in the hands of the company (TA 1988, Sch 25, paras 1–4). Where the company fulfils these conditions for a particular accounting period, that period is called an 'ADP exempt period' (TA 1988, Sch 24, para 1(6)).

Acceptance. (1) In CONTRACT LAW, acceptance of an offer may be made by express words or may be inferred from conduct showing an unqualified intention to accept. A mere intention to accept not shown by words or conduct is insufficient.

(2) If a LEASE for more than three years is made verbally it is normally invalid for not being in writing, but acceptance of rent from the LESSEE if he obtained possession will create a tenancy from year to year binding on the LESSOR; and on the same principle, acceptance of rent may confirm a lease, which has been put an end to by notice, the acceptance here operating as a withdrawal, WAIVER or abandonment of the notice.

(3) A buyer is deemed to have accepted goods when he intimates to the seller that he has accepted them, or when the goods have been delivered to him, and he does any act in relation to them which is inconsistent with the ownership of the seller, or when after the lapse of a reasonable time he retains the goods without intimating to the seller that he has rejected them (see Sale of Goods Act 1979, s 35).

Accident. In the Social Security Contributions and Benefits Act 1992 the word is used in the popular and ordinary sense and means a mishap or untoward event, not expected or designed.

Account. A statement of the transactions concerning a fund of property, especially the funds of a trust or a company, or of credits and liabilities between contracting parties. Regarding the latter, an open, or current, account is one of which the 'balance', ie the concluding statement of the account which expresses the current position of the account, is not 'struck', ie not accepted by all interested parties. A stated account is no longer open or current, but closed by the statement, agreed to by both the parties, of a balance due to the one or other of them. A stated account is settled where balances due to one party or another are paid, closing the account.

Account, action of, claim for an. An action of account or claim for an account is a case in which the CLAIMANT demands an accounting by the defendant of his stewardship over a fund of property, most typically, a claim by the BENEFICIARY of a TRUST for a trustee to account for his transactions with the trust property. The trustee will be liable for any misdealings with the trust property that the account reveals, and so the action of account is typically brought as a means of remedying a breach of trust, and a trustee's general liability to beneficiaries can be called his 'liability to account'.

Accounting bases. The methods developed for applying fundamental accounting concepts to financial transactions and items, for the purpose of financial accounts, and in particular (*a*) for determining the accounting periods in which revenue and costs should be recognised in the profit and loss account and (*b*) for determining the amounts at which material items should be stated in the balance sheet. [SSAP 2 – Disclosure of accounting policies]

Accounting concepts. *See* FUNDAMENTAL ACCOUNTING CONCEPTS.

Accounting date. The date to which a company makes up its accounts (TA 1988, s 843).

Accounting entity. A fundamental accounting concept is to identify the entity for which accounts are constructed. Sometimes, this will be an entity that in law is recognised as a 'person', such as a limited company or a Scottish partnership. Frequently, an accounting entity is not a 'person' in law. It may be the business of a sole trader, an English partnership, a division of a company, a fund in a trust or a particular appeal made by a charity. When accounts are drawn up for an accounting entity, accounting practice is to treat the trade of the accounting entity as separate from any other activities. This means that a transaction between an individual in his personal capacity, for example, and the trade he carries on as a sole trader is recognised in the accounts, with debtors and creditors appearing in the Balance Sheet to show sums due one from the other. Similarly, rent paid by a partnership to one or more individual partners is recognised as an expense of the partnership trade.

Accounting equation. The equation that forms the basis of accounting practice:
Opening balance sheet + Profits – Drawings = Closing balance sheet

Accounting period. (1) A company's liability to corporation tax is on the profits of an accounting period (TA 1988, s 8(3)). An accounting period is usually one of a number of successive periods for which the company makes up its accounts. An accounting period cannot exceed 12 months. When the company makes up accounts for a period of account exceeding 12 months, the accounting period will end 12 months after the start of the company's period of account and a new one begins. When a company draws up accounts, the accounting date to which the accounts are drawn determines the accounting period(s) for assessment of the company's profits. The Revenue have no power to substitute an accounting period which they would prefer. Once an assessment is raised for an accounting period, that assessment cannot be revised by virtue of the inspector wishing to use a different period as the accounting period (*Kelsall v Stipplechoice Ltd [1995] STC 681, CA*).

(2) For insurance premium tax an accounting period is a three-month period. This will be the period notified on the taxpayer's certificate of registration or, if the taxpayer is not registered, a calendar quarter (FA 1994, s 54 & SI 1994/1774, reg 2).

(3) For landfill tax an accounting period is a three-month period. This will be the period notified on the taxpayer's certificate of registration or, if the taxpayer is not registered, a calendar quarter (FA 1996, s 49 & SI 1996/1527, reg 2(1)).

Accounting policies. (1) The specific accounting bases selected and consistently followed by a business enterprise as being, in the opinion of the management, appropriate to its circumstances and best suited to present fairly its results and financial position. [SSAP 2 – Disclosure of accounting policies]

(2) The specific principles, bases, conventions, rules and practices applied by an entity in order to reflect the effects of transactions and other events through recognising, selecting measurement bases for, and presenting assets, liabilities, gains, losses and changes to shareholders' funds. Accounting policies do not include estimation techniques. [FRED 21 – Accounting policies]

Accounting profit. The amount of profit for an accounting entity calculated by using accounting principles without any adjustment to confirm to specific rules for taxation. Before computing accounting profit it is first necessary to decide which accounting policies are most appropriate for the particular accounting entity and the particular purpose for which accounting profit is to be measured.
See PROFITS.

Accounting standard. *See* FINANCIAL REPORTING STANDARD.

Accruals concept. A fundamental basis of accounting. Revenue and costs are accrued (that is, recognised as they are earned or incurred, not as money is received or paid); matched with one another so far as their relationship can be established or justifiably assumed, and dealt with in the profit and loss account of the period to which they relate; provided that where the accruals concept is inconsistent with the 'prudence' concept, the latter prevails. The accruals concept implies that the profit and loss account reflects changes in the amount of net assets that arise out of the transactions of the relevant period (other than distributions or subscriptions of capital and unrealised surpluses arising on revaluation of fixed assets). Revenue and profits dealt with in the profit and loss account are matched with associated costs and expenses by including in the same account the costs incurred in earning them (so far as these are material and identifiable). [SSAP 2 – Disclosure of accounting policies]

Accrue. *Lit* to grow to, as interest accrues to principal.

Accrued benefits. The benefits for service up to a given point in time, whether the rights to the benefits are vested or not. They may be calculated in relation to current earnings or projected final earnings. [SSAP 24 – Accounting for pension costs]

An accrued benefits method of actuarial valuation is a valuation method in which the actuarial value of liabilities relate at a given date to: (*a*) the benefits, including future increases promised by the rules, for the current and deferred pensioners and their dependants; and (*b*) the benefits which the members assumed to be in service on the given date will receive for service up to that date only. Allowance may be made for expected increases in earnings after the given date, and/or for additional pension increases not promised by the rules. The given date may be a current or future date. The further into the future the adopted date lies, the closer the results will be to those of a prospective benefits valuation method. [SSAP 24 – Accounting for pension costs]

Accumulation. When the income of a TRUST fund, eg bank account interest or dividends on shares, instead of being paid over to some person or persons as it arises, is invested so as to be reserved for the benefit of some person or persons in the future, the income is said to be accumulated. For a trust under English law (other than a charitable trust), income arising can be accumulated for the first 21 years only by virtue of the rules against perpetuities, and the Law of Property Act 1925, ss 164–166. Income arising more than 21 years after the creation of the trust must be distributed. (Case law seems to indicate that the distribution should be within 18 months of the end of the year in which the income arises.) For a trust under Jersey law, income can be accumulated throughout the 100 years for which a trust is allowed to exist.
See PERPETUITY; TRUST.

Accumulation and maintenance settlement. When a trust satisfies the conditions for an accumulation and maintenance settlement, the property in trust is not 'relevant property' and so the ten-year and exit charges are not imposed (IHTA 1984, s 58). In addition the legislation provides that there is to be no charge where the beneficiary becomes beneficially entitled to, or to an interest in possession in, settled property on or before attaining the age specified in the trust deed; similarly there is to be no charge on the death of a beneficiary before attaining the specified age (IHTA 1984, s 71(4)). Unlike transfers into most other trusts, a transfer to an accumulation and maintenance trust by an individual is a potentially exempt transfer (IHTA 1984, s 3A(3)). An accumulation and maintenance trust is narrowly defined as a settlement that fulfils three conditions: Condition (1) one or more persons (in this paragraph referred to as beneficiaries) will, on or before attaining a specified age not exceeding 25, become entitled to, or to an interest in possession in, the settled property or part of it; Condition (2) no interest in possession subsists in the settled property or part and the income from it is to be accumulated so far as not applied for the maintenance, education or benefit of a beneficiary; and Condition (3) either: (*a*) not more than 25 years have elapsed since the day on which the settlement was made or, if it was later, since the time (or latest time) when conditions 1 and 2 above became satisfied with respect to the property (ie 25 years since the settlement was created or it became an accumulation and maintenance settlement); or (*b*) all the persons who are or have been beneficiaries are or were either grandchildren of a common grandparent or children, widows or widowers of such grandchildren who were themselves beneficiaries but died before the time when, had they survived, they would have become entitled as mentioned in condition 1 (above) (IHTA 1984, s 71(2)).

Condition 1 causes one to be wary of wide powers of appointment and of their exercise. Thus in *Inglewood v IRC* (*[1983] STC 133*) the fact that the appointment in favour of a beneficiary could be revoked and resettled on trusts outside these rules meant that it was not certain that he would become entitled and so the reliefs did not apply.

Acknowledgment. A declaration or avowal of an act or document so as to give it legal validity (OED, 1651).

(1) Of debt, if in writing signed by the debtor or his agent, will prevent the limitation period from running except as from the date of such acknowledgment. Similarly, as regards acknowledgment of title to land (see Limitation Act 1980, s 29).

(2) Of signature to a will by testator. If the signature is not made in the presence of two witnesses, its subsequent acknowledgment in their presence will satisfy the Wills Act 1837.

Acquisition. A business combination that is not a merger. [FRS 6 – Acquisitions and mergers]. FRS 7 – Fair values in acquisition accounting requires that the business combination be accounted for by using the acquisition method of accounting.

Acquisitions. Operations of the reporting entity that are acquired in the period. [FRS 3 – Reporting financial performance]

Act of God. An extraordinary occurrence or circumstance which could not have been foreseen and which could not have been guarded against; an accident due to natural causes, as eg a destructive storm, or a sudden and unforeseen death.

Active market. A market of sufficient depth to absorb the investment held without a significant effect on the price. [FRS 1 – Cash flow statements (revised 1996)]

Active trust. A trust requiring some active duties on the part of the trustee.
See BARE TRUST; TRUST.

Actuarial gains and losses. Changes in actuarial deficits or surpluses that arise because: (*a*) events have not coincided with the actuarial assumptions made for the last valuation (experience gains and losses) or (*b*) the actuarial assumptions have changed. [FRED 20 – Retirement Benefits]

Actuarial liability. The value placed on the liability of a defined benefit scheme for outgoings due after the valuation date. An actuarial liability measured using the projected unit method reflects the benefits that the employer is committed to provide for service up to the valuation date. [FRED 20 – Retirement Benefits]

Additional voluntary contributions. The maximum contribution to an exempt approved occupational pension scheme is normally limited to 15% of the employee's annual remuneration (or the earnings cap, if lower). Most employers operate schemes that make regular contributions that are less than 15% and, in any event, remuneration for the purpose of the limit includes commissions, bonuses and taxable benefits charged under Schedule E whereas employee contributions required under an employer's scheme rules are usually based on salary alone. Consequently many employees are able to make additional contributions to those required under the scheme rules without exceeding the 15% of remuneration limit. Such contributions are termed 'additional voluntary contributions' or AVCs. For many years the majority of exempt approved schemes have offered the employee the facility of making AVCs and the Social Security Act 1986, s 12 made it mandatory for members to be given this opportunity as of right from 6 April 1988.

The Government as part of its overall policy of giving employees greater freedom of choice in how they provide for their retirement has taken steps to enable employees to make AVCs to new freestanding schemes. Such schemes are governed by supplementary practice notes (IR 12) and first became available as from 26 October 1987. A freestanding AVC scheme is one which is established by the employee and is completely separate from the employer's scheme. A freestanding AVC scheme is a form of exempt approved scheme: a distinguishing feature is that only the employee (and if the scheme is used for contracting out of SERPS, the DSS) can make contributions.

Ad valorem (according to the value). A duty, the amount of which depends on the value of the property taxed, is called an *ad valorem* duty. Stamp duties are divided into ad valorem duties (such as the duty at ½% on the consideration given for the purchase of shares) and fixed duties (typically £5 on any stampable document on which there is not ad valorem duty).

Ademption of a legacy. The implied revocation of a BEQUEST in a WILL by some subsequent act of the testator, eg when a specific CHATTEL is bequeathed, and the testator afterwards sells it, the gift is said to adeem, and can, of course, not take effect; ademption also occurs when a parent bequeaths a legacy to his child and afterwards makes a separate provision for the child in satisfaction of it.

Adjudication. The special nature of stamp duties is illustrated by the adjudication process which enables the correct amount of duty to be determined—usually conclusively—by the Revenue. Any person may require the Commissioners to express their opinion on the liability to duty or the amount due. In some instances adjudication is compulsory: (*a*) conveyance in contemplation of sale; (*b*) orders made under the Variation of Trusts Act 1958; and (*c*) orders made under the Companies Act 1985, s 427. It is also required when relief or exemption is claimed under: (*a*) FA 1930, s 42 (transfer between associated companies); (*b*) FA 1980, s 98 (maintenance funds for historic buildings); (*c*) FA 1980, s 102 (conveyances in consideration of a debt); (*d*) FA 1982, s 129 and FA 1983, s 46 (for conveyances, transfers or leases to charities or the National Heritage Memorial Fund or the Historic Buildings and Monuments Commission for England); (*e*) FA 1986, ss 75–77 (reconstruction of companies and acquisition of share capital); (*f*) FA 1995, s 151 (lease or tack or agreement for lease or tack between associated bodies); (*g*) FA 1997, s 96 (demutualisation of insurance companies). Apart from satisfying statutory requirements the main advantages in requesting adjudication is that the instrument is—if duly stamped under the adjudication process—admissible for all purposes; thus it is the most that can be done to convince third parties. The process is also the first step in disputing the Stamp Office's view of the correct amount of duty.

Adjudication stamp. Following adjudication, the instrument *may* be stamped with the amount of duty determined and a further stamp—the adjudication stamp—denoting that it is duly stamped or with a stamp to show that it is not chargeable. There is in general no statutory obligation to pay the duty assessed subject, however, to a fine of £300 if the duty assessed following an adjudication has not been paid within 30 days, under SA 1891, s 12A(2).

Adjusting events. Post balance sheet events which provide additional evidence of conditions existing at the balance sheet date. They include events which because of statutory or conventional requirements are reflected in the financial statements. [SSAP 17 – Accounting for post balance sheet events]

Adjustment. In INSURANCE law, the settling of the amount of the loss, and of the INDEMNITY which the assured is entitled to receive, and, in the case of several UNDERWRITERS, of the proportion which each underwriter is liable to pay in respect thereof.

Administration. (1) The administration of a deceased's estate; ie, getting in the debts due to the deceased, and paying his creditors to the extent of his assets, and otherwise distributing his estate to the persons who are by law entitled to it. The person charged with this duty is spoken of as 'executor' or 'administrator', according as he has been appointed by the deceased in his will, or by the Chancery Division. See also the Administration of Estates Act 1925, and the Supreme Court Act 1981. Also applied to the execution of a trust.

(2) The affairs of a bankrupt are in administration when administered by his trustee. *See* EXECUTOR.

(3) The Queen's ministers, or collectively the Government are often called the *Administration*, as charged with the administration or management of public affairs. The administration of justice by judges, magistrates, etc.

Administration period. The period from the date of death to the completion of the administration of the estate (TA 1988, s 695(1)). The administration is 'completed' when the personal representatives have ascertained all assets and liabilities.

Admissibility. The failure to stamp a document (unlike a failure to pay income tax) is not an offence and, in general, the Crown cannot sue for duty on an unstamped instrument. However, an unstamped document has reduced admissibility. The Stamp Act 1891 imposes a number of restrictions in respect of unstamped or insufficiently stamped instruments (SA 1891, ss 14, 17).

It is expressly provided that an instrument which is not duly stamped in accordance with the law in force at the time when it was first executed 'shall not, except in criminal proceedings, be given in evidence, or be available for any purpose whatsoever . . .' (SA 1891, s 14(4)). This cannot be remedied by the consent of the parties (*Nixon v Albion Marine Insurance Co (1867) LR 2 Exch 338*). The instrument is not admissible whether directly or for a collateral purpose (*Fengl v Fengl [1914] P 274*); nor is secondary evidence of the instrument admissible (*Hamilton Finance Co Ltd v Coverley Westray Waltaum & Toseti Ltd [1969] 1 Lloyd's Rep 53*); cross-examination upon an unstamped document is not allowed (*Baker v Dale (1858) 1 F & F*) but unstamped instruments are admissible to refresh a witness's memory (*Birchall v Bullough [1896] 1 QB 325*) and to prove fraud (*Re Shaw (1920) 90 LJ KB*) or an act of bankruptcy (*Re Gunsbourg (1919) 88 LJ KB 204*). It has also been held that a plaintiff need not stamp an instrument when he was trying to prevent the transaction from being implemented and was arguing that the agreement was void (*Mason v Motor Traction Co [1905] 1 Ch 419*). The prohibition on admissibility does not extend to criminal proceedings, nor apparently, to rent tribunals since these are not courts of law. This reasoning could be extended to proceedings before the Commissioners of Income Tax but not to the High Court on appeal by way of case stated. The words 'available for any purpose whatever' mean that one party cannot compel another to rely on and accept as having legal effect an instrument which is not duly stamped (*Marx v Estates and General Investments [1975] 3 All ER 1064 at 1072*). In practice, the Inland Revenue will refuse to give effect to unstamped instruments. For example, the Stamp Office will not accept that fixed duty is payable on a transfer of land on the basis that the beneficial interest in the land has been conveyed by an unstamped instrument held overseas: if the assignment of the beneficial interest is on sale, the transfer will be assessed with ad valorem duty calculated by reference to the consideration for the sale. This view has been confirmed as correct by the Court of Appeal (*Parinv (Hatfield) Ltd v IRC [1998] STC 305*). The effect of the general rule as to late stamping on payment of a penalty is that the defect of non-stamping is inherently remediable. One consequence of this is that it is unprofessional for counsel to object to the admissibility of the document for non-stamping unless the case is a revenue case or the defect goes to the validity of the document (Boulton, *Conduct and Etiquette at the Bar* (6th edn) p. 70).

Administration order. An order directing that, during the period for which it is in force, the affairs, business and property of a company are to be managed by an administrator appointed for the purpose by the Court (see Insolvency Act 1986, s 8(2)). The Court may make such an order if it is satisfied that a company is or is likely to become unable to pay its debts and considers that the making of an order would be likely to achieve eg the survival of the company as a going concern or a more advantageous realisation of its assets than would be effected on a winding up (see ibid, s 8(1), (3)).

Administration suit. A suit instituted for the ADMINISTRATION of a deceased's ESTATE. This suit may be instituted by an executor or administrator, or any person interested in the deceased's estate as CREDITOR, legatee, NEXT OF KIN, etc.

Administrative law. A branch of public law which deals with the rightful exercise of the powers of the various organs of the state or other public bodies, in particular the power of courts to control the action of these bodies by reviewing their actions or decisions by the process known as judicial review, ie the assessment by a judge or judges of a superior court of the legality or correctness of an inferior tribunal or administrative agency's actions. Administrative law concerns the rules and procedures by which the courts give effect to that settlement in a detailed way as a matter of day-to-day oversight to ensure that particular organs of the state do not act in excess of their powers, or fail to act to carry out their duties. In particular, administrative law concerns the power of the courts to control the conduct of various local authorities, commissions, tribunals, agencies, and other bodies given powers to act under statutes, ie by Act of Parliament, to ensure that they act in accordance with the powers granted them, and so many cases in administrative law concern claims by affected individuals that a public body has acted *ultra vires*, ie in excess of the powers granted it by Parliament. With respect to administrative agencies or tribunals which are not courts of justice but which act in a *quasi*-judicial capacity, ie render decisions which have an adjudicative nature, the courts have sometimes required such bodies to observe the rules of 'natural justice', chiefly to act fairly in good faith, and in particular so as to ensure that adjudicators are not biased in favour of one side or the other and that each party has an opportunity to adequately state his case (the principle of *audi alteram partem*, hear the other side). Traditionally, the three most important administrative law actions were actions for the prerogative orders of *certiorari, mandamus*, and prohibition.

Administrator. A person to whom the administration of the estate of a deceased is committed by letters of administration from the Chancery Division in cases where the deceased left no will, or when the executor acting under a will is out of the realm, where the validity of the will itself is questioned, or *cum testamento annexo*, where the testator has left a will and has not appointed an executor, or where the testator has appointed an executor who is either unable or unwilling to act.

If a stranger, ie a person who is neither administrator nor executor, takes the goods of the deceased, and administers of his own wrong, he may be charged and sued not as an administrator but as an executor *de son tort. See* EXECUTOR DE SON TORT.

See ADMINISTRATION.

Administratrix. A woman to whom administration is granted.

See ADMINISTRATION; ADMINISTRATOR.

Adult. A person who has attained full age, now 18.

Adverse opinion. Where an audit is required, whether by company law or by other controlling regulations, the auditor is required to report as to whether, in his opinion, the financial statements give a true and fair view of the profits and loss and state of affairs of the accounting entity for the period stated. If the auditor considers that the financial statements do not give a true and fair view, he is required to state this in his audit report. Such a statement is an 'adverse opinion'.

See QUALIFIED REPORT; AUDITORS' REPORT.

Agent. A person authorised, expressly or impliedly, to act for another (called the principal) and who is, in consequence of, and to the extent of, the authority delegated by him, bound by the acts of his agent. This term includes most kinds of agents, eg factors and brokers, and the stewards of landowners. Agents may be either *general*, who can bind their principals in all matters of a class, or *special*, in a particular transaction only. The agent is not usually personally liable.

Agent of necessity. A person who pledges the credit of another when urgent reasons make it necessary to do so, eg the master of a ship purchasing goods necessary for the continuance of the voyage. Such acts are binding on the principal.

Aggregates Levy. Aggregates Levy is a levy on the commercial exploitation of aggregate (FA 2001, ss 17(1) & 18). It is introduced to tackle the environmental costs of quarrying and to encourage the use of recycled materials.

Aggregates Levy applies to rock, sand and gravel and substances incorporated in the rock, sand or gravel, or naturally occurring substances mixed with rock, sand or gravel, extracted in the UK or its territorial waters (FA 2001, s 48(1) & (3)). Recycled aggregate does not attract the Aggregates Levy. Aggregate becomes liable to the Levy when it is commercially exploited. In practical terms this means earliest of:

(a) physical removal from the site where it was extracted (FA 2001, s 48(3)) (except when it is moved to another site which is registered (FA 2001, s 24) in the same name as in the originating site (FA 2001, s 20);
(b) sale to another person;
(c) use for construction purposes (FA 2001, s 48(2));
(d) mixing with anything which is not chargeable aggregate or water.

Anyone commercially exploiting aggregate in the UK is affected. Usually this is the operator (FA 2001, s 21) of the site where the aggregate is extracted (FA 2001, s 48(3)), although it could be the owner of the aggregate. Anyone importing aggregate from outside the UK and agreeing to supply it or using it for construction purposes (FA 2001, s 48(2)) is also affected. Exports of aggregate are relieved, while imports of aggregate are taxed on their first sale or use in the UK.

Aggregates Levy is administered by HM Customs and Excise. The law is contained in FA 2001, ss 16–19 and Schs 4–10. The Levy is due to come into force on a date to be specified by statutory instrument. This is likely to be 1 April 2002.

Agreement. The consent or joining together of two minds in respect of anything done or to be done; also the written evidence of such consent. An agreement, or *contract*, exists either where a promise is made on one side, and assented to on the other; or where two or more persons enter into an engagement with each other, by a promise on either side.

See CONTRACT.

Agreement to sell. A contract of sale whereby the transfer of the property in the goods is to take place at a future time or subject to some condition later to be fulfilled: Sale of Goods Act 1979, s 2(5). The agreement becomes a sale when the time elapses or the conditions are fulfilled subject to which the property in the goods is to be transferred: ibid, s 2(6).

Agricultural Buildings Allowance. A capital allowance which may be claimed by a person with a major interest in agricultural land who incurs capital expenditure on the construction of farmhouses, farm buildings, cottages, fences and other works, eg drainage (CAA 2001, ss 361, 369, 370, 371). The allowance takes the form of a writing-down allowance over 25 years, ie 4% pa straight line (CAA 2001, s 373(1)). The expenditure must have been incurred for the purposes of husbandry (CAA 2001, s 362(1)(a)).

Agricultural holding. The aggregate of the land (whether agricultural land or not) comprised in a contract of tenancy (see the Agricultural Holdings Act 1986, s 1(1)).
See AGRICULTURAL LAND.

Agricultural land. Land used for agriculture and so used for the purposes of a trade or business (see Agricultural Holdings Act 1986, s 1(4)). It is also defined by the General Rate Act 1967, s 26(3), as extended by the Rating Act 1971, to mean any land used as arable meadow or pasture ground only, land used for a plantation or wood, etc, certain cottage gardens, orchards, allotments, livestock buildings, buildings occupied in connection with bee-keeping, etc, but excluding other classes of land such as parks, pleasure grounds and racecourses.

Agricultural property. Agricultural property attracts 100% relief for inheritance tax. Agricultural property is defined as meaning agricultural land or pasture and as including the woodlands (as distinct from the timber) and buildings for intensive fish-farming or livestock-rearing if occupied with such land or pasture (IHTA 1984, s 115(2)). Short rotational coppice is agricultural land for this purpose. Stud farms qualify, but a meadow used for horses to graze does not qualify, where the horses are not used to pull the plough or otherwise in connection with agriculture (*Wheatley v IRC [1998] STC (SCD) 60*). Sport is not agriculture (*Earl of Normanton v Giles [1980] 1 WLR 28*) but land in habitat schemes qualifies (IHTA 1984, s 124C). Such property also includes such cottages, farm buildings and farm houses as are of a character appropriate to the property.

Agricultural value. IHT agricultural property relief is given against the agricultural value of property; no relief is given against any additional value that the property may have, such as an increased value of land in the hope that development for non-agricultural purposes may occur. For IHT purposes, the agricultural value is the value that the property concerned would have if it were subject to a perpetual covenant prohibiting its use otherwise than as agricultural property (IHTA 1984, s 115(3)).

Agriculture. Includes horticulture, fruit growing, seed growing, dairy farming and livestock breeding and keeping, the use of land as grazing land, meadow land, osier land, market gardens and nursery grounds and the preparation of land for agricultural use (see Health and Safety at Work etc Act 1974, s 53(1)).

Allocation. A portion of revenue, etc, assigned to a special person or purpose (OED, 1658)

(1) In drawing up a set of accounts, it is necessary to allocate costs to a cost centre. This is particularly important in cost accounting. If a particular cost cannot be allocated to a single cost centre, the cost is reflected in the accounts by the technique of apportionment or the technique of absorption.

(2) The number of shares allotted to an investor in a new issue of shares by a company.

Allotment. When a company intends to issue new shares, it may make the issue available to existing members pro-rata to their existing shareholders, or may advertise the issue of shares by means of a prospectus, or may make the issue in connection with the granting of shares to employees, as approved by the members. In any of these cases, the company is required to send each person to whom shares are to be issued a letter of allotment stating how many shares have been allotted. In the case of an allotment made by a listed company in respect of shares that are listed or are to be listed, it is a requirement that the shareholder's application be accompanied by a cheque for the full value of the shares and the letter of allotment must enclose a cheque for any unallotted balance. Where applications have been received by the company for a number of shares in excess of that which is to be issued (ie there has been over-subscription), it is acceptable for allotment to be made by a proportional allocation or alternatively by a random draw.

Allotment letter. Of shares in a company concluding the contract to take shares.

Allowance. *See* PERSONAL ALLOWANCES.

Alteration in deeds or other documents generally vitiates the instrument if made in a material part after execution. In deeds an alteration is presumed to have been made before or at the time of execution; in wills, after execution; and see Wills Act 1837, s 21. As to bills of exchange, see the Bills of Exchange Act 1882.

Amalgamation. The combination of two or more companies or their businesses into one company or into the control of one company. *See* Companies Act 1985, ss 425–427.

Ambiguity. Uncertainty of meaning in the words of a written instrument. Where the doubt arises on the face of the instrument itself, eg a blank is left for a name, the ambiguity is said to be *patent*, as distinguished from a *latent* ambiguity, where the doubt is introduced by collateral circumstances or extrinsic matter, the meaning of the words alone being *prima facie* sufficiently clear and intelligible.

Amendment. A correction of any errors in writ or pleadings in actions or prosecutions. Large powers of amendment have been given by modern statutes.

Amortisation. (1) Where an accounting entity has incurred an expense that relates to more than one period of account, the expense is amortised over a number of periods. The term 'depreciation' is usually applied to the process of spreading cost when the purchase has been of a tangible asset. The term 'amortisation' is used when the purchase has been of a leasehold interest, or other intangible right. It is customary to amortise the premium on a lease over the period of the lease, or the period to the next rent review. If the expense has been, for example, a payment that allows use of a brand name over a specified period, it may be more appropriate to amortise the expense over the period by reference to the sales of the brand made in each period of account. (In the US the word 'depreciation' is not used; the word 'amortization' is used for both tangible and intangible assets.)

See DEPRECIATION.

(2) A repayment of a debt instalment, each payment being interest arising from the date of payment plus a partial payment of the capital.

(3) Where a fee is charged by a bank, etc, for a loan extended to the accounting entity, the initial charge may be amortised over the period of the loan.

(4) The redemption of stock by a sinking fund.

Annual exempt amount. The capital gains that can be made in a fiscal year before capital gains tax is chargeable (TCGA 1992, s 3).

Annual general meeting. Every company is required to call an annual general meeting of its shareholders. The maximum time permitted between annual general meetings is 15 months and shareholders must be given 21 days' notice of the meeting. The usual business transacted at an AGM is presentation of the company's annual accounts, the appointment of any new directors and re-appointment of any directors retiring, by rotation or otherwise, the appointment of auditors and fixing of their remuneration, and the approval of a dividend recommended by the directors. Other business may be transacted at an AGM if notice of the other business has been given to the shareholders, but not otherwise (Companies Act 1985, s 366). Any meeting of the shareholders of a company that is not the annual general meeting is an extraordinary general meeting.

Annual interest. *See* YEARLY INTEREST.

Annual return. A return to be made by a company every year giving various details relating to eg its registered office, registers of members and debenture holders, shares, director and secretary (see the Companies Act 1985, ss 363 and 364).

Annual value. A value placed upon hereditaments for the purpose of assessing liability to income tax or rates.

Annuity. A yearly sum payable. A life annuity is an annual payment, eg under the terms of a will. Annuity is not defined in the Taxes Acts. It has been judicially described as meaning 'where an income is purchased with a sum of money and the capital has gone and has ceased to exist, the principal having been converted into an annuity' (per Watson B in *Foley v Fletcher and Rose (1858) 3 H & N 769 at 784*).

Anton Piller order. An order permitting an individual to search and take possession of the property of another in order to further justice in a civil action (which takes its name from *Anton Piller KG v Manufacturing Processes Ltd [1976] 1 All ER 779, CA*). Following the CIVIL PROCEDURE RULES 1998, such an order is to be known as a 'search order'.

Appeal. An appeal may be made against a Revenue notice or assessment by giving notice to the inspector within thirty days of its issue (TMA 1970, s 31). An appeal can be against: (*a*) an assessment on the individual (TMA 1970, s 31); (*b*) a notice (TMA 1970, s 32); (*c*) an Inland Revenue amendment of the self-assessment (TMA 1970, s 31(1)); (*d*) a penalty assessment (TMA 1970, s 29(8)); (*e*) a notice requiring the production of documents (TMA 1970, s 19A(6)); and (*f*) delay in completing enquiries into a self-assessment (TMA 1970, s 28A(6)).

The appeal will be made either to the General Commissioners, a body of lay persons assisted by a qualified clerk, or the Special Commissioners, who are highly qualified persons. The current rules about Special Commissioners restrict eligibility for future appointments to persons who are legally qualified and to make it usual for a Commissioner to sit on his or her own (FA 1984, Sch 22). Sometimes the legislation reserves a particular appeal to one or other body; where this is not so the choice lies with the taxpayer. The choice for a hearing to be before the Special Commissioners should be exercised by a notice combined with the notice of appeal within the normal time limit for the appeal (TMA 1970, s 46(1)). Alternatively, the taxpayer and Revenue can apply to the General Commissioners for the case to be transferred to the Special Commissioners (TMA 1970, s 44(3)).

An appeal is to the Lands Tribunal where the matter under appeal concerns a chargeable gain and the question in dispute is a question of the value of land in the UK (TMA 1970, s 47).

Other methods of appeal include seeking the opinion of the court (as in *A-G v National Provincial Bank Ltd (1928) 14 TC 111*). It is also sometimes possible to enter an originating summons as in *Buxton v Public Trustee (1962) 41 TC 235*, which concerns the charitable nature of trusts.

Appointed day. The day on which legislation becomes effective. Some Acts of Parliament specify particular provisions, stating that these will come into effect on an appointed day, which is later specified in a statutory instrument.

Appointment. Besides its ordinary meaning, to appoint is to cause to be transferred property, under a *power of appointment*. Eg, under a TRUST, an individual given a power of appointment (called the 'donee' of the power of appointment) is entitled to have the TRUSTEE transfer (some amount of the) property held on trust to persons who are referred to as the OBJECTS of the power. *See* POWER.

Apportionment. The dividing of a legal right into its proportionate parts, according to the interests of the parties concerned. The word is generally used with reference to the adjustment of rights between two persons having successive interests in the same property, eg a TENANT FOR LIFE and the REMAINDERMAN. By the Apportionment Act 1870 it is provided that all rents, annuities, dividends, and other periodical payments in the nature of income, are to be considered as accruing from day to day, and are apportionable in respect of time accordingly.

Appropriation. Special attribution (OED 1690).

(1) Any part of the real or personal estate of a deceased person may be appropriated in its actual conditions in or towards satisfaction of a legacy or share of residue. See the Administration of Estates Act 1925, s 41.

(2) The application of a particular payment for the purpose of paying a particular debt. The debtor at the time of paying has the right of appropriation, but, as a general rule, the creditor may apply the payment if the debtor does not; if neither does so, the law usually appropriates earliest payment to earliest debt (*Clayton's case*).

Approved share option scheme. If Inland Revenue approval is given to an employee share option scheme, the gain made by the employee is subject to capital gains tax (with the benefits of the annual exempt amount) instead of a charge arising to income tax under Schedule E. By virtue of TA 1988, ss 135 & 140A–E and FA 1988, s 78. Currently, Inland Revenue approval can be obtained for three types of share option scheme:

(1) A scheme allowing options to be given to selected employees where the employee is required to pay the price on exercise that is 85% or more of the value of the shares when the option is granted (TA 1988, Sch 9).

(2) A scheme available to all employees under which shares can be granted without payment (FA 2000, Sch 8).

(3) Enterprise management incentives, whereby selected full-time employees can be given options of up to £100,000 each (FA 2000, Sch 14).

Arbitration. Where two or more parties submit all matters in dispute to the judgment of *arbitrators*, who are to decide the controversy; and if they do not agree, it

is usual to add, that another person be called in as *umpire*, to whose sole judgment it is then referred. Frequently there is only one arbitrator originally appointed. The decision, in any of these cases, is called an *award*. The Arbitration Act 1950 consolidated the earlier law with respect to arbitration. Amendments to it were made by the Arbitration Act 1979, concerning the judicial review of arbitration awards and the abolition of the procedure of stating a case for the decision of the High Court.

Arising basis. The basis for the charge to income tax and to capital gains tax on an individual who is resident in the UK and domiciled within the UK, being a charge on all income (and all gains) arising during the fiscal year.

Arrangements between debtors and creditors are agreements under which the debtor's affairs are to be conducted so as to provide for the payment of debts owing to creditors, so as to maximise the payment of those debts, but by which the agreeing creditors will not proceed at law to have the debtor declared bankrupt. Arrangements must be in accordance with the Deeds of Arrangement Act 1914.

As to arrangements within the bankruptcy law, see the Insolvency Act 1986, Part VIII.

Articles of association. Regulations governing the mode of conducting the business of an incorporated company and its internal organisation. These must usually accompany the Memorandum of Association, which sets out the objects and capital, etc, of the company. In the case of a company limited by shares, Table A of the Companies Act 1985 may be taken as the articles of the company.

See TABLE A.

Artificial person. *See* PERSON.

Assent. Consent. The executor's assent to a bequest is essential to perfect a legatee's title. Provisions as to assents are contained in the Administration of Estates Act 1925, s 36. To pass the legal estate it must be in writing, signed by the personal representative, and must name the person in whose favour it is given. The statutory covenant against incumbrances may be implied if the assent is expressed to be given 'as personal representative' (see s 36(3)).

Assessors. Persons who assist a judge with their special knowledge of the subject which he has to decide. By the Supreme Court Act 1981, s 70 the High Court or Court of Appeal may call in the aid of one or more assessors specially qualified, and may try and hear the matter in question with their assistance. See now the Civil Procedure Rules 1998, 35.15.

Asset. (1) For a charge to capital gains tax to arise, there must be a disposal (or deemed disposal) of an asset. All forms of property are assets whether situated in the UK or not (TCGA 1992, s 21(1)). Property is not further defined. Assets are however stated to include (*a*) options, debts and incorporeal property generally, (*b*) any currency other than sterling, and (*c*) any form of property created by the person disposing of it, or otherwise coming to be owned without being acquired. Property owned without being acquired covers items such as generated goodwill. Property created includes not only such items as paintings but also copyrights, patents and crops. Rights under contractual licences or rights of registration under the Matrimonial Homes Act 1983 may equally be 'property' and sums received on the redemption of a rentcharge, the release of a covenant and for the release of a right to occupy the matrimonial home may all give rise to CGT. The rights of an employer to the services of an employee was held by the House of Lords to be an asset in *O'Brien v Benson's Hosiery (Holdings) Ltd ([1979] STC 735)*. The fact that the rights could not be assigned by the employer was irrelevant. It was sufficient that they could be 'turned to account'.

It is probably the case that an unenforceable promise is not an asset for the purpose of the CGT legislation. (See *A-G v Murray [1904] 1 KB 165* where proceeds of an insurance policy were held not to be part of the deceased's estate for the pur-

pose of estate duty and the insurance policy was void.) However, the attitude of the court has, in more recent years, been characterised by the maxim 'where there is fruit there must be a tree'. *Emmet on Title* suggests that a claim is not an asset until it is proved to be well founded. It is, however, the frequent experience of practitioners that a commercial payment is made to dispose of the nuisance value of a claim, even where it is thought that the claim would not succeed before the court. It has been argued by the Revenue in correspondence and in court proceedings that such a claim, however unfounded, constitutes an asset. The view taken is that the receipt of money by the claimant is sufficient evidence of his having a right, even though that right may not have been recognised by the court.

Similar obscurity surrounds the position of rights barred by statute. However, it is frequently the case that statute barred rights can be enforced indirectly and the acknowledgement of a claim can revive a right that would otherwise be statute barred. On this analysis, therefore, a receipt arising on a claim that is statute barred attracts a charge to CGT under TCGA 1992, s 22 as 'a capital sum derived from an asset'.

A distinction must be made between the ownership of part of an asset, on one hand, and ownership of the whole of an asset, subject to a charge, on the other hand. This distinction was explored in *Editor v Inspector of Taxes ([2000] STC (SCD) 337)*.

(2) In respect of the estate of a deceased person, by *assets* is meant such property as is available for the payment of the debts of an individual or company, or of a person deceased.

Formerly, it was important that the assets of a deceased person were divided into *real estate*, and *personal assets*, consisting of what is called *personal estate*, which were administered according to different rules.

Under the Administration of Estates Act 1925, s 32, the real and personal estate, whether legal or equitable, of a deceased person, are made assets for the payment of his debts, whether by specialty or simple contract. This section virtually abolishes any distinction between legal and equitable assets. Realty and personalty are alike equally liable for the payment of debts, and vest in the personal representatives, who have a power of sale. See generally the Administration of Estates Act 1925, as amended by the Administration of Estates Act 1971.

(3) Rights or other access to future economic benefits controlled by an entity as a result of past transactions or events. [FRS 5 – Substance of transactions]

Assign. (1) to make over a right or interest to another; (2) to point out, or set forth.

Assignee, or **Assign.** A person who is appointed by another to do any act in his own right, or who takes the rights or title of another by assignment, as distinguished from a *deputy* who acts in the right of another. Such an assignee may be either *by deed*, ie by act of party, eg when a lessee assigns his lease to another, or *in law*, the person whom the law so makes, without any appointment of the person, as an administrator who is the assignee in law to the intestate.

Assignor. One who transfers or assigns property to another.
See ASSIGNEE.

Associate. An entity (other than a subsidiary) in which another entity (the investor) has a participating interest and over whose operating and financial policies the investor exercises a significant influence (Companies Act 1985, Sch 4A, para 20). [FRS 9 – Associates and joint ventures]

Associated company. Associated company. But for express provision, it would be easy to exploit the benefit of the lower rates of corporation tax applied to the first £10,000 of profit (the 'starting rate' of 10%) and the first £300,000 of profit (the 'small companies rate' of 20%) by dividing a business between many companies. It is therefore provided that when the company has one or more associated companies in the accounting period the

figures of £50,000, £300,000 and £1,500,000 are divided by the total number of companies which are associated with each other (TA 1988, ss 13AA & 13(3)). This technique of crude division by the number of companies rather than division according to the size of profits, has the effect that two associated companies each with a profit of £300,000 will together pay less tax than if one had profits of £599,000 and the other of £1,000. For this purpose, overseas companies under common control are treated as 'associated companies', even if the overseas company has no liability to UK tax.

Companies are associated if at the relevant time, or at any time within one year previously, one has control of the other or both are under the control of the same person or persons (TA 1988, s 416(1)). A person has control if he exercises or is able to exercise or is entitled to acquire control over the company's affairs, a phrase which could mean:
(1) the power to carry a resolution at a general meeting, including the power to elect the board of directors; or
(2) more narrowly, the power to run the company's affairs, that is power at the director level, the point being that the general meeting cannot usually tell its directors how to manage the day-to-day affairs of the company.

In *Steele v EVC International NV [1996] STC 785* the Court of Appeal preferred (1) to (2). Control of the affairs of a company meant control at the level of general meetings of shareholders, as control at that level carried with it the power to make the ultimate decisions as to the business of a company and in that sense to control its affairs.

Control is, however, declared by TA 1988, s 416(2) to exist in defined circumstances although these are without prejudice to the broad principle. These circumstances are where one possesses or is entitled to acquire:
(1) the greater part of the share capital or issued share capital of the company or of the voting power of the company; or
(2) such part of the share capital as would entitle him to the greater part of the

income of the company were it all distributed ignoring any loan capital; or

(3) such rights as would entitle him in the event of the winding up of the company to the greater part of the assets of the company.

In applying these rules there is to be attributed to a person any rights held by a nominee for him and also the rights held by any associate of his, a wide term including any relative or partner. There may also be attributed to him all the powers of any company of which he has control whether by himself or with associates. The Court of Appeal has determined that the attribution of rights by the Revenue is discretionary and not mandatory (*R v IRC, ex p Newfields Developments Ltd [2000] STC 52, CA*).

Associated employments. Two or more employments held by one individual with either the same employer or with employers who are associated with each other. If the employments are with two or more companies, these are treated as associated if one company controls the other or both companies are under the control of the same person or persons (TA 1988, s 416(1)). If the employers are individuals or partnerships, these are treated as associated if one has control of the other or both are under control of the same person (TA 1988, s 840). Where employments are associated, the employee is treated as a higher rate employee for the purpose of the benefit in kind provisions if his emoluments in aggregate exceed £8,500.

Associated operations. Inheritance tax is charged on a disposition. Where there are associated operations, the disposition on which inheritance tax is charged is treated as the value of the donor's estate before the associated operations less the value of his estate after the associated operations. Thus, such operations are elided; all are treated as made at the time of the last. Broadly such operations are either two or more affecting one piece of property or one paving the way for another. More precisely, they are defined as: 'any two or more operations of any kind whether effected by the same person or by different persons and whether or not simultaneous being (*a*) operations which affect the same property or one of which affects some property and the other or others affect property which represents, directly or indirectly, that property or income arising from that property or any property representing accumulations of such income or (*b*) any two operations of which one is effected with reference to the other or with a view to enabling the other to be effected or facilitating its being effected and any further operations having a like relation to any of those two and so on . . .' (IHTA 1984, s 268(1)).

Association, Articles of. *See* ARTICLES OF ASSOCIATION.

Association, Memorandum of. *See* MEMORANDUM OF ASSOCIATION.

Astronaut. A person who escapes taxation by not being resident in any territory, by virtue of spending insufficient time in any one country to qualify as resident under the rules in force in that country.

At arm's length. When a person is not, or having been, ceases to be, under the influence or control of another, he is said to be 'at arm's length' with him, eg a CESTUI QUE TRUST and TRUSTEE.

Attachment of debts. *See* GARNISHEE.

Attachment of earnings. A court may make an attachment of earnings order to secure payment of an order of the court, such as a JUDGMENT DEBT. The debtor must give particulars of his earnings and anticipated earnings, and attend the court hearing at which the deduction rate from earnings will be decided. The debtor's employer must then, under the court order, deduct the specified amounts from the debtor's wages or salary, and pay them to the collecting officer of the court (see Attachment of Earnings Act 1971).

Attestation. The subscription by a person of his name to a deed, will, or other document executed by another, for the purpose of testifying to its genuineness.

(1) Deed of document *inter vivos*. A deed ought to be duly attested, ie show

that it was executed by the party in the presence of a witness or witnesses. In most cases this is rather for preserving the evidence, than for constituting the essence, of the deed, but attestation is essential for the validity of bills of sale (Bills of Sale Act 1878, and Bills of Sale (Amendment) Act 1882), and for deeds executing powers of appointment (Law of Property Act 1925, s 159), and in a few other cases.

See BILL OF SALE.

(2) Will. Every will except a military will must, by the Wills Act 1837, be made in the presence of two or more witnesses present at the same time, such witnesses *attesting* and subscribing the will in the presence of the testator, though not necessarily in the presence of each other.

See WILL.

Attestation clause. The clause in which a witness to a deed, will, or other document certifies to its genuineness. It is not legally essential, even for a will (Wills Act 1837, s 8), but it is the simplest evidence of due execution and is universally included.

See ATTESTATION.

Attested copy. A copy of a document verified as correct.

Attributable profit. That part of the total profit currently estimated to arise over the duration of the contract, after allowing for estimated remedial and maintenance costs and increases in costs so far as not recoverable under the terms of the contract, that fairly reflects the profit attributable to that part of the work performed at the accounting date. (There can be no attributable profit until the profitable outcome of the contract can be assessed with reasonable certainty.) [SSAP 9 – Stocks and long-term contracts]

Audit. Company law requires an audit of the statutory annual accounts of every limited company, unless it fulfils the criteria for a small company or a medium sized company (Companies Act 1985, ss 235 and 246). An audit is an independent examination of, and the subsequent expression of

opinion on, financial statements of an organisation. An audit is required to be performed in accordance with auditing standards which specify that the auditor collects evidence by means of compliance tests (tests of control) and substantive tests (tests of detail). An audit is required for a small or medium sized company if requested by any shareholder holding 10% or more of the nominal value of any class of the company's shares in issue (or shareholders who, together hold 10% or more of the share capital) (Companies Act 1985, s 249B(2)). An audit may also be required by an organisation's constitution, such as the deed of trust establishing a charity or the rules of a club.

Audit opinion. An opinion contained in an Auditors' Report. An audit opinion must express the view as to whether or not the financial statements that are the subject of the Audit Report show a true and fair view, are in accordance with relevant legislation and have used appropriate accounting policies. There are three types of audit opinion. If the auditor is satisfied on these points and that the accounts have been drawn up in accordance with appropriate accounting standards, the auditor gives an unqualified opinion. If the auditor considers that the accounts are not in accordance with any one of the relevant requirements and the difference is material, the auditor gives a qualified opinion. If the auditor considers that the accounts fail to give a true and fair view or he has (for whatever reason) been unable to obtain sufficient evidence to satisfy himself of the veracity of the accounts, the auditor gives an adverse opinion.

Auditor. A person appointed to check the accounts of local authorities, companies, partnerships, trusts, etc.

Auditor General. *See* COMPTROLLER AND AUDITOR GENERAL.

Auditors' report. A report prepared by the auditors relating to the financial state of a company.

It must state whether the annual accounts have been properly prepared in accordance with the Companies Act 1985, s 235(1). It must be signed by them: ibid, s 236. In preparing the report the auditors must carry out such investigations as will enable them to form an opinion as to whether proper accounting records have been kept by the company: ibid, s 237(1).

Authorised capital. The total amount of capital which a company is authorised by its memorandum of association to offer to subscribers, as distinguished from its *issued* capital, or capital actually taken up by such subscribers.

Authorised minimum capital of a public company means £50,000 or such other sum as the Secretary of State may by order made by statutory instrument specify instead (see Companies Act 1985, s 118(1)).

Authorised share capital. *See* NOMINAL SHARE CAPITAL.

Authority. (1) Power given by one person to another enabling the latter to do some act. *See* AGENT.
(2) a governing body, eg county council or local authority;
(3) grounds for some legal proposition, eg judicial decisions, or opinions of authors.

Autre droit, in. In right of another. A person may hold property in his own right or in right of another, eg trustee in right of *cestui que trust*, or an executor or administrator in right of the deceased and his legatees, devisees, or the persons entitled on his intestacy.

Average clause. A clause in an insurance policy stating that if at the time of the loss the sum insured is less than the value of the subject-matter of insurance, the assured is to be regarded as his own insurer for the difference and is to bear a rateable proportion of the loss accordingly.

Average remaining service life. A weighted average of the expected future service of the current members of the scheme up to their normal retirement dates

or expected dates or earlier withdrawal or death in service. The weightings can have regard to periods of service, salary levels of scheme members and future anticipated salary growth in a manner which the actuary considers appropriate having regard to the actuarial method and assumptions used. [SSAP 24 – Accounting for pension costs]

Averaging. Averaging is a method of reducing the income tax burden when the profits generated fluctuate greatly from year to year. The intention of the averaging provisions is primarily to reduce the income taxed at higher rate in a year of abnormally high profits, where the taxpayer is customarily subject to a charge at basic rate only. Averaging is available for two kinds of activities only. First, for the profits of the trade of farming (TA 1988, s 96). Second, for the profit of the profession or vocation of a 'creative artist', which is defined by statute as one where the taxpayer's profits are derived wholly or mainly from 'literary, dramatic, musical or artistic works or designs created by the taxpayer personally or . . . in partnership' (TA 1988, Sch 4A, para 2). If the profits of either year are nil or less than 70% of the other, the profits may be equalised. If the profit of one year is between 70% and 75% of that of the other, averaging is not available but a claim can be made to adjust the profits of the two years by shifting from the higher year to the lower year an amount equal to three times the difference between the two, less 3/4 of the higher figure.

Avoidance. 'The hallmark of tax avoidance is that the taxpayer reduces his liability to tax without incurring the economic consequences that Parliament intended to be suffered by any taxpayer qualifying for such reduction in his tax liability. The hallmark of tax mitigation, on the other hand, is that the taxpayer takes advantage of a fiscally attractive option afforded to him by the tax legislation, and genuinely suffers the economic consequences that Parliament intended to be suffered by those taking advantage of the option.' (per Lord Nolan in *IRC v Willoughby [1997] STC 995 at 1003–1004* considering the application of

TA 1988, s 741 which provides an exemption from s 739 if avoiding a liability to tax is not one of the purposes of the transaction).
See TAX AVOIDANCE.

Award. The decision of an arbitrator.
See ARBITRATION.

B

'B' List. A list of the past members of the company within the last 12 months of a winding-up order made out by the liquidator.

BES. Business Expansion Scheme.

BIMBO. Buy In Management Buy Out.

Back duty. If an investigation shows that tax has been underpaid as a consequence of underdeclaration or misdeclaration of income by the taxpayer, Revenue practice is to favour a contract settlement under which a sum in settlement of the back duty agreed to be due is offered by the taxpayer and the contract is made by the Board of Inland Revenue accepting the offer. In practice, the investigating officer often drafts the letter of offer from the taxpayer, specifying an amount which would be acceptable to the Board, this amount being calculated to include tax underpaid, interest on the underpayment and penalties calculated as a percentage of the tax underpaid. Where there is a contract settlement of a taxpayer's back duty, it is usual for the Revenue to completely mitigate (that is, choose not to charge) the fixed sum penalties given in statute for failures to make returns. Once a settlement has been entered into, the sum that is payable under the settlement is no longer a payment of tax, but is a payment due under a contract, quite separate from the payment of tax, interest and penalties from which the contractual debt is calculated (*A-G v Midland Bank Executor & Trustee Co Ltd (1934) 19 TC 136*).

The conduct of back duty cases is a skilled art. The Revenue may have been tipped off or may simply disbelieve the taxpayer's return. Sources of information that are used include returns made by banks, etc, evidence given in court, government contracts, a customer suspicious on being asked for a bearer cheque, and even a reported robbery; informers may be rewarded.

Once alerted the Revenue may require a complete statement of means and a satisfactory explanation of all sums appearing in bank accounts or supporting a luxurious lifestyle. To this end the Revenue are reported to keep records of all horse racing results and details of wins on the National Lottery.

Park J describes the process of back duty and the use of capital statements:

'Sophisticated points of tax law rarely arise in back duty cases. Back duty is the area where the Revenue, having conducted an investigation into a taxpayer, form the view that the income which he had been declaring for tax was lower than his true income. In back duty investigations the Revenue frequently prepare (as they did in this case) "capital statements".

Capital statements are useful. It is a fact—unfortunate but true—that there are people who cheat on their taxes, and capital statements are a technique which ferrets out the case where the taxpayer has had more money to spend than his declared income suggests he should have had.'(*Hurley v Taylor [1998] STC 202 at 213 f, g*).

Bad debt. An amount that is due to be received at the accounting date but it is considered that it is unlikely that the sum will ever be received. The accounting principle of prudence requires that a debt should be written off to the profit and loss account as soon as it is judged that the debt will be bad.

Bailment. A delivery of goods by one person, called the *bailor*, to another person, called the *bailee*, for some purpose, under an agreement, express or implied, either for CONSIDERATION or GRATUITOUSLY that, after the purpose has been fulfilled, they shall be redelivered to the bailor, or otherwise dealt with according to his directions, or kept until he reclaims them.

Bailments are of six kinds:

1. the bare deposit of goods with another, for the exclusive use of the bailor.
2. the lending of goods for the use or convenience of the bailee.
3. the placing of goods with the bailee on hire.
4. the pawning or pledging of goods.
5. the delivery of goods to a carrier to a person who is to carry out some services in respect of them for payment.
6. similar to the last, but where the carriage or services are to be gratuitous.

Bailor. A person who entrusts goods to another by way of bailment.
See BAILMENT.

Balancing allowance. (1) Industrial buildings allowance: A balancing allowance or charge arises if within 25 years of the building being first used, the relevant interest is sold or the building is demolished or destroyed or altogether ceases to be used (CAA 2001, s 314(4), (5)). The charge or allowance depends upon the 'residue of expenditure' which is the original cost minus the allowances made, whether initial or writing down (CAA 2001, s 313). This residue is set against any sale, insurance compensation or salvage monies (CAA 2001, s 316(1)). Should the residue exceed those sums, the difference is the subject of the balancing allowance. Should these sums exceed the allowance the difference is the subject of the balancing charge subject to the rule that the charge may not exceed the allowances made (CAA 2001, ss 352, 353).

(2) Plant and machinery: A balancing allowance (or charge) is made whenever one of the following events occurs: (*a*) the asset ceases to belong to the claimant; (*b*) if he loses possession of it in circumstances in which it is reasonable to assume the loss is permanent; (*c*) the asset ceases to exist as such (as a result of destruction, dismantling or otherwise); (*d*) the asset begins to be used wholly or partly for purposes other than those of the trade; or (*e*) the trade is permanently discontinued. If the qualifying expenditure (the cost less capital allowances given) exceeds the disposal value, the excess is a balancing allowance. If the disposal value exceeds the qualifying expenditure, a balancing charge equal to that excess is made.

(3) Agricultural buildings allowance: A balancing allowance or balancing charge arises on the happening of a 'balancing event' which is defined as arising when the relevant interest is transferred and where the building is demolished, destroyed or otherwise ceases to exist (CAA 2001, ss 376, 382). However, there will only be a balancing event if an election is made (CAA 2001, ss 381(1), 382(6), (7)).

Balance Sheet. A statement of all assets and all liabilities of an enterprise, drawn up at a date that is specified, usually the last day of a period of account. Company law requires that every company draw up a balance sheet, irrespective of the size of the company. The balance sheet must give a true and fair view of the state of affairs of the company at the date displayed. Companies Act 1985, Sch 8A gives regulations for the format of a statutory Balance Sheet.

Balance Sheet audit. An audit that is limited in its scope to the verification of the existence, ownership and value of the items shown on the balance sheet.

Balance Sheet format. Companies Act 1985, Sch 8A gives two alternative formats for the presentation of a balance sheet designed to be part of a company's financial statements to be placed on the public record at the Registrar of Companies. The first format is a vertical format; the second format is a horizontal format. The former requires the disclosure of net current assets and liabilities, which is not required in the latter format. Schedule 8A specifies 20 items that are required on a balance sheet, grouped into 11 categories.

Balance Sheet value. The total of the balance sheet, which is the value of assets measured at historical cost, less accumulated depreciation from which the full value of liabilities has been deducted.

Bank. An entity whose business is to receive deposits or other repayable funds from the public and to grant credits for its own account (Companies Act 1985, s 262 &

Banking Act 1987). The Tax Acts refer to banks, building societies and others as, collectively, 'deposit takers'.

Bank credit. The sum agreed between the bank and its customer, up to which the customer may draw by means of overdraft or on a fixed loan. The borrowing may be secured on the assets of the customer, or unsecured. Colloquially, reference is often made to unquantified credit: 'My credit is good'.

Bank interest. (1) A charge made by a bank to an individual or an enterprise, usually calculated on the daily overdraft balance or the balance on a loan. The rate of interest is often calculated as bank base rate plus a stated percentage.

(2) Interest credited to a money deposit at a bank or other deposit taker. Such interest received is subject to income tax under Schedule D Case III (TA 1988, s 18(3)).

Bank of England. The central bank for the UK. Owned by the Crown, the Bank of England acts as the Government's banker issuing Government stock (gilts) to raise funds for the Exchequer. In 1997 the bank was given responsibility for setting the Bank of England base rate; prior to that date this had been the responsibility shared between the Bank of England and the Chancellor of the Exchequer.

Bankers' books. The Bankers' Books Evidence Act 1879 makes a copy of an entry in a banker's book *prima facie* evidence of such entry on proof that the copy has been checked by comparison with the original entry.

Bankruptcy. A debtor, who by reason of some act or circumstance indicating a failure to meet his liabilities may be adjudged a 'bankrupt' by the High Court or by a County Court exercising bankruptcy jurisdiction.

Proceedings are commenced by the presentation of a bankruptcy petition by a creditor or by the debtor himself (see Insolvency Act 1986, ss 267–275). The Court may then make a bankruptcy order (ss 271 & 274). The bankruptcy order continues until the bankrupt is discharged (s 278). On the making of the order the bankrupt's estate vests in his trustee in bankruptcy or, in the case of the Official Receiver, on his becoming trustee (s 306). There are restrictions on a bankrupt disposing of his property (s 284). He may have to face a public examination (s 290). The duties of the trustee in bankruptcy are to acquire, control, realise and distribute the bankrupt's estate among his creditors (ss 305–335). A bankrupt may be convicted of bankruptcy offences, eg concealment of property, absconding, gambling (ss 353–362). In certain cases a criminal bankruptcy order may be made against him (see Powers of Criminal Courts Act 1973, ss 39–41, Sch 2).

Bare trust. (1) A trust under which the TRUSTEE, called a bare trustee, holds property for the beneficial owner and is obliged to deal with the property according to the beneficial owner's directions.

(2) For CGT purposes, where assets are held by a trustee for another person who is absolutely entitled as against the trustee, or for two or more persons who are so entitled, the property is not settled and the acts of the trustee are treated as the acts of the beneficiary and disposals between them are disregarded (TCGA 1992, s 60(1)). All gains and losses and consequent liability concern the beneficiary and not the trustee.

The beneficiary is absolutely entitled if he has the exclusive right, subject only to satisfying any outstanding charge, lien or other right. These words refer to some personal right of indemnity and are not apt to cover another beneficial interest arising under the same instrument (per Walton J in *Stephenson v Barclays Bank Trust Co Ltd [1975] STC 151 at 163*). Charges are included in this list because of the estate and powers of the mortgagee to direct how that asset shall be dealt with (TCGA 1992, s 60(2) and per Goff J in *Crowe v Appleby [1975] STC 502 at 510*). This definition sits oddly with the trust doctrine that a beneficiary who is absolutely entitled has the right to end the trust but no power to direct the trustee how his discretion shall be exercised.

It appears that a right to call for the conveyance of the trust asset to the beneficiary meets this test even though the beneficiary cannot control the trustee in other ways. If the test is whether the beneficiary can call upon the trustees for the transfer of the trust property, the answer may well turn on the nature of the trust property. Thus, a co-owner of land has no right to call for the land itself because of the trust for sale. Similar problems arise with certain shares in a private company and to mortgage debts. In *Stephenson v Barclays Bank Trust Co Ltd [1975] STC 151* Walton J said (*at 163*) that one of several co-owners would, in these circumstances, have to wait until the property was sold before being entitled to call for the transfer of his or her share. When there is co-ownership of shares, it is necessary to determine the terms of the co-ownership (*Booth v Ellard [1980] STC 555*). However, it appears likely that such technical points will not be accepted by the courts and that therefore such property is not settled. In *Jenkins v Brown [1989] STC 577*, land comprised in a pool held by trustees was conveyed to beneficiaries according to their interests prior to the trust being created.

There is a bare trust not only where the person is absolutely entitled as against the trustee, but also where he would be so entitled but for being an infant or other person under a disability. However, this must be the only reason for his not being absolutely entitled. In *Tomlinson v Glyn's Executor and Trustee Co (1970) 45 TC 607*, property was held 'for such of the beneficiaries as shall attain the age of 21 years or marry under that age' (21 was then the age of majority). The beneficiary, even if he had not been an infant, would not have been absolutely entitled, since his interest was contingent upon attaining his majority (or marrying before that time). What would have happened if the beneficiary had married and so satisfied the condition precedent while still an infant? Semble that there is a disposal under TCGA 1992, s 71.

A further reason was that the interests of the beneficiaries might be defeasible *pro tanto* if other children were born so that it could not be said that these infants had 'vested indefeasible interests in possession'.

The dividing line between CGT being charged on trustees by virtue of property being settled property and CGT being charged on individuals by virtue of the

trustees being mere nominees was considered by the court in *Booth v Ellard [1980] STC 555*. In that case, 12 members of the same family held 72% of the issued share capital of their family company. In 1972 they entered into a written agreement which was expressed to last for 15 years only and which could be brought to an end after ten years by any nine of the family members deciding to terminate the agreement. Under the agreement, the shares held by the 12 individuals were transferred to trustees who were given elaborate instructions as to the way they should exercise their voting rights, deal with bonus and rights issues as well as a pre-emption right being given to the individuals on any disposal by the trustees.

Goulding J held that the shares had not become settled property under the agreement and, instead, fell to be treated as the property of the 12 family members as co-owners. Goulding J held that property held for 'a plurality of beneficial owners' is to be treated as nominee property under the terms of (now) TCGA 1992, s 60 if two conditions are fulfilled:

(1) the interests of the beneficial owners are concurrent and not successive. This is in contrast to, for example, interest of a life tenant on the one hand and a remainderman on the other;

(2) the interests of co-owners are the same (*[1980] STC 555 at 572*).

The right given to the trustees to deal with the shares did not prevent the arrangement being a bare trust.

See BENEFICIAL INTEREST; NOMINEE SHAREHOLDER; TRUST.

Barometer stock. An equity that is regarded by investment analysts as an indication of the overall financial health of the stock market.

Base rate. The rate at which the Bank of England lends to discount houses. The fixing of the base rate is now a matter for the Bank of England alone. The clearing banks and other financial institutions frequently specify that interest charged to a customer on a loan is a specified percentage above base rate and that interest credited to an account is a specified percentage below base rate. For this calculation, each financial institution specifies its own base rate; however, the rate is usually identical to that of the Bank of England base rate.

Basic e.p.s. The earnings per share calculated by dividing the profits generated by a company by the number of shares in issue, no adjustment being made for any options that have been granted that would create further shares.

Basic rate. The basic rate of tax is specified in each year's Finance Act (eg FA 2001, s 50(b)). The basic rate of tax applies to income of an individual that falls into the band of income specified in TA 1988, s 1(2), which is amended for each fiscal year by statutory instrument (if the increase is in accordance with inflation) or by that year's Finance Act, if the increase is other than the inflationary increase. (Thus, the lower end of the basic rate band for 2001/02 is given by FA 2001, s 51(1) but the upper end is given by SI 2001/638, art 2(b).) For a person who is not an individual (such as a trustee, personal representative or a foreign company subject to income tax), the basic rate of income tax is applied to the total income liable to UK taxation. Basic rate is also applied to the withholding of tax on the payment of an annuity or a royalty (TA 1988, s 3). *See* RATE OF TAX.

Basic wage. The wage paid to an employee excluding payments for any bonus, holiday pay, overtime or employer's national insurance.

Basis of apportionment. Where an overhead is not directly attributable to a particular cost centre (such as rent), a basis of apportionment must be specified so that the cost is shared between cost centres.

Basis period. For income tax, each fiscal year has a basis period, so that income arising during the basis period is brought into the charge to tax in that particular fiscal year. For income generally, the basis period is the fiscal year, from 6 April to the following 5 April. For profits of a trade, profession or vocation, the normal basis

period is the 12 months to the accounting date that ends in the fiscal year (TA 1988, s 60(3)). There is a different basis period for the first year of trading, at cessation of the trade and when the business changes its accounting date.

Batch costing. An approach taken in cost accounting under which costs are expressed on the basis of each batch produced. The method is typically applied where production is of large numbers of low value items.

Bear, on the Stock Exchange, is a seller of stock which he cannot deliver; ie one who speculates for the fall in price of stock which he does not possess, thus enabling him to buy it subsequently for less than he has previously sold it for.
See BULL.

Bear market. A market in which prices are primarily influenced by sellers.

Bearer. Money payable under a cheque or security may be expressed to be payable to a certain person or bearer, in which case anyone who presents the cheque or security may claim payment, and, in case of transfer, endorsement will not be necessary.

Bearer share. A bearer share is one where the bearer is entitled to dividends and any entitlement on a winding-up, or other capital transaction. This is in contrast to a registered share, where the rights attach to the person named in the company's share register. Bearer shares are uncommon in the UK but are frequently used overseas. Ownership of a bearer share is transferred by delivery of the share certificate; a share transfer document is not required. Thus, there is no stampable document. There is a special charge to stamp duty at 1.5% on the issue of a bearer instrument by a UK company, whether or not the issue is in the UK, and on the issue of a bearer instrument in the UK by a foreign company (FA 1999, Sch 15). There is, then, no stamp duty payable on the transfer of the bearer instrument. For stamp duty, a bearer instrument is defined by FA 1999, Sch 15, para 3 as:

(1) A marketable security transferable by delivery.
(2) A share warrant or stock certificate to bearer or instrument to bearer (by whatever name called) having the like effect as such a warrant or certificate.
(3) A deposit certificate to bearer.
(4) Any other instrument to bearer by means of which stock can be transferred.
(5) An instrument issued by a non-UK company that is a bearer instrument by usage.

Beatles clause. 'The Beatles clause' was introduced in 1969 to prevent one form of converting future taxable income into present untaxable capital and is now TA 1988, s 775. The clause subjects to income tax a capital sum received for the sale of an individual's future earnings.

Prior to enactment of the clause in 1969, considerable tax advantage could be gained from the sale of future earnings. Suppose that a film is about to be made and that £1m is available for the star's services. A company acquires the star's services in return for an option to take shares. The company would pay the star say £50,000 by way of living allowance so as to cover his expenses, these being taxable to the individual under Schedule E but deductible by the company. The company would sell the star's services to a film company in return for £1m, would receive that sum and would suffer corporation tax. Similarly, a company could be formed to promote the career of a potential star over a number of years, shares in the new company being issued to the star in exchange for a contract giving the company exclusive rights over the potential star for a stated number of years. Once the star is well launched, the star would sell his shares in the company at a large capital gain, on which CGT at a low effective rate is charged instead of the income tax charge that would have been imposed on the star's earnings.

Bed and breakfast. The sale of shares followed closely by repurchase is termed 'bed and breakfast'. An individual may have made disposals out of his share portfolio during a fiscal year that have triggered gains and, hence, a liability to capital gains tax, but shares remaining in the portfolio are standing at a price below the acquisition cost. The investor may wish to retain these shares but would like to reduce or eliminate his CGT liability by triggering the loss. Prior to 17 March 1998, this could have been achieved by the investor selling the shares standing at a loss and repurchasing them the following day, a procedure known as 'bed and breakfast'. The identification rule in TCGA 1992, s 106A(5) now negates the tax effect of bed and breakfasting as a purchase is identified with a sale made up to 30 days before the purchase. It is, however, still possible to have the same effect by bed and breakfasting an asset other than a share. Alternatively, the husband can sell his shareholding and the wife purchase a holding in the same company, without triggering the anti-avoidance legislation.

Belong. In order to claim a capital allowance, the asset must belong to the person in consequence of the payment (CAA 2001, ss 167–170). The word 'belong' is interpreted strictly by reference to property law concepts. So in *Stokes v Costain Property Investments Ltd [1984] STC 204, CA* where plant (lifts) was installed by a tenant and immediately became the property of the landlord under general land law principles, the tenant was not entitled to the allowances as the lift did not belong to the tenant. This case is no authority on fixtures which remain the property of the tenant. It has now been held in *Melluish v BMI (No. 3) Ltd [1994] STC 802, CA* that where the asset becomes a fixture it cannot still belong to the person installing it. The concept of a fixture which remains personal property is a contradiction in terms and an impossibility in law. It follows that a contractual right to remove the fixture cannot prevent it becoming part of the land and so ceasing to belong to the installer.

Belonging in a country. The VAT Acts provide that services (but not goods) are supplied in the country where the supplier 'belongs' (VATA 1994, s 7(10)). This is the place where the supplier has a business establishment or some other fixed establishment, a foreign trader being deemed to 'belong' in the UK if he has a branch or agency in the UK through which he trades (VATA 1994, s 9(5)). If the supplier has no business or fixed establishment, he 'belongs' where he is resident; in the case of a company, this is, for VAT purposes, the country of incorporation (VATA 1994, s 9(5)(b)).

Below the line. Entries on a company's profit and loss account that show how the profit is distributed (or the source from which funds are used to finance a loss). This is contrasted with entries above the line, which show how the profit has been generated.

Beneficial interest. A right of substantial enjoyment or interest, as opposed to merely nominal ownership or interest. Thus if A holds lands in trust for B, A holds the legal title, and B, who is called the BENEFICIARY or *cestui que trust*, holds the equitable title or equitable interest. Because, under the rules of trust law, the trustee must hold his legal title to secure the benefits of the property to the beneficiary (or beneficiaries) under the terms of the trust, the beneficiary is said to have the beneficial interest or beneficial title in the property. Where, however, A holds the legal title to property for his own benefit, ie not as a trustee for anyone else, A is said to have a beneficial legal interest or title in the property.

Beneficial occupation. Occupation of land which is to the benefit of the occupier. The word 'beneficial' does not connote pecuniary profit, but means 'to the advantage of'.

Beneficial owner. English law distinguishes between legal title and an equitable interest. The beneficial owner (ie holder of the equitable interest) is the person who has the benefit of the asset, being entitled to the income arising and is able to direct the disposal of the asset, even though the asset may be registered in the name of another person, the holder of the legal title.

Contrast BARE TRUST; NOMINEE SHAREHOLDER.

Beneficiary. (1) Generally, one who benefits from a circumstance or legal arrangement. Thus a third-party beneficiary of a contract is one who, though not a party to a contract, benefits from the performance of it.

(2) The modern term used in place of *cestui que trust*, ie a person for whom trust property is held, having rights against the TRUSTEE to enforce the trust, ie ensure that the trustee carries out the trust according to its terms.

See BENEFICIAL INTEREST; TRUST.

Benefits in kind. TA 1988, s 154 requires there to be treated as income of the director or employee sums spent in or in connection with the provision of accommodation, other than living accommodation, of entertainment, of domestic or other services or other benefits or facilities of whatsoever nature. The section charges the director or employer on the cash equivalent of the benefit. This will usually be the cost of the benefit (TA 1988, s 156(1)). The persons providing the benefit are those at whose cost the provision is made (TA 1988, s 154(3)).

Bequest. A gift made by a will.

Bid. (1) To offer a price for a thing which is being sold. May be withdrawn before acceptance except where under SEAL.

(2) An approach made by one company to the shareholders of another company to purchase their shares (either for cash or for shares) with a view to a takeover.

Bid price. The price at which a market maker will buy shares (or a unit trust company will buy units from an investor). Where two prices are stated for a security, the lower is the bid price and the higher is the offer price.

Bilateral contract. One in which the parties are under an obligation reciprocally towards each other, eg sale, where one party becomes bound to deliver the thing sold and the other to pay the price.

Contrast UNILATERAL CONTRACT.

Bill. This word has several meanings:

(1) An account delivered by a creditor to his debtor in respect of goods supplied or work done. Thus, a *bill of costs* is a bill furnished by a solicitor to his client.

(2) Bill in Parliament. A measure submitted to either House of Parliament for the purpose of being passed into law. When a measure has been actually passed into law, it is called an 'Act'. Hence, a few weeks after the Chancellor's Budget Day speech, the annual Finance Bill is laid before the House of Commons. This is then debated in committee and on the floor of the House, and amendments made. The amended bill is then sent to the House of Lords and, thence, to the Queen. By giving the Royal Assent, the Finance Bill becomes the Finance Act. When the Speaker of the House certifies a bill as 'a finance bill', the House of Lords has no power to amend the bill.

Bill of exchange. Bills of exchange are written documents which facilitate dealing with credit, the payment of debts, etc. A bill of exchange is defined by the Bills of Exchange Act 1882, s 1 as an unconditional order in writing, addressed by one person (the drawer) to another (the drawee, and afterwards acceptor), signed by the person giving it, requiring the person to whom it is addressed to pay on demand, or at a fixed or determinable future time, a sum certain in money to, or to the order of, a payee, who is either a specified person, or the bearer of (anyone who possesses) the bill. For example, a cheque is an unconditional order by a person (the drawer) to a banker (the drawee) to pay money; the bank 'accepts' the cheque when it honours the order and makes payment, to the payee, generally a third party. The bank will accept the order embodied in the cheque in view of its pre-existing contractual relationship with the drawer, usually the contractual relationship whereby the drawer maintains a current account with the bank providing the drawer with a cheque-writing facility. Bills of exchange are typically negotiable instruments, though by various forms of writing and marking (ie by 'crossing' cheques) their negotiability can be curtailed.

See CHEQUE; NEGOTIABLE INSTRUMENTS.

Bill of sale. An assignment under seal of chattels personal, ie a DEED by which title to chattels is transferred without a transfer of possession. The Bills of Sale Act 1878 applies now only to absolute bills of sale, eg a transfer where the donor remains in possession, but the retention of possession is not to secure the payment of a debt, in which case the bill of sale is one 'by way of mortgage'. The Bills of Sale (1878) Amendment Act 1882 applies to every bill of sale by way of mortgage. Both classes must be registered within seven days and re-registered every five years, and those under the Act of 1882 must set out the consideration for which it was made, and must not be for less than £30 or they will be void. The Act of 1882 also makes void every bill of sale unless it is made in a form scheduled to the Act. See also the Bills of Sale Acts 1890, 1891; also the Law of Property Act 1925, s 189(1), which provides that a power of distress given by way of indemnity against a rent payable in respect of any land, or against the breach of any covenant or condition in relation to land, is not a bill of sale within the meaning of the above Acts.

Binding contract for sale. For inheritance tax, it is a condition for both business property relief and for agricultural property relief that there is no binding contract for sale over the property concerned (IHTA 1984, ss 113 and 124). Inland Revenue Statement of Practice SP12/80 gives the Revenue view as to the types of 'buy and sell' agreements commonly made between partners of a partnership which constitute a binding contract for sale.

Blackacre. A fictitious piece of land, used as an example in much legal discourse.

Blank acceptance. An acceptance written on blank stamped paper, and acting as a *prima facie* authority by the acceptor to complete a bill of exchange for any amount the stamp will cover (see the Bills of Exchange Act 1882, s 20).

Blank transfer. A transfer form relating to shares without the name of the transferee being inserted.

Board. The directors of a company.

Board of Customs & Excise. The government department with responsibility for the customs duties, excise duty and value added tax. The first Commissioners of Customs were appointed by Charles II in 1671. The Board of Customs has existed continuously since that date. (By contrast, the Board of Inland Revenue was created more than 300 years later.)

Board of Inland Revenue. The eight-member Board of Inland Revenue has statutory responsibility for the administration of income tax, corporation tax, capital gains tax, inheritance tax and stamp duties and the collection of National Insurance contributions (TMA 1970, s 1(1)). Under the direction given by TMA 1970, s 1(2), the Board of Inland Revenue appoints inspectors and collectors of taxes. The Board can delegate its statutory functions to an inspector (*R v IRC, ex p Ulster Bank Ltd [2000] STC 537* and *R v IRC, ex p Davis Frankel & Mead (a firm) [2000] STC 595*). The Taxes Acts specify that certain claims must be made to the Board and not to an inspector (such as a claim that an individual is not domiciled within the United Kingdom). Where the claim is specified as being to the Board, any appeal against its refusal is to the Special Commissioners, the General Commissioners having no authority (TMA 1970, s 46C(1)(a)).

Body corporate. A company, whether incorporated in Great Britain or elsewhere (Companies Act 1985, s 740). A Scottish partnership is not regarded as a body corporate, nor is a corporation sole.
See CORPORATION.

Bona fide commercial reasons. The income tax charge on a 'transaction in a security' (TA 1988, s 703) does not apply if the taxpayer shows that the transaction was carried out for bona fide commercial reasons (see *Laird Group plc v IRC [1999] STC (SCD) 86*). In determining what are bona fide commercial reasons, the word commercial includes non-financial reasons. Hence a view that to retain family control of a company is important for the

future prosperity of the company, whether in the context of company–customer or employer–employee relationships can be good commercial reasons so that steps taken to preserve that control will escape TA 1988, s 703 (*IRC v Goodwin [1976] STC 28, HL*). In *Lewis v IRC [1999] STC (SCD) 349* the trustees of a pension fund held shares in a company that was shortly to be floated. After flotation, the value of that shareholding would have been over 35% of the assets in the pension fund, which was considered by the trustees to be an unacceptably high percentage. The trustees sold part of the shareholding to the company for £2,532,937. By making a capital sale to the company, the tax saved by the pension fund was £633,234. The Special Commissioner quashed an assessment in this sum, holding that the trustees 'were aware of the possible tax benefits of choosing this option but the obtaining of a tax advantage was not the main object ... the tax benefit was "the cherry on the cake"'. The main object was the desired reduction in the size of the shareholding. The trustees 'reacted to the situation by taking the simplest and cheapest option available to them and in doing so in our judgement were acting in the ordinary course of managing investments'. In deciding whether there are commercial reasons it is not necessary for the taxpayer to show that those reasons are connected with the company concerned. So in *Clark v IRC [1978] STC 614* the taxpayer, a farmer, decided to sell shares in a controlled company in order to raise money with which to buy another farm; his claim to use this defence was upheld.

Bona fide purchaser. Common abbreviation of '*bona fide* purchaser for value of a legal interest without notice, actual, imputed, or constructive, of an equitable interest'. Also known as 'equity's darling'. In general, a person who gives valuable CONSIDERATION for a legal title, or a legal interest in property, such as a legal mortgage over land, will take that title or interest free of any pre-existing *equitable interests* in the property, so long as he was, at the time of the sale, actually unaware of such interests, and had no constructive notice of them, ie knowledge of them he would have acquired through diligent investigation of his seller's title prior to sale, and no imputed notice of them, ie the actual or constructive notice of them of any agent acting for him in the transaction (eg a solicitor). Thus the owner of this unnoticed equitable interest will not be able to enforce his prior rights in the property against this purchaser. By contrast, a purchaser will be bound to give effect to any pre-existing legal interests in the property. This regime of notice, by which interests in property are protected or may be lost in the course of transactions with the property, is now largely obsolete with respect to transactions with land, having been replaced by a system under which interests and titles to land are protected by registration in public registers. However, with respect to personal property held on trust this rule of bona fide purchase, sometimes called the 'doctrine of notice', continues to operate.

Bond. (1) An instrument under SEAL, whereby a person binds himself to do or not to do certain things; this is a *single* bond. The person so binding himself is called the *obligor*. The person to whom he is bound, who is entitled to enforce the bond, is called the *obligee*. In some cases the obligor binds himself to pay a certain sum, called a *penal sum* or *penalty*, to which a condition is added, that, if he does or does not do a particular act (ie, if he complies with the conditions which the bond is intended to secure), the bond shall be void, otherwise it is to be of full force and effect. This is a *double* bond. The obligee, however, cannot recover the whole penalty, but only the actual loss proved to have been suffered.

(2) A tradeable security issued by government, a bank or a company giving the holder the right to receive a stated rate of interest calculated on the nominal value of the bond (which is usually, but not always, the sum paid to the borrower when the bond was originally issued). A bond usually has a repayment date on which the nominal value (perhaps with a specified increase) will be paid to the holder. Some government bonds are undated; building societies also issue irredeemable bonds.

(3) A savings product issued by a life assurance society which entitles the holder to withdraw cash from the fund (5% of the original sum invested can be withdrawn each year, without a charge to income tax). *See* SEAL; DEED.

Bond creditor. A creditor whose debt is secured by a bond.
See BOND.

Bond washing. Dividends and interest payments only become income when they are due and payable and there is no apportionment of that dividend over the period in respect of which it is declared. This gives the opportunity for one individual who is taxed at higher rate to sell his shares after declaration of a dividend to an individual who is subject to tax at basic rate (and, hence, not required to pay tax on a dividend received), who then sells the shares stripped of their dividend, back to the original purchaser, all this being planned under the original agreement. In this way the bonds or shares are said to be washed of their dividend or interest. This arrangement is now subjected to income tax by TA 1988, s 737A and, for interest on government stock, by the accrued income scheme.

Bonus. A sum added to that insured under a policy accruing after the policy has been in force for a specified period (see *Prudential Insurance Co Ltd v IRC [1904] 2 KB 658* (per Channell J)).

Bonus share. A share given by the company free to a shareholder, usually in proportion to his present shareholding, eg one bonus share for every share at present held by him.
See SHARE PREMIUM ACCOUNT.

Branch. A foreign company is subject to UK tax on the profits of its branch in the UK (TA 1988, s 18(1)(a)(iii)). Although a non-resident is not normally subject to UK capital gains tax, a charge is imposed on the disposal of assets by a non-resident where those assets have been used in the trade of a UK branch (TCGA 1992, s 10(1)). In the Taxes Acts, the definition is given of 'branch or agency', being: 'any factorship, agency, receivership, branch or management' (TMA 1970, s 118(1); TA 1988, s 834(1) and TCGA 1992, s 12(3)). Hoffmann J, in *IRC v Brackett [1986] STC 521 at 533* said:

'Looking at the matter broadly it seems to me that the intention is to bring within the charge to tax a foreign resident whose trade, though possibly centred abroad, includes operations conducted in this country through an establishment or permanent representative here.'

This approach was used to justify a decision that the disposal of the goodwill of a restaurant in Bedfordshire was the disposal of an asset used in a UK branch (*White (Paul) v Carline [1995] STC (SCD) 186*). Where the entire trade of a non-resident is carried on in the UK, that trade has been held to be correctly described as 'a branch' (*Puddu v Doleman [1995] STC (SCD) 236*).

Breach. An invasion of a right or violation of a duty. The word is specially used in the following expressions:

(1) *Breach of contract.* Failure to act as required by a contract.

(2) *Breach of covenant.* A non-fulfilment of a covenant.

(3) *Breach of trust.* A violation by a trustee of the duty imposed on him by the instrument creating the trust.

Break up value. The aggregate of all sums that would be expected to be received for the piecemeal sale of the assets of a business, on the assumption that the business would be broken up, less the payments that would be required to settle the liabilities arising on the break up of the business, including redundancy pay for all employees.

Bridging loan. A short term loan to finance the purchase of one asset (commonly property) before another is sold.

British citizenship. A person born in the United Kingdom is a British citizen if at the time of the birth his father or mother is (*a*) a British citizen; or (*b*) settled in the United Kingdom (see the British Nationality Act 1981, s 1(1)).

British citizenship may also be acquired by adoption, descent, registration and naturalisation (see ibid, ss 1–6). British citizenship may be renounced (see ibid, s 12). It may also be resumed (see ibid, s 13).

British citizens are entitled to personal allowances, even if not resident in the UK (TA 1988, s 278). Citizenship is not generally taken as a test of taxability in the UK, although holding British nationality may give entitlement under a double tax agreement and it may also be a factor that is taken into account in determining the domicile of an individual.

British subject. A person who has the status of a Commonwealth citizen under the British Nationality Act 1981 (see British Nationality Act 1981, s 51(1)(b)).

Broker. An agent between the contracting parties in business transactions, paid by a commission, or brokerage. *See* FACTOR; STOCKBROKER.

Budget. The financial statement of the national revenue and expenditure for each year, submitted to Parliament by the Chancellor of the Exchequer.

Budget day election. An election under TCGA 1992, Sch 2, para 17(1) that the chargeable gain arising on a disposal is computed by reference to the value of the asset at 6 April 1965 and not by time apportionment. (Rebasing GCT to 31 March 1982 has greatly reduced the relevance of this election. However, the election continues to be of relevance where the gain computed is then less than the gain that would be computed by taking the value at 31 March 1982.)

Building lease. A LEASE of land for a long term, usually ninety-nine years, at a rent called a ground rent, the lessee covenanting to build on it.

By the Law of Property Act 1925, s 99 either a mortgagor or mortgagee in possession can (in case of mortgage made after 1925) make a valid building lease for up to 999 years. Under the Settled Land Act 1925, s 41 a tenant for life may make a building lease for up to 999 years (see also ss 44 and 46 of that Act).

Building society. A society whose purpose or principal purpose is that of raising, primarily by the subscriptions of the members, a stock or fund for making to them advances secured on land for their residential use (see Building Societies Act 1986, s 5). Each person investing in a 'share account' of a building society is a shareholder of the society, as is each person accepting a secured loan ('a mortgage') from the society. A share in a building society is an asset for CGT purposes but no indexation allowance is available (FA 1988, s 113(1)(a)). A permanent interest-bearing share issued by a building society is a qualifying corporate bond (TCGA 1992, s 117(4) & (5)). In 1997, four old established building societies, whose members were those depositing money on 'share accounts', converted to banks (being quoted companies), the members then holding conventional voting shares. The Special Commissioners held that the trade of the building societies was carried on in the same way, and by the same people, before and after the conversion. Hence, the conversion costs (which totalled £359,600,000) were revenue and deductible for corporation tax purposes (*Halifax plc v Davidson [2000] STC (SCD) 251, Woolwich plc v Davidson [2000] STC (SCD) 302, Northern Rock v Thorpe [2000] STC (SCD) 317, Alliance & Leicester v Hamer [2000] STC (SCD) 332*).

Bull. On the Stock Exchange, is one who *buys* stock for settlement at a future date, without intending to take delivery, but with a view to gain by a rise in price in the interval.
    See BEAR.

Bull market. A market in which prices are primarily influenced by buyers.

Bunny bond. A bond issued under terms so that the investor can choose whether to receive interest or additional bonds.

Business. It appears that an activity is a 'business' for the purposes of the UK VAT legislation if it amounts to an 'economic activity' within the meaning of Directive 77/388/EEC art 4 (the Sixth Directive) as interpreted by the EC Court of Justice (*Wellcome Trust Ltd v Customs and Excise Comrs (1994) VAT decision 12206*). The leading UK case on the meaning of 'business' (*Customs and Excise Comrs v Morrison's Academy Boarding Houses Association [1978] STC 1*) was decided before the Sixth Directive was adopted and many of the subsequent cases made no reference to it. They do not, therefore, provide an authoritative interpretation of the Sixth Directive, although they may provide useful guidelines on matters not expressly covered by it and possible answers to questions not yet considered by the Court of Justice.

It has been said that it will never be possible or desirable to define the word exhaustively and that it does not have the same meaning wherever used in the VAT legislation (*Singer & Friedlander Ltd v Customs and Excise Comrs [1989] VATTR 27*). However, the earlier UK case law suggests that the following considerations should be taken into account in deciding whether an activity amounts to a business, although they are not principles which are conclusive in every case:

(1) Whether the activity is a 'serious undertaking earnestly pursued' or 'a serious occupation not necessarily confined to commercial or profit making undertakings'.

(2) Whether the activity is an occupation or function actively pursued with reasonable or recognisable continuity.

(3) Whether the activity has a certain measure of substance as measured by quarterly or annual value of taxable supplies made.

(4) Whether the activity is conducted in a regular manner and on sound and recognised business principles.

(5) Whether the activity is predominantly concerned with the making of taxable supplies to consumers for a consideration.

(6) Whether the taxable supplies are of a kind which, subject to differences of detail, are commonly made by those who seek to profit by them (*Customs and Excise Comrs v Lord Fisher [1981] STC 238, [1981] 2 All ER 147*).

Activities do not need to be carried on with the object of making a profit in order to amount to a business (*Customs and Excise*

Comrs v Morrison's Academy Boarding Houses Association [1978] STC 1).

Business asset. When a disposal is made of a business asset, taper relief at a preferential rate is applied to the capital gain arising on the disposal in order to compute the sum on which capital gains tax is charged. For periods of ownership from 6 April 2000 onwards, the following are treated as business assets:

(1) all shares and securities in unlisted trading companies;

(2) all shares and securities in a listed trading company where the individual is an employee or an officer (including those involved on a part-time basis);

(3) all shares and securities in a listed trading company where the individual is able to exercise at least 5% of the voting rights in the company;

(4) an asset used for the purposes of the trade of an unlisted trading company;

(5) an asset used for the purposes of trade carried on by the taxpayer, either alone or in partnership; and

(6) an asset held for the purposes of an office or employment.

(TCGA 1992, Sch A1, para 5).

Where there is a disposal by personal representatives or trustees the rule as to the nature of the asset is parallel to that for an individual. Thus, for a disposal made by a personal representative, an asset qualifies as a business asset if it is a shareholding of the appropriate description or if it is an asset used in a trade carried on by the personal representatives.

Assets held by trustees are treated as business assets if they fulfil the requirements outlined above for individuals. In addition, where a trust has a beneficiary with an interest in possession who is employed by the company whose shares are held by the trustees, the beneficiary's employment is imputed on the trustees for the purpose of determining the status of the trustees' shareholding. Thus, from 6 April 2000 onwards, a trustees' shareholding in a quoted trading company is treated as a business asset if the individual who is entitled to all income arising from those shares is in the employment of that company.

Examples of assets that are treated as business assets for the purpose of taper relief include: goodwill of a business; a freehold property let to a partnership of which the taxpayer is a member; a list of contact names purchased by an individual on being appointed as a salaried insurance agent; a patent exploited by an individual's personal company.

Business combination. The bringing together of separate entities into one economic entity as a result of one entity uniting with, or obtaining control over the net assets and operations of, another. [FRS 6 – Acquisitions and mergers & FRS 7 – Fair values in acquisition accounting]

Business entertainment. The cost of business entertainment is not allowable as a deduction in computing a liability to income tax or corporation tax (TA 1988, s 577(1)). VAT charged on business entertainment is not deducted from output VAT in calculating the VAT payable of a registered trader (SI 1992/3222, art 5(3)). Business entertainment is entertainment and hospitality of any kind provided by the trader, or by a member of his staff, but does not include anything provided by him for bone fide members of his staff unless its provision for them is incidental to its provision also for others (TA 1988, s 577(5)).

Business Expansion Scheme (BES). This is a scheme that was available from 1983 until 1993, under which an investor could obtain full relief against income tax for sums paid for shares in an unquoted trading company. The shares could be newly issued or purchased from another shareholder. The Business Expansion Scheme has been succeeded by the Enterprise Investment Scheme (EIS).

Business name. A name used by a person in the course of his business.

Any person (whether an individual or a company) has the right to carry on a trade under his own name. If he chooses to carry on a trade under a different name, a 'business name', the requirements of Business Names Act 1985 must be satisfied. Regulations under s 2 of the Act prohibit certain business names and under s 3 allow certain names only by approval of the Secretary of State.

Where a business name is used, the actual name of the person, company or partnership using it must be stated on all business letters and on invoices and receipts issued in the course of the business: (s 4(1)). A notice to the same effect must be displayed in a prominent position in any premises where the business is carried on: (s 4(1)).

Business property. Inheritance tax relief at either 100% or 50% is applied to transfers of certain business property provided (*a*) the asset is relevant business property, (*b*) the business is a qualifying business, (*c*) the asset has been held for the minimum period of ownership, and (*d*) the asset is not an excepted asset. A legacy that can only be satisfied by resort to an identified asset which is subject to business property relief is entitled to this relief (*Russell v IRC [1988] STC 195, [1988] 2 All ER 405*). The relief is applied to the value transferred, not the chargeable transfer and not the property (IHTA 1984, ss 103 & 104(1)). It is therefore applied before other relief, eg for CGT borne by the donee. Where the property is the subject of a chargeable transfer but the donor dies within seven years (so that additional tax may be due) or is the subject of a potentially exempt transfer (so that tax may become due) the benefit of the relief may, in those terms, be clawed back unless further conditions are satisfied at the time of the death.

There are six categories of relevant business property of which the first three qualify for 100% relief, the others for 50% relief (IHTA 1984, s 104(1)). The categories of property are:

(1) A business or an interest in a business, other than an excluded business (IHTA 1984, s 105(1)(a);

(2) *unquoted* shares (but not securities) in any company, unless the company carries on an excluded business (IHTA 1984, s 105(1)(bb);

(3) *quoted* shares or securities which give the transferor *control* of the company either by themselves or with other shares or securities owned by the transferor (IHTA 1984, s 105(1)(cc));

(4) *unquoted* securities of a company in which the transferor had a controlling interest before the transfer (IHTA 1984, s 105(1));

(5) any land or building, machinery or plant which, immediately before the transfer, was used wholly or mainly for the purposes of a business carried on by a company of which the transferor then had *control* or by a partnership of which he was then a partner (IHTA 1984, s 105(1)(d));

(6) land or buildings used for the purposes of a business carried on by the transferor where the property is settled but the transferor had a beneficial interest in possession at the time of the transfer (IHTA 1984, s 105(1)(e)).

In deciding whether shares are quoted or unquoted for the purpose of this relief one asks whether they are quoted on a recognised stock exchange (IHTA 1984, s 105(12A)). For the purposes of this relief a USM or AIM company is treated as unquoted so enabling the holding to qualify for 100% relief under (2) or (4) above (IHTA 1984, s 228(5)). Where an individual has lent money to finance an unquoted trading company, 100% can be available in respect of that loan, where the company has issued a debenture and the investor has a 51% shareholding in the company (that is, he is able to cast more than half of the votes at any general meeting—IHTA 1984, ss 105(1)(b), 169(1)). If, however, the investor does not have control of the company, no business property relief is available on the debenture. It is a matter of considerable significance when considering passing the family company to the next generation; it is often desirable for the debentures to be passed before transferring a tranche of shares that would cause a loss of control.

Business property relief is excluded if the company carries on an excluded business.

The relief is designed to alleviate the tax consequences of the transfer of a business. For this reason the transfer of property subject to a binding contract for sale is not relevant business property save where the property is a business or an interest in a business and the sale is to a company which is to carry on that business and is made in consideration wholly or mainly of shares or securities in that company (IHTA 1984, s 113).

Business rates. All property that is not domestic property is liable to business rates. Rates are payable by the occupier to the local authority and are computed by reference to the 'rateable value' of the property. Responsibility for determining the rateable value is with the District Valuer, an officer of Inland Revenue. His determination is subject to an appeals procedure. Each local authority specifies a rate (ie a number of pence) in each pound of rateable value, as the amount payable for the financial year by occupiers of property in the administrative area for local authority. A charity has an automatic relief of 50% applied to its liability to business rates; a local authority is authorised to increase this to 100% at its discretion. Special reliefs also apply to agricultural land.

Buy In Management Buy Out (BIMBO). A type of management buy out where investment is by the existing managers plus third party venture capitalists, who typically exercise managerial control after the BIMBO.

C

CA. Court of Appeal.

CAP. The Common Agricultural Policy.

CGT. Capital gains tax.

CIMA. Chartered Institute of Management Accountants.

CIOT. Chartered Institute of Taxation.

CIPFA. Chartered Institute of Public Finance and Accountancy.

Call. (1) Instalments whereby the capital in companies is gradually paid up by the shareholders (see the Companies Act 1985, s 8(1)).

(2) The conferring on students of the degree of barrister.

(3) The right to demand the allotment or transfer of shares at or before a given date at a given place.

See OPTION (2).

Called-up share capital. In relation to a company means, unless the contrary intention appears, so much of its share capital as equals the aggregate amount of the calls made on its shares (whether or not those calls have been paid), together with any share capital paid up without being called and any share capital to be paid on a specified future date under the articles, the terms of allotment of the relevant shares or any other arrangements for payment of those shares (see Companies Act 1985, s 737(1), (3)). 'Uncalled share capital' is to be construed accordingly (see ibid, s 737(2)).

Calls on contributories. Demands made by a company, or its official liquidator, on persons liable to contribute to its assets.

See CONTRIBUTORY.

Capita, distribution per. A distribution of an intestate's estate, in which each claimant has a share in his own right as in equal degree of kindred to the deceased, and not as representing another person, ie distribution *per stirpes*.

See STIRPES, DISTRIBUTION PER.

Capital allowance. An allowance which may be made for the purpose of income tax and corporation tax in respect of capital expenditure in case of eg machinery and plant, ships, agricultural buildings. See the Capital Allowances Act 1990.

See CORPORATION TAX; INCOME TAX.

Capital clause. A clause in a company's memorandum of association stating the amount of share capital with which the company proposes to be registered and the division of it into shares of a fixed amount.

Capital distribution. A company makes a capital distribution if it makes any distribution in money or money's worth which would not be treated as income in the hands of the recipient for purposes of income tax (TCGA 1992, s 122(5)(b)). A capital distribution is a disposal or part disposal of the shares held, the consideration being the amount received by the shareholder (TCGA 1992, s 122(1)). However, there is relief from tax where the capital distribution consists of shares or securities issued as part of a capital reorganisation (such as a scrip or rights issue) or, on election, where the capital distribution is 'small'. Taxable capital distributions commonly include distributions in liquidation (TA 1988, s 209(1)), repayment of share capital (TA 1988, s 209(2)(b)), repurchase by a company of its own share capital (TA 1988, s 219) and certain capital distributions by foreign companies.

Capital expenditure. Capital expenditure is not deductible in computing profits even though incurred wholly and exclusively for business purposes; such expenditure may qualify for relief under the capital allowance system. The task of distinguishing revenue from capital expenditure is not easy; and the problem has been made difficult by the inevitable fact that words or formulae that have been found useful in one set of facts may be neither relevant nor significant in another (per Lord Radcliffe in *Taxes Comr v Nchanga Consolidated Copper Mines Ltd [1964] 1 All ER 208 at 212*). While the courts have provided different tests at different times, none is paramount (see *Caledonian Paper plc v IRC [1998] STC (SCD) 129 at 134*). The latest test, reinforced by the House of Lords in *Tucker v Granada Motorway Services Ltd [1979] STC 393* requires first that one isolate the asset on which the sum has been spent; sums spent on an asset of a capital nature may be capital while sums spent on other things will not be. If that asset is of a capital nature, one then considers the nature of the particular expense; so sums spent on acquiring the capital asset will be capital while sums spent maintaining or repairing it will be revenue. This approach was followed by the Privy Council in *Auckland Gas v CIR [2000] STC 527, PC*. Gas leaked from old iron pipes. Instead of repairing the iron pipes, a network of polyethylene pipes was installed. The work was capital.

The costs of acquiring a business are capital expenses. Expenses shortly after acquiring a business will not be deductible if they are part of the acquisition cost (*Royal Insurance Co v Watson [1897] AC 1, 3 TC 500*). Facilities for and reorganisation of business are clearly capital of the business so expenditure on them may be capital. Thus the building of a factory is a capital expense and there will also be so classified ancillary works such as the provision of a water supply (*Boyce v Whitwick Colliery Co Ltd (1934) 18 TC 655*), of drainage (*Bean v Doncaster Amalgmated Collieries Ltd (1944) 27 TC 296*) and roads (*Pitt v Castle Hill Warehousing Co Ltd [1974] STC 420*. See also *Ounsworth v Vickers Ltd [1915] 6 TC 671*). Likewise the cost of sinking a mine shaft is a capital expense (*Bonner v Basset Mines Ltd (1912) 6 TC 146*) as is the cost of reconverting an oil rig at the end of its lease period (*RTZ Oil and Gas Ltd v Elliss [1987] STC 512*) or the cost of acquiring a waste tipping site (*Rolfe v Wimpey Waste Management Ltd*

[1989] STC 454, CA), The expense of moving from one set of business premises to another is a capital expense (*Granite Supply Association Ltd v Kitton (1905) 5 TC 168*) although the costs of removing trading stock are not so regarded. Once and for all expenditure on reorganisation may be capital. This was so in *Watney Combe Reid & Co Ltd v Pike [1982] STC 733* where a brewery made *ex gratia* payments to tenants under a scheme by which separate management companies were substituted for tenants; the purpose was to make the assets more profitable but it was important that the scheme involved a new corporate structure and a new way of doing business.

The expense of an application for planning permission over land is generally capital since the land is a capital asset and this expense is more than mere maintenance (*ECC Quarries Ltd v Watkis [1975] STC 578*). Likewise the premises are capital assets and so where a brewer applies for a licence for new premises the legal cost of applying for the new licence is capital expenditure (*Morse v Stedeford (1934) 18 TC 457*).

A payment for getting rid of a permanent disadvantage or onerous burden may be an enduring benefit and so a capital expense. So in *Alexander Howard & Co Ltd v Bentley (1948) 30 TC 334* the taxpayer paid a lump sum to be rid of a contingent liability to pay an annuity to the widow of its governing director. A payment to settle a capital liability is clearly a capital payment. So where a company had agreed to buy a ship to use in its trade a payment made on cancellation of the contract was a capital expense (*Countess Warwick Steamship Co Ltd v Ogg (1924) 8 TC 652*).

Contrast REPAIRS AND RENEWALS.

Capital gains tax. Capital gains tax is charged on chargeable gains 'accruing to' a person, other than a company, during a year of assessment (TCGA 1992, s 1).

Chargeable gains accrue only on chargeable disposals of chargeable assets. Certain events are treated as disposals, eg the complete loss or destruction of an asset (TCGA 1992, s 24(1)).

Although a number of the machinery provisions relating to returns, self-assessments, appeals and so on, are common to both taxes, CGT is a tax separate from income tax. This is still the case, notwithstanding the unification of the rates of CGT and income tax from 1988/89. Any gain liable to income tax is excluded from CGT and losses available for set off against income are not allowable losses for CGT. Conversely, an excess of capital losses cannot be set off against income liable to income tax. Further, deductions that are or would be allowable for income tax are not generally allowable for CGT.

CGT was introduced in 1965 and applies only to gains accruing since 5 April 1965. For disposals on or after 6 April 1988, CGT is effectively imposed only on gains accruing since 31 March 1982, subject to certain restrictions (TCGA 1992, s 39). The application of these restrictions involves computing the gain under the pre-6 April 1988 rules, including the special assumptions made in order to calculate gains in respect of assets owned on 6 April 1965. The restrictions may be disapplied if the taxpayer so elects.

To remove from the charge to tax increases in value which are purely as a result of inflation, a measure of relief (termed 'indexation relief') is applied for the period April 1982 to April 1998. Taper relief applies from April 1998.

For a liability to capital gains tax to arise:

1   there must be a disposal of a type relevant to CGT;
2   of an asset of a type relevant to CGT;
3   by a person chargeable to the tax;
4   on which a chargeable gain which is computed under the Act arises.

The scheme of the legislation is to distinguish a gain from a chargeable gain. It is only the latter that is subjected to tax. As we have just seen, the legislation does not specify how a gain should be computed. Rather, it specifies what costs can be deducted from the consideration (TCGA 1992, s 53(1)). These costs, in turn, attract an indexation allowance which statute specifies as 'allowed against the unindexed gain so as to give the gain for the purposes of this Act' (TCGA 1992, s 38). This is a strange formulation in an Act that does not instruct the taxpayer how to compute an 'unindexed gain'. The next step is to deduct any relief that arises by virtue of the nature of the asset (such as principal private residence relief) or a relief that arises from the use of the proceeds (rollover relief, deferral relief). Finally, the computational relief, taper relief, is deducted in order to compute the chargeable gain.

Capital instruments. All instruments that are issued by reporting entities as a means of raising finance, including shares, debentures, loans and debt instruments, options and warrants that give the holder the right to subscribe for or obtain capital instruments. In the case of consolidated financial statements the term includes capital instruments issued by subsidiaries except those that are held by another member of the group included in the consolidation. [FRS 4 – Capital instruments & FRS 13 – Derivatives and other financial instruments]

Capital redemption reserve. A reserve to which the amount by which a company's issued share capital is diminished on the cancellation of shares redeemed or purchased by a company is transferred (see Companies Act 1985, s 170(1)).

Carry over. A term used on the Stock Exchange signifying the postponement of the completion of a contract to buy or sell shares.

Cash. Cash in hand and deposits repayable on demand with any qualifying financial institution, less overdrafts from any qualifying financial institution repayable on demand. Deposits are repayable on demand if they can be withdrawn at any time without notice and without penalty or if a maturity or period of notice of not more than 24 hours or one working day has been agreed. Cash includes cash in hand and deposits denominated in foreign currencies. [FRS 1 – Cash flow statements]

Cash accounting. A method of accounting for VAT based on amounts paid and amounts received during the period of the

VAT return. Relief for bad debts is, thus, automatically granted by the scheme. In order to qualify to use cash accounting, the business cannot have taxable supplies that are expected to exceed £350,000 in the 12 month period.

Cash basis. Prior to 1999/2000, many professionals, including some very large professional partnerships, drew up their accounts on what was termed as a 'conventional' basis. In practice, there were many different accounting bases that were adopted. Some partnerships drew up true 'cash accounts'; that is, no income was recognised until it was received and no expenditure until it was paid—this meant there was no work in progress, debtors or creditors. More commonly, creditors and debtors were recognised but not work in progress. In some cases, accounts were drawn up recognising creditors but not debtors nor work in progress. Where work in progress was recognised, the accounting treatment ranged from a valuation at charging rates for all work undertaken, including that by the principals, to a purely nominal sum that had its basis in history and nothing else. Good arguments could be—and were—put forward for the use of such accounting concepts. For barristers, for example, the fact that it is not possible to sue for fees charged for representation at proceedings provided a justification that the only proper way of accounting was to recognise those fees only when they were received.

From 2000/01, a profession is required to draw up its accounts, for tax purposes, using opening and closing balance sheets that are in accordance with accounting standards. The effect of this is that the accounts for the period that forms the first period under the new rules are drawn up with the opening position being the closing balance sheet for the preceding period (FA 1998, Sch 6, para 3). The closing position is, however, a balance sheet in accordance with Accounting Standards. Where a conventional basis has been used in the past the effect of this is that the profit of the basis period for the first period under the new rules is increased by the difference between the balance sheet total at the end

of that period and the total that would have been computed had the conventional basis been followed. This is termed the 'adjustment charge' (FA 1998, Sch 6, para 2(1)). This 'adjustment charge' is then spread over ten years (FA 1998, Sch 6, para 4).

Cash flow. An increase or decrease in an amount of cash. [FRS 1 – Cash flow statements]

Cash-settled commodity contract. A commodity contract (including a contract for the delivery of gold) which, though having contract terms that require settlement by physical delivery, is of a type that is normally extinguished other than by physical delivery in accordance with general market practice.

'Commodities' in this context means hard commodities (such as metals) and soft commodities (such as oils, grains, cocoa, coffee, cotton, soya beans and sugar). It is not intended that cash or government securities should be treated as commodities for the purposes of the FRS. [FRS 13 – Derivatives and other financial instruments]

Certificate. A writing made in any court, to give notice to another court of anything done in it.

Certificate, land. A certificate drawn up by the Land Registry and containing particulars of registered land, and delivered to the registered proprietor or deposited in the Registry as the proprietor may prefer.

Certificate, share. See SHARE CERTIFICATE.

Certificate of incorporation. A document signed by the Registrar of Companies showing that the company to which it relates has been formed.

On the registration of a company's memorandum, the Registrar must give a certificate that the company is incorporated and, in the case of a limited company, that it is limited (see Companies Act 1985, s 13(1), (2)). Where he registers a company's memorandum which states that the company is to be a public company, the certificate of incorporation must contain a statement that the company is a public company (see ibid, s 13(6)).

See LIMITED COMPANY; PUBLIC COMPANY.

Certificate of value. For transfers of property other than stock or marketable securities where the consideration does not exceed £60,000 the stamp duty chargeable is £nil. The nil rate of duty operates only if the instrument is certified as being for a consideration not exceeding the sum of £60,000 (FA 1999, Sch 13, Part I, para 6). Certification requires that the instruments contain a statement certifying that the transaction does not form part of a large transaction or series of transactions in respect of which the amount or value, or aggregate amount or value of the consideration exceeds the relevant figure.

Similar certificates certifying that the consideration does not exceed £250,000 or £500,000 are required for the 1% and 3% rates respectively to operate.

Certification of transfer. A certification indorsed on a transfer form showing that a share certificate has been lodged with a company representing more shares than the transferor wants to transfer.

Certum est quod certum reddi potest (that is certain which can be rendered certain). The law imposes requirements of certainty upon the terms of various transactions in order for those transactions to be valid, eg terms of contracts, of trusts, of leases, and so on. However this does not entail that all aspects of a transaction must be known in their particulars from the outset; it is sufficient that all necessary particulars will be certain when it is essential that they are known. For example, an *income* BENEFICIARY under a TRUST is entitled to be paid income on the trust property; nevertheless that the amount of income on property is not known in advance before it arises (eg the exact value of dividends on shares before they are declared, etc) does not make the trust void for uncertainty of subject matter (uncertainty about the property which is the subject of the trust), because the income will be known exactly when it arises and must be paid to the beneficiary.

Chairman. The person elected by the directors of a company to be chairman of their meetings, including a person who, though not so elected, holds any office carrying similar functions. Generally, any person elected to take charge of and control meetings, as, eg, of a local council. He may have a casting vote.

Chancery Division. One of the three Divisions of the High Court of Justice, superseding the former High Court of Chancery. The causes and matters assigned to the Division include the administration of estates, partnership actions, actions relating to mortgages, portions and charges on land, trusts, etc, and bankruptcy business. The companies court and the patents court are also situated in this Division.

Charge. A word used in various senses:

(1) A charge on land is a SECURITY INTEREST in land. Charges on land are typically called incumbrances, for they 'incumber' the title to land. Charges on land are mortgages, either legal or equitable, or charging orders, made by a court to secure the payment of a JUDGMENT DEBT. As to the only charges on land which are capable of subsisting at law, see the Law of Property Act 1925, s 1(2), and as to mortgages, see the Law of Property Act 1925, Part III, and Sch 1, Parts VII and VIII.

(2) Expenses or costs.

Charge by way of legal mortgage. A mortgage created by charge. One of the only two ways in which a legal mortgage can be created. The mortgagee, under such a charge, does not get any legal term. But the effect of such a charge is to give him the same protection, powers and remedies as if a mortgage term by demise or subdemise were vested in him (see the Law of Property Act 1925, s 87, and Form No 1 in Sch V to the Act).

See MORTGAGE; SECURITY.

Charge on income. A charge on income is an income expense that is an annuity or annual payment payable otherwise than in respect of any of the company's loan relationships, but not including sums which are, or, but for any exemption would be, chargeable under Schedule A (TA 1988, s 338(3)). A payment which is deductible in computing profits, is not to be treated as a charge on income. However it is also enacted that no deduction may be made in computing income from any source in respect of sums falling within the definition above. The line between a charge on profits and a deductible expense is important, first because some items, eg patents and mining royalties, can only be treated as charges; second, because charges are deducted when made and not on an accruals basis (this means that a charge may be paid at the due date or early or late with consequent effect) and third, because an expense deductible in computing income affects trading income and so trading losses whereas a charge can be set off against all types of profit, whether income or capital gain.

A qualifying donation to a charity (such as a gift aid donation) is a charge on income (TA 1988, ss 338(2)(b) & 339(1)).

Chargeable asset. An asset on which capital gains tax is charged on a disposal. Every asset is a chargeable asset, other than the following exempt assets: (a) Debts other than the debt on a security, (b) Covenants, (c) Wasting assets, (d) Private residence, (e) Government stock, (f) Qualifying corporate bonds, (g) EIS shares and certain BES shares, (h) Woodlands.

Chargeable business asset. CGT holdover relief on a gift of shares is limited to the proportion of the value of the shares that the value of chargeable business assets in the company bears to total chargeable assets (TCGA 1992, Sch 7, para 7). A chargeable asset is a chargeable business asset if it is used for the purposes of a trade, profession or vocation carried on by the company, or another company in the group (TCGA 1992, Sch 7, para 7(2)(a)).

Chargeable event. Income tax at higher rate only is charged on the proceeds received from a life assurance policy (not being an approved exempt policy) at a chargeable event. A chargeable event occurs on: (a) death, (b) maturity of the policy, (c) surrender of the policy and (d)

assignment of the policy for money or money's worth (TA 1988, s 540(1)).

Chargeable transfer. Inheritance tax is a tax on a chargeable transfer (IHTA 1984, s 1). A chargeable transfer is any transfer of value made by an individual after 26 March 1974 other than an exempt transfer (IHTA 1984, s 2(1)) or a potentially exempt transfer made after 17 March 1986 (IHTA 1984, s 3A(1)).

At a technical level it is necessary to distinguish (a) the value transferred by a transfer of value from (b) the value transferred by a chargeable transfer. This is because (a) is calculated ignoring the exempt transfer rules and without regard to grossing up.

See TRANSFER OF VALUE.

Charitable purposes. Purposes recognised in law as being of a charitable nature. CHARITIES may only direct their funds to such purposes. Charitable purposes are of a varied nature, and derive from a list of such purposes found in the Preamble to the Charitable Uses Act 1601, sometimes known as the Statute of Elizabeth. The scope of charitable purposes has grown by analogy from the list in the Preamble, thus any purpose mentioned in the Preamble is charitable, and the courts have expanded the list to include those purposes analogous to those found there. Charitable purposes have been characterised as falling under four heads: (i) the relief of poverty; (ii) the advancement of education; (iii) the advancement of religion; and (iv) other purposes beneficial to the community not falling under the above heads (*IT Special Purposes Comrs v Pemsel (1891) 3 TC 53 at 94* per Lord McNaughten and, more recently, the decision of the High Court in *IRC v Oldham Training and Enterprise Council [1996] STC 1218*).

Charitable trust. A trust for charitable purposes. Unlike trusts for persons, charitable trusts may be perpetual. Charitable trusts are also relieved of many tax liabilities to which trusts for persons are subject.

Charity. A 'Charity' is defined in TA 1988, s 506(1) for the purpose of the income tax and corporation tax exemptions as 'any body of persons or trust established for charitable purposes only'. It is clear that to be a charity it is not necessary for the body to be registered with the Charity Commissioners, although such a registration is irrefutable evidence that the body is a charity. When a body is correctly regarded as a 'charity' the capital gains tax reliefs in TCGA 1992, ss 256, 257 are applicable.

Charity Commissioners. A body of commissioners for England and Wales, originally established by the Charitable Trusts Acts 1853–1860. There is a Chief Charity Commissioner and two other Commissioners; at least two of the three must be barristers or solicitors. One or two additional Commissioners may be appointed if necessary. The Commissioners have the general function of promoting the effective use of charitable resources by encouraging the development of better methods of administration, by giving information and advice, and by investigating and checking abuses.

Chartered Association of Certified Accountants. The Association was founded in 1904 and has 79,000 qualified members. Members use the designatory letters ACCA (Associates) and FCCA (Fellows). The majority of members work in industry, although a significant number are in public practice. Website: www.acca.org.uk

Chartered Institute of Management Accountants. CIMA was founded in 1919 and was granted its Royal Charter in 1975. The Institute has 50,000 qualified members, who use the designatory letters CMA. The majority of members work in industry. Website: www.cima.org.uk

Chartered Institute of Public Finance and Accountancy. CIPFA was founded in 1885 and was granted its Royal Charter in 1959. The Institute has 13,500 members, who use the designation CPFA. The majority of members have posts in central or local Government. Website: www.cipfa.org.uk

Chartered Institute of Taxation. CIOT is the senior professional institute in the

UK specialising in taxation. Founded in 1930 and granted its Royal Charter in 1994, the Institute has 11,000 members, of which 515 are Fellows (FTII) and 10,500 are Associates (ATII). Website: www.ciot.org.uk

Chattels. The name given to things which in law are deemed personal property. Chattels are divided into *chattels real* and *chattels personal*; chattels real being interests less than a freehold in land which devolved (after the manner of personal estate) as leaseholds. As opposed to freeholds, they are regarded as personal property. But as being interests in real estate, they are called *chattels real* to distinguish them from movables, which are called *chattels personal*.

Formerly, the distinction between real and personal property was important for the devolution of estates on intestacy (*see* SUCCESSION), but now the rules as to devolution apply equally to real and personal property.

In normal legal parlance, chattels do not comprise the entire spectrum of personal property, but only CHOSES in possession, ie tangible objects. Thus intangible personal property, CHOSES in action of various kinds, intellectual property, and so forth, are not chattels.

The Administration of Estates Act 1925, s 55(1)(x) defines 'personal chattels' as meaning carriages, horses, stable furniture and effects (not used for business purposes), motor cars and accessories (not used for business purposes), garden effects, domestic animals, plate, plated articles, linen, china, glass, books, pictures, prints, furniture, jewellery, articles of household or personal use or ornament, musical and scientific instruments and apparatus, wines, liquors and consumable stores.

See REAL AND PERSONAL PROPERTY.

Cheque. A written order addressed by a person (the drawer) to a banker (the drawee) to pay money, generally to some third party (the payee). It is defined by the Bills of Exchange Act 1882, s 73 as a bill of exchange drawn on a banker payable on demand.

See BILL OF EXCHANGE.

A cheque may be drawn in favour of a specified person, or payable to his order, in which case it may be transferred to another party by endorsement and delivery, or payable to bearer (ie to any one currently holding it), in which case it is transferable by mere delivery. If properly transferred to him or her, the transferee acquires the same right as had the original payee or bearer to demand payment from the drawee.

The law of cheques is codified in the above-mentioned Act, and in the Cheques Acts 1957 and 1992, all of which are to be construed as one.

A *certified* cheque is a cheque which the bank on which it is drawn has certified that it will accept and pay on presentation.

Uncrossed cheques are transferable, and count as NEGOTIABLE INSTRUMENTS. The transferee may demand payment from the drawee (the bank upon which a cheque is drawn) upon presentation of the cheque. However, by various means the transferability of cheques may be restricted. A *crossed* cheque is a cheque crossed with two lines, between which may be inserted *either* the name of a bank *or* the words 'and company' in full or abbreviated. In the former case the banker on whom it is drawn must not pay the money for the cheque to any person other than the banker named; in the latter case he must not pay it to any person other than a banker. A *non-transferable* cheque is a crossed cheque bearing the words 'account payee' or 'a/c payee' either with or without the word 'only', and operates similarly to the latter-mentioned crossed cheque. In all of these cases an individual may only receive payment under the cheque via a banker, who will present the cheque to the drawee bank.

Child. The meaning varies, eg in the Children and Young Persons Act 1933, the word means a person under the age of 14 years (s 107(1)). But in the Children Act 1989 it means a person under the age of 18 years (s 105(1)).

Chinese walls. Invisible divisions between different functions of financial conglomerates. They are designed to prevent CONFLICT OF INTEREST.

Chose. A thing, specifically, any asset other than land. *Choses* are of two kinds— *choses in possession* and *choses in action*. A *chose in possession* is an item of property which can be possessed, and therefore all objects, clothes, furniture, food, animals, books, and so on are *choses in possession*. A *chose in action* is a thing of which a person has not any means of possessing, but merely a right to claim it (if withheld) by action, ie by process of law. Thus, the right to be paid the balance of one's account at a bank, or the right to be paid money owed one by a debtor, is a *chose in action*. *Choses in possession* are transferred by delivery with the intention that the receiver shall henceforward be the owner, or by DEED of gift. *Choses in action* are transferred by assignment in writing, signed by the assignor, absolute in terms, and to be effective notice must be given in writing to the debtor (see Law of Property Act 1925, s 136(1)).

City Code on Take-overs and Mergers. A code operated by the Stock Exchange relating to the take-overs and mergers of listed companies. It is not a code of law but of business practice. A Panel on Take-overs and Mergers is responsible for its operation.

Civil. A term variously opposed to criminal, ecclesiastical, military, or common law. The civil law and procedure and civil actions, etc as opposed to the criminal law and procedure and actions etc concerns non-penal actions under which individuals seek redress for wrongs, eg damages for breach of contract. The civil law as opposed to the ecclesiastical law is the law generated by the law courts and Parliament, rather than the law generated by the Church. As opposed to military law, the civil law is the law applying to civilians, ie those not serving in the army, navy, or air-force. As opposed to the laws of England, the members of the Commonwealth, and the United States, whose legal systems are based on the COMMON LAW, civil refers to those systems of law, such as the French or German, whose law derives from Roman CIVIL LAW JURISDICTION and is generally embodied in 'civil codes'.

Civil Law Jurisdiction. The system of law that is based on codification (such as

French law), by contrast to Common Law, which is based on precedent.

Civil procedure. The procedures by which litigants initiate and maintain proceedings in a civil action or case, and the specific means of governing of this process by judges and other officials of the court. The day-to-day processes of litigation, from the filing of claims, the setting down of hearing dates, the specifying of particular forms for different documents, time periods for the giving of notices, and so on, are generally set down in the 'rules of court' for particular courts which are amended from time to time, and usually published anew annually.

Civil Procedure Act 1997. An Act embodying reforms in the law of civil procedure proposed by a Committee headed by Lord Woolf (generally known as the 'Woolf Reforms'), which are intended to promote the early settlement of claims and to expedite the legal process in advance of trial and make it less expensive, in particular through the greater oversight of judges.

Civil Procedure Rules. The new form of the rules of court, made under the Civil Procedure Act 1997, which apply both to county courts and to the High Court generally.

Civil remedy. A remedy available to a person by action, as opposed to a criminal prosecution.

Claim. A challenge of interest in anything that is in the possession of another person, or at least out of the possession of the claimant.

Claimant. One who makes a legal claim. In accordance with the CIVIL PROCEDURE RULES, claimant is to be the preferred term in lawyerly use for the party previously called the plaintiff.

Class 1 NIC. National insurance contributions charged on the earnings of 'employed earners'. A primary contribution is required from the employee. A secondary contribution is required from the employer.

Class 1A NIC. Class 1A contributions secure no benefits for employees under the contributory scheme. The contributions secure unemployment, incapacity, maternity and long-term benefits, mainly retirement pension and bereavement benefits.

Class 1B NIC. National insurance contributions payable by employers in respect of PAYE Settlement Agreements.

Class 2 NIC. National insurance contributions payable by all self-employed earners. The contributions secure incapacity, maternity and long-term benefits, mainly retirement pension and bereavement benefits.

Class 3 NIC. Voluntary national insurance contributions which can only be paid by those not otherwise securing benefits through contributions and secure only the long-term benefits.

Class 4 NIC. National insurance contributions payable on business profits between a lower and upper threshold which are immediately derived by an individual from carrying on a trade, profession or vocation. Business profits for this purpose are ascertained as for income tax and collection is through the income tax system.

Class of business. A distinguishable component of an entity that provides a separate product or service or a separate group of related products or services. [SSAP 25 – Segmental reporting]

Class of intangible assets. A category of intangible assets having a similar nature, function or use in the business of the entity. [FRS 10 – Goodwill and intangible assets]

Class of tangible fixed assets. A category of tangible fixed assets having a similar nature, function or use in the business of the entity. [FRS 15 – Tangible fixed assets]

Client. A person who consults a solicitor. A solicitor, also, in reference to the counsel he instructs is spoken of as a client. The word is also used in reference to other professions.

Climate change levy. Climate change levy is imposed on supplies for industrial and commercial purposes of energy in the form of electricity, gas, petroleum gas and other gaseous hydrocarbons supplied in a liquid state, and any other taxable commodity, such as coal. The levy is specified in FA 2000, s 30 and Sch 6. It applies to supplies made after 5 April 2001. The levy applies to industry (including fuel industries), commerce, agriculture, public administration and other services. It does not apply to domestic or charity use, fuel for transport, energy used to produce another energy produce (eg coal used to generate electricity), and use to manufacture feedstocks etc. Exemptions also apply to electricity generated in combined heat and power plants and by renewable sources such as wind and solar power.

With some exceptions, the person liable to account for the levy is the supplier. The levy is charged at the half-rate for horticultural producers and at a reduced rate of 20% where a supplier in an energy-intensive sector has concluded an approved climate-change agreement.

Close company. A company is designated a close company if it satisfies any one of three tests. The tests are:
(*a*) that it is controlled by five or fewer participators,
(*b*) that it is controlled by its directors,
(*c*) five or fewer participators, or participators who are directors, together possess or are entitled to acquire such rights as would, in the event of the winding-up of the company entitle them to receive the greater part of the assets of the relevant company which would then be available for distribution among the participators. (To apply this test, the rights of loan creditors are disregarded.)
(TA 1988, s 414).

Certain companies are not close companies:
(1) a non-resident company, even if controlled by a resident company,
(2) a company controlled by one (or more) open companies, unless it is treated as close by the application of one of the other tests,
(3) a company which is only close because

it has one or more open companies as loan creditors with control under that rule which gives control to one entitled to the greater share of the assets on a winding-up,
(4) a company controlled by the Crown.

Close family. Close members of the family of an individual are those family members, or members of the same household, who may be expected to influence, or be influenced by, that person in their dealings with the reporting entity. [FRS 8 – Related party disclosures]

Close investment holding company. A close investment holding company cannot use the reduced rate of corporation tax. All profits are taxed at the full corporation tax rate of 30% (TA 1988, s 13A).

A close investment holding company is defined by exception. Every close company is a close investment holding company, and hence, does not have the lower rates of tax available, unless the company exists wholly or mainly for any one or more of six specified purposes (TA 1988, s 13A(1) & (2)).

The first qualifying purpose is carrying on a trade or trades on a commercial basis. (This definition does not extend to professions.) The second purpose is that of making investments in land where the land is, or is intended to be, let to unconnected persons. The remaining qualifying purposes embroider the first two. Thus a company will escape close investment company status if its purpose is to hold shares in and securities of or making loans to a qualifying company or to co-ordinate the administration of two or more qualifying companies. It may also exist for the purposes either (*a*) of a trade carried on, on a commercial basis, by a company which controls it or by a qualifying company, or (*b*) of making investments by a company which controls it or by another qualifying company.

Closing rate. The exchange rate for spot transactions ruling at the balance sheet date and is the mean of the buying and selling rates at the close of business on the date for which the rate is to be ascertained. [SSAP 20 – Foreign currency translation]

Club. A voluntary association, for social and other purposes, of a number of persons who pay a certain sum either to a common fund for the benefit of the members or to a particular individual. In the former case it is a 'members' club and in the latter a 'proprietary' club. In a proprietary club the expenses and risk are borne by a contractor who takes all profits. A members' club is usually managed by a steward under the superintendence of a committee, and the members, merely as such, are not liable for debts incurred by the committee or for goods supplied to the club. A club as a body has no position recognised in law. It is not a partnership, nor a company, nor a society subject to statutory rules, except under the Licensing Acts. As to the sale of intoxicating liquor in clubs, see the Licensing Act 1964, ss 39 *et seq*.

For the taxation status of a club, *see* UNINCORPORATED ASSOCIATION.

Codicil. A schedule or supplement to a will, when the testator desires to add, explain, alter, or retract anything. It must be executed with the same formalities as a will under the Wills Act 1837. *See* WILL.

Collective investment scheme. Any arrangements with respect to property of any description, including money, the purpose or effect of which is to enable persons taking part in the arrangements to participate in or receive profit arising from the acquisition, holding, management or disposal of the property or sums paid out of such profits or income (see Financial Services Act 1986, s 75(1)).

Commercial Court. A court constituted as part of the Queen's Bench Division, to take causes and matters entered in the Commercial List (see Administration of Justice Act 1970, s 3(1)).

Commercial law. Also known as mercantile law, a branch of the laws of CONTRACT and PROPERTY dealing with business transactions. The main subject areas are the SALE OF GOODS, the law of BILLS OF EXCHANGE, NEGOTIABLE INSTRUMENTS and documents of title, and the law of credit transactions, in particular secured credit transactions. Sales of goods are the most common commercial contractual transaction, by which a money payment (or the promise to make one) is exchanged for a chattel or CHATTELS. They are thus contracts for the exchange of property, and so involve the law of both. The law of sale of goods is particularly concerned with the express or implied terms of the contract concerning the seller's good title to the goods or authority to sell them and the quality of the goods and their fitness for the buyer's purposes, in particular where sold (wholly or in part) on the basis of a description or sample; the property or title aspects of a contract for sale, in particular the time when and circumstances in which the buyer obtains title to the goods (eg at the time the contract is made and before actual delivery of the goods, or upon delivery, or sometime following delivery (eg when the purchase price is paid for goods transferred on credit, etc), and the rights of THIRD PARTY purchasers of the goods in these circumstances; and the seller's and buyer's remedy for breach of contract. Bills of exchange, negotiable instruments, and documents of title all concern the '*reification*' (the turning of an abstract thing into something tangible) *of rights* to be paid certain sums of money or to be delivered property, *into* documentary form. An example of the former is a PROMISSORY NOTE, which embodies the right to be paid a certain sum of money, and of the latter, a bill of lading, which embodies the right to the cargo on board a ship. These documents are typically transferable so as to confer upon the transferee the right they embody, and much of the law in this area concerns the rights of transferees to enforce such rights in different circumstances, eg where the transferee in good faith takes from a transferor who obtained the document fraudulently, or where the transaction or relationship between the original parties to the creation of the document is such as to affect the force of the right the document purportedly embodies. Notice again the connection between the law of contract and the law of property. Voluntarily-created contractual obligations, by being embodied in a document that may be transferred in theory to anyone, become of a species of property right, and so the rights of THIRD

PARTY transferees become an issue. The law of credit transactions concerns the rules governing the relationship of creditor and debtor, and in particular, the law of secured debt transactions, ie transactions by which the creditor takes a SECURITY INTEREST in the property of the debtor. This law is often much involved in the law of the sale of goods, for many sales of goods are also secured credit transactions. For example, a seller may deliver and pass title to goods to a buyer on credit, but take a security interest in the goods so delivered; if the buyer does not pay the price under the contract, ie his debt to the seller, in the specified time, the seller will be able to exercise a right to repossess the goods, and sell them on to a THIRD PARTY to make up the deficiency in the price paid.

Following the creation of legislation to protect consumers in commercial dealings, commercial law can also encompass CONSUMER LAW.

Commodity contract and cash-settled commodity contract. A commodity contract is a contract that provides for settlement by receipt or delivery of a commodity. [FRS 13 – Derivatives and other financial instruments]

Common, tenancy in. One of the two basic forms of co-ownership, the other being joint tenancy. A tenancy in common is sometimes referred to as ownership of 'undivided shares', as its basic rationale is that though each co-owner is each an owner of the whole of the property, each holds his or her own interest in the property separately. Thus, upon death, a tenant in common's right to the property can be passed under his or her will, and if not given by will, devolves under the rules of intestate SUCCESSION.

As regards land, this tenancy is possible only in EQUITY (see ss 34–39 and Sch 1, Part IV to the Law of Property Act 1925 (as amended by the Law of Property (Amendment) Act 1926)), however, co-owners may hold movable property as tenants in common.

See JOINT TENANCY.

Common Law. The ancient unwritten law of England, which has been exported to former colonies, including the United States of America.

The term 'Common Law' is used in various senses:

(1) Of the ancient law above mentioned embodied in judicial decisions as opposed to statute law, ie the law enacted by Parliament.

(2) Of the original and proper law of England, formerly administered in the Common Law Courts, ie the superior court of Westminster, and the Nisi Prius Courts, as opposed to the system called Equity, which was administered in the Court of Chancery. Since the Judicature Act 1873 all courts administer law and equity concurrently (see now the Supreme Court Act 1981, s 49).

(3) Of the municipal law of England as opposed to the Roman Civil Law, or other foreign law.

Commorientes. Persons dying of the same accident or on the same occasion. Under the provisions of the Law of Property Act 1925, s 184 the younger is deemed to have survived the elder.

Company. (1) A body of persons associated together for the purposes of trade or business. Companies are formed (1) by charter, (2) by special Act of Parliament, (3) by registration at Companies House.

Companies are regulated chiefly by the Companies Act 1985.

For the different types of companies, see the entries below.

(2) In the Corporation Taxes Acts, a 'company' means any body corporate or unincorporated association (TA 1988, s 832(1), (2) and see *Frampton (Trustees of the Worthing Rugby Football Club) v IRC [1987] STC 273* and *Blackpool Marton Rotary Club v Martin [1988] STC 823*), but does not include a partnership, a local authority or a local authority association. Individuals who invest a joint account, eg as members of an investment club, are not treated as a company carrying on business together. Authorised unit trusts are treated as if they were companies (TA 1988, s 468).

(3) Includes any enterprise which

comes within the scope of statements of standard accounting practice. [SSAP 17 – Accounting for post balance sheet events, SSAP 20 – Foreign currency translation & SSAP 21 – Accounting for leases and hire purchase contracts]

Company, close. *See* CLOSE COMPANY.

Company, holding. *See* HOLDING COMPANY.

Company, limited. *See* LIMITED COMPANY.

Company, private limited. *See* PRIVATE LIMITED COMPANY.

Company, public. *See* PUBLIC COMPANY.

Company, small. *See* SMALL COMPANY.

Company, subsidiary. *See* SUBSIDIARY COMPANY.

Company, unlimited. *See* UNLIMITED COMPANY.

Company law. The law governing companies, one of the two most prevalent forms of business organisation, the other being PARTNERSHIPS. Companies may be public, limited either by shares or by guarantee, or private, which may be limited by shares or unlimited.

See PUBLIC COMPANY; PRIVATE LIMITED COMPANY; COMPANY LIMITED BY GUARANTEE; COMPANY LIMITED BY SHARES; UNLIMITED COMPANY.

There are two related, central principles which underlie the general shape of company law. The first is the principle of corporate personality. Companies are corporations, which means that the company has a distinct personality in law from those of its members (cf PARTNERSHIPS). Thus a company can sue or be sued in its own name, and holds its own property. The members are not entitled to treat the company's property as property co-owned by them all. Their interest in the company is limited by the rights they have under the company's charter or rules of association: typically, the holder of ordinary shares in a company limited by shares has the right to be paid dividends as and when

declared by the company's board of directors (ie governing officers) and the right to participate in the governance of the company at general meetings of the shareholders and in the election of the board of directors. So, for example, if a company brings an action against someone for breach of contract, any damages it receives become the property of the company—they are not distributed to the members as if they were joint plaintiffs (claimants) in the legal action. Similarly, if the company is itself liable to an outside party, only the assets of the company itself (including any rights it holds to make monetary demands, or *calls*, on others, eg its members) are available to meet that liability. The members are not themselves personally liable to the company's creditors. The second principle is limited liability. Although unlimited companies exist, the vast majority of trading companies exploit the facility of limited liability. This liability refers to the liability of members of the company to meet its liabilities after the company's own assets are used up. If one holds fully paid up shares in a company, one has no further liability to the company, and thus no liability indirectly to its creditors.

Besides dealing with the effects of limited liability and corporate personality in a company's dealing with outside parties, company law concerns the incorporation (or birth) of companies and their winding-up (termination), the law governing the issuance of shares, and the rights provided by different shares to shareholders and the relations between different classes of shareholders, the rights of shareholders vis-à-vis the company itself and against the directors, the election of directors and the taking over of control of a company, and the duties of directors.

Company limited by guarantee. A company having the liability of its members limited by the memorandum of association to such amount as the members may respectively thereby undertake to contribute to the assets of the company in the event of its being wound up (see Companies Act 1985, s 1(2)(b)).

Company limited by shares. A company having the liability of its members limited by the memorandum of association to the amount, if any, unpaid on the shares respectively held by them (see Companies Act 1985, s 1(2)(a)).

Company secretary. An officer of a company dealing with the running of it from day to day and its general administration.

A company registered in England and Wales is required to specify a company secretary, being the person responsible for the submission of the annual return to the Registrar of Companies; a sole director must not also be secretary (Companies Act 1985, s 283(1), (2)). The name and address of the company secretary must be included in the register of directors and secretaries (s 288). There are no qualifications (nor any minimum age) specified for the company secretary of a private company. A public company is required to appoint a company secretary who holds one of the qualifications specified in Companies Act 1985, s 286.

Compensation for loss of employment. Such compensation will not be earnings for National Insurance contribution purposes if it represents compensation for breach by the employer of the terms of the employment contract (*Du Cros v Ryall (1935) 19 TC 444*). Compensation in this sense implies that either the employee is in a position to seek redress before the employment tribunal (or the court) or is actually doing so. In either case the compensation is to satisfy an actual or potential claim against the employer. It is not necessary that the employee should threaten to take legal action, or even that he should be aware that he could bring a claim against the employer: what is required is that there should be at the least a potential claim. The DSS guidance referred to the compensation payment being 'made voluntarily'. The guidance is correct if what is meant is making a payment to discharge a potential claim before the employee has considered making such a claim.

Compensation of this kind must be distinguished from that which arises under the terms of the employment contract, eg where the contract provides for an amount payable on premature termination. Because compensation of this kind is contractual, it is a profit derived from the employment and is therefore rightly to be included in earnings for contributions purposes. This follows the distinction made in the employment law case, *Delaney v Staples [1991] 2 QB 47, [1991] 1 All ER 609, CA*. However, the House of Lords' judgment in *Mairs v Haughey [1993] STC 569, HL* brings that point into question.

The Revenue guidance indicates that where it is the normal practice to make non-contractual compensation payments on termination of the employment, they should be 'treated as earnings'. This is because it is considered that such payments will have become part of the contractual arrangements if there is such a normal practice but this is not necessarily the case: one test is whether the employee could sue for the payment if it was not made in his or her own case.

Complaint. The act by which civil proceedings are set in motion in the magistrates' courts, as distinguished from an information in respect of a criminal offence (see Magistrates' Courts Act 1980, ss 50, 51).

Completion. The finalisation of a contract, especially one for the sale of land. The vendor delivers up the land contracted to be sold with a good title. The purchaser pays the price and takes possession. Completion normally takes place at the office of the vendor's solicitor at an agreed period after the exchange of contracts.

Compliance audit. An audit of procedures operated by the enterprise. For example, a set of dispatch notes can be traced back to the original orders and the posting into the sales ledger. A compliance test of this nature is important in establishing the degree to which the auditor can rely on the entries in the financial statements of the enterprise being a proper reflection of the activities of the enterprise.

Composition. A sum of money agreed to be accepted by the creditors of a debtor in satisfaction of the debts due to them from the debtor. A composition may be a private one effected by deed and registered under the Deeds of Arrangement Act 1914, when only creditors assenting to it will be bound; or a composition in bankruptcy proceedings under the Insolvency Act 1986, when, if passed by the creditors and approved by the court, it will bind all creditors entitled to prove, and of course no registration under the Deeds of Arrangement Act 1914 is necessary.

Deeds of arrangement affecting land may be registered under s 7 of the Land Charges Act 1972, in the name of the debtor.

See ARRANGEMENTS.

Compound settlement. Where land is settled by a series of separate deeds, the deeds together form one settlement which is called a 'compound settlement'. The commonest example of this occurs in the case of a resettlement, which requires several deeds. The fee simple is first settled on the father for life with remainder to his eldest son in tail; the entailed interest is barred by the son with the consent of his father as protector; and, finally, the land is resettled, generally, on the father for life, then on the son for life, with remainder to the son's eldest son in tail. In this case the three deeds may be read as one, being together called a 'compound settlement'. The Settled Land Act 1925, s 1(1), proviso, provides that the word 'settlement' is to be construed as referring to such a compound settlement where it exists.

See SETTLEMENT.

Compromise. An adjustment of claims in dispute by concession, either without resort to legal proceedings, or on the condition of abandoning them if already commenced.

Comptroller and Auditor General. An official appointed under the National Audit Act 1983 whose function is to carry out examinations into the economy, efficiency and effectiveness with which Government departments and bodies supported by public funds have used their resources in discharging their functions (see ss 6 and 7 of the Act).

He has a right of access to all such documents as he may reasonably require for carrying out an examination (National Audit Act 1983, s 8). He must report to the House of Commons the results of any examination: ibid, s 9.

Condition. The term condition has several meanings:

(1) In contract law, a condition is a term of a contract. If a condition of a contract is not met, then the innocent party may treat the contract as at an end, refuse further performance of his obligations under it, and bring an action against the other party for DAMAGES for breach.

See CONTRACT LAW; WARRANTY.

(2) In property law, a condition is a term of a GRANT, which either sets a requirement for the grant taking effect, a condition precedent, or provides for the termination of the estate granted upon the happening of an event, a condition subsequent.

See CONDITIONS PRECEDENT AND SUBSEQUENT.

Conditional fee, otherwise called a fee simple conditional, properly comprises every estate in fee simple granted on condition. But the term is usually understood to refer to that particular species called a 'conditional fee' at Common Law, which is an estate restrained in its form of donation to some particular heirs (exclusive of others): eg, to the heirs of a man's body, or to the heirs male of his body. The judges of earlier days construed it, not as an estate descendible to some particular heirs, but as an estate on condition that the land was to revert to the donor, if the donee had no heirs of his body. Once, therefore, an heir was born to the donee, the court would hold that the condition was met, and on the principle that once a condition was met it was utterly gone, the donee would then be regarded as having a fee simple absolute. This construction of gifts of lands was put a stop to by the Statute of Westminster the Second (1285), commonly called the statute *De Donis Conditionalibus*, which provided that henceforth the will of the donor should be observed *secundum formam in carta doni expressam* (according to the form expressed in the charter of gift), under which entailed estates or fees tail could thenceforward be granted. Under the Law of Property Act 1925 legal estates tail are converted into equitable estates tail, and such last-mentioned estates may be created in any property, real or personal (see ss 1(1) and (3), 130, and Sch 1, Part I).

See ESTATE.

Conditional sale agreement. An agreement for the sale of goods under which the purchase price or part of it is payable by instalments, and the property in the goods is to remain in the seller (notwithstanding that the buyer is to be in possession of the goods) until such conditions as to the payment of instalments or otherwise as may be specified in the agreement are fulfilled (see the Consumer Credit Act 1974, s 189(1)).

See HIRE-PURCHASE AGREEMENT.

Conditions of sale. The terms stated in writing, on which an estate or interest is to be sold by public auction. The Law of Property Act 1925, s 45, applies certain conditions of sale to all contracts, unless otherwise expressly stated. In the exercise of his powers under s 46 of the Act, the Lord Chancellor has prescribed a Statutory Form of Conditions of Sale which also apply to contracts by correspondence, unless excluded or modified.

Conditions precedent and subsequent. A condition *precedent*, in a conveyance or disposition of an estate, is a condition which must happen or be performed before the estate or interest can vest. A condition *subsequent* is a condition on the failure or non-performance of which an estate already vested may be defeated.

Conflict of interest, Conflict of interest and duty. In equity, the situation where a fiduciary's own interests conflict with his duty to act in the best interests of his principal. The 'no conflict rule' forbids a fiduciary from placing himself in a position where his own interest and his duty to his principal conflict in this way.

Conflict of laws. The discordance between the laws of one country and another, as applied to the same subject-matter, eg in the case of a contract made in one country and intended to be executed in another. Rules of law have been developed to deal with conflicts of laws, in particular rules for determining which country's courts are the appropriate forum for the dispute, and which country's law is the appropriate law for the resolution of the dispute. Because the law governing these disputes was developed largely in respect of PRIVATE LAW claims regarding contracts, torts, property, and the validity of marriages, the law of conflicts is also called 'private international law', to distinguish it from the law of nations, or 'public' international law.

Connected person. (1) Where the person making the disposal is connected with the person acquiring the asset, they are treated as parties to a transaction otherwise than at arm's length (TCGA 1992, s 18) and market value is substituted for any consideration actually paid for the purpose of calculating the capital gain arising on the disposal (TCGA 1992, s 17).

Connected persons for the purposes of capital gains tax are those within the following five categories given in TCGA 1992, s 286:

(a) Relatives

A taxpayer is connected with his/her spouse, brother, sister, ancestor or lineal descendant. A taxpayer is also connected with the spouse of any one of those individuals. Further, an individual is connected with the relations in the foregoing list of his husband or wife. This definition differs from the definition used for inheritance tax in IHTA 1984, s 272 in that, unlike inheritance tax, an individual's uncle, aunt, nephew and niece, are not connected persons for CGT purposes.

In this definition, a husband or wife means an individual who is married to the taxpayer, whether or not they are living together. A spouse, thus, ceases to be a connected person, and the spouse's relatives cease to be connected, only at decree absolute.

(b) Trustees

A trustee is connected with the settlor of the settlement of which he is trustee and also he is connected with any person who is, himself, connected with the settlor.

In addition, a trustee is connected with any close company of which the trustees of the settlement are participators, any company controlled by such a company and any company that fulfils this definition, but is not close solely by virtue of not being resident in the UK.

A connection can only be made through an individual while he is alive. Thus, after the death of the settlor of a trust, the trustees are not connected under these provisions with any individuals.

(c) Partners

A person is connected with any person with whom he is in partnership, with the spouse of any partner and with the brother, sister, ancestor or lineal descendant of any partner. However, this connection does not apply 'in relation to acquisitions or disposals of partnership assets pursuant to bona fide commercial arrangements'.

(d) Connected companies

A company is connected with another company:
(i) if the same person has control of both, or a person has control of one and persons connected with him, or he and persons connected with him, have control of the other; or
(ii) if a group of two or more persons has control of each company, and the groups either consist of the same persons or could be regarded as consisting of the same persons by treating (in one or more cases) a member of either group as replaced by a person with whom he is connected.

(TCGA 1992, s 286(5)).

(e) Individual and company connected

A company is connected with an individual if that individual has control of it or where a group of individuals who are connected persons have control of the company. Further, any two or more persons acting together to secure and exercise control of a company are treated in relation to that company as connected with each other.

(2) For Companies Act disclosure requirements, shareholdings of a director's spouse, his minor child or a company with which he is associated, or a trust from which he benefits are required to be recorded in the Directors' Report (Companies Act 1985, Sch 7, para 2(3)).

Consent presupposes a physical power, a mental power and a free and serious use of them. If consent is obtained by fraud or undue influence, it is not binding.

Consequential damage or injury is damage or injury arising by *consequence* to one person, from the culpable act or omission of another.

Consideration. Value that passes in exchange for something promised or done.

(1) Valuable consideration is necessary to make an agreement binding in law (though obligations may be made binding by expressing them in writing SEAL, ie in a DEED). It need not be adequate, but must be of some value in the eye of the law and cannot be illegal. It must also be present or future, but it must not be past, ie a value given before the agreement was made.

(2) There is also a consideration of natural love and affection for a spouse or near relation. This is, for some purposes, deemed a *good* consideration, but it is not *valuable* consideration, so as to support an action on a simple contract. It is sometimes called *meritorious* consideration.

(3) For capital gains tax, a gain is computed by deducting expenditure from consideration (or deemed consideration). Unless statute otherwise provides, the consideration for the disposal is the actual amount received, in money or money's worth.

Any receipt is potentially liable to be treated as consideration. Where there is a complex arrangement for the disposal, such as frequently arises on commercial deals when companies are sold or reorganised, the approach to be adopted was given by Lightman J in *Spectros International plc v Madeen [1997] STC 114 at 138b* as:

'The critical issue is to identify the consideration agreed and allocated to the disposal of the shares . . . I must approach the question before me as a matter of construction of the composite of the three documents . . . I must identify and give effect to the form of transaction which the parties have entered into and which they have sought to do; and in this process I must have regard first and foremost to the terms and language of the composite documents read as a whole in their proper context, but I am also to take into account business sense and reality and most particularly the value of the shares.'

Where the consideration includes an asset (eg a right) that will be valued at the date of the disposal that is being taxed, the value of the disposal consideration will then become the acquisition cost of the asset (see *Marren v Ingles [1980] STC 500*).

The valuation of any consideration must be taken as at the date of disposal; hindsight is not permitted (see *Fielder v Vedlynn Ltd [1992] STC 553*).

(4) For VAT, a transaction amounts to a supply only if a consideration is given for it (VATA 1994, s 5(2)(a)). However, a transfer, disposal or use of business goods or services without consideration is specifically stated to be a supply of goods or a supply of services (so as to be chargeable to tax) in specified circumstances.

Consideration may comprise money (ie cash), something other than money (ie a barter deal) or partly money and partly something else (eg a part exchange deal for a new motor car) (VATA 1994, s 19(2), (3)). A consideration in something other than money must be capable of being expressed in money (*Staatssecretaris van Financiën v Coöperatieve Aardappelenbewaarplaats GA (case 154/80) [1981] ECR 445, ECJ*). It may arise from the terms of a contract or from a general promise (see *Granada Group plc v Customs and Excise Comrs [1991] VATTR 104*). The money or other thing may be provided by the customer or a third party. It may be paid or given to the supplier or to someone other than the supplier. There must be a direct link between what has been provided and the consideration received (*Naturally Yours Cosmetics Ltd v Customs and Excise Comrs (case 230/87) [1988] STC 879, ECJ*). A sum of money received by a trader amounts to consideration only if there is a corresponding supply and the trader is free to deal with the sum as his own or receive some benefit from it (*H J Glawe Spiel-und Unterhaltungsgeräte Aufstellungsgesellschaft mbH & Co KG v*

Finanzamt Hamburg-Barmbek-Uhlenhorst (case C-38/93) [1994] STC 453).

The consideration for a transaction is that which is given, and this is determined objectively upon the facts of the transaction by reference to the terms agreed. Thus, the fact that a trader does not obtain the best possible bargain does not mean that his forbearance to charge a higher price amounts to consideration (*Exeter Golf and Country Club Ltd v Customs and Excise Comrs [1979] VATTR 70*). On the other hand, the fact that a trader does not make a profit on a supply does not mean that there is no consideration for it (*Heart of Variety Ltd v Customs and Excise Comrs [1975] VATTR 103*). The determining factor is whether a consideration is due, not whether it has been received (VATA 1994, s 25(1)). Thus, cash received for a retail sale amounts to consideration whether it is placed in the till or diverted by an employee before getting as far as the till (*Benton v Customs and Excise Comrs [1975] VATTR 138*).

A charge imposed under a statutory rather than a contractual obligation is not consideration where the payee receives no more than an indirect benefit from services supplied by the statutory body concerned (*Apple and Pear Development Council v Customs and Excise Comrs (case 102/86) [1988] STC 221, ECJ*).

See CONTRACT LAW.

Consignment. The act of sending goods; also the goods themselves so sent. The person who consigns the goods is called the consignor, and the person to whom they are sent is called the consignee.

Consistency concept. A fundamental basis of accounting. There is consistency of accounting treatment of like items within each accounting period and from one period to the next. [SSAP 2 – Disclosure of accounting policies]

Consolidated financial statements.
(1) The financial statements of a group prepared by consolidation. [FRS 2 – Accounting for subsidiary undertakings]
(2) Companies Act 1985, Sch 4 requires a consolidated balance sheet for any holding

company of a group, subject to certain *de minimus* exemptions. A consolidated balance sheet must give a true and fair view of the state of affairs of the group. In order to construct a consolidated balance sheet, any turnover and any profit on intra-group transactions must be excluded.

Consolidated Fund. A fund formed by the union, in 1787, of three public funds, then known as the *Aggregate* Fund, the *General* Fund, and the *South Sea* Fund. This Consolidated Fund of Great Britain was combined with that of Ireland by the Consolidated Fund Act 1816, s 1, as the *Consolidated Fund of the United Kingdom.* The United Kingdom now means Great Britain and Northern Ireland only.

The Consolidated Fund constitutes almost the whole of the ordinary public income of the United Kingdom, is pledged for the payment of the whole of the interest on the National Debt, and is also liable to several specific charges imposed upon it from time to time by Act of Parliament.

Consolidation. The process of adjusting and combining financial information from the individual financial statements of a parent undertaking and its subsidiary undertaking to prepare consolidated financial statements that present financial information for the group as a single economic entity. [FRS 2 – Accounting for subsidiary undertakings]

Consolidation Act. An Act of Parliament which repeals and re-enacts with amendments, if and where necessary, a number of previous enactments. Statutory provision is made for making corrections and minor improvements in consolidation by the Consolidation of Enactments (Procedure) Act 1949.

Consolidation of mortgages. A mortgagee, whether original or by assignment, who held more than one mortgage by the same mortgagor, had a right in equity to compel the mortgagor to redeem all the mortgages if he sought to redeem one of them. See as to consolidation of mortgages, the Law of Property Act 1925, s 93.

Consolidation of shares. A conversion of a number of shares of a certain nominal value into a smaller number of shares of a larger nominal value, eg the conversion of twenty 5 pence shares into one £1 share.

Consolidation order. An order for consolidating the actions, invented by Lord Mansfield, the effect of which is to bind the plaintiff or defendants in several actions by the verdict in one, where the questions in dispute, and the evidence to be adduced, are the same in all. The application for such an order is most frequently made in actions against underwriters on policies of insurance.

Consols. Funds formed by the consolidation of Government annuities.

Consortium. Consortia are particularly common in advanced technology projects and the extension of group income and group relief concepts to them allows for the pooling of resources and of risks. Consortium relief is available to a UK resident company with a shareholding in a loss making company even where all other shareholders in the loss making company are not resident in the UK.

A consortium exists if 75% of the ordinary share capital of a company is directly and beneficially owned between the consortium members, each owning at least 5% (TA 1988, s 413(6)). The test must be satisfied in respect of entitlement to divisible income and also to assets on a winding-up (TA 1988, s 413(8)).

Construction. Interpretation as, for example, the construction of statutes or the construction of the terms of a contract reduced to writing.

Constructive obligation. An obligation that derives from an entity's actions where:
(a) by an established pattern of past practice, published policies or a sufficiently specific current statement, the entity has indicated to other parties that it will accept certain responsibilities; and
(b) as a result, the entity has created a valid expectation on the part of those other parties that it will discharge those responsibilities.

[FRS 12 – Provisions, contingent liabilities and contingent assets]

Constructive trust. A trust raised by construction of a court of equity, in order to satisfy the demands of justice. It differs from an implied trust, which arises from the implied or presumed intention of a party. (*See*, eg RESULTING TRUST.) A constructive trust may arise without reference to the presumed intention of any party. Thus, eg, a constructive trust may arise where a person, who is only joint owner, permanently benefits an estate by repairs or improvements. A trust may arise in his favour in respect of the sum he has expended in such repairs or improvements. Or a constructive trust may arise *in reference* to the intentions of parties, but without giving effect to their exact intentions. Thus a constructive trust may arise where A, the legal owner of an estate in land, is married to B, and A and B have some common intention to share the land, and in virtue of B's detrimental reliance on that intention, acts to her detriment: A will be regarded as holding the legal estate on trust for himself and B in appropriate shares. Occasionally, in order to avoid a fraud, the courts will give effect to an intended trust which fails for want of compliance with a statute imposing formalities on the creation of a trust, for example a requirement that the declaration of trust be evidenced in writing under s 53(1)(b) of the Law of Property Act 1925; but this is better regarded as an express trust enforced by Equity despite the statute on the principle that Equity will not allow a statute intended to prevent frauds from being used as an instrument of fraud, rather than as a constructive trust. The most prevalent example of the constructive trust is the *contractual* constructive trust. Where A and B enter into a contract for the sale of land, or for a unique chattel, as soon as the contract is made, but before transfer of title to the property, equity will regard the seller as holding the property on trust for the buyer. The trust evaporates when the legal title to the property is transferred under the contract of sale, and B becomes the legal owner of it.

Consumer credit agreement. A personal credit agreement by which the creditor provides the debtor with credit not exceeding £15,000 (Consumer Credit Act 1974, s 8(2)).

See PERSONAL CREDIT AGREEMENT; CREDIT.

Consumer hire agreement. An agreement made by a person with an individual ('the hirer') for the bailment of goods to the hirer which (*a*) is not a hire-purchase agreement, (*b*) is capable of subsisting for more than three months, and (*c*) does not require the hirer to make payments exceeding £15,000 (Consumer Credit Act 1974, s 15).

See HIRE-PURCHASE AGREEMENT.

Contingent asset. A possible asset that arises from past events and whose existence will be confirmed only by the occurrence of one or more uncertain future events not wholly within the entity's control. [FRS 12 – Provisions, contingent liabilities and contingent assets]

Contingent legacy. One bequeathed on a contingency; eg if the legatee shall attain the age of 21 years.

Contingent liability.
(*a*) A possible obligation that arises from past events and whose existence will be confirmed only by the occurrence of one or more uncertain future events not wholly within the entity's control; or
(*b*) a present obligation that arises from past events but is not recognised because:
   (i) it is not probable that a transfer of economic benefits will be required to settle the obligation; or
   (iii) the amount of the obligation cannot be measured with sufficient reliability.
[FRS 12 – Provisions, contingent liabilities and contingent assets]

Continuing partners. Partners remaining and carrying on a partnership after the retirement of one or more of their fellow partners.

Contract. A contract has been variously defined. Thus, it is said to be 'an agreement between competent persons, upon a legal consideration, to do or abstain from doing some act'; or more shortly as 'an agreement enforceable at law'. The agreement may be by *parol*, ie by word of mouth, or writing not under seal, or it may be by specialty (ie by writing under seal) (although see CONTRACT LAW, for the fundamental distinction between contracts and obligations under seal); in which case it is more properly termed a *covenant*. Where a contract is not a specialty, it is called a *parol* or *simple contract*, to distinguish it from a contract by specialty. A simple contract may be either *written* or *verbal*. A simple contract must be made on a *consideration*, in order that an action may be founded on it.

See CONSIDERATION; DEED; SEAL.

An action of contract, or *ex contractu*, is an action in which the wrong complained of is a *breach of contract*, and is opposed to an action of *tort*, which is brought for a wrong *independent of contract*.

See CONTRACT LAW.

Contract law. The law governing agreements. A contract is an agreement that the law will enforce, and so by making a contract the parties undertake obligations to each other and confer rights upon each other that these obligations will be fulfilled, and upon failure to do so, to enforce these obligations at law.

Contracts are formed by the agreement of the parties, in all essential matters. The standard analysis of the formation of a contract is in terms of offer and acceptance: a contract is formed when an offer by one party is accepted by another. An 'acceptance' in which a party accepts certain aspects of the offer but proposes changes to others is a counter-offer, not a true acceptance. Offers must be distinguished from 'invitations to treat', ie invitations to make an offer or negotiate. Generally, advertisements expressing the willingness to sell goods at specified prices, or the display of goods at specified prices, are at law invitations to treat only, not offers, thus the advertiser or displayer is not bound by contract to a person attending to buy the goods on the terms of the advertisement or display.

The contractual *doctrine of privity* flows from the nature of contracts as agreements; only those 'privy' to an agreement, ie the agreeing parties, have rights and obligations under it.

Contracts end upon the completion of performance by both sides, by agreement of the parties, by frustration (by unexpected events making the contract impossible to perform), or by a serious breach by one party.

The standard remedy for breach of contract is DAMAGES, ie a money award which puts the innocent party, so far as money can do so, in the position he or she would have been in had the contract been performed. In exceptional circumstances, a plaintiff may be awarded an order of specific performance, an injunction by the court to the defaulting party to perform his or her contractual obligations.

Contract note. The note sent by a broker or agent to his principal advising him of the sale or purchase of any stock or marketable security.

Contributory. Every person liable to contribute to the assets of a company in the event of its being wound up (see Insolvency Act 1986, s 79). In the case of a company limited by shares no contribution can be required from any member exceeding the amount unpaid on his shares (see ibid, s 74(2)). A past member is not liable to contribute if he has ceased to be a member for one year before the commencement of winding-up (see ibid, s 74(2)).

Present members who are liable to contribute are placed on the 'A' list and are primarily liable. Past members who are liable to contribute are placed on the 'B' list and are secondarily liable.

Control. (1) The ability of an entity to direct the operating and financial policies of another entity with a view to gaining economic benefits from its activities. [FRS 5 – Substance of transactions & FRS 9 – Associates and joint ventures]

(2) The ability of an undertaking to

direct the financial and operating policies of another undertaking with a view to gaining economic benefits from its activities. [FRS 2 – Accounting for subsidiary undertakings & FRS 8 – Related party disclosures]

(3) For tax purposes, a person is taken to control a company if he exercises or is able to exercise now or as of right in the future, or is entitled to acquire (now or as of right in the future) control over the company's affairs. 'Control over the company's affairs' is not defined and may mean control at a general meeting or control of those matters which are within the discretion of the directors. Precise analysis is probably unnecessary since statute gives certain instances which are, however, not to detract from the generality of the principle:

(i) the greater part of the share capital or of the issued share capital; or

(ii) the greater part of the voting power of the company; or

(iii) such part of the share capital as would entitle him to receive the greater part of the income of the company if, ignoring the rights of loan creditors, it were all distributed among the participators; or

(iv) such rights as would enable him to receive the greater part of the assets of the company in the event of a winding-up or in any other circumstances.

(TA 1988, s 416(2)).

(4) Control in the context of an asset: The ability to obtain the future economic benefits relating to an asset and to restrict the access of others in those benefits. [FRS 5 – Substance of transactions]

See CONTROLLED FOREIGN COMPANY.

Controlled foreign company. If in any accounting period a company is resident outside the UK but is controlled by persons resident in the UK and the company is subject to a lower level of taxation in that country of residence, special rules, known as Controlled Foreign Company (CFC) rules apply. These rules apportion the total *income* profits of the foreign company computed as for UK corporation tax (its chargeable profits) and any creditable tax among all the persons who had an *interest* in the company during the accounting period.

A charge can only be made on a company resident in the UK which has a minimum 25% interest in the CFC (TA 1988, s 747(5)). The CFC rules only allow attribution to a UK company but the rules apply when the foreign company is controlled by any persons (companies, individuals, or trustees, etc) resident in the UK. So if a company is resident outside the UK but has 30% non-UK shareholders, 40% UK corporate shareholders and 30% UK individual shareholders, the company is controlled by persons resident in the UK, and the tax charge is levied on the 40% UK corporate shareholders (but no tax charge is levied on the UK-resident individuals).

The legislation only applies where the company is not resident in the UK but is resident in a country with a lower rate of tax (TA 1988, s 747(1)(c)). The basic rule is that a company is regarded as resident in any territory in which throughout the relevant accounting period it is liable to tax (whether or not it actually pays any) by reason of its domicile, residence or place of management (TA 1988, s 749(1)). If no territory of residence can be found under these rules then the company is presumed to be resident in a territory with a lower rate of tax (TA 1988, s 749(5)). Control is generally determined as for close companies (TA 1988, s 756(3)); one looks to see whether 51% of those with interests in the company are resident in the UK as opposed to being in the hands of five or fewer participators (TA 1988, s 756(3)). Whether a person has an interest in a company is determined as for close companies. One looks at share capital, or voting rights or a right to receive distributions or to secure that income or assets may be applied directly or indirectly for someone's benefit (TA 1988, s 749B(1), (3) & (4)). Apart from the exclusion of loan creditors (TA 1988, s 749B(2)), the only softening is that where a person's entitlement to secure the application of a company's income or assets for his benefit is contingent upon a default of the company under any agreement, this is an interest in the company only if the default has occurred (TA 1988, s 749B(4)).

Conventional basis. *See* CASH BASIS.

Conveyance. (1) The transfer of the owner-ship of property, especially land, from one person to another; or the written instrument whereby such transfer is effected.

(2) As used in the Law of Property Act 1925, 'conveyance' includes a mortgage, charge, lease, assent, vesting declaration, vesting instrument, disclaimer, release, and every other assurance of property or of an interest therein by any instrument, except a will. 'Convey' has a similar meaning (see s 205(1)(ii)).

(3) Stamp duty legislation imposes duty on 'a conveyance on sale', which it defines as including 'every instrument, and every decree or order of a court or Commissioners, by which any property, or any estate or interest in property, is, on being sold, transferred to or vested in the purchaser, or another person on behalf of or at the direction of the purchaser' (FA 1999, Sch 13, Part I, para 1(2)). If therefore the instrument transfers property and does so on sale, duty will be chargeable.

Corporate personality, principle of. A principle that a company is in law a different person from its members, eg (i) a member of a 'one-man' company can lend money to it on the security of its assets and gain priority over the unsecured creditors, for he and the company are separate per-sons (see *Salomon v Salomon & Co Ltd [1897] AC 22, HL*); (ii) a member has no insurable interest in the property of the company (see *Macaura v Northern Assurance Co [1925] AC 619, HL*); (iii) the nationality of a company does not depend on that of its members (see *Janson v Driefontein Consolidated Mines Ltd [1902] AC 484, HL*).

But in certain cases the Court will 'lift the veil' of corporate personality and look at the reality of the situation.

See LIFTING THE VEIL.

Corporate venturing scheme. From 1 April 2000, for a ten-year period, the cor-porate venturing scheme provides an equivalent investment arrangement for companies to that which is available to individuals under the enterprise investment scheme. A company can invest by sub-scribing for new shares in an unquoted trading company and obtain a reduction in corporation tax at 20% as long as the shares are retained for at least three years. On any disposal of the shares thereafter, the chargeable gain arising can be rolled into a further investment that qualifies under the scheme. Where the disposal of shares gives rise to a loss, this is allowable against cap-ital gains subject to corporation tax. The loss is computed as net of the investment relief obtained on the original investment (FA 2000, s 63 and Schs 15 & 16).

As with the EIS, there are three reliefs available to the corporate investor. These are relief against corporation tax (FA 2000, Sch 15, paras 1–6), relief against company profits for losses incurred on disposal of shares to which investment relief is attrib-utable (FA 2000, Sch 15, para 7) and the deferment of a chargeable gain where there is reinvestment into shares qualifying under the corporate venturing scheme (FA 2000, Sch 15, para 8).

Relief under the corporate venturing scheme is restricted to companies that carry on a trade, other than in financial services (FA 2000, Sch 15, paras 10 and 11). Exceptionally, a non-trading company is able to use the scheme if it is a member of a trading group (FA 2000, Sch 15, para 10(5)). The investor company must not own more than 30% of the ordinary share capital of the target company, nor must there be arrangements in place under which it is entitled to require more than that percentage.

Corporation. A number of persons united and consolidated together so as to be con-sidered as one person in law, possessing the character of perpetuity, its existence being constantly maintained by the succession of new individuals in the place of those who die, or are removed. Corporations are either *aggregate* or *sole*. Corporations aggregate consist of many persons, several of whom are contemporaneously members of it, eg a limited company or the mayor and com-monalty of a city, or the dean and chapter of a cathedral. Corporations sole are such as consist, at any given time, of one person only, eg the Queen, a bishop, a vicar, etc. A corporation must sue, or be sued, in its corporate name.

Corporation tax. Corporation tax is chargeable on the profits of companies. Profits means the aggregate of income and chargeable capital gains after the deduction of brought forward capital losses, management expenses and charges on income (TA 1988, s 6(4); see *MEPC Holdings Limited v Taylor [2000] STC (SCD) 504*). The same rate of tax is now charged on all profits, whether income or capital gain.

The charge to corporation tax excludes any charge to income tax and capital gains tax. Where profits accrue in the course of winding-up, corporation tax is payable notwithstanding the fact that fiduciary obligations are owed to the shareholders.

The rate of corporation tax is imposed for a 'financial year', which is the twelve months beginning on 1 April (Interpretation Act 1978, Sch 1). Hence 'financial year 2001' is 1 April 2001 to 31 March 2002.

Corporation Tax Acts. The enactments relating to the taxation of income and chargeable gains of companies and of company distributions (including provisions relating to income tax) (Interpretation Act 1978, Sch 1).

Cost. Cost is defined in relation to the different categories of stocks as being that expenditure which has been incurred in the normal course of business in bringing the product or service to its present location and condition. This expenditure should include, in addition to cost of purchase, such costs of conversion as are appropriate to that location and condition. [SSAP 9 – Stocks and long-term contracts]

Cost benefit analysis. A technique for judging the worth of a proposed project, that was much favoured in the 1960s by national Government, for example in the consideration of the siting of the possible third airport for London. The technique consists of ascribing a cost to every item brought into consideration, including non-financial items such as amenity and time spent by private individuals.

Cost of conversion.
(a) Costs which are specifically attributable to units of production, eg direct labour, direct expenses and sub-contracted work;
(b) production overheads;
(c) other overheads, if any, attributable in the particular circumstances of the business to bringing the product or service to its present location and condition.
[SSAP 9 – Stocks and long-term contracts]

Cost of purchase. Purchase price including import duties, transport and handling costs and any other directly attributable costs, less trade discounts, rebates and subsidies. [SSAP 9 – Stocks and long-term contracts]

Council tax. A tax introduced by the Local Government Finance Act 1992. A local authority must levy and collect it (Local Government Finance Act 1992, s 1(1)). It is payable in respect of dwellings situated in its area (ibid, s 1(1)). There are different amounts for dwellings in different valuation bands (ibid, s 5). The persons liable to pay tax are set out in ibid, ss 6–9. The amount of tax payable is calculated in accordance with ibid, ss 10–13.

The local authority must compile a valuation list showing which of the valuation bands is applicable to the dwelling (ibid, ss 22, 23). It must set the amounts of tax for different categories of dwellings (ibid, s 30).

The Secretary of State has power to limit the amount of tax payable (ibid, s 53).

Counterclaim. A defendant in an action may set off or set up by way of counterclaim any right or claim whether such set-off or counterclaim sounds in damages or not. Such set-off or counterclaim has the same effect as a statement of claim in a cross action so as to enable the court to pronounce a final judgment in the same action both on the original and on the cross claim. But if in the opinion of the court such set-off or counterclaim cannot be conveniently disposed of in the same action or ought not to be allowed, the court may refuse permission to the defendant to avail himself of it. *See* SET-OFF.

Counterpart. When the several parts of an indenture are interchangeably executed by the parties to it, that part of copy which is executed by the grantor is called original, and the rest are counterparts.

See INDENTURE.

Countersign. The signature of a secretary or other person to vouch for the authenticity of a document signed by a superior.

Coupons. Dividend and interest certificates. Generally attached to bonds or other certificates of loan. When the interest is payable, they are cut off and presented for payment.

Court of Appeal. The Court of Appeal is now a superior court of record consisting of two Divisions, the Civil Division and the Criminal Division. The Court of Appeal consists of the Lord Chancellor (president of the Court); ex-Lord Chancellors; any Lord of Appeal in Ordinary who, at the date of his appointment, would have been qualified to be appointed to an ordinary judge of the Court of Appeal or who, at that date, was a judge of that court; the Lord Chief Justice; the Master of the Rolls; the President of the Family Division; and not more than 18 ordinary members of that court, called Lords Justices of Appeal (see Supreme Court Act 1981, s 2(2)). Generally speaking, appeals lie to the Court of Appeal from all orders and judgments of the High Court; although in certain circumstances an appeal may lie directly to the House of Lords from proceedings in the High Court under the Administration of Justice Act 1969.

Court of Session. The superior court, in Scotland, of law and equity, divorce and admiralty, having a general civil jurisdiction.

Covenant. A clause of an agreement contained in a deed whereby a party stipulates for the truth of certain facts, or binds himself to give something to another, or to do or not to do any act.

See DEED; RECITAL.

Credit includes a cash loan and any other form of financial accommodation (Consumer Credit Act 1974, s 9(1)).

Credit broker. A person acting in the course of a business of credit-brokerage carried on by him (Supply of Goods and Services Act 1982, s 18(1)).

Credit-token. A card, check, voucher, coupon, stamp, form, booklet or other document or thing given to an individual by a person carrying on a consumer credit business, who undertakes

(*a*) that on the production of it, he will supply cash, goods and services on credit, or

(*b*) that, where on the production of it to a third party, the third party supplies cash, goods and services, he will pay the third party for them, in return for payment to him by the individual (Consumer Credit Act 1974, s 149(1)).

Credit union. A society whose objects are

(i) the promotion of thrift among its members by the accumulation of their savings;

(ii) the creation of sources of credit for the members' benefit at a fair and reasonable rate of interest;

(iii) the use of the members' savings for their mutual benefit; and

(iv) the training and education of the members in the wise use of money (Credit Unions Act 1979, s 1(3)).

Credit unions can be registered under the Industrial and Provident Societies Act 1965, s 1(1).

Creditor. One to whom another person owes money.

Creditors' voluntary winding-up. A winding-up in the case of which a declaration of solvency has not been made in accordance with the Insolvency Act 1986, s 89 (see Insolvency Act 1986, s 90).

See DECLARATION OF SOLVENCY.

Crossed cheque. *See* CHEQUE.

Crown. A word often used for the King and Queen as being the Sovereign of the realm, ie in the public capacity of representative of the State as a constitutional monarchy. So understood, the Crown is distinguishable from the individual King or Queen, and in this respect, the 'Crown never dies'.

Crown copyright. Copyright existing where the Crown is the first owner of any copyright in a work (Copyright, Designs and Patents Act 1988, s 163). The Crown is entitled to copyright in every Act of Parliament or Measures of the General Synod of the Church of England (ibid, s 164).

Cum dividend. With the dividend. A term used in connection with the purchase of shares resulting in the buyer having a right to the dividend in respect of them.
See DIVIDEND; SHARE.

Cum rights. With the rights. A term used to denote the fact that a buyer of shares is entitled to subscribe for further shares in proportion to the number bought.
See RIGHTS ISSUE; SHARE.

Cum testamento annexo. 'With the will annexed.' A person is administrator *cum testamento annexo* when he is appointed to administer the estate of the deceased in accordance with the will, but was not named as executor in that document. The situation arises when the only named executor has died or is incapacitated.
See ADMINISTRATOR.

Cumulative preference shares. Where preference shares are cumulative, then if the profits of the company in any year are insufficient to pay the fixed dividend on them, the deficiency must be made up out of the profits of subsequent years. Preference shares are presumed to be cumulative and ambiguous language in the articles will not be enough to make them non-cumulative (see *Foster v Coles and MB Foster & Sons Ltd (1906) 22 TLR 555.*

Currency contract. Contracts to buy and sell currency are taxed on the accruals basis (FA 1993, ss 126(1), 157). The rules require that a qualifying company, A Ltd,

enter into a contract under which it is entitled and obliged to receive payment at a specified time of a specified amount of one currency (eg $1,000 on 1 December) and to pay at the same time a specified amount in another currency (eg £600). If on 1 December it requires £700 to buy $1,000 there is an initial exchange gain of £100.

This definition of currency contract includes the re-exchange of principal under a currency swap arrangement at the end of the transaction but not the payment of fees. The definition also includes contracts providing for net payments (FA 1993, s 126(1A)).

Currency note.
(*a*) Any note which
  (i) has been lawfully issued in England and Wales, Scotland, Northern Ireland, any of the Channel Islands, the Isle of Man or the Republic of Ireland;
  (ii) is or has been customarily used in the country where it was issued; and
  (iii) is payable on demand; or
(*b*) any note which
  (i) has been lawfully issued in some country other than those mentioned above; and
  (ii) is customarily used as money in that country (see Forgery and Counterfeiting Act 1981, s 27(1)).

Current funding level valuation. A consideration as to whether the assets would have been sufficient at the valuation date to cover liabilities arising in respect of pensions in payment, preserved benefits for members whose pensionable service has ceased and accrued benefits for members in pensionable service, based on pensionable service to and pensionable earnings at, the date of valuation including revaluation on the statutory basis or such higher basis as has been promised. [SSAP 24 – Accounting for pension costs]

Current service cost. The increase in the actuarial liability expected to arise from employee service in the current period. [FRED 20 – Retirement benefits]

Current value. The current value of a tangible fixed asset to the business is the lower of replacement cost and recoverable amount. [FRS 15 – Tangible fixed assets]

Curtailment. An event that reduces the expected years of future service of present employees or reduces for a number of employees the accrual of defined benefits for some or all of their future service. Curtailments include:

(*a*) termination of employees' services earlier than expected, for example as a result of closing a factory or discontinuing a segment of a business; and

(*b*) termination of, or amendment to the terms of, a defined benefit scheme so that some or all future service by current employees will no longer qualify for benefits or will qualify only for reduced benefits.

[FRED 20 – Retirement benefits]

Custom of merchants (*Lex Mercatoria*). The branch of law which comprises the rules relating to bills of exchange, partnership and other mercantile matters. In mercantile custom, universality is of far greater importance than immemorial antiquity.

D

DCF. Discounted cash flow.

DTI. The Department of Trade and Industry.

Damages. The pecuniary, ie monetary, satisfaction awarded by a Judge or jury in a civil action for the wrong suffered by the plaintiff.
See EXEMPLARY DAMAGES.

Date of acquisition. The date on which control of the acquired entity passes to the acquirer. This is the date from which the acquired entity is accounted for by the acquirer as a subsidiary undertaking under FRS 2 'Accounting for Subsidiary Undertakings'. [FRS 7 – Fair values in acquisition accounting]

Date on which the financial statements are approved. The date on which the financial statements are approved by the board of directors is the date the board of directors formally approves a set of documents as the financial statements. In respect of unincorporated enterprises, the date of approval is the corresponding date. In respect of group accounts, the date of approval is the date when the group accounts are formally approved by the board of the directors of the holding company. [SSAP 17 – Accounting for post balance sheet events]

Day book. A primary book of account. A commercial enterprise would typically have a purchase day book, in which sums that will eventually fall due for payment on purchases made are recorded, and a sales day book, on which payments due on sales made are recorded.

Debenture. A loan for a fixed period (typically five or more years) made to a company, usually secured on the assets of the company from time to time (a floating charge), but, occasionally, secured on defined assets (a fixed charge). Most debentures pay a fixed rate of interest. Frequently, the rate of interest on a debenture is specified as a fixed percentage above bank base rate from time to time. Sometimes, a debenture carries no interest but a premium is paid on the maturity of the debenture. (Where a company wishes to lend money on such deferred interest payment terms, it is usually preferable for the company to issue zero-rated preferred dividend shares, as these attract a CGT charge in the hands of the individual investor, as opposed to the income tax charge that applies on a zero-rated debenture.) Debenture stock is frequently irredeemable and usually transferable in any amount. The issue of debenture stock in the case of companies incorporated by Act of Parliament is regulated either by their special Acts or by the Companies Clauses Act 1863. A company is required to make a return to the Registrar of Companies when it issues a debenture, see the Companies Act 1985, ss 190, 191.

Debenture-holders' action. An action brought by a debenture-holder on behalf of himself and all other debenture-holders of the same class to enforce their rights under the debentures.

Debenture trust deed. A deed charging specific property of a company by a legal mortgage or legal charge in favour of trustees for the debenture-holders and charging the rest of the assets of the company by a floating charge.
See DEBENTURE; FLOATING CHARGE.

Debit card. A card the use of which by its holder to make a payment results in a current account of his at a bank, or at any other institution providing banking services, being debited with the payment.

Debt. (1) A certain sum due from one person to another either (1) by *record*, eg, judgment, (2) under *specialty*, or deed, or (3) under *simple* contract by writing or oral. With the exception of certain preferred debts, all debts are payable *pari passu* in bankruptcy (see the Insolvency Act 1986, s 328). In the administration of the estate of a deceased person the order is (1) Crown debts, (2) rates, taxes, etc, (3) judgments, (4) recognisances and statutes, (5) specialty and simple debts, (6) voluntary debts, but when the estate is insolvent the order follows that of bankruptcy (see the Administration of Estates Act 1925, s 34(1), and Sch I, Part I).

(2) Capital instruments that are classified as liabilities. [FRS 4 – Capital instruments]

(3) A debt is exempt from CGT, unless it is a debt on a security (TCGA 1992, s 251(1)). In the context of this exemption, Lord Fraser said:

'The meaning of the word debt depends very much on its context. It is capable of including a contingent debt which may never be payable . . . It is also capable of including a sum of which the amount is not ascertained. But . . . does not apply to the obligation of the purchaser under this agreement, which was described by Templeman LJ as "a possible liability to pay an unidentical viable sum at an unascertainable date". The words to which I have given emphasis bring out the three factors of this obligation which cumulatively prevent its being a debt in the sense of [TCGA 1992, s 251].' (*Marren v Ingles [1980] STC 500 at 524*).

See DEBT ON A SECURITY.

Debt-adjusting, in relation to debts due under consumer credit agreements or consumer hire agreements, means
(i) negotiating with the creditor or owner terms for the discharge of a debt; or
(ii) taking over the debtor's obligations to discharge a debt; or
(iii) any similar activity concerned with the liquidation of a debt (Consumer Credit Act 1974, s 145(5)).

See CONSUMER CREDIT AGREEMENT; CONSUMER HIRE AGREEMENT.

Debt-collecting. The taking of steps to procure payment of debts due under consumer credit agreements or consumer hire agreements (Consumer Credit Act 1974, s 145(7)).

See CONSUMER CREDIT AGREEMENT; CONSUMER HIRE AGREEMENT.

Debt collection period. The period that an enterprise takes to collect the money owed to it. The calculation is typically undertaken at the balance sheet date and consists of dividing the trade debtors at that date by the annual sales turnover, expressed as a number of days. For example, if debtors are £100,000 and sales are £400,000, the debt collection period is 91 days.

Debt equity ratio. The ratio between the borrowing of a company (both short-term and long-term) and the equity of the company. Where there is a large amount of debt by comparison to equity, a company is referred to as 'highly geared'.

Debt on a security. A debt on a security is an asset on which a chargeable gain or an allowable loss for CGT can arise (TCGA 1992, s 251(1)). That section states that the definition in TCGA 1992, s 132(2)(b) is to be used. This defines 'security' as 'includes any loan stock or similar security whether of the Government of the UK or any other government, or of any public or local authority in the UK or elsewhere, or of any company, whether secured or unsecured'.

The current judicial view seems to be that a debt on a security must be something in the nature of an investment. In *Cleveleys Investment Trust Co v IRC (1971) 47 TC 300* Lord Cameron said:

'Once the terms of [TCGA 1992, s 132] are examined, it becomes abundantly plain that the word "security" in [TCGA 1992, s 251(1)] is a substantive and refers to those securities which are or can be subject to a conversion.' (*at 318D*)

In his dissenting judgment, Lord Migdale said:

'I think that the words "the debt on a security" refer to an obligation to pay or repay embodied in the share or stock certificate issued by a government, local authority or company, which is evidence of the ownership of the share or stock and solves the right to receive payment . . . "The debt on a security" means a debt evidenced in a document as a security. I cannot see any similarity between the letter of acceptance or the bill of exchange in this case and loan stock or, for that matter, an unsecured debenture.' (*at 315E*)

In *Aberdeen Construction Group Ltd v IRC [1978] STC 127* the taxpayer company contracted to sell a subsidiary. The terms of the sale were that the share capital in the company was sold for £250,000 on condition that the company wrote off loans totalling £500,000 that had been made to its subsidiary. Aberdeen Construction Group Ltd contended that the loans it had made constituted a 'debt on a security' so that an allowable loss accrued. The Court of Session and the House of Lords rejected the argument that the loans constituted a 'debt on a security'. The clearest statement was made by Lord Emslie in the Court of Session who said:

'What then is "a security" within the meaning of TCGA 1992, s 251(1)? Reference to s 132(3) shows that it is concerned with "conversion of securities" and with the word "security" itself . . . On a proper construction of that subsection, I am persuaded that what is in contemplation is the issue of a document or certificate by the debtor institution which would represent a marketable security, as that expression is commonly understood, the nature and character of which would remain constant in all transmissions.' (*[1977] STC 302 at 309f*).

A different approach was taken by the court in *W T Ramsay Ltd v IRC [1981] STC 174, HL*. The House of Lords, in that case, considered a complex tax avoidance scheme that for its efficacy relied on a debt being assigned for £393,750 more than its cost. The taxpayer contended that no chargeable gain resulted as it was not a debt on a security. The House of Lords ruled that the loan was a debt on a security and, hence, the tax avoidance scheme failed. Lord Wilberforce said:

'It can be seen, however, in my opinion, that the legislature is endeavouring to distinguish between mere debts, which normally (although there are exceptions) do not increase but may decrease in value and debts with added characteristics such as may enable them to be realised or dealt with at a profit. But this distinction must still be given effect through the words used.

Of these, some help is gained from a contrast to be drawn between debts simpliciter, which may arise from trading and a multitude of other situations, commercial or private, and loans, certainly a narrower class, and one which presupposes some kind of contractual structure . . .

With all this lack of certainty as to the statutory words, I do not feel any doubt that in this case the debt was a debt on a security. I have already stated its terms. It was created by contract the terms of which were recorded in writing; it was designed, from the beginning, to be capable of being sold, and, indeed, to be sold at a profit.' (*at 184b-f*).

In *Tarmac Roadstone Holdings Ltd v Williams [1996] STC (SCD) 409* the Special Commissioner held that the distinguishing feature of a debt on security is that it is in the nature of an investment which can be dealt with as such. The distinction between a debt and a debt on a security is, in the Special Commissioner's judgment, not to be found by looking at TCGA 1992, s 134 alone and must be based on the definition in s 82(3)(b) (*at 418c*).

See DEBT.

Debt restructuring. The issue of new debt (typically new debentures) in exchange for old debt, there being a difference between the terms applicable to the old and new debt. Thus, for example, a company that has 7% debentures in issue that mature in six months' time, may offer to restructure the debt by exchanging each existing debenture for a new debenture at 7½% repayable after ten years.

Declaration, statutory. *See* STATUTORY DECLARATION.

Declaration of solvency. A statutory declaration by the directors, where it is proposed to wind up a company voluntarily, to the effect that they have made a full inquiry into the affairs of the company, and that, having done so, they have formed the opinion that the company will be able to pay its debts in full within such period not exceeding twelve months from the commencement of the winding-up as may be specified in the declaration (see the Insolvency Act 1986, s 89(1)).

A declaration of solvency has no effect unless:

(a) it is made within the five weeks immediately preceding the date of the passing of the resolution for winding-up or on that date but before the passing of that resolution; and

(b) it embodies a statement of the company's assets and liabilities as at the latest practicable date before the making of the declaration (ibid, s 89(2)).

Declaration of trust. The essential operative act by which a trust is created. A declaration of trust whereby a person admits that he holds property on trust for another is called a *self-declaration of trust*. Typically, however, a person who creates a trust will transfer property *on trust* to someone who will hold the legal title to the property as trustee, and before or at the time of transfer will declare the trust, either orally or in writing. A trust is only *constituted*, made actual, when the trustee acquires the legal title to the trust property. A declaration of trust of land, whether freehold or leasehold, must, by the Law of Property Act 1925, s 53, be evidenced in writing, and signed by the party declaring the trust. But declarations of trust of money, or personal chattels, need not be so evidenced. For the form of trust instrument on settlement of land see the Settled Land Act 1925, Sch I, Form No 3.

Deduction at source. When A makes a payment to B out of income which has been brought into charge to income tax and the payment is an annuity or annual payment, and so B's income within Schedule D, Case III, A has a right to deduct basic rate tax. So if A is due to pay B £100 he will deduct £22 and pay only £78. The authority for this is TA 1988, ss 348 & 349. Only payments which are taxed on the recipient under Schedule D, Case III are subject to this rule.

Deduction at basic rate applies to annuities and annual payments other than interest and to payments in respect of patent royalties within TA 1988, s 119; all other payments within the scheme in ss 348 & 349 now suffer deduction at the lower rate of 20%.

The scheme thus has two functions. The first is to collect tax from B by allowing A to deduct basic rate tax at source; this may be called the withholding function. The second is to give effect to A's right to deduct this payment in computing total income by first making A pay tax at basic rate on this part of his income and then permitting A to recoup that tax on making this payment; this may be called the relief function.

Deed. An ancient creature of the common law, the deed is a formal written instrument which *acted* at law to alter the rights and duties of the parties to it, hence the term *deed*. Deeds could, for example, bind someone at law to carry out a promise expressed in it, or transfer title to property. At common law a deed, to be effective, needed to be SEALed and delivered, hence the use of the phrase a document, promise, etc 'under seal'. The seal was all important – if the seal fell off, the deed was ineffective. As long as the parties to the deed were clear, and the party bound under the deed affixed his seal, there was no need for a signature, and rare was the person who could make one given the general inability to write. The requirement of signature came later, so that a deed to be effective needed to be signed, sealed and delivered. Delivery is also essential. The mere writing, signing, and sealing of a deed did not make it effective; a person obtaining an advantage under a deed needed to attain possession of it by delivery, ie the creator needed to transfer possession of the deed to that person with the intention of making it legally binding.

See DELIVERY OF A DEED.

Deeds no longer require a seal, so that strictly speaking it is now incorrect to refer to promises, etc 'under seal'; by the Law of Property (Miscellaneous Provisions) Act 1989, deeds must be signed by the party or parties bound by them, and *attested* by two witnesses. The requirement of delivery remains. By properly signing, sealing, and delivering a deed, or now by signing, having attested, and delivering a deed, a person is said to *execute* a deed. Execution in the case of a corporation requires the affixing of the seal of the corporation.

Deeds are of two general forms, either a *deed poll* or a *deed indented*. If a deed is made by more parties than one, there ought to be as many copies of it as there are parties; multiple copies of the deed were thus made by copying, or engrossing, the words of the deed as many times as necessary on one parchment, and the copies then separated by cutting in irregular acute angles on the top or side, ie along *indented* lines, and such deeds are called indentures. Because the different copies of the deed could be shown to tally or correspond with one another by placing them side by side, this method of making deeds served as a device to prevent fraud. By the Law of Property Act 1925, s 56(2), a deed between parties, to effect its objects, has the effect of an indenture though not indented or expressed to be an indenture. A deed made by one party only is not indented, but *polled* or shaved quite even, and is therefore called a *deed poll,* or a single deed.

Deeds may be described as deeds, or as conveyances, trust instruments, settlements, mortgages, etc, according to their nature (see the Law of Property Act 1925, s 57).

Deed of covenant. Covenants are often entered into by separate deed, eg a deed of covenant for production of deeds (now generally replaced by an acknowledgement).

Deed of Variation. A deed of variation of an estate made within a two-year period from the date of death gives the right to an election so that the variation is not a disposal and the CGT rules apply as if the allocation of the estate specified in the deed of variation had been made by the deceased (TCGA 1992, s 62(6) & (7)). The deed must be an instrument in writing.

See DISCLAIMER.

Default surcharge. A VAT registered trader is liable to default surcharge if he fails to furnish a VAT return, or pay any tax shown

to be due thereon, in respect of a prescribed accounting period falling within a 'surcharge period' notified to him in a surcharge liability notice (VATA 1994, s 59(1)–(3)). Default surcharge is the greater of £30 and a percentage of outstanding tax, the rate being governed by the number of previous failures to pay tax during the surcharge period. The specified percentages are: 2% (no previous failures), 5% (one previous failure), 10% (two previous failures) and 15% (three or more previous failures).

A trader is not liable to default surcharge if he satisfies the Commissioners or, on appeal, a VAT Tribunal, that any of the following apply: (1) he did not receive a surcharge liability notice (see *Customs and Excise Comrs v Medway Draughting and Technical Services Ltd [1989] STC 346*); (2) the surcharge liability notice is invalid (see *Dow Chemical Co Ltd v Customs and Excise Comrs [1996] V & DR 52*); (3) he posted his return and remittance before the due date (VATA 1994, s 59(7)(a); see, for example, *Halstead Motor Co v Customs and Excise Comrs [1995] V & DR 201*); or (4) he has a reasonable excuse for the failure (VATA 1994, s 59(7)(b); see *Customs and Excise Comrs v Palco Industry Co Ltd [1990] STC 594*).

Deferral relief. Deferral relief can be used to reduce or extinguish the capital gain arising on any gain, whether on the disposal of an asset, or on a gain arising on a deemed disposal. The taxpayer can choose the amount of the gain to be relieved. Deferral relief is designed to assist a new business in raising funds. Deferral relief gives relief to a taxpayer only when the taxpayer subscribes for new shares (TCGA 1992, Sch 5B, para 1(2)(a)) and the target company fulfils the requirements for the enterprise investment scheme (TCGA 1992, Sch 5B, para 1(2)(e)). The investor can be connected with the company, unlike the requirements for income tax relief on EIS investment (TA 1998, s 291(1)(b)).

When CGT deferral relief is claimed, the gain arising on disposal is calculated in the usual way, including the application of taper relief. The gain charged on the disposal is then reduced by the amount of the deferral (TCGA 1992, Sch 5B, para 2(1)). The amount of the deferral is the lowest of the following three sums: (*a*) the gain that would otherwise be chargeable on the disposal; (*b*) the consideration for the qualifying investment; (*c*) the amount the taxpayer chooses to claim (TCGA 1992, Sch 5B, para 2(1), (3)).

When there is a disposal of the qualifying investment, or another event causing clawback of relief, the deferral is brought into charge at that date (TCGA 1992, Sch 5B, para 4(1)(a)). The amount brought into charge is the sum that was deferred; there is no further taper relief applied by reference to the period since the original disposal (TCGA 1992, Sch 5B, para 4(1)(b)).

Death does not cause a clawback of deferral relief (TCGA 1992, Sch 5B, para 3(5)).

Deferred debt. A debt (eg one in respect of which a rate of interest varying with the profits of a business is payable) which has to be paid after the preferred debts and the ordinary debts have been paid in full.

Deferred shares or stock. Stock or shares in a company, the holders of which have a right to participate in the net earnings of the company, but the right is *deferred* until the prior claims of preferred and ordinary stock or shareholders have been met.

Deferred tax. A fundamental principle in the preparation of the financial statements is matching. Liabilities arising from the activities of an enterprise over a period of account should be shown in the financial statements for that period. A quoted company will normally produce interim accounts for shareholders reporting on the trading for a six-month period. That period is not a basis period for the imposition of corporation tax; however, accounting practice requires that a calculation be made of a tax charge that can fairly be attributed to the trading profit for the six-month period and the liability thus arising is shown as a liability in the company's balance sheet. Other taxation charges are more subtle. If the company has investment property, the value of the property will be shown in the financial statements as its current market value (see SSAP 19). A sale of an investment property at the balance sheet value is likely to trigger a tax charge on the capital gain arising. Revaluation of an investment property, thus creates a potential liability. The function of the deferred tax account is to recognise this potential liability. If the enterprise has traded at a loss, that loss is likely to be available for tax purposes to be put against the profit of a subsequent period and thereby reduce the tax payable. There is, thus, a potential asset available to the enterprise. Again, it is the function of the deferred tax reserve to recognise this potential asset, as appropriate. In the UK tax system, depreciation is not a tax allowance, instead, capital allowances are provided. Whenever there is a difference between the rate of depreciation and the rate at which a capital allowance is given, there is a timing difference. It is the function of the deferred tax account to reflect such a timing difference.

There are three distinct and different approaches that can be taken in computing a provision for deferred tax.

(*a*) In October 1978, the Accounting Standards Committee issued Statement of Standard Accounting Practice (SSAP) 15. The SSAP adopts the 'partial provision' approach under which the SSAP requires that deferred tax be accounted for in respect of the net amount by which it is probable that any payment of tax will be temporarily deferred or accelerated by the operation of timing differences which will reverse in the foreseeable future without being replaced. The SSAP requires that deferred tax be provided only where it is probable that tax will become payable as a reversal of timing differences. When an enterprise is not expected to reduce the scale of its operation significantly and it is judged that the payment of tax will be permanently deferred, the SSAP requires that deferred tax is not provided.

(*b*) In 1996 International Accounting Standard (IAS) 12 was issued. This requires full provision for deferred tax. Under the full provision approach, deferred tax is to be provided for both timing and permanent differences (although in practice IAS 12 makes exception for most of the latter) hence, for example, IAS 12 requires provision for deferred tax on rolled over capital gains, even where the cost is only deducted for tax purposes on a sale and the enterprise has no current proposals for a sale of the asset.

(c) In August 1999, the Accounting Standards Board issued a Financial Reporting Exposure Draft (FRED) 19 – Deferred Tax that requires provision to be made for deferred tax on timing differences, but only when the resulting deferred tax can be justified as representing an asset or liability in its own right. The critical point, as stated by the Board in this exposure draft, is that deferred tax should be provided for as a liability only when the reporting entity has an *obligation* to pay more tax in the future as a result of *past* events. FRED 19 continues to be merely an exposure draft and one that, moreover, incorporates a contrary view that was held by a minority of members of the Accounting Standards Board. The current position is, thus, that the standard in force in the UK, continues to be SSAP 15, which is the 'accounting standard' for UK companies under the terms of Companies Act 1985, Part VII but this is in conflict with the international standard. Thus, if a UK company is, for example, a member of a US group, that company is required to compute a deferred tax provision in two separate ways for the purpose of reporting its results in the two separate jurisdictions.

Deferred tax is described by ASB as:

(1) The tax attributable to timing differences. [SSAP 15 – Accounting for deferred tax]

(2) The tax that is estimated to be payable or recoverable in future when timing differences reverse. [FRED 19 – Deferred tax]

See PERMANENT DIFFERENCES; TIMING DIFFERENCES.

Defined benefit scheme. A pension or other retirement benefit scheme where the scheme rules define the benefits independently of the contributions payable, and the benefits are not directly related to the investments of the scheme. The scheme may be funded or unfunded. [SSAP 24 – Accounting for pension costs & FRED 20 – Retirement Benefits]

Defined contribution scheme. A defined contribution scheme is a pension scheme in which the benefits are directly determined by the value of contributions paid in respect of each member. Normally, the rate of contribution is specified in the rules of the scheme. [SSAP 24 – Accounting for pension costs & FRED 20 – Retirement Benefits]

Delayed remittance. An individual who is domiciled within the UK is subject to UK income tax and capital gains tax on income and gains made worldwide, in the period in which the income arises or the gain is crystallised. Where a foreign country has exchange control regulations, it is possible that the income or the sale proceeds on the disposal will be blocked by the foreign country and not able to be remitted to the UK. Where this is the case, TA 1988, s 584 (for income) and TCGA 1992, s 279 (for CGT) provide relief for the delayed remittance, so that the income (or gain) is brought into charge as income (or gain) of the fiscal year in which the relevant authorities in the foreign jurisdiction release the funds for remittance to the UK (or, if earlier, the date they are actually brought into the UK).

Delivery of a deed. This is held to be performed by the person who executes the deed placing his finger on the seal, and saying 'I deliver this as my act and deed'. A deed takes effect only from delivery. A delivery may be either absolute, to the other party or grantee himself; or to a third person, to hold until some condition is performed by the grantee; in which latter case it is called an *escrow*.

See DEED.

Demerger. A demerger of a company's activities takes place when a company that carries on two or more trades is split to create two or more separate companies. After the split, each separate company then carries on one of the trades. A demerger of a group takes place when one or more of the companies in the group leave the group to carry on one or more of the trades in one or more companies outside the group.

Until 1980 it was difficult—but not impossible—to split a group up. The difficulty was that the transfer of the piece being split off would cause the value received by the shareholder to be treated as a qualifying distribution supra; in addition there were capital gains and stamp duty problems when a company or assets left the group. As part of a campaign to free British industry from unnecessary constraints Parliament included certain provisions— now TA 1988, ss 213–218—to encourage the process of 'demerging' by removing some of the obstacles.

There are three types of demerger provided by the Act. These are:

(1) where a company spins off a subsidiary directly to its shareholders, ie where it distributes shares in a subsidiary to its shareholders so that those shareholders control the former subsidiary directly and no longer through the distributing company;

(2) where a company spins off a subsidiary indirectly to its shareholders, ie where it transfers shares in a subsidiary to another company in exchange for shares but the shares are not held by the subsidiary but distributed to the shareholders of the parent; and

(3) where a company spins off a trade to its shareholders but indirectly, ie where it transfers a trade to another company in exchange for shares and those shares are not held by the parent but distributed to its shareholders.

Department of Trade and Industry. A government department responsible for general overseas policy, commercial relations, exports, tariffs, companies and insurance legislation.

Deposit. (1) The act of entrusting money to a bank is called a *deposit* in a bank; and the amount of the money deposited is also called the *deposit*.

(2) A type of bailment by which a

person entrusts another with a chattel to keep it safely without reward.

See BAILMENT.

(3) Money paid as earnest or security for the performance of a contract, eg the money paid by the purchaser on signature of a contract for sale.

Deposit-taker. The system of deducting tax at source is applied to interest on 'relevant deposits' made with a 'deposit-taker'. 'Deposit-taker' is the Bank of England, any institution authorised under the Banking Act 1987, the Post Office, a local authority and any person who receives deposits in the course of his business and recognised as such by the Treasury. (The bodies within the last category are listed in statutory instruments SI 1984/1801, SI 1985/1696 & SI 1992/3234.)

Depreciable amount. The cost of a tangible fixed asset (or, where an asset is revalued, the revalued amount) less its residual value. [FRS 15 – Tangible fixed assets]

Depreciated replacement cost (of tangible fixed assets other than property). The cost of replacing an existing tangible fixed asset with an identical or substantially similar new asset having a similar production or service capacity, from which appropriate deductions are made to reflect the value attributable to the remaining portion of the total useful economic life of the asset and the residual value at the end of the asset's useful economic life.

Costs directly attributable to bringing the tangible fixed asset into working condition for its intended use, such as costs of transport, installation, commissioning, consultants' fees, non-recoverable taxes and duties, are included in depreciated replacement cost. The deductions from gross replacement cost should take into account the age and condition of the asset, economic and functional obsolescence, and environmental and other relevant factors. [FRS 15 – Tangible fixed assets]

Depreciation. (1) The measure of the cost or revalued amount of the economic benefits of the tangible fixed asset that have been consumed during the period.

Consumption includes the wearing out, using up or other reduction in the useful economic life of a tangible fixed asset whether arising from use, effluxion of time or obsolescence through either changes in technology or demand for the goods and services produced by the asset. [FRS 15 – Tangible fixed assets]. The depreciation charge in a set of financial statements is designed to reduce the cost of the asset to £nil (or, sometimes, its value as scrap) over the useful economic life of the fixed asset. The term 'depreciation' applies to tangible fixed assets; the term 'amortisation' is used for intangible fixed assets. Various methods of calculating depreciation include the straight line method, the reducing balance method and the sum of the digits method. (In the US, the word 'depreciation' is not used; instead, the word 'amortization' is applied to both tangible assets and intangible assets.)

(2) Reduction in value of one currency in relation to another currency.

Derivative. A financial instrument, such as a financial future or a financial option, where the instrument gives rights at a specified future date to acquire an asset or to receive a payment computed by reference to the price of an asset. The derivative market of the London Stock Exchange is the London International Financial Futures and Options Exchange (LIFFE). Underlying items include equities, bonds, commodities, interest rates, exchange rates and stock market and other indices.

ASB defines derivative financial instruments to 'include futures, options, forward contracts, interest rate and currency swaps, interest rate caps, collars and floors, forward interest rate agreements, commitments to purchase shares or bonds, note issuance facilities and letters of credit.' [FRS 13 – Derivatives and other financial instruments]

Descendant. A relation in a succeeding generation. A direct or lineal descendent is a child, a child of that child (ie grandchild) and so on. A collateral descendent is one whose relationship is traced through a common ancestor, ie one's nephew is one's relation as being a child of one's brother or sister, who shares one's parents.

Destination of turnover is the geographical segment to which products or services are supplied. [SSAP 25 – Segmental reporting]

Dilapidations. A tenant repairing lease will typically provide that the outgoing tenant is required to pay a sum in respect of dilapidations at the end of the period of the lease and also, commonly, on transfer of the leasehold interest. The sum payable by the outgoing tenant is often valued by an independent assessor, who is charged with the task of computing the cost of putting the premises back to the condition in which they were at the start of the lease.

Direct costs. Costs that are directly applicable to a unit, as compared to overhead costs.

Director. (1) A person who conducts the affairs of a company.

A private company must have at least one director (Companies Act 1985, s 282(3)). A public company must have at least two directors (ibid, s 282(1)). The company must keep a register of directors (ibid, s 288). A director must hold a qualification share if the articles of association so require (ibid, s 291). Generally, a person cannot be appointed a director of a public company if he is aged 70 at the time of his appointment (ibid, s 293(2)). A director can be removed (ibid, s 303).

Fair dealings by directors can be enforced, eg there are restrictions on a director taking financial advantage (ibid, ss 311–322A); certain share dealings by a director or his family are prohibited (ss 323–329); and there are restrictions on a company's powers to make loans to a director (ibid, ss 330–334).

Directors are not entitled to any remuneration apart from express agreement. But the articles of association usually provide that their remuneration shall be determined by an ordinary resolution of the company.

A director becomes disqualified if he does anything which by the articles of association amounts to a disqualification, eg if he becomes bankrupt or is suffering from mental disorder.

A court may make a disqualification

order under the Company Directors Disqualification Act 1986.

A director is under a duty in the performance of his functions to have regard to the interests of the company's employees in general as well of those of its members (Companies Act 1985, s 309(1)).

A director is under a duty of care towards the company, the standard of which is that of an ordinary person in the conduct of his own affairs.

(2) Directors include the corresponding officers or organisations which do not have directors. [SSAP 17 – Accounting for post balance sheet events]

Director, disqualification order against. An order by the court under the Company Directors Disqualification Act 1986.

Such an order can be made if eg

(i) he is convicted of an indictable offence (s 2);

(ii) he is guilty of persistent breaches of companies legislation (s 3);

(iii) he is guilty of fraudulent trading (s 4);

(iv) he has been a director of an insolvent company (s 6).

If a person acts in contravention of a disqualification order, he is guilty of an offence (s 13), and he is personally liable for the company's debts (s 14).

A register of disqualification orders is kept (s 18).

Director, managing. See MANAGING DIRECTOR.

Director, shadow. See SHADOW DIRECTOR.

Director General of Fair Trading. An officer appointed by the Secretary of State for the purpose of performing the functions stated in the Fair Trading Act 1973. These duties are (i) to keep under review the carrying on of commercial activities in the United Kingdom which relate to goods supplied to consumers or which relate to services supplied to them, and to collect information with respect to such activities, and the circumstances relating to practices which may adversely affect the interests of consumers; and (ii) to receive and collate evidence becoming available to him with respect to such activities (ibid, s 2(1)).

Director's qualification share. See QUALIFICATION SHARE.

Directors' register. A register kept at the company's registered office containing particulars showing, eg, the name, address and business occupation of each director (Companies Act 1985, ss 288, 289).

Directors' report. A report by the directors concerning the finances and general activities of the company during the preceding financial year. It must be attached to the balance sheet and contain a fair review of the development of the business of the company during the financial year and its position at the end of it, and stating the amount, if any, which they recommend should be paid as dividend, and the amount, if any, which they propose to carry to reserves (see the Companies Act 1985, s 234(1)).

Dirty Dogs Act. Attributed to Laddie J: 'This is a case for section 1 of the Dirty Dogs Act. The English Court knows a scoundrel when it sees one and will act accordingly.'

Discharge. A word used in various senses:

(1) Of the discharge of a bankrupt under the Insolvency Act 1986, s 280, by which he is freed of all debts and liabilities provable under the bankruptcy, with certain specified exceptions.

(2) Of the discharge of a surety, whereby he is released from his liability as surety.

(3) Of the payment of a debt whereby the debtor is freed from further liability.

(4) Of the release of lands, or money in the funds, from an incumbrance, by payment of the amount to the incumbrancer, or otherwise by consent of the incumbrancer. As to discharge of mortgage by means of indorsed receipt, see the Law of Property Act 1925, s 115, and Form No 2 set out in Sch III to that Act.

Disclaimer. A renunciation, denial, or refusal. It is used:

(1) Of any act whereby a person refuses to accept an interest in property, eg of estate which is attempted to be conveyed to

him, as where land is conveyed to an intended trustee without his consent, and he refuses to accept it. This is called the disclaimer of an estate. Powers of disclaimer are given by the Administration of Estates Act 1925, s 23 to the personal representative of a tenant for life of the trust estate. A disclaimer of a benefit arising under a will or intestacy, if made within a two-year period from the date of death, is treated as if the benefit had never been conferred and the CGT rules apply as if the allocation of the estate specified in the deed of variation had been made by the deceased (TCGA 1992, s 62(6)). In contrast to a deed of variation, no election is required to treat the disclaimer as not being a disposal. To have this effect for CGT, the disclaimer must be an instrument in writing.

See DEED OF VARIATION, cf GRATUITOUS TRANSFERS OF VALUE.

(2) Of the refusal by the trustee in a bankruptcy to accept a burdensome lease or other onerous property of the bankrupt (see the Insolvency Act 1986, s 315).

(3) Of disclaimer of a trade mark under the Trade Marks Act 1938, s 14.

(4) Of disclaimer of powers. Under the Law of Property Act 1925, s 156 a person to whom any power, whether coupled with an interest or not, is given may by deed disclaim the power.

(5) Of the refusal by a liquidator of a company to accept a burdensome lease or other onerous property (see the Insolvency Act 1986, s 178).

Disclosure. The revealing of information. More specifically, the disclosure of documents which may serve as evidence in a trial, by one side to the other in advance of trial. Disclosure of documents was formerly termed 'discovery of documents'. For the rules concerning disclosure see the Civil Procedure Rules 1998, Part 31.

Discontinued Operations. Operations of the reporting entity that are sold or terminated and that satisfy all of the following conditions.

(a) The sale or termination is completed either in the period or before the earlier of three months after the commencement of the subsequent

period and the date on which the financial statements are approved.

(b) If a termination, the former activities have ceased permanently.

(c) The sale or termination has a material effect on the nature and focus of the reporting entity's operations and represents a material reduction in its operating facilities resulting either from its withdrawal from a particular market (whether class of business or geographical) or from a material reduction in turnover in the reporting entity's continuing markets.

(d) The assets, liabilities, results of operations and activities are clearly distinguishable, physically, operationally and for financial reporting purposes.

Operations not satisfying all these conditions are classified as continuing. [FRS 3 – Reporting financial performance]

Discount. (1) An allowance made to bankers or others for advancing money on bills of exchange before they become due.

See BILL OF EXCHANGE.

(2) An allowance frequently made at the settlement of accounts, by way of deduction from the amount payable.

Discounted cash flow (DCF). A method of financially appraising a capital project by predicting a stream of cash flows, which are expressed in net present value by the application of a chosen interest rate (the 'discount rate').

Discounted security. There is a charge to income tax under Schedule D, Case III on the capital gain made on the transfer or redemption of a 'relevant discounted security' or a gilt strip (FA 1996, Sch 13, paras 1 & 14).

A 'relevant discounted security' is one where the issue price is less than the amount payable on redemption by more than $\frac{1}{2}$% of the issue price times the number of years between issue and redemption, unless the security is issued for a period in excess of thirty years, when the security is a 'relevant discounted security' if the discount exceeds 15% irrespective of the number of years (FA

1996, Sch 13, para 3). One is required to look at every possible occasion and not just the earliest; if the gain is or would or might be deep on any one of those occasions the security is 'relevant' and so comes within these rules (FA 1996, Sch 13, para 3(1)). An exception is made where the holder's option to redeem arises because of a default by the issuer—provided a redemption is unlikely.

Discovery. The term describing the processes by which one party to an action discovered or acquired information from the other side about the evidence upon which that other would rely at trial. Discovery was

(1) Of *facts*, obtainable by either party to an action, in the form of answers on oath to questions known as interrogatories administered by the other party after approval of the court, and on payment of deposit as security for the costs. The answers, or any of them, might be put in as evidence at the trial, and are obtained with the object of getting admissions or discovery of such material facts as relate to the case of the party interrogating.

(2) Of *documents*, obtained as above. The party against whom an order for discovery of documents was made was required to file an affidavit setting out all the documents relating to the action which are or have been in his possession or power.

Under the Civil Procedure Rules 1998, documentary discovery is called the disclosure and inspection of documents, found in Part 31, and rules concerning witness statements and depositions are found in Parts 32 and 34.

Discovery is also used in reference to the disclosure by a bankrupt of his property for the benefit of his creditors.

'Discovery' assessment. Under self-assessment, the Revenue can raise an enquiry (under TMA 1970, s 9A) into a tax return, which may lead to undisclosed income or understated income being brought into the charge to tax. However, an enquiry cannot be commenced more than 12 months after the due date for submission of a return, unless the return was submitted late. The only mechanism for the Revenue

charging tax after the 'enquiry window' has closed, is by means of a 'discovery' assessment. If an inspector 'discovers' that profits have not been assessed or the assessment has become insufficient or that excessive relief has been given, he may make an assessment under TMA 1970, s 29. Where the taxpayer has made a self-assessment return, no 'discovery assessment' can be made unless one of two alternative conditions is fulfilled. The first alternative is that the self-assessment charges too little tax (or overstates a claim) as a result of fraudulent or negligent conduct by the taxpayer or a person acting on his behalf (TMA 1970, s 29(4)). The second alternative is that at the end of the period allowed for an enquiry (or the completion of the enquiry, where there was one) the Revenue officer could not have been reasonably expected, on the basis of information supplied to him, to be aware that the self-assessment charges too little tax (or overstates a claim) (TMA 1970, s 29(5)). The term discovery has been given a wide ambit by the courts; the words are apt to cover any case in which for any reason it newly appears that the taxpayer has been undercharged (per Viscount Simonds in *Cenlon Finance Co Ltd v Ellwood (1962) 40 TC 176 at 204*). So an assessment may be made where the Revenue decide that a company should be treated as a dealing company rather than an investment company (*Jones v Mason Investments (Luton) Ltd (1966) 43 TC 570*) or where a new inspector takes a different view of the law from his predecessor or to correct an arithmetical error in the computation (*Parkin v Cattell (1971) 48 TC 462*). Since the validity of the new assessment is a question of law, the Revenue may justify it even though it refers to an incorrect provision (*Vickerman v Personal Representatives of Mason [1984] STC 231*). It is open to the Revenue to issue a second (additional) assessment rather than seeking an increase in the first on appeal (*Duchy Maternity Ltd v Hodgson [1985] STC 764*).

Discretionary trust. A trust under which the trustees have a discretion to apply the income and the capital of the trust as they wish.

See TRUST.

Dispensation. More properly known as a 'notice of nil liability', a dispensation for benefit in kind is a notice provided by Inland Revenue to an employer that payments made in accordance with arrangements that have been specified may be omitted from the P11D return that is required following each fiscal year of benefits extended to employees and may, similarly, be omitted from the employees' personal tax returns. A dispensation is given when the Revenue are satisfied that the deduction that could be claimed by the employee under TA 1988, s 198 is equal to (or exceeds) the value of the benefit in kind that arises under TA 1988, ss 145–154 in respect of the payment made by the employer. It is common for a dispensation to be given in respect of travel costs; a dispensation can cover any other matter within the benefit in kind legislation, and also any cash payments made to an employee that are direct reimbursements of an employee's expenditure. From 6 April 2002 onwards, no dispensations are provided in respect of mileage allowances paid to employees (FA 2001, s 58). Instead, the statutory scheme in TA 1988, ss 197AD–197AH is applied, which allows a fixed sum to be paid per mile irrespective of the size of the car and without reference to the actual cost borne by the employee.

Disposal. Capital gains tax charges tax on a gain arising on a disposal. The concept of disposal is not defined in statute, but nor has it yet caused much reported litigation. It has been suggested that any form of transfer or alienation of the beneficial title to an asset (whether legal or equitable) from one person to another involves a disposal by the one and an acquisition by the other. A sale by personal representatives in the course of administration is clearly a disposal on this definition since beneficial title passes to the purchaser and the fact that the disposer is not himself beneficially entitled is quite irrelevant. A disclaimer does not constitute a disposal (TCGA 1992, s 62(8)(a); see *Re Paradise Motor Co Ltd [1968] 2 All ER 625*).

An exchange of assets is a disposal of each asset involved. An example is where a farm is owned by two brothers, each having an undivided share in the whole and they decide that they will construct a boundary so that the first brother has sole ownership of the land north of the boundary, leaving the land to the south in the sole ownership of the second brother. This is a disposal by the first brother of his half interest in the land to the south and a disposal by the second brother of his half interest in the land to the north. Each brother has made a disposal, the consideration for which is the value of the land acquired from the other. Another example is the surrender of a lease in exchange for a new one; in order to avoid CGT it is common to grant the new lease subject to the existing lease and perhaps increasing the rent under the existing lease. (Where the new lease and the old lease are identical in the sense of relating to the same property and having the same terms, the Revenue, by concession, do not treat the surrender as involving any disposal.)

There is no general exclusion for involuntary disposals.

The concept of disposal is extended to certain deemed disposals and by treating certain shifts of economic value as disposals even though no asset is disposed of. In deciding what is the subject matter of a disposal undertaken in steps as part of a scheme, it is permissible to look at the effect of the whole scheme.

Disposals may realise a gain or realise a loss.

Disposition. Inheritance tax is charged on a chargeable transfer. This is defined as a transfer of value (other than an exempt transfer or potentially exempt transfer), which is, in turn, stated to be a disposition as a result of which an individual's estate is reduced. The word 'disposition' is not defined in the legislation (although it is stated to include a disposition effected by associated operations). The word 'disposition' is not the same as the word 'disposal' used in CGT nor is it the same as a 'gift' in the IHT legislation dealing with a gift with reservation. A disposition need not be of any existing property so that distinctions between the creation and the disposition of interests are quite immaterial; all that is required is some act or, in some situations, an omission, which results in a loss in value to a person's estate. To be a disposition, however, there must be property. A disposition of services would not cause a charge to tax whereas the disposition of a right to be paid for services would be a transfer of value.

From this it might appear to follow that deliberately to destroy an asset, for example a picture or stamp, would be a disposition as would an accidental destruction, although the absence of an intent to confer a benefit will usually prevent a charge arising. The notion of a transfer, however, suggests the need for a transferee so that one could argue that even deliberate destruction could not be a disposition. Against this one may point out that the word 'transferee' was almost completely removed in the 1984 consolidation and that the word to be construed is 'disposition', not 'transfer'. Destruction of an asset by disclaimer was held to be a disposition in *IRC v Buchanan (1957) 37 TC 365*, with reference to TA 1988, s 660B.

See CHARGEABLE TRANSFER; TRANSFER OF VALUE.

Dissection. The duality rule does not prevent the dissection of expenditure and subsequent deduction of that part of the expenditure which is wholly and exclusively for business purposes. Thus, if a professional man uses one of his rooms in his house as an office, the expenses of that office are deductible, and this will be so even though the electricity, rates and other bills apply to the house as a whole and have to be dissected in order to discover the part attributable to the office. In these cases, the sum is dissected in order to discover that part which is wholly for business purposes, wholly being a matter of quantum, and the test of exclusive business purpose is then applied to that part (*Gazelle v Servini [1995] STC (SCD) 324*). The rule is frequently applied when a business loan is obtained and part of the sum borrowed is used for personal expenditure, which may be evidenced by excess drawings being made from the business (*Silk v Fletcher [1999] STC (SCD) 220* and *Silk v Fletcher (No 2) [2000] STC (SCD) 565*). Dissection has also been applied where an unreasonable amount of

remuneration was paid to an employee, the court allowing the employer to deduct that part which would have been reasonable (*Copeman v William J Flood & Sons Ltd (1941) 24 TC 53*). However, it could not be applied to the air fare paid in *Bowden v Russell and Russell (1965) 42 TC 301* since one could not identify the precise point in mid-Atlantic at which the solicitor ceased to be travelling for personal reasons and began to travel for business reasons.

See DUALITY; WHOLLY AND EXCLUSIVELY.

Distraint. If a person neglects or refuses to pay the sum charged, the Inland Revenue are empowered to distrain (TMA 1970, s 61(1), (2)). A justice of the peace may issue a warrant in writing authorising a collector to break open, in the daytime, any house or premises, calling to his assistance any constable.

In *Nixon v Freeman (1860) 5 H & N 647* the court held that a bailiff in collecting tax was entitled to enter premises through an open window, and may also further open a window which was already partly open. However, three years later, in *Hancock v Austin (1863) 14 CBNS 634* it was held that a bailiff was not entitled to open a window catch without a warrant authorising him to 'break open' the premises. The saga continued in *Miller v Tebb (1893) 9 TLR 515, CA* where the court held that a bailiff was entitled to enter premises through a partially open skylight. In *Long v Clark [1894] 1 QB 119, CA*, the court held that a bailiff had no right to break into premises without a warrant but, even without a warrant, was entitled to climb over a wall or fence from adjoining premises. Certain items cannot be distrained. In *Morley v Pincombe (1848) 2 Exch 101* it was held that food is exempt from distraint, on the grounds that, being perishable, it is incapable of being returned in the same condition as when distrained upon. In *Nargett v Nias (1859) 1 E & E 439*, it was held that distraint could not be levied on a trader's tools.

Distributable reserves. The accumulated profits of a company that are, by law, able to be distributed as dividends to shareholders. Such profits are the realised profits;

revaluation reserves, for example, are not distributable.

Distribution. When a distribution is made by a company resident in the UK, the recipient is assessable to income tax under Schedule F (TA 1988, s 20). Distributions are not deductible in computing the profits of the company (TA 1988, s 337(2)). If the distribution is to another company subject to corporation tax there is no charge to income tax; however, there is no charge to corporation tax either (TA 1988, s 208). Such a receipt is called franked investment income.

Statute defines a distribution as:

(1) Dividends, including a capital dividend (TA 1988, s 209(2)(a));

(2) Any other distribution out of the assets of the company, in cash or otherwise, made in respect of shares (TA 1988, s 209(2)(b));

(3) The issue of any redeemable share capital or any security issued by the company in respect of shares or securities unless made wholly or in part for new consideration (TA 1988, s 209(2)(c));

(4) Interest that represents more than a reasonable commercial return (TA 1988, s 209(2)(d));

(5) Interest that it is attributable to the phenomenon known as thin capitalisation (TA 1988, s 209(2)(da));

(6) Interest on a debenture where the debenture is more like a share than a genuine debenture (TA 1988, s 209(2)(e));

(7) An asset passed by the company to a shareholder (the distribution is the market value of the asset less any consideration paid) (TA 1988, s 209(6));

(8) Certain repayments of share capital (TA 1988, s 211);

(9) A bonus issue that follows repayment of share capital (TA 1988, s 210).

Payments which are not distributions include distributions in respect of share capital in a winding-up (TCGA 1992, s 122) (even if the payments represent arrears of undeclared cumulative preference dividends: *Re Dominion Tar and Chemical Co Ltd [1929] 2 Ch 387*), covenanted donations to charity (TA 1988, s 339(6), (7)), certain payments by an industrial provident society(TA 1988, s 486(10), (11)), building society (TA 1988, s 476) or a mutual trading society (TA 1988, s 490) as well as certain group payments.

Dividend. (1) The periodical income arising from stocks, shares, etc.

(2) The proportion of a creditor's debt payable to him on the division of a bankrupt's or insolvent's estate.

Dividend cover. The ratio between the post-tax profit of a period of account and the dividend paid in respect of that period. Dividend cover is a measure that is widely applied in stock market analysis and is likely to be reflected in the share price.

Dividend stripping. Dividend stripping can be achieved in the following way. A has shares in company X. A sells those shares to B. B uses his voting power to compel the company to pay a large dividend to B. B then sells the shares back to A or to someone else. At first sight there is nothing inequitable about this. If B's marginal rate is simply lower than that of A there is a loss of tax. This lower rate may be achieved if B is either an exempt person or is simply less well off than A. If however B is a dealer in securities he may claim that, while the dividend paid out is undoubtedly his income, that must be set off against the loss he incurs when the shares he had bought are resold, the loss being due to the payment out of the cash reserve of the company. The effect is that the payment will have been drawn out free of tax, while A has received a sum which reflects the value of those cash reserves and that sum will be treated as a capital payment only.

Such arrangements can be attacked by TA 1988, s 730, which imposes a charge under Schedule D, Case VI on income that would otherwise be a dividend.

Dividend yield. The ratio between the dividend paid for a period of account and the market value of shares in the company.

Domicile. An individual who is domiciled in a jurisdiction within the UK is subject to UK income tax and UK capital gains tax on foreign income and gains on foreign assets as they arise. An individual who is not domiciled within the UK is subject to UK income tax on foreign income that is remitted to the UK and not on foreign income that remains (or is spent) outside the UK; similarly, a non-UK domiciled individual is not subject to UK CGT on foreign gains if the proceeds are not remitted to the UK.

A person is domiciled where he has or is deemed by law to have his permanent home. He must have a domicile; but may not have more than one domicile. Subject to two qualifications, the test of domicile is that developed by the general rules of the conflict of laws. For recent examples, see *Anderson (Anderson's Executor) v IRC [1998] STC (SCD) 43* and also *Re Clore (No 2), Official Solicitor v Clore [1984] STC 609.*

The first qualification is that for tax purposes the question is whether or not a person is domiciled within the UK (eg TA 1988, ss 19(1), 65(4), 739). For general conflict of law purposes the question will be whether a person is domiciled in England and Wales, or Scotland or some other separate jurisdiction. Although generally a person domiciled in the UK will be domiciled in one of its constituent parts this is not necessarily so since a person with a domicile of origin in France who decides to live in the UK but is undecided as between Scotland and England may have a UK domicile for UK tax purposes and a French domicile for conflict of laws purposes. However, it is understood that the Revenue do not take this point and would treat the person as still domiciled in France.

The second qualification is that for tax purposes an individual's registration on the UK electoral roll as an overseas voter is to be disregarded in determining domicile (FA 1996, s 200). This rule applies as from 6 April 1996 and can itself be disregarded if the individual so wishes (FA 1996, s 200(4)).

The primary test of domicile is the domicile of origin. If it is alleged that this has been superseded by domicile of choice, the onus of proof relies on the party alleging that a change of domicile has occurred (*Winans v A-G [1904] AC 287 at 288 and 289* per the Earl of Halsbury). In *F v IRC [2000] STC (SCD) 1*, the Special Commissioner ruled that the Revenue failed to demonstrate that an Iranian who came to England in 1949 at the age of 19 and remained until his death in 1992 had made such a fundamental change in his way of life as to demonstrate the acquisition of a domicile of choice in England and Wales. This case, which arises in the context of CGT, gives a very useful review of the law on domicile.

Dominant influence. Influence that can be exercised to achieve the operating and financial policies desired by the holder of the influence, notwithstanding the rights or influence of any other party.

(*a*) In the context of FRS 2, the right to exercise a dominant influence means that the holder has a right to give directions with respect to the operating and financial policies of another undertaking with which its directors are obliged to comply, whether or not they are for the benefit of that undertaking.

(*b*) The actual exercise of dominant influence is the exercise of an influence that achieves the result that the operating and financial policies of the undertaking influenced are set in accordance with the wishes of the holder of the influence and for the holder's benefit whether or not those wishes are explicit. The actual exercise of dominant influence is identified by its effect in practice rather than by the way in which it is exercised. [FRS 2 – Accounting for subsidiary undertakings]

Donee. *See* DONOR.

Donor. A person who makes a gift to another; and the person to whom the gift is made is called the *donee.*

Dormant partner. A person who takes no active part in the partnership affairs, and is not known to the world as a partner, but who receives the profits of the partnership. *See* PARTNERSHIP.

Double entry. A system of bookkeeping in which the entries are made so as to show the debit and credit of every transaction.

Double taxation agreement. The UK today has treaties with over 100 countries, including the Isle of Man, Jersey, and Guernsey (including Alderney). In 1997 the UK was the first country to reach this century; at that time there were over 1,300 treaties worldwide. There are UK treaties with nearly all Western European countries, with most members of the Commonwealth and with countries such as Japan and Israel. However there are no treaties with many of the Arab countries such as Yemen, nor with tax havens such as the Cayman Islands and Liechtenstein. Arrangements with some countries are limited to transport profits and employees, eg Argentina, Brazil, Ethiopia and Iran.

Double taxation relief. Relief given against a UK tax liability in recognition of a liability to a foreign tax. There are three methods of giving relief:

(1) The UK has entered into double taxation agreement with over 100 other territories, a process authorised by TA 1988, s 788. Treaty relief may exempt some income from tax in one country and give credit for foreign taxes on other income. Section 788 only allows the Revenue to propose Orders in Council if they are consistent with the purposes there spelt out. For this reason it is thought that the UK treaties may only relieve from tax and not increase it.

(2) Relief can unilaterally be given to allow the foreign tax paid as a credit against the UK tax liability. This is permitted by TA 1988, s 790. The rules which the foreign tax must satisfy in order to qualify as a tax credit are the same whether the credit arises under treaty or unilaterally.

(3) Relief can be given by deducting the foreign tax in computing the profits of the business, thus treating the foreign tax like any other business expense. This is permitted by TA 1988, s 811.

Draft. A cheque or bill of exchange, or other negotiable instrument; also the rough copy of a legal document before it has been engrossed.

Duality. TA 1988, s 74(1)(a) prohibits the deduction of expenses not being money

'wholly and exclusively laid . . . for the purposes of the trade'. When calculating tax assessable profits, this duality rule prevents the deduction of expenditure for mixed purposes. This usually arises where the expenditure has mixed business and personal purposes. The leading case is the decision of the House of Lords in *Mallalieu v Drummond [1983] STC 665, HL* in which a lady barrister sought to deduct the cost of clothes bought for wear in court, such clothes being required by court etiquette. The undisputed evidence was that the taxpayer's expenditure was motivated solely by thoughts of court etiquette and not at all by mere human thoughts of warmth and decency. Counsel for the taxpayer disclaimed any reliance on his client's dislike of black clothing and the question was reduced to this: if clothing is purchased for use only on business occasions and such clothes are only so used (or for proceeding to and from work) is the expense deductible? The House of Lords said no. In addition to the business purpose there were the other purposes of warmth and decency. As Lord Brightman said: 'I reject that notion that the object of a taxpayer is inevitably limited to the particular conscious motive in mind at the moment of expenditure.'

See DISSECTION; WHOLLY AND EXCLUSIVELY.

Duration of lease. A premium paid for a lease of over 50 years is capital. The recipient is subject to CGT; the payer has a CGT base cost. A premium paid for a lease of under 50 years is part capital and part income (TA 1988, s 34(1)). The recipient is subject to income tax on a part of the premium; the payer has a revenue expense. The definition of a 50-year lease takes full account of the commercial realities. Thus if a tenant has a 40-year lease with an option to extend it for a further 20 years, account may be taken of the circumstances making it likely that the lease will be so extended. Likewise if a tenant, or a person connected with him, has the right not to extend the existing lease but instead has the right to a further lease of the same premises or part of them, the term may be treated as not expiring before the end of the further lease.

If any of the terms of the lease (whether relating to forfeiture or to any other matter) or any other circumstances render it unlikely that the lease will continue beyond a date falling short of the expiry of the term of the lease, the lease shall be treated as if it ended not later than that date, provided that the premium would not have been substantially greater had the lease been expected to run its full term (TA 1988, s 34(1)). Thus a 51-year lease with an option to the landlord to terminate it after five years would be treated as a five-year lease, as would one which provided that after five years the rent, originally a full commercial rent, should be quintupled. The question of what is unlikely is judged at the time the lease is granted (TA 1988, s 38). The rule by focusing on what is likely or unlikely means that a lease for life falls within these rules if actuarial tables show that the life is unlikely to last more than 50 years. (This is despite the imposition of a 99-year lease by virtue of the Law of Property Act 1925, s 149.)

Dwelling. A building or part of a building occupied or intended to be occupied as a separate dwelling, together with any yard, garden, outhouses, and appurtenances belonging to or usually enjoyed with that building or part of it. It implies a building used or capable of being used as a residence by one or more families and provided with all necessary parts and appliances, eg, floors, staircases, windows, etc.

E

EC. European Community.

EGM. Extraordinary general meeting.

EIS. Enterprise Investment Scheme.

E&OE. Errors and omissions excepted. A phrase extended to an account stated, to excuse slight mistakes or oversights.

ESOP. Employee share ownership plan.

ESOT. Employee share ownership trust.

EU. European Union.

Earned income. Earned income is defined in three main categories:

(1) Any income arising in respect of any remuneration from any office or employment including pensions, superannuation or other allowances, deferred pay or compensation for loss of office.

(2) Any income from any property which is attached to or forms part of the employment of any office or employment of profit held by the individual.

(3) Any income which is charged under Schedule D if it is immediately derived by the individual from a trade, profession or vocation carried on by him as an individual or as a partner personally acting in the partnership (TA 1988, s 833(4); the list is supplemented in s 833(5), (6)).

(4) Certain other types of income are declared to be earned income. These are income in respect of a Civil List pension, voluntary pensions (TA 1988, s 133), maternity benefits and other social security benefits (TA 1988, s 617) and certain annuities granted under Agriculture Act 1967. Also declared to be earned income are post cessation receipts, income from the sale of patent rights for an invention actually devised by the taxpayer and golden handshakes. Pensions to former employees are earned income. Enterprise allowance payments are earned income (TA 1988, s 127(3)), as is income from furnished holiday lettings (TA 1988, s 503(1)).

Earnings. The basic definition of earnings for national insurance contribution (as well as benefit) purposes is that 'earnings includes any remuneration or profit derived from an employment' (SSCBA 1992, s 3(1)). The expression 'an employment' refers both to employment as an 'employed earner' and to employment as a 'self-employed earner' (SSCBA 1992, s 2(1)(a), (b)). 'Remuneration' is a term appropriate to the wages, salaries, fees etc. earned by an employee, whereas 'profit' is appropriate to the business profits of a self-employed person. Nevertheless an employee's earnings can also include 'profit' as is apparent from the provisions dealing with the collection of Class 1 contributions through the PAYE system. There 'emoluments'—in this context the earnings on which contributions have to be paid through the PAYE system—are defined as 'so much of a person's remuneration or profit derived from employed earner's employment as constitute earnings for the purposes of the Act' (SI 2001/1004, Sch 4, para 1).

It is on the basis that an employee's earnings include profit that the authorities consider that such items as benefits in kind (in so far as not subject to the payment in kind exclusion) and round sum allowances give rise to Class 1 contribution liability.

However, before the profit can be included in the employee's earnings, it must be derived from the employment. In *Hochstrasser v Mayes (1957) 38 TC 673 at 705*, Upjohn J said: 'in my judgment not every payment made to an employee is necessarily made to him as a profit arising from his employment. Indeed in my judgment the authorities show that to be a profit arising from the employment, the payment must be made in reference to the services the employee renders by virtue of his office and it must be in the nature of a reward for services past, present or future.'

Certain payments are specifically required to be included in 'remuneration' and so are within the definition of earnings for contribution purposes. They are:

(1) statutory sick pay and statutory maternity pay (SSCBA 1992, s 4(1)(a));

(2) sickness payments under arrangements made by the employer where the employer has made or is liable to make contributions to fund such payments (SSCBA 1992, s 4(1)(b));

(3) payments for restrictive covenants where a tax liability arises under TA 1988, s 313.

Earnings available for ordinary shareholders. A company's post-tax profit for the period that is available for distribution as a dividend to the holders of ordinary shares, after deducting sums payable to debenture-holders and holders of preference shares.

Earnings per share. E.p.s. is calculated by taking the net profit or loss for the period, after all exceptional and extraordinary items. From the profit is then deducted the tax charge for the period, payments due to debenture-holders, preference share holders and minority interests.

There are then two separate measures of earnings per share. In order to calculate the basic earnings per share, the earnings calculated as above are divided by the weighted average number of ordinary shares in issue during the period of account. In order to calculate the diluted earnings per share, the earnings are divided by the weighted average number of ordinary shares in issue during the period plus the weighted average number of ordinary shares that would be issued if all share options had been exercised, all other employee rights to share capital had been allocated and any convertible debt or equity had been converted into ordinary shares. The calculation is undertaken on the assumption that each option had been called, and each conversion made, in accordance with the terms of the option or conversion, on the first day of the period of account. Exceptionally, where the option or conversion right has been granted during the period of account, the calculation is performed as if the option had been exercised or the conversion made on the date of grant of the option or conversion right. [See FRS 14 – Earnings per share]

Earnings retained. The accumulated profit of a company after dividends have been paid.

Earnings yield. The percentage calculated by the earnings per share against the market price of the share.

Earn-out agreement. When a business is sold, a frequent arrangement is for a lump sum to be payable on the sale and a further sum paid after a specified period, the payment of the second sum to be conditional on specified profit targets being achieved. Where the amount of the second payment cannot be known at the date of the agreement (because it is, for example, a percentage of post sale profits), the capital gains tax treatment follows the principle laid down in *Marren v Ingles*. That is, there are two CGT disposals: the first disposal on the sale, the value of the right to the further sum is treated as part of the consideration received; the second disposal when the further consideration is received, the value of the right is put against this to compute the second gain.

Easement. A particular kind of INCORPOREAL HERIDITAMENT, ie an intangible right in land. An easement is a right enjoyed by a person over his neighbour's property, eg a right of way, or a right of passage for water, which is a privilege without a *profit*; that is, the easement owner enjoys some right over the land of another but which does not allow him to take anything away such as soil or timber. Generally an easement belongs to a person as being the owner of a specific house or land, which is then called the *dominant tenement*, the land in which the easement owner has a right being called the *servient tenement*. An easement may be positive or negative; a positive easement is a right to do some thing on the servient tenement, such as pass over it (a right of way) or park a car there, to run telephone lines over it, etc. A negative easement does not allow the easement owner to act in any way, but prevents the owner of the servient tenement from acting in a certain way, eg an easement of light prohibits the servient owner from building in such a way as to prevent light reaching the dominant owner's windows. Under the Law of Property Act 1925 an easement at law must be for an interest equivalent to an estate in fee simple absolute in possession or a term of years absolute. After 1925, all other easements are equitable only (see the Law of Property Act 1925, s 1).

Ejusdem generis (of the same kind or nature). Where in a statute, etc, particular classes are specified by name, followed by general words, the meaning of the general words that follow is generally restricted to the categories represented by the particular words, and the general words are taken to apply to only those things not specifically mentioned in the statute, etc, that are *ejusdem generis* with the particular classes.

Emergency tax code. The code applied by an employer for a new employee who does not produce form P45 from a previous employer during the fiscal year. The code is the personal allowance (without addition) divided by 10 and is applied on a Week 1 or Month 1 basis. Where salary is paid monthly, the effect of using the emergency tax code is that income tax is deducted from the monthly payment in so far as it exceeds one-twelfth of the annual personal allowance.

Emoluments. Emoluments 'includes all salaries, fees, wages, perquisites and profits whatsoever' (TA 1988, s 131). A perquisite is merely a casual emolument additional to regular salary or wages (per Lord Guest in *Owen v Pook [1970] AC 244 at 225*). Case law makes it clear that not all payments from employers to employees fall within this definition and that some payments from non-employers do. The test is one of causation; an emolument is a payment in return for acting as or being an employee (per Lord Radcliffe in *Hochstrasser v Mayes [1960] AC 376 at 389, 392*). The word 'emoluments' covers also certain payments in kind. A payment in kind will only

be taxable if in addition to being an emolument it is convertible into money, although a wider test applies to employees earning £8,500 a year or more and to directors (TA 1988, s 154).

Employee share ownership scheme. An ESOP is a trust created by a company that buys shares in that company (usually with funds provided by the employer). The shares are then allocated to employees on a pre-determined basis, which may be related to the achievement of performance targets. An ESOP acquires existing shares; it therefore does not cause dilution of the company's share capital.

Employees share ownership trust. An ESOT is a trust established by a company to acquire shares in that company and distribute them to employees. If the conditions of TA 1988, s 186 are satisfied, which require that all employees can benefit from the distribution of shares after a stated period in employment, the payments to the ESOT by the company are tax deductible. The ESOT arrangement is superseded by the provisions of FA 2000.

Employers' liability insurance. A type of insurance protecting the insured against his liability to pay damages for injuries sustained by persons in his employment.

Employment. An employment was once described as a post and as something 'more or less analogous to an office' (per Rowlatt J in *Davies v Braithwaite [1931] 2 KB 628 at 635*) but modern cases take a different tack and equate employment with a contract of service (per Lightman J in *Barnett v Brabyn [1996] STC 716 at 724c*, approving *Hall v Lorimer [1994] STC 23*). A ship's master, a chauffeur and a reporter on the staff of the newspaper are all employed under a contract of service and so come within Schedule E whereas a ship's pilot, a taxi-man and a newspaper contributor are employed (by the owner, the hirer or the newspaper) under a contract for services (*Stevenson, Jordan and Harrison Ltd v Macdonald and Evans [1952] 1 TLR 101 at 111*, per Lord Denning) and so do not. A consultant under the National Health

Service is taxed under Schedule E in respect of that employment or office whether the arrangement is whole time or part time (*Mitchell and Edon v Ross [1959], 40 TC 11* (Upjohn J)). By contrast a person under contract to provide clerking services to a set of barristers' chambers was held to be an independent contractor on the particular facts (*McMenamin v Diggles [1991] STC 419*). If no services are to be performed, the contract is not one of employment; however, the remuneration may be brought within Schedule E by virtue of it arising from 'an office' (TA 1988, s 314).

Endowment. Permanent provision for any institution or person. The word is frequently used for a charity's funds, to distinguish the fund that has been established from the (usually original) donation that established the charity and which is essential for the continuing ability of the charity to perform its functions from donations that the charity expects to spend in furthering its charitable objects.

Endowment insurance. A type of insurance whereby a specified sum becomes payable not on the death of the insured but on the arrival of a specified date, the insured being still alive.

Endowment policy. *See* ENDOWMENT INSURANCE.

Enduring power of attorney. A power of attorney which is not revoked by any subsequent mental incapacity of the donor (see the Enduring Powers of Attorney Act 1985, s 1).
See POWER OF ATTORNEY.

Engagement letter. On appointment, an auditor should write an engagement letter to the organisation concerned, giving written confirmation of the auditor's acceptance of the appointment and specifying the scope of the audit, the form of report and detailing any work to be undertaken in addition to the audit.

Enlarge. To *enlarge an estate* is to increase a person's interest in land, eg where there is an estate in A for life, with remainder to B and his heirs, and B releases his estate to A, A's estate is said to be *enlarged* into a fee simple.

Enquiry. It is of the essence of self-assessment that the taxpayer makes his own assessment and payment follows from the self-assessment, not from action by the Revenue. The corollary to self-assessment by the taxpayer is a statutory regime for the Revenue to test the veracity of self-assessments by a process of Revenue enquiries. About one tax return in every one thousand returns submitted is selected at random for a Revenue enquiry under TMA 1970, s 9A. This selection process takes place before tax returns are sent to taxpayers with selection being based on stratified sampling applied to the previous year's returns. By this method, the Revenue centrally collects information on compliance by around 7,500 taxpayers. Many more enquiries commence as a result of either information on the tax return or information from a third party.

An enquiry under self-assessment is a formal procedure that commences with written notification served on the taxpayer by the Revenue officer. Such notification can only be given during the 'enquiry window' which starts with the date of receipt of the self-assessment return by the Revenue and ends on 31 January, 22 months after the end of the fiscal year for which the return is made. The time limits are interpreted strictly. In *Holly v Inspector of Taxes [2000] STC (SCD) 50* the Special Commissioner held that a notice posted by the Revenue on Monday 25 January 1999 by second class post was not a valid notice of commencement of enquiry under TMA 1970, s 9A as it was not actually received until 3 February 1999. In *Wing Hung Lai v Bale [1999] STC (SCD) 238*, the notice was posted by the Revenue on Wednesday 27 January 1999 by second class post. Under the Post Office code of practice, delivery of that notice would be in the ordinary course of post on Monday 1 February. On this basis, the notice was held to be invalid.

On giving notice under TMA 1970, s 9A(1), 11B(1) or 12AC(1), a Revenue officer is empowered to require the taxpayer to produce to the officer 'such documents as are in the taxpayer's possession or power and as the officer may reasonably require for the purpose of determining whether and, if so, the extent to which the return is incorrect or incomplete or the amendment is incorrect' (TMA 1970, s 19A(2)). The notice from the Revenue must specify the time in which the taxpayer is required to produce the documents. The time given to the taxpayer must not be less than 30 days. This time limit is interpreted strictly. A notice that gave 30 days from the date it was posted by the Revenue was held to be invalid, as the taxpayer could not have had 30 days from the date of receipt of that notice (*Self-assessed v Inspector of Taxes [1999] STC (SCD) 253*).

At the completion of an enquiry, the Revenue officer is required to issue a 'closure notice' informing the taxpayer that he has completed his enquiry and stating his conclusions (TMA 1970, s 28A(1)). The closure notice must either state that no amendment of the return is required or makes an amendment of the return. The effect of a 'closure notice' is, thus, to amend the taxpayer's self-assessment without any action by the taxpayer.

The taxpayer can then make an appeal against the amendment of his self-assessment (TMA 1970, s 31(1)).

Enterprise investment scheme (EIS).
Relief given under the enterprise investment scheme is a reduction in the income tax liability for the year, computed as 20% of the sum invested in subscribing for newly-issued shares in an unquoted company (TA 1988, s 289A(1) & (2)). The shares must be issued in order to raise money for the purpose of a qualifying business activity, and the money raised must be used for the purpose of that activity, 80% being used within 12 months of the issue and the remaining 20% within 24 months (TA 1988, s 289). The shares must be issued in exchange for cash (TA 1988, s 289(1)(a)).

The shares must be eligible shares. Shares are eligible if they are new ordinary shares which, throughout the period of five years beginning with the date on which they are issued, carry no present or future preferential right to dividends or to a company's assets on its winding-up and no present or future preferential right to be redeemed (TA 1988, s 289(7)).

The enterprise investment scheme requires that the company must exist wholly for the purpose of carrying on one or more qualifying trades. A holding company may also qualify since the rule includes a company whose business consists wholly of holding shares or securities in, or making loans to, one or more qualifying subsidiaries. A trade is a qualifying trade unless it is an excluded trade: the list includes dealing in land, in commodities or futures, or in shares, securities or other financial instruments; others featured include the provision of legal and accounting services, banking, insurance and leasing (TA 1988, s 297(2)).

Where a person has made a chargeable gain on the disposal of any asset, on or after 29 November 1994, and in the period beginning 12 months before and ending three years after the date on which the gain accrued, he subscribes for shares in a company that qualifies under the EIS, then the amount of the chargeable gain equal to the amount of the EIS investment is treated as postponed (TCGA 1992, Sch 5B).

Enterprise management incentive.
Enterprise management incentives (EMIs) are designed to help small companies attract and retain the key people they need and to reward employees for taking a risk by investing their time and skills in helping small companies achieve their potential. The company may grant EMI share options over shares with a value of up to £3,000,000 in total and up to £100,000 to an individual employee (FA 2000, Sch 14, paras 10 & 11). The grant of the option is then free of an income tax charge (and, also, free of both employee's and employer's NIC), as is the exercise of the option. The gain made on sale is subject to CGT, not income tax, and CGT taper relief is calculated from the date of grant of the option, not the later date of exercise. This will mean that, usually, tax is charged on only 25% of the gain.

This scheme is meant to apply to small high-risk companies. The company must be a qualifying company, ie one which is an independent, trading company with gross assets not exceeding £15 million (£30 million from 6 April 2002) (FA 2000, Sch 14, paras 13, 16 & 17). The trade must be carried on in the UK but the company need not be resident here (FA 2000, Sch 14, para 18). Only the parent company of a group can grant EMI options.

The option cannot be exercised for three years and must be capable of being exercised within ten years (FA 2000, Sch 14, para 39). There are no rules directing the conditions under which the shares may be issued; so the shares may be non-voting or subject to pre-emption rights on the part of the company. This is to allow the company to protect its independence.

Entire contract. A contract in which everything to be done on one side is the consideration for everything to be done on the other. This is opposed to a severable or apportionable contract.

See CONSIDERATION.

Entirety. The whole, as distinguished from a moiety, etc.

See MOIETY.

Entity. A body corporate, partnership, or unincorporated association carrying on a trade or business with or without a view to profit. The reference to carrying on a trade or business means a trade or business of its own and not just part of the trades or businesses of entities that have interests in it. [FRS 9 – Associates and Joint Ventures]. Under FRS 5 – Reporting the substance of transactions, where all significant matters of operating and financial policy are predetermined in a contractual arrangement, if one party gains the benefits arising from the net assets of that arrangement and is exposed to the risks inherent in them, then that party possesses control and the arrangement is that party's quasi-subsidiary.

Entry. (1) Putting down a business transaction in a book of account.

(2) The taking possession of lands or tenements. See the following entries.

Equitable estate. Any estate, interest or charge in or over land which is not a legal estate takes effect as an equitable interest (see the Law of Property Act 1925, s 1(3)).

See ESTATE; EQUITY.

Equitable lien. *See* LIEN; EQUITY.

Equitable mortgage. A mortgage recognised in equity but not at law.

See MORTGAGE; EQUITY.

Equitable mortgages may be effected either by a written instrument or by a deposit of title deeds with or without writing. The right to effect such an equitable mortgage is preserved by the Law of Property Act 1925 (see ss 2(3), 13).

See TITLE DEEDS.

Equity. (1) A singular feature of the development of English law is that this general equitable jurisdiction came to form the basis of a body of law separate from the rules of common law, administered by a separate court, called the Court of Equity. Where the Common Law courts might provide no remedy for a plaintiff in a just cause, or might otherwise provide a harsh result, it became customary for suitors to apply to the medieval Chancellor, who as 'keeper of the King's conscience' would give equitable relief. Over time, the principles of equitable intervention crystallised into a second body of law, known as Equity; the principles of this body of law have often been framed in terms of a series of equitable maxims (see below); and it is important to realise that equity has always been a 'gloss' on the law, a departure from the common law in certain circumstances to better provide justice, but not a comprehensive body of law in its own right. Nevertheless, the Court of Chancery created one entire substantive branch of law, the law of trusts, as well as the law of fiduciary obligations, and much of the current law governing property in land. The orders of the Court of Chancery also gave rise to legal remedies unavailable at common law, in particular the injunction.

By the Judicature Acts of 1873–75 the Court of Chancery and the Courts of Common Law were fused, so that the rules of both the Common Law and Equity were thenceforward applied in one court. The

Court of Chancery became the Chancery Division of the High Court, and for convenience certain matters of equitable jurisdiction are still assigned to it; but by the Supreme Court Act 1981, s 49 both law and equity are to be administered in all Divisions of the High Court and in the Court of Appeal. But where there is any conflict between the rules of Common Law and the rules of equity, the latter are to prevail.

A few of the 'maxims' of equity may be briefly stated, as follows:

(1) 'Equity acts *in personam*', ie against a specific person rather than against property, and so compels performance of contracts, trusts, etc.

(2) 'Equity follows the law', ie does not depart unnecessarily from Common Law principles.

(3) 'Equity delights in equality', ie attempts to adjudicate fairly or equally between the parties.

(4) 'He who seeks equity must do equity', or a plaintiff must himself be prepared to see justice done.

(5) 'He who comes into equity must come with clean hands', ie must not have been guilty of improper conduct in regard to the subject-matter of litigation.

The most significant continuing effect of equity is the law of trusts.

See TRUST.

(2) The share capital of a company. The business of a company is financed by equity and borrowing. The funds invested as equity are at risk in that borrowing will be repaid in priority to equity on a winding-up. The ratio between equity capital and borrowing is the company's gearing; a company is highly geared if it has large borrowings compared to its equity. Equity shares are defined in Accounting Standards simply as 'shares other than non-equity shares' [FRS 4 – Capital instruments, FRS 6 – Acquisitions and mergers & FRS 13 – Derivatives and other financial instruments]. For the purpose of the Companies Act equity share capital is defined as: 'a company's issued share capital, excluding any part of that capital which, neither as respects dividends nor as respects capital, carries any right to participate beyond a specified amount in a distribution' (Companies Act 1985, s 744).

Equity dilution. A reduction in a shareholder's percentage shareholding, caused by the issue of further equity.

Equity dividend. Dividends relating to equity shares as defined in paragraph 7 of FRS 4 – Capital Instruments. [FRS 1 – Cash flow statements]

Equity dividend cover. The ratio between the profits of a company available for distribution and the dividend paid.

Equity instrument. An instrument that evidences an ownership interest in an entity, ie a residual interest in the assets of the entity after deducting all of its liabilities. 'Equity instrument' has a wider meaning than equity shares because it includes some non-equity shares, as well as warrants and options to subscribe for or purchase equity shares in the issuing entity. [FRS 13 – Derivatives and other financial instruments & FRS 14 – Earnings per share]

Equity method. (1) A method of accounting for an investment that brings into the consolidated profit and loss account the investor's share of the investment undertaking's results and that records the investment in the consolidated balance sheet at the investor's share of the investment undertaking's net assets including any goodwill arising to the extent that it has not previously been written off. [FRS 2 – Accounting for subsidiary undertakings]

(2) A method of accounting that brings an investment into its investor's financial statements initially at its cost, identifying any goodwill arising. The carrying amount of the investment is adjusted in each period by the investor's share of the results of its investee less any amortisation or write-off for goodwill, the investor's share of any relevant gains or losses, and any other changes in the investee's net assets including distributions to its owners, for example by dividend. The investor's share of its investee's results is recognised in its profit and loss account. The investor's cash flow

statement includes the cash flows between the investor and its investee, for example relating to dividends and loans. [FRS 9 – Associates and joint ventures]

Equity of a statute. The sound interpretation of a statute, the words of which may be too general, too special or otherwise inaccurate and defective.

Escrow. A scroll or writing sealed and delivered to a person not a party to it, to be held by him until some condition or conditions were performed by the party intended to be benefited by it; and, on the fulfilment of those conditions, to be delivered to such party, and to take effect as a deed to all intents and purposes. The word is commonly used when a contract has been signed by one party, but not dated. That party's solicitor then holds the document 'in escrow' and dates the document when the other party has signed the contract. The procedure is routine for the exchange of contracts on a sale and purchase of land.

Essence of a contract. In contracts certain stipulations, eg as to time, are sometimes stated to be *of the essence of the contract*. This means that such stipulations must in all circumstances be strictly complied with.

Estate. (1) The largest kind of INTEREST in land, ie an ownership interest. An estate is 'time in the land', ie a period of rightful ownership. Before the reorganisation of land law by the PROPERTY ACTS 1925, three basic estates were recognised at law: the fee simple, the fee tail, and the life estate. The length of time in the land of each was determined by the terms under which the land could be inherited, and an estate the length of which was determined by inheritance was called a fee. A fee simple was the largest estate, and was created by a GRANT 'to A and his heirs'. Thus the estate lasted so long as any person could inherit from the current estate owner. (Originally, there was some question as to whether the estate depended on there being persons alive who might have inherited from A, the original grantee. Thus, if A sold the land to B, and during B's ownership A's genealogical line died out so A had no general

descendants or 'heirs', it might have been argued that the estate came to an end, as the original time in the land was determined by the continuing existence of A's line. However it was settled early on that 'and his heirs' would apply to any fee simple owner for the time being; thus the estate would only terminate if the present owner died without heirs, ie general descendants.) A fee tail was an estate created by a grant to 'A and the heirs of his body' (sometimes limited to male or female heirs only). This estate could only be inherited by direct, or lineal, descendants, and unlike the fee simple, by the statute *De Donis Conditionalibus* (*see* CONDITIONAL FEE), when the lineal descendants of the original grantee failed, the estate terminated. A life estate was one granted to a person for his or her life only. Only fees and life estates were properly considered estates, and acquired the name of freeholds. Time in the land determined by a fixed period, ie a term of years, also called a LEASE, was distinguished as a leasehold interest, but came to be regarded as an estate of ownership in its own right.

By the Law of Property Act 1925, s 1, the only estates in land which are capable of subsisting or of being conveyed or created at law are:

(*a*) an estate in fee simple absolute in possession (ie a fee simple which is subject to no CONDITIONS, ie 'absolute', and one 'in possession', ie not a future interest);

(*b*) a term of years absolute.

(2) For inheritance tax, the notion of an estate is a concept central to the scheme of the tax charge because a disposition only gives rise to IHT if it causes a reduction in the value of the transferor's estate (IHTA 1984, s 3(1)) and also because on death a person is treated as having made a transfer of value equal to the value of his estate immediately before death (IHTA 1984, s 4(1)).

An estate is the aggregate of all the property to which the person is beneficially entitled. Allowable deductions should also be made (IHTA 1984, s 5(1)). Property held in a fiduciary capacity is not included. Property is widely defined as 'including rights and interests of any description'. It covers not only tangible property, but also equitable rights, debts and other choses in action, and indeed any rights capable of being reduced to a money value. If the terms of a settlement give the settlor the right for assets to be passed back to him, the right to receive those assets back is property and remains in the settlor's estate (*Melville v IRC [2000] STC 638*).

A person beneficially entitled to an interest in possession in settled property is treated as beneficially entitled to the property in which the interest subsists and not to the interest itself (IHTA 1984, s 49(1)). Thus the tenant for life of a fund worth £300,000 whose free estate is worth £10,000 will on death make a chargeable transfer of £310,000.

A person's estate will include property (other than settled property) over which he has a general power which enables him, or would if he were *sui juris* enable him, to dispose of it; he is treated as beneficially entitled to the property (*O'Neill v IRC [1998] STC (SCD) 110*).

There is no rule which prevents an asset from being in two estates at the same time. Where A makes a revocable gift of personalty to B, the property appears to form part of the estate of both of them. It forms part of the estate of A since there are no restrictions on the right to revoke; A can therefore revoke the gift and dispose of the property as he thinks fit. It forms part of the estate of B since B gets good title subject to A's right to revoke.

(3) One's estate on death, distributable under one's WILL or, where there is no will, or the will is insufficient to dispose of all of one's estate, under the rules of intestate succession.

(4) The sum total of one's property available for distribution to one's creditors in a bankruptcy.

Estimation techniques. The methods and estimates adopted by an entity to arrive at monetary values, corresponding to the measurement bases selected, for assets, liabilities, gains, losses and changes to shareholders' funds.

Estimation techniques include, for example:

(a) methods of depreciation, such as straight-line and reducing balance, applied in the context of a particular measurement basis, used to estimate the proportion of the economic benefits of a tangible fixed asset consumed in a period;

(b) methods used to estimate the present value of a provision, such as the discounting of expected cash flows; and

(c) estimates of the proportion of trade debts that will not be recovered, particularly where such estimates are made by considering a population as a whole rather than individual balances.

[FRED 21 – Accounting policies]

Estop, to. *See* ESTOPPEL.

Estoppel. The law in some cases estops or prevents a person from alleging certain facts, which then cannot be proved by him. 'An estoppel', says Blackstone, 'happens where a man hath done some act or executed some deed which estops or precludes him from averring anything to the contrary'.

Estoppels may be divided into four kinds:

(1) Estoppel by record. The rule that a person may not deny the fact of a judgment of a court which has previously been decided against him, appears to be based on two maxims – *Interest reipublicae ut sit finis litium* and *Nemo debet bis vexari pro eadem causa*. It applies generally to all civil and criminal courts.

(2) Estoppel by DEED. The rule that a party to a deed is not permitted to deny facts stated in it affords an illustration of the importance of a seal in English law. There is no such estoppel in the case of ordinary signed documents, unless it comes within the definition of estoppel by conduct.

(3) Estoppel by conduct. A person who, by his words or conduct, wilfully causes another person to believe in the existence of a certain state of things, and induces him to act in that belief, so as to alter his position for the worse, is estopped from setting up against the other person a different

state of things as existing at the time in question.

(4) Estoppel *in pais*. A tenant of land is estopped from disputing the title of the landlord by whom he was let into possession of whom he has acknowledged by the payment of rent.

Et seq. Et sequentes: 'and that which follows'.

Euro. The currency adopted jointly on 1 January 1999 by 11 countries of the European Union, being Austria, Belgium, Finland, France, Germany, Ireland, Italy, Luxembourg, Netherlands, Portugal and Spain and adopted by Greece on 1 January 2001. Euro bank notes and coins are introduced on 1 January 2002. The national currencies of the 12 'Euroblock' countries cease to be legal tender on a timetable specified by each individual country, with the last date of acceptance being not later than 28 February 2002. The Euro notes, which are in values from 5 Euros to 500 Euros are identical in all countries. The Euro coins, which have values from 1 Euro cent to 2 Euros, carry a common design on the face but each member state has its own motif on the reverse. Coins issued by any of the participant counties are equally acceptable in all 12 countries.

European Commission. The term generally used now to describe the EUROPEAN COMMUNITY COMMISSION, following the Maastricht Treaty of 1991, 'The Treaty on European Union'.
See EUROPEAN UNION; EUROPEAN UNION, LAW OF.

European Community. This association of European States, formerly known as the European Economic Community, and often referred to as 'the Common Market', was established by the Treaty of Rome on 25 March 1957. Following the successful customs union of the Benelux countries (Belgium, Holland and Luxembourg) immediately following the war, the Treaty of Rome admitted France, Germany, Italy, the United Kingdom, Denmark, Greece, the Irish Republic, Spain, Portugal, Austria, Finland, and Sweden to membership.

The purpose was economic, with the aim of creating one big market area. The prime means of achieving this were the abolition of customs barriers and quantitative restrictions, the freedom of citizens of the community to work and establish businesses throughout the Community. There is a common agricultural policy, cartels and monopolies are controlled, and there is co-ordination of policies in the spheres of commerce and finance. With the creation of the monetary union with the euro as currency, the aim to establish a common currency is on its way to being met, though some member states, including the UK at present, are not currently participating.

Following the Maastricht Treaty of 1991, 'The Treaty on European Union' (see European Communities (Amendment) Act 1993), the term European Community has been more or less replaced by the term European Union, although the European Community, as well as the European Coal and Steel Community and the European Atomic Energy Community, have not been abolished or superseded as specific entities.
See EUROPEAN UNION; EUROPEAN UNION, LAW OF.

European Community Commission. The Commission must formulate recommendations or deliver opinions on matters dealt with in the Treaty of Rome (art 155). It must exercise the powers conferred on it by the Council for the implementation of the rules laid down by the Council (ibid, art 155). Following the Maastricht Treaty of 1991, 'The Treaty on European Union', generally called the European Commission.
See EUROPEAN COMMUNITY COUNCIL.

European Community Council (of Ministers). A Council made up of ministerial representatives of the various member states, the appropriate minister of the government from each state for the subject under discussion, eg the Council is composed of finance ministers when taxation policy is under discussion. The Council's duty is to ensure co-ordination of the general economic policies of the Member States (Treaty of Rome, art 145). It can confer on the Commission powers for the implementation of the rules which it lays down (ibid, art 145). Now called the Council of the European Union following the Maastricht Treaty of 1991, 'The Treaty on European Union', or commonly, just the Council.

See EUROPEAN COMMUNITY COMMISSION; EUROPEAN UNION; EUROPEAN UNION, LAW OF.

European Community directive. A directive issued by the Council or the Commission binding, as to the result to be achieved, on each member state to which it is addressed, but leaving to the national authorities the choice of form and methods: Treaty of Rome, art 189.

See EUROPEAN COMMUNITY COMMISSION; EUROPEAN COMMUNITY COUNCIL.

European Community margin of solvency. The margin of solvency of an insurance company computed by reference to the assets and liabilities of the business carried on by it in member states (taken together) (Insurance Companies Act 1982, s 32(5)(b)).

European Community regulation. A regulation issued by the Council or the Commission having general application. It is binding in its entirety and directly applicable in all member states (Treaty of Rome, art 189).

See EUROPEAN COMMUNITY COUNCIL; EUROPEAN COMMUNITY COMMISSION.

European Court of Justice. A court whose duty is to ensure that in the interpretation and application of the Treaty of Rome the law is observed (Treaty of Rome, art 164). It consists of 13 Judges (ibid, art 165). It is assisted by 6 Advocates-General (ibid, art 166).

European Economic Interest Grouping. An EEIG is a form of business entity set up by enterprises of two or more member states (TA 1988, s 510A). It is intended to be an attractive vehicle for international co-operation within the EC among enterprises which may include companies and other bodies subject to corporation tax or partnerships or sole traders, which are subject to income tax. The purposes for which the EEIG may be formed include such activities as packaging, processing, marketing or research which are ancillary to the business of and which are for the common benefit of members of the EEIG. An EEIG may not be formed in order to make profits for itself. The scope for using EEIGs is therefore very limited.

The principle to be applied in charging an EEIG to tax is fiscal transparency; the grouping is simply an agent for its members (TA 1988, s 510A(2)). Any profits of the EEIG are to be taxed in the hands of the members only and not at the level of the EEIG. Where it carries on a trade or profession it is treated as a partnership (TA 1988, s 510A(6)).

This simple outline of the legislation masks many conceptual and practical problems. These entities are the subject of their own Inland Revenue manual.

European Investment Bank. A bank whose task is to contribute, by having recourse to the capital market and utilising its own resources, to the balances and steady development of the common market in the interests of the EC (Treaty of Rome, art 130).

European Parliament consists of representatives of the peoples of the EC Member States and exercises the advisory and supervisory powers conferred upon it by the Treaty of Rome (Treaty of Rome, art 107). It is, for the most part, a consultative body, which renders advice to the Council and Commission on proposed legislation, though via a new 'Co-decision Procedure' introduced in the Maastricht Treaty of 1991, the Parliament and the Council may, in effect, legislate together.

European Union. The term European Union is now generally applied to the association of European states known as the European Community, following the Maastricht Treaty of 1992, 'The Treaty on European Union'. However, the term is broader than European Community, intended to form an umbrella term for it and the European Coal and Steel Community and the European Atomic

Energy Community, and the European Union is said to be founded upon the other three communities, although it appears that initiatives which create new law, develop the institutions of the European Community, or create new bodies which further the political, economic, and monetary union of the member states, although the results of the acts of the European Community institutions may be regarded as initiatives of the European Union operating through the institutions of one of the communities. In this way, the European Community might eventually be regarded as having been superseded by the European Union.

European Union, Law of. The Law of the European Union (or EU) is generally divided into two parts, the law of EU institutions, and substantive law of the EU. The former is the law governing the constitution, powers, and inter-relationships of EU bodies such as the European Commission, the Council, the European Parliament, and the European Court of Justice, and the general framework of the European polity as originally laid out in the Treaty of Rome and since modified by subsequent treaties, in particular the Maastricht Treaty of 1991. One can regard this as the *constitutional* law of the EU. Recent developments have concerned the rights of nationals of one member state to vote in the national elections of another, so as to begin to create rights for individuals as citizens not only of their member state but as citizens of the EU. The projected expansions of the EU will also involve changes in this part of EU law. The substantive law of the EU consists of those laws issuing from the institutions which govern the behaviour of the subjects of the European Union, either by EUROPEAN COMMUNITY REGULATION or by EUROPEAN COMMUNITY DIRECTIVE, eg environmental law, competition law, and so on, although this law is enforced by the regulatory agencies, courts, etc of the several member states. Ultimately, questions concerning the meaning of EU laws and their interactions with the municipal laws of the member states may be resolved by the European Court of Justice. The European Court of Justice has developed

and reinforced many times the doctrine of 'primacy', the doctrine that EU laws are superior to the municipal laws of the member states, and so in any clash between them the law of the EU will prevail. The bulk of the substantive law of the European Union predominantly flows from the Union's origins in the European Economic Community, and is therefore concerned to ensure the operation of a single market for all member states, and other economic matters. In consequence, there has been much law generated on the free movement of persons, both to work as employees and to establish business throughout the Union, on the free movement of goods, freedom from restrictions on the provisions of services, competition, and the harmonisation of taxation. However, there is also EU law concerning the environment, social policy, and police cooperation.

Evasion. *See* TAX EVASION.

Evidence. That which, in a court of justice, makes clear, or ascertains the truth of, the very fact or point in issue, either on the one side or on the other.

Any matter, lawfully deposed to on oath or affirmation, which contributes (however slightly) to the elucidation of any question at issue in a court of justice, is said to be *evidence*.

Evidence is either *written* or *parol*; written evidence consists of records, deeds, affidavits, or other writings: *parol* or *oral evidence* consists of witnesses personally appearing in Court, and in general swearing to the truth of what they depose. Evidence may also be primary, ie best evidence, or secondary; direct, circumstantial, or hearsay; real or intrinsic.

Examination. (1) The interrogation of witnesses. The *examination-in-chief* of a witness is the interrogation of a witness, in the first instance, by the counsel of the party calling him. His examination by the opposing counsel is known as his *cross-examination*; and his further examination by his own side, on points arising out of the cross-examination, is his *re-examination*.

(2) The examination of a bankrupt is the interrogation of a bankrupt, by a court having jurisdiction in bankruptcy, as to the state of his property.

Except for. A phrase in an Auditors' Report indicating a qualified report.
See QUALIFIED REPORT.

Exceptional items. Material items which derive from events or transactions that fall within the ordinary activities of the reporting entity and which individually or, if of a similar type, in aggregate, need to be disclosed by virtue of their size or incidence if the financial statements are to give a true and fair view. [FRS 3 – Reporting financial performance]

Excess clause. A clause in an insurance policy specifying that the insured must bear liability up to a specified sum if a loss occurs, eg the first £200. Only after this limit has been reached are the insurers liable and then only for the sum by which the limit is exceeded.

Excess policy. A policy in respect of a subject-matter which is also insured under another policy, stating that the insurer is under no liability until the insured has been paid in full under that other policy.

Exchange control. A restriction on the purchase and sale of foreign currency, which may include a restriction on the purchase of goods sold in a foreign currency. The UK abolished exchange control in 1979.

Exchange gain/loss. The gain (or loss) arising when items are converted into the domestic currency for the purpose of incorporating in the organisation's accounts.

Exchange rate. The rate at which two currencies may be exchanged for each other at a particular point in time; different rates apply for spot and forward transactions. [SSAP 20 – Foreign currency translation]

Exchequer. The Department of State having the management of the royal revenue. It consisted formerly of two divisions, the first being the office of the receipt of the Exchequer, for the collection of the royal revenue; the second being a court for the administration of justice.

Excise. A name formerly confined to the imposition on beer, ale, cider, and other commodities manufactured within the realm, being charged sometimes on the consumption of the commodity, but more frequently on the retail side of it.

Under recent Acts of Parliament, however, many imports have been classed under excise. Such is the case with regard to the licence which must be taken out by every one who uses a gun, or deals in game. See particularly the Customs and Excise Management Act 1979.

Excluded property. Inheritance tax is not charged on excluded property. The following is excluded property:
(1) property, other than settled property, situate outside the UK provided the person beneficially entitled to it is an individual domiciled outside the UK (IHTA 1984, s 6(1));
(2) settled property situate outside the UK provided the settlor was domiciled outside the UK when the settlement was made (IHTA 1984, s 48(3));
(3) a reversionary interest in settled property provided the person beneficially entitled to it is not domiciled in the UK (IHTA 1984, s 6(1));
(4) certain other reversionary interests in settled property (IHTA 1984, s 48(1)).
(5) certain types of property situated in the UK owned by persons domiciled elsewhere.

Exclusion clause. A term of a contract by which a party excludes a legal liability he would otherwise have, for example liability for negligently caused injury in the course of providing a service contracted for.
See CONTRACT.

Ex dividend. Without the dividend. A term used in connection with the purchase of shares resulting in the buyer not having a right to the dividend in respect of them.
See CUM DIVIDEND; SHARE.

Execution. (1) The putting in force the sentence of the law in a judicial proceeding. It is styled *final process*.

(2) The signing of a deed or will, or other written instrument, in such manner as to make it (so far as regards form) legally valid (see, eg the Law of Property (Miscellaneous Provisions) Act 1989, s 1).

(3) The carrying out of a trust.

Executive. The branch of government which is entrusted with carrying the laws into effect. The supreme executive power is vested in the King or Queen for the time being who by convention acts on ministerial advice.

Executive share option scheme. Available from 6 April 1984, an executive share option scheme is an arrangement under which options can be granted to persons chosen by the company management (typically directors only) and receive the benefit of an approved Inland Revenue scheme, with the consequent exemption from income tax and NIC charges. In FA 1996, a restriction was introduced so that no individual can have options over shares of a value of more than £30,000 and enjoy the tax benefits of an executive share option scheme. For smaller companies, share options available under the Enterprise Management Initiative legislation introduced in 2000 have effectively superseded the executive share option scheme.

Executor. One to whom another, by his last will and testament, commits the execution of his directions and dispositions of it. His duties are:

(1) to bury the deceased in a manner suitable to the estate which he leaves behind him;

(2) to prove the will of the deceased;

(3) to make an inventory of the goods and chattels of the deceased, and to collect the goods so listed; and for this purpose, if necessary, to take proceedings against debtors to his testator's estate;

(4) to pay, *first*, the debts of his testator and *then* the legacies bequeathed by his will; and to distribute the residue, in default of

any residuary disposition, among the persons entitled to it on an intestacy.

An executor is the legal personal representative of his testator, and the testator's rights and liabilities devolve for the most part upon him. A person appointed executor is not on that account bound to accept the office. See, generally, the Administration of Estates Act 1925 and the Supreme Court Act 1981, Pt V.

Executor de son tort. One who, without any just authority, intermeddles with the goods of a deceased person, as if he has been duly appointed executor. An *executor de son tort* is liable to the burden of an executorship without its advantages. He cannot bring an action himself in right of the deceased, but actions may be brought against him (see the Administration of Estates Act 1925, ss 28, 29).

Executrix. Feminine of executor.

Exemplary damages. Damages on a high scale, given mainly in respect of tortious acts, committed through malice or other circumstances of aggravation, which exceed the amount required merely to compensate the plaintiff for the loss or injury suffered by him or her.

Exempli gratia (abbr eg). For the sake of example.

Exempt distribution. A distribution by a company in a demerger that satisfies the conditions in TA 1988, s 213. An exempt distribution is free from income tax, corporation tax and capital gains tax. Stamp duty may, however, be levied.

See DEMERGER.

Exempt lifetime transfer. Inheritance tax is not charged on an exempt transfer. Lifetime transfers that are exempt are:

(1) Transfers not exceeding £3,000 in a fiscal year (IHTA 1984, s 19)

Each tax year a person may make transfers of value up to £3,000 without incurring any liability to tax. Such transfers are exempt. Where several transfers are made in one year, the exemption is given according to the date of the transfer, the earlier transfers enjoying the exemption.

(2) Small gifts to the same person (IHTA 1984, s 20)

Transfers of value made by a transferor in any one year by outright gifts to any one person are exempt to the extent that the values transferred, without grossing up, do not exceed £250. There is no rollover of any unused portion of £250. This is intended as a *de minimis* exception and so cannot be used to exempt the first £250 of a larger transfer.

(3) Normal expenditure out of income (IHTA 1984, s 21)

A transfer is exempt to the extent that it is shown that:

(a) it was made as part of the normal expenditure of the transferor; and

(b) that taking one year with another it was made out of income; and

(c) that after allowing for all transfers forming part of his normal expenditure, the transferor was left with sufficient income (after tax) to maintain his usual standard of living.

(4) Marriage gifts (IHTA 1984, s 22)

Three rules apply:

(a) The first £5,000 of a transfer of value made by gift made in consideration of marriage by the parent of either party to the marriage is exempt from tax.

(b) Where the transferor is a remoter ancestor or is a party to the marriage, the first £2,500 is exempt.

(c) The first £1,000 of a marriage gift made by a person other than a party to the marriage or his or her parent or remoter ancestor, is also exempt.

Exempt supply. No VAT is charged when a supply is specified by VATA 1994, Sch 9 as an exempt supply. As VAT is a European tax, subject to EC legislation, an exemption under UK law is either a reflection of the general EC exemption in EC Sixth Council Directive of 17 May 1997 Articles 13–16 or is given as a derogation to the UK under Article 27 of that Directive. VATA 1994 specifies exempt supplies in 15 categories, namely:

Group 1 – land*
Group 2 – insurance
Group 3 – postal services
Group 4 – betting, gaming and lotteries
Group 5 – finance
Group 6 – education
Group 7 – health and welfare
Group 8 – burial and cremation
Group 9 – trade unions, professional and other public interest bodies
Group 10 – sport and physical education
Group 11 – works of art, etc
Group 12 – fund-raising events
Group 13 – cultural services
Group 14 – certain supplies, the input tax on which was irrecoverable
Group 15 – investment gold

* A taxpayer can elect, under certain conditions, to charge standard rate VAT on land (VATA 1994, Sch 10, para 3(2)).

The consequences of exemption are as follows:

(1) A person is neither liable nor entitled to registration by reference to the exempt supplies he makes. This arises from the fact that it is taxable supplies which are taken into account for registration purposes (VATA 1994, Sch 1, para 1(1), (2) & (9)). Thus, a trader is unable to become registered if his supplies consist wholly of exempt supplies.

(2) A taxable person is not normally entitled to credit for input tax attributable to an exempt supply.

(3) An acquisition is not a taxable acquisition, and is therefore excluded from the charge to tax, if the goods were supplied under an exempt supply (VATA 1994, s 31(1)).

Exercise of significant influence. (1) The investor is actively involved and is influential in the direction of the investee through his participation in policy decisions covering aspects of policy relevant to the investor, including decisions on strategic issues such as:

(a) the expansion or contraction of the business, participation in other entities or changes in products, markets and activities of its investee; and

(b) determining the balance between dividend and reinvestment.

For the purpose of applying this presumption, the shares held by the parent and its subsidiaries in that entity should he aggregated. The presumption is rebutted if the investor does not fulfil the criteria for the exercise of significant influence set out above. The reference to shares is to allotted shares in an entity with a share capital, to rights to share in the capital in an entity with capital but no share capital, and to interests conferring any right to share in the profits, or imposing a liability to contribute to the losses or giving an obligation to contribute to debts or expenses in a winding-up for an entity without capital. Dividends are not the only way a beneficial interest can be enjoyed: there are other ways of extracting benefit, for example, through a management contract with a fee based on performance (making the receiver of the fee more than just a manager). [FRS 9 – Associates and joint ventures]

(2) The Companies Acts provide that an entity holding 20% or more of the voting rights in another entity should be presumed to exercise a significant influence over that other entity unless the contrary is shown (Companies Act 1985, s 260).

Ex gratia. (1) As a matter of favour.

(2) An ex gratia pension, or a discretionary pension, or an ex gratia increase in a pension, is one which the employer has no legal, contractual or implied commitment to provide. [SSAP 24 – Accounting for pension costs]

Exit charge. A charge to inheritance tax arises when property leaves a discretionary trust (IHTA 1984, s 65). The exit charge is a proportionate ten-year anniversary charge designed to compensate the Revenue for the fact that this property will not be relevant property when the next ten-year anniversary comes round.

The first situation covered by this rule is that in which the property ceases to be comprised in the settlement. Property transferred to a beneficiary under a power of appointment or of advancement or simply distributed from the discretionary settlement could give rise to a charge under this rule. Where the property is transferred to an individual absolutely it is to be presumed that the transfer is chargeable and cannot be potentially exempt.

The second situation is that in which the property remains comprised in the settlement but ceases to be relevant property, as where the beneficiary is given a life interest in a fund. There will be a charge under the present rule. If the property is still held for the beneficiary when the ten-year anniversary comes round, that part cannot be charged under the principal charge as it is not then relevant property—hence the present charge.

Another way in which the property ceases to be relevant property is where there is still no qualifying interest in possession but the trust falls within the list of excluded trust. One example would be when an accumulation and maintenance settlement arises.

Ex parte. (1) Of the one part, one-sided. Thus, an *ex parte* statement is a statement of one side only. So, an injunction granted *ex parte* is an injunction granted after hearing one side only.

See INJUNCTION.

(2) The phrase '*ex parte*' preceding a name in the heading of a reported case indicates that the party whose name follows is the party on whose application the case is heard.

Expectancy, Estates in. Interests in land which are limited or appointed to take effect in possession at some future time.

Expectation of life. In matters of life insurance, and the granting of annuities, this expression means the length of time that any specified person may expect, according to the table of averages, to live.

Expected rate of return on assets. The average rate of return, including both income and changes in market value, expected over the remaining life of the related obligation on the actual assets held by the scheme. [FRED 20 – Retirement benefits]

Expected return on assets. The expected rate of return multiplied by the market value of the scheme assets. [FRED 20 – Retirement benefits]

Experience surplus or deficiency. That part of the excess or deficiency of the actuarial value of assets over the actuarial value of liabilities, on the basis of the valuation method used, which arises because events have not coincided with the actuarial assumptions made for the last valuation. [SSAP 24 – Accounting for pension costs]

Expert witness. A skilled witness called to give evidence in the subject with which he is specially conversant. As to the rules of court relating to, and the admissibility of, expert opinion, see the Civil Procedure Rules 1998, Part 35.

Export Guarantees. Guarantees given by the Secretary of State for Trade and Industry to persons carrying on business in the United Kingdom in connection with the export, manufacture, etc of goods. There is an Export Guarantees Advisory Council (see the Export Guarantees Act 1975).

Exposure draft. *See* FINANCIAL REPORTING EXPOSURE DRAFT.

Express. That which is not left to implication, eg an express promise or covenant.

Express contract or convention. A contract or agreement expressed in words, or by signs which custom or usage has made equivalent to words.

Express trust. A trust which is clearly expressed by its author or may fairly be collected from a written document.
See TRUST.

Expropriation. The compulsory taking of land by a public authority, with compensation to be fixed by a board or court.

Ex rights. Without the rights. A term used to denote the fact that a buyer of shares is not entitled to subscribe for further shares in proportion to the number bought.
See CUM RIGHTS; SHARE.

Extraordinary general meeting. An EGM is any meeting of shareholders other than an annual general meeting. An EGM can be called by the directors, or by members who together hold at least 10% of the share capital, or by a resigning auditor or by the court.

Extraordinary items. Material items possessing a high degree of abnormality which arise from events or transactions that fall outside the ordinary activities of the reporting entity and which are not expected to recur. They do not include exceptional items nor do they include prior period items merely because they relate to a prior period. [FRS 3 – Reporting financial performance]

Extraordinary resolution. Any resolution put to the shareholders in either an annual general meeting or an extraordinary general meeting, where the articles of the company specify that 75% of the votes cast are required for the resolution to be passed. Notice must be given of the intention to propose the resolution as an extraordinary resolution (Companies Act 1985, s 378(1)).

Extra-statutory concession. Extra-statutory concessions are issued by the Inland Revenue. 241 concessions are published (and indexed), but further concessions relating to particular groups of taxpayers are not stated in the published documents. The Revenue state that concessions are used 'to deal with what are, on the whole, minor or transitory anomalies . . . and to reduce cases of hardship at the margins of the code when a statutory remedy would be difficult to devise or would run to a length out of proportion to the intrinsic importance of the matter' (Inland Revenue press release, 16 February 1989). The published concessions are tightly written and legislative in form. One crucial difference from a statutory provision was thought to be that the Revenue could withhold the benefit of the concession if they were so minded without legal—as distinct from political or administrative—consequences. However, the development of administrative law remedies suggests that an assessment made on the basis of withholding a concession could be quashed on the basis of breach of the duty to act fairly as between different taxpayers (see *R v IRC, ex p J Rothschild Holdings [1987] STC 163*; *R v Inspector of Taxes, ex p Brumfield [1989] STC 151* and *R v IRC, ex p Kaye [1992] STC 581*). The booklet of published concessions states in its inside front cover: 'A concession will not be given in any case where an attempt is made to use it for tax avoidance'. In *R v IRC, ex p Fulford-Dobson [1987] STC 344*, McNeill J held that this is an integral part of each of the [now 241] separate concessions in the booklet and refused an application by the taxpayer to discharge an assessment to CGT that would not have been made if extra-statutory concession D2 had been applied by the Revenue.

The courts have not always been appreciative of Revenue concessions. Sir Richard Scott V-C in *Steibelt v Paling [1999] STC 594* quoted extra-statutory concession D24 as being the way in which a court would probably have constructed the statutory language and commented: 'I am not satisfied that in publishing D24 the Revenue is making any concession at all'.

F

FCA. Fellow of the Institute of Chartered Accountants in England and Wales.

FIFO. First in first out cost allocation method.

FOB (free on board). A term inserted in contracts for the sale of goods to be shipped. It signifies that the cost of shipping, ie putting on board at a port or place of shipment, is to be paid by the seller.

FRED. Financial Reporting Exposure Draft.

FRS. Financial reporting standard.

FRSSE. Financial Reporting Standard for Smaller Entities.
See FINANCIAL REPORTING STANDARD.

FTII. Fellow of the Chartered Institute of Taxation. *(When established in 1930, the letters stood for Fellow of the Taxation Institute Incorporated.)*

FURBS. Funded unapproved retirement benefits scheme.

Factor. An agent remunerated by a commission, who is entrusted with the possession of goods to sell in his own name as apparent owner. The Factors Acts were amended and consolidated by the Factors Act 1889.

Factorage. Also called 'commission'. An allowance given to factors by a merchant.
See FACTOR.

Factory. Any premises in which persons are employed in manual labour in any process for or incidental to (*a*) the making of any article or of part of any article, or (*b*) the altering, repairing, ornamenting, finishing, cleaning or washing or breaking up or demolition of any article, or (*c*) the adapting for sale of any article, or (*d*) the slaughtering of cattle, etc, or (*e*) the confinement of such animals in certain premises whilst awaiting slaughter, being premises in which the work is carried on by way of trade or for purposes of gain, and over which the employer has the right of access or control. See the Factories Act 1961, s 175, which also specifies a number of classes of premises, eg, shipyards, dry docks, laundries, etc, which are to be included in the expression 'factory'.

Fair value. The amount at which an asset or liability could be exchanged in an arm's length transaction between informed and willing parties, other than in a forced or liquidation sale. When any grants are receivable towards the purchase or use of the asset, the market value is net of the sum receivable. [SSAP 21 – Accounting for leases and hire purchase contracts, FRS 7 – Fair values in acquisition accounting, FRS 13 – Derivatives and other financial instruments, FRS 14 – Earnings per share]

Family. A word with various meanings, according to the context in which it is found. Thus, in one sense it may mean a whole household, including servants and perhaps lodgers. In another it means all persons descended from a common stock, ie all blood relations. In a third, the word includes children only; thus, when a man speaks of his wife and family, he means his wife and children (see *Re Makein [1955] 1 All ER 57*).

Fee simple. An estate limited to a man and his heirs; the most absolute interest which a subject can possess in land, ie equivalent to full ownership. A 'fee simple absolute in possession' is one of the two legal estates in land which are now capable of subsisting under the Law of Property Act 1925, s 1(1); and by s 60 of that Act, a conveyance of freehold land without words of limitation passes the fee simple, unless a contrary intention appears.
See ESTATE.

Fiduciary. A person with a legal power to alter the legal position of another, generally called the fiduciary's *principal* and one who must use his or her discretion in exercising that power so as to serve the principal's best interests and, in particular, so as never to serve his own interests to the detriment of his principal. Examples are agents, who are fiduciaries to their principals, and trustees, who are fiduciaries to the beneficiaries of the trust, and company directors to their companies. The law of fiduciaries is the product of EQUITY, and one of its chief concerns is to prevent and deal with situations where the fiduciary's own interests conflict with his duty to serve the best interests of his principal.

See AGENT; TRUSTEE; CONFLICT OF INTEREST; EQUITY.

Fiduciary estate. The estate or interest of a trustee in lands or money, as opposed to the beneficial interest or enjoyment thereof.

Film, in relation to copyright, means a recording on any medium from which a moving image may by any means be produced (Copyright, Designs and Patents Act 1988, s 5(1)). Copyright does not subsist in a film which is a copy taken from a previous film; ibid, s 5(2).

Final dividend. A dividend recommended by the directors of a company and approved at the annual general meeting. It may be paid in addition to one or more interim dividends.

See INTERIM DIVIDEND.

Final remuneration. There are two alternative methods of calculating a pension payable under an occupational pension scheme. In a 'money purchase scheme', the pension is calculated from the fund that has been built up. In a 'defined benefits scheme', the pension is calculated from the employee's final remuneration. Inland Revenue are required by TA 1988, s 590(2) to give mandatory approval for a pension scheme where the benefit is a pension on retirement at an age between 60 and 75, and that the pension does not exceed x/60 of the employee's final remuneration, meaning the average annual remuneration over the previous three years where x is the number of years of service (not exceeding

40 years), to a maximum of 2/3rds of final remuneration. The scheme may allow a lump sum of up to 3x/80 of the final remuneration, where x is the number of years of service (not exceeding 40 years), to a maximum lump sum of 1½ times the final remuneration. (There are other conditions to be satisfied for approval.)

Finance charge. The amount borne by the lessee over the lease term, representing the difference between the total of the minimum lease payments (including any residual amounts guaranteed by him) and the amount at which he records the leased asset at the inception of the lease. [SSAP 21 – Accounting for leases and hire purchase contracts]

Finance costs. The difference between the net proceeds of an instrument and the total amount of payments (or other transfers of economic benefits) that the issuer may be required to make in respect of the instrument. Finance costs include:
(*a*) interest on bank overdrafts and short-term and long-term debt;
(*b*) amortisation of discounts or premiums relating to debt; and
(*c*) amortisation of ancillary costs incurred in connection with the arrangement of debt.
[FRS 4 – Capital instruments & FRS 15 – Tangible fixed assets]

Finance lease. A lease that transfers substantially all the risks and rewards of ownership of an asset to the lessee. It should be presumed that such a transfer of risks and rewards occurs if at the inception of a lease the present value of the minimum lease payments including any initial payment, amounts to substantially all (normally 90% or more) of the fair value of the leased asset. The present value should be calculated by using the interest rate implicit in the lease. If the fair value of the asset is not determinable, an estimate thereof should be used. The presumption that a lease should be classified as a finance lease may in exceptional circumstances be rebutted if it can be clearly demonstrated that the lease in question does not transfer substantially all the risks and rewards of ownership (other than legal title) to the lessee. By contrast, a lease that does transfer substantially all the risks and rewards of ownership (other than legal title) to the lessee, should be treated as a finance lease, even if the other conditions for such a treatment are not fulfilled. [SSAP 21 – Accounting for leases and hire purchase contracts]

Financial accounting. Financial accounting (as contrasted with cost accounting) is concerned with the drawing up of accounts (usually annual accounts) for an enterprise under the relevant accounting standards, in order to give a true and fair view of the activities of the business to a person outside the business. For the accounts of a company, it is necessary for the financial accounting to be in accordance with the requirements of the Companies Act 1985.

Financial asset. Any asset that is:
(a) cash;
(b) a contractual right to receive cash or another financial asset from another entity;
(c) a contractual right to exchange financial instruments with another entity under conditions that are potentially favourable; or
(d) an equity instrument of another entity. [FRS 13 – Derivatives and other financial instruments]

Financial instrument. Any contract that gives rise to both a financial asset of one entity and a financial liability or equity instrument of another entity. Financial instruments include both primary financial instruments—such as bonds. debtors, creditors and shares—and derivative financial instruments. [FRS 13 – Derivatives and other financial instruments & FRS 14 – Earnings per share]

Financial liability. Any liability that is a contractual obligation:
(a) to deliver cash or another financial asset to another entity; or
(b) to exchange financial instruments with another entity under conditions that are potentially unfavourable.

[FRS 13 – Derivatives and other financial instruments]

Financial Reporting Exposure Draft. Before a statement of the Accounting Standards Board is brought into force, the text of the proposed Financial Reporting Standard (FRS) is issued as a Financial Reporting Exposure Draft (FRED). There are currently four Financial Reporting Exposure Drafts in issue:
FRED 19 – Deferred tax
FRED 20 – Retirement benefits
FRED 21 – Accounting policies
FRED 22 – Accounting policies (Compliance with statement of recommended practice)

Financial Reporting Standard. An FRS is an accounting standard issued by the Accounting Standards Board which was created as a standard setting body for the purposes of Companies Act 1985, s 256(1), with effect from 20 August 1990. Its creation is given statutory effect by the Accounting Standards (Prescribed Body) Regulations 1990 (SI 1990/1667). Financial Reporting Standards issued by the Accounting Standards Board are applicable to financial statements of any reporting entity that are intended to give a true and fair view of its state of affairs at the balance sheet date. An FRS need not, however, be applied to immaterial items. An FRS (and also any SSAP adopted by the Accounting Standards Board) is an 'accounting standard' within the meaning of Companies Act 1985, Schs 4, 9 and 9A. There are currently 16 Financial Reporting Standards in issue:
FRS 1 – Cash flow statements
FRS 2 – Accounting for subsidiary undertakings
FRS 3 – Reporting financial performance
FRS 4 – Capital instruments
FRS 5 – Reporting the substance of transactions
FRS 6 – Acquisitions and mergers
FRS 7 – Fair values in acquisition accounting
FRS 8 – Related party disclosures
FRS 9 – Associates and joint ventures
FRS 10 – Goodwill and intangible assets
FRS 11 – Impairment of fixed assets and goodwill

FRS 12 – Provisions, contingent liabilities and contingent assets

FRS 13 – Derivatives and other financial instruments: disclosures

FRS 14 – Earnings per share

FRS 15 – Tangible fixed assets

FRS 16 – Current tax

In addition, the Accounting Standards Board has issued the Financial Reporting Standards for Smaller Entities (FRSSE).

Financial statements. Balance sheets, profit and loss accounts, statements of source and application of funds, notes and other statements, which collectively are intended to give a true and fair view of financial position and profit or loss. [SSAP 15 – Accounting for deferred tax, SSAP 17 – Accounting for post balance sheet events & SSAP 20 – Foreign currency translation]

Financial year. Corporation tax is charged on the profits of the corporation during the financial year (TA 1988, s 6(1)). The 'financial year' is the year starting on 1 April (Interpretation Act 1978, Sch 1). Hence 'financial year 2001' is 1 April 2001 to 31 March 2002 (TA 1988, s 834(1)). However, assessments are made by reference to accounting periods (TA 1988, s 8(3)). Where the accounting period does not correspond with the financial year the profits of the period are apportioned to compute the tax liability. Where the rate changes from one financial year to the next, each rate is applied to that portion of the accounting period falling within it.

The financial year is relevant only to the rate of tax. If the method of computing income or capital gains and so corporate profits changes from one year to the next, the accounting period is treated as if it were a year of assessment, although various provisions (eg change of ownership) require an accounting period to be split for specific purposes (TA 1988, s 9(1)).

Firm. A partnership.

Firm name. The name under which their business is carried on by persons who have entered into partnership with one another (see Partnership Act 1890, s 4(1)).

First in first out (FIFO). One of the two basic methods of valuing stocks, or finished goods. The value of goods in stock is calculated on the assumption that the withdrawals from stock represent items that have been in stock for the longest time.
Contrast: LIFO.

Fiscal year. For income tax and CGT, the tax year runs from 6 April to 5 April (TA 1988, s 2(2)), so that the year from 6 April 2002 to 5 April 2003 is known as fiscal year 2002/03. (Different rules apply to corporation tax.) The reason for these dates is that the financial year originally began on Lady Day, 25 March; this was changed in 1752 when the calendars were changed. Since income tax is an annual tax and is imposed by a charge in each year's Finance Act, difficulties arose where the Finance Act had not become law by the start of the tax year (6 April). The Finance Acts of 1909, 1910 and 1911 reached the statute book 13, 7 and 7 months after the start of the financial year. Tax could not be levied lawfully simply on the basis of a resolution of the House of Commons (*Bowles v Bank of England [1913] 1 Ch 57*). The Provisional Collection of Taxes Act 1968 was enacted to give temporary statutory effect to tax charging resolutions of the House of Commons. The resolutions if passed in March or April expire on 5 August next and if passed in any other month expire after four months. New taxes are expressly excluded.

Fixed assets. An asset of an enterprise that is intended for continuing use, normally one that generates profits for the enterprise, as opposed to circulating assets, such as stock. On a company's balance sheet, fixed assets are classified as tangible fixed assets, intangible fixed assets or investments. Tangible fixed assets include land, buildings, plant, machinery, fixtures and fittings. Intangible fixed assets include goodwill, patents and trademarks. An investment (which may be in a quoted or an unquoted holding) includes investment in a subsidiary, or undertaken for the purpose of the trade (such as in a farmers co-operative) as well as investment of the company's funds. An investment is normally shown at its current market value, although, in some circumstances, historic cost is acceptable. Other fixed assets must be written off over their useful economic lives by depreciation (of tangible fixed assets) or amortisation (of intangible fixed assets).

Fixed profit car scheme. Where an employer pays a mileage allowance to an employee using his own car for business any profit element will be taxable under general principles. As an alternative, for years up to and including 2001/02, there is a voluntary administrative arrangement known as the fixed profit car scheme. Under this scheme, where an employee uses his private car for travel on his employer's business, the employer can pay the employee a mileage allowance of any sum up to the figure given in the Revenue 'FPCS' table, without the receipt being treated as a taxable emolument. This scheme covers only sums paid for business travel. Where the payment by the employer exceeds the FPCS figure, only the excess is treated as a taxable emolument. Where the payment made by the employer is less than the FPCS figure, the employee can claim the shortfall as a tax-deductible cost.

From 6 April 2002 the extra-statutory administrative arrangements of the FPCS are replaced by the new statutory regime of TA 1988, ss 197AD–AH & Sch 12AA. Whereas FPCS gives mileage rates that are higher for larger cars, the new statutory 'mileage allowance' is a fixed sum that applies irrespective of the size of the car and, thus, reflects environmental concerns by a deliberate use of the tax system to disadvantage the user of a larger car.

See MILEAGE ALLOWANCE; QUALIFYING TRAVELLING EXPENSES.

Fixtures. Things of an accessory character, annexed to houses or lands; including not only such things as grates in a house, or steam engines in a colliery, but also windows and palings. To be a fixture, a thing must not constitute part of the principal subject, eg in the case of the walls or floors of a house; but on the other hand, it must be in actual union or connection with it, and not merely brought into contact with it, eg in the case of a picture suspended on hooks

against a wall. As a general rule, the property, by being annexed to the land, immediately belongs to the freeholder, but there are three exceptions to the rule: (*a*) in favour of trade fixtures; (*b*) for agricultural purposes (see the Agricultural Holdings Act 1986, s 13); (*c*) for ornament and convenience.

Flat. A separate and self-contained set of premises, whether or not on the same floor, constructed for use for the purposes of a dwelling and forming part of a building from some other part of which it is divided horizontally.

A 100% first year capital allowance is available for the conversion of property above commercial premises into flats, or the refurbishment of decayed and empty flats over commercial premises (CAA 2001, ss 393A–393W). The new provisions were recommended by the Urban Task Force, chaired by Lord Rogers, in the report 'Towards an Urban Renaissance' and the intention of the legislation is described by the Treasury as enabling property owners and occupiers 'to obtain up front tax relief for their capital expenditure on recycling former residential space over shops . . . (being) part of a package of measures being introduced to encourage the regeneration of urban areas' (H M Treasury Explanatory Notes to the Finance Bill 2001, 30 March 2001).

The allowance is given to a person who has a 'relevant interest' in property that is converted into a 'qualifying flat' and who incurs 'qualifying expenditure'. Where the conditions are fulfilled, that person is entitled to claim an initial allowance of 100% of the qualifying expenditure.

The intention behind the legislation is, clearly, to grant an allowance for the creation of low price, privately let accommodation. This is achieved by the restrictive definition of a 'qualifying flat', being one within a qualifying building, with its own entry, having not more than four rooms, that is suitable for letting as a dwelling and held for the purpose of short-term letting (CAA 2001, ss 393G(2), 393D(1)(a), (d) & (c)). In addition, the flat must be such that the rent that could reasonably be expected for a shorthold letting to an unconnected tenant is less than £480 per week, if in Greater London, or £300 per week if elsewhere in the UK (lower limits are imposed for flats of less than four rooms).

Floating capital. Capital retained for the purpose of meeting current expenditure.

Floating charge. A charge created by a company by a debenture on its assets for the time being. It gives the debenture-holders no immediate right *in rem* over the assets that it affects; but leaves the company a free power of disposition over the whole of its property.
See CHARGE; DEBENTURE; SECURITY INTEREST.

'A floating charge is ambulatory and hovers over the property, until some event occurs which causes it to settle and crystallise into a specific charge' (see *Barker v Eynon [1974] 1 All ER 900*).

Floating rate financial assets and financial liabilities. Financial assets and financial liabilities that attract an interest charge and have their interest rate reset at least once a year. Financial assets and financial liabilities that have their interest rate reset less frequently than once a year are to be treated as fixed rate financial assets and financial liabilities. [FRS 13 – Derivatives and other financial instruments]

Floating rate loan. A loan, where the interest varies, such as a loan that is specified as a fixed percentage above bank base rate.

Flotation. The launching of a public company by inviting the public to subscribe for its shares. The subscription may be effected by means of an introduction, an issue by tender, an offer for sale, a placing or a public issue. Shares issued on a flotation can be traded in a Stock Exchange.

Foreclosure. The forfeiture by a mortgagor of his equity of redemption, by reason of his default in payment of the principal or interest of the mortgage debt within a reasonable time. For a mortgagee to initiate proceedings for foreclosure is the most extreme remedy available to him or her for the mortgagor's default, for not only is the mortgagor's right to redeem the mortgaged land extinguished, the mortgagor remains liable to repay the whole of the outstanding mortgage debt. For this reason, mortgagees are typically limited to the remedy of an order for the possession of the property so as to exercise a power of sale, the proceeds of sale going to reduce the outstanding mortgage loan (after deduction of the costs of sale, etc) and so reducing the mortgagor's liability under the mortgage loan to the extent of the value of the land.
See MORTGAGE.

Foreign branch. Either a legally constituted enterprise located overseas or a group of assets and liabilities which are accounted for in foreign currencies. [SSAP 20 – Foreign currency translation]

Foreign emoluments. Emoluments are foreign only if they belong to a person not domiciled in the UK and are from a non-resident employer (TA 1988, s 192).

Foreign enterprise. A subsidiary, associated company or branch whose operations are based in a country other than that of the investing company or whose assets and liabilities are denominated mainly in a foreign currency. [SSAP 20 – Foreign currency translation]

Foreign law. The law of a foreign state. In cases where the court determines that the law properly to be applied to the case is foreign law, eg where a contract is in dispute and the contract specifies that the contract will be governed by the law of a named foreign state, the court will hear from those with expertise of the foreign law and its application to the case; it is thus a question of fact which must be proved by the evidence of expert witnesses (see the Foreign Law Ascertainment Act 1861). See also Civil Evidence Act 1972, s 4, Civil Procedure Rules 1998, 33.7.
See CONFLICT OF LAWS.

Foreseeable losses. Losses which are currently estimated to arise over the duration of the contract (after allowing for estimated remedial and maintenance costs and increases in costs so far as not recoverable under the terms of the contract). This estimate is required irrespective of:

(*a*) whether or not work has yet commenced on such contracts;

(*b*) the proportion of work carried out at that accounting date;

(*c*) the amount of profits expected to arise on other contracts.

[SSAP 9 – Stocks and long-term contracts]

Forfeiture of share. An expropriation by a company of a member's share. Shares can only be forfeited for non-payment of calls (*see* CALL) or for similar reasons. An attempt to forfeit shares for other reasons is illegal (see *Hopkinson v Mortimer, Harley & Co Ltd [1917] 1 Ch 646*).

Forward contract. An agreement to exchange different currencies at a specified future date and at a specified rate. The difference between the specified rate and the spot rate ruling on the date the contract was entered into is the discount or premium on the forward contract. [SSAP 20 – Foreign currency translation]

Founder's share. A share allotted to a person who first founded the company. The issue of such shares is now rare. The holder of such a share is usually entitled to a proportion of the profits if the dividend on the ordinary shares has been paid up to a specified amount.

Fraud. Civil penalties are provided for the non-statement, or understatement, of tax liabilities by fraud. Criminal sanctions are also imposed.

The modes of fraud are infinite, and it has been said that the courts have never laid down what constitutes fraud, or any general rule beyond which they will not go in giving equitable relief on the ground of fraud. Fraud is, however, usually divided into two large classes: (i) actual fraud; and (ii) constructive fraud.

An actual fraud may be defined as something said, done or omitted by a person with the design of perpetrating what he must have known to be a positive fraud.

Constructive frauds are acts, statements or omissions which operate as virtual frauds on individuals or which, if generally permitted, would be prejudicial to the public welfare, and yet may have been unconnected with any selfish or evil designs; eg, bonds and agreements entered into as a reward for using influence over another, to induce him to make a will for the benefit of the obligor. For such contracts encourage a spirit of artifice and scheming and tend to deceive and injure others.

'To amount to fraud, conduct must be deliberately dishonest' (see *R v Sinclair [1968] 3 All ER 241*).

Fraudulent trading. Trading by a company in defraud of creditors or for a fraudulent purpose (see the Insolvency Act 1986, s 213).

Freehold. Freehold estates were those titles to the ownership of land worthy of acceptance by a free man during the medieval period when the basic structure of English land law was developed, being the fee simple, the fee tail, or the life estate.

The term freehold is used at present in opposition to leasehold.

Friendly Society. A savings association for the purpose of affording relief to the members in sickness, and assistance to their widows and children on their deaths (see the Friendly Societies Act 1992).

Full age. The age of majority was formerly twenty-one, but is now eighteen (Family Law Reform Act 1969, s 1).

Full rate. *See* RATE OF TAX.

Full-time working officer or employee. A full-time working officer or employee is defined as an individual 'who is required to devote substantially the whole of his time to the service of that company, or the companies taken together, in a managerial or technical capacity' (TCGA 1992, Sch 6, para 1(2)). In *IRC v D Devine & Sons Ltd (1963) 41 TC 210*, the court considered parallel provisions relating to profits tax. Mrs Devine worked three days a week—

the Court of Appeal held that she was not a full-time working director.

Inland Revenue practice in interpreting the 'full-time' requirement is given in the Capital Gains Manual paras CG63621-63623 which state:

'In practice, you should consider whether someone devotes substantially the whole of his time to the service of the company by reference to the normal working week. For a company which has other full-time employees this can be taken to mean at least ¾ of the full normal working hours.

Note that it is not relevant if the officer/employee only works for a small number of hours but considers that that is the maximum hours which is required, or which he is able to devote to those duties.

Where the officer/employee is absent through illness, they should not be treated as having ceased to work full-time until a reasonable period of absence has elapsed. The period to allow should normally be the shortest of:

- the period of the illness, or
- 12 months from the start of the illness, or
- the period during which they continue as an officer/employee and no action is taken which suggests that full-time working will not resume (for example, if the company agrees that the employee will be able to go back to work on a part-time basis).

You may also accept that full-time working did not cease if the period of illness is slightly in excess of one year, provided that:

- during the period of absence no action is taken suggesting that full-time working will not resume,

and

- the employee does in fact resume full-time working before the disposal of the relevant shares or securities.'

The 'full time' requirement has given difficulty for the courts. In the decision of the majority of the Court of Appeal in *Palmer v Maloney [1999] STC 890*, Clarke LJ said: 'There seems to be much to be said for a rule of thumb such as that adopted by the Revenue' (*at 900a*).

Functional currency. The currency of the primary economic environment in which an entity operates and generates net cash flows. [FRS 13 – Derivatives and other financial instruments] (SSAP 20 'Foreign currency translation' uses the term 'local currency' rather than the term 'functional currency', although the definitions of the two terms are identical.)

Fund, Consolidated. *See* CONSOLIDATED FUND.

Fundamental accounting concepts. The broad basic assumptions which underlie the periodic financial accounts of business enterprises. At the present time the four following fundamental concepts (the relative importance of which will vary according to the circumstances of the particular case) are regarded as having general acceptability:

(*a*) going concern;
(*b*) consistency;
(*c*) prudence;
(*d*) matching.

Funded scheme. A pension scheme where the future liabilities for benefits are provided for by the accumulation of assets held externally to the employing company's business. [SSAP 24 – Accounting for pension costs]

Funded unapproved retirement benefits scheme. With a funded unapproved scheme, payments by the employer to a third party, eg the trustees in the case of a trust arrangement, to provide relevant benefits are assessable under Schedule E on the employee (TA 1988, s 595(4)). When pension payments are made, they are chargeable to tax under Schedule E in the ordinary way; lump sum commutation payments, however, are not taxable so long as the lump sum is attributable to an employer's contribution (or contributions) on which the employee has been subject to tax (TA 1988, ss 189 & 596A(8)).

A particular attraction of a funded unapproved scheme under trust (commonly known as a FURBS—ie a funded unapproved retirement benefit scheme) is that income on investments held by the trustees may be subject to income tax at only the basic rate of 23%. However, as a result of the changes for trust taxation, from 6 April 1998 capital gains within a FURBS attract tax at 34%.

A number of FURBS were established with non-resident trustees with the view of securing complete freedom from UK tax on investment income and gains.

Funding level. The level of funding is the proportion at a given date of the actuarial value of liabilities for pensioners' and deferred pensioners' benefits and for members' accrued benefits that is covered by the actuarial value of assets. For this purpose the actuarial value of future contributions is excluded from the value of assets. [SSAP 24 – Accounting for pension costs]

Funding plan. The timing of payments in an orderly fashion to meet the future cost of a given set of benefits. [SSAP 24 – Accounting for pension costs]

Fund-raising business. Any business carried on for gain and wholly or primarily engaged in soliciting or otherwise procuring money or other property for charitable, benevolent or philanthropic purposes (Charities Act 1992, s 58(1)).

Such a business is controlled by the Charities Act 1992, ss 59–64.

Funeral expenses. It is the first duty of an executor or administrator to bury the testator in a manner suitable to the estate which he has left, and the expenses will form a first charge on the estate; if, however, he is extravagant, he commits a *devastavit*, for which he is answerable to the creditors or legatees.

Fungibles. Movable goods which may be estimated by weight, number or measure, eg grain or coin. They are opposed to jewels, paintings, etc.

Furnished holiday lettings. Furnished holiday lettings are treated as if they were a trade for most purposes of income tax and also capital gains tax. Thus, for income tax, loss relief is available (with modified provisions for opening years) and the income is relevant earnings for pension contribution

purposes. For capital gains tax, the following reliefs are available in respect of furnished holiday lettings:

(a) rollover relief under TCGA 1992, ss 152–157;

(b) retirement relief under TCGA 1992, ss 163 & 164, Sch 6;

(c) holdover relief under TCGA 1992, s 165;

(d) relief for loans to traders under TCGA 1992, s 253.

TA 1988, s 504 requires the following conditions to be fulfilled for a property to be regarded as furnished holiday accommodation:

(1) The property is let commercially to the public generally.

(2) The property is available for letting for not less than 140 days in a year.

(3) The property is actually let for at least 70 days in a year.

(4) For any period of seven months it is not normally occupied by the same person for a continuous period exceeding 31 days.

The 'year' for which the test is applied is:

(1) Where the property is first let during the fiscal year concerned, a period of 12 months starting with the date of the first letting.

(2) Where the property ceases to be let during the fiscal year concerned, the 12 months ending on the date the property is last let under conditions that fulfil the requirements for a furnished holiday letting.

(3) In any other case, for an individual for the fiscal year; for a company, it is a period of account of 12 months.

The treatment afforded to furnished holiday accommodation is not dependent on profits being made (*Walls v Livesey [1995] STC (SCD) 12*).

Furniss v Dawson principle. The courts have the power to ignore the steps inserted for no commercial purpose and to levy tax on the basis that the end result had been achieved without the intermediate result. In order to ignore a step in a transaction: 'First, there must be a preordained series of transactions; or, if one likes, a single composite transaction. This composite transaction may or may not include the achievement of a legitimate commercial (ie business) end . . . Secondly, there must be steps inserted which have no commercial (business) purpose apart from the avoidance of a liability to tax—not "no business effect".' (per Lord Brightman in *Furniss v Dawson [1984] STC 153*). This is probably better called 'the Ramsay principle' after *Ramsay v IRC [1981] STC 174*. The scope of the principle has been substantially reduced by the decisions of the House of Lords in *MacNiven v Westmoreland Investments Ltd [2001] STC 237*.

See INTERPRETATION OF STATUTE.

Further advance or **charge.** A second or subsequent loan of money to a mortgagor by a mortgagee, either on the same or on an additional security.

See MORTGAGE.

Further assurance. Covenant for further assurance, in a deed of conveyance, means a covenant to make to the purchaser any additional 'assurance' which may be necessary to complete his title. It is *implied* on the use of the appropriate words, eg 'as beneficial owner', in conveyances made on and after 1 January 1882, by virtue of the Conveyancing Act 1881 (see now, as to implied covenants for title, s 76 of, and Sch II to, the Law of Property Act 1925).

See ASSURANCE (INSURANCE).

Future estate. An estate to take effect in possession at a future time. The expression is most frequently applied to contingent remainders and executory interests; but it would seem to be also applicable to vested remainders and reversions.

Future goods. Goods to be manufactured or acquired by the seller after the making of the contract of sale (Sale of Goods Act 1979, s 61(1)). Where by a contract of sale the seller purports to effect a present sale of future goods, the contract operates as an agreement to sell the goods: ibid, s 5(3).

See AGREEMENT TO SELL.

G

Gambling. Profits arising from gambling transactions do not fall within the definition of income taxed under Schedule D, Case VI. Such transactions are merely irrational agreements. The event which entitles the gambler to his winnings does not of itself produce the profit. There is no increment, no service, but merely an acquisition. This has to be distinguished from an organised seeking after profits which may create a trade and so a subject matter which bears fruit in the shape of profits or gains. Hence it has been held that while gambling may be a way of life—indeed in *Graham v Green (1925) 9 TC 309* it was the taxpayer's sole means of livelihood—it is not a trade and so its winnings escape Cases I, II and VI. Such views however do not prevent courts from holding that a bookmaker is carrying on a vocation and is therefore taxable under Case II, the distinction being that a bookmaker has an organisation (*Partridge v Mallandaine (1886) 18 QBD 276*).

Speculation is distinguished from mere gambling. Thus a person who buys shares on the stock exchange or cotton futures in the hope of an increase in capital value is a speculator and not a gambler—the distinction being that the contract to buy or sell the cotton is a very real one from the point of view of the vendor and gives rise to very real contractual rights whereas in a gambling transaction both parties regard the matter as a mere wager (*Cooper v Stubbs (1925) 10 TC 29*). Also to be distinguished are payments for the provision of services. So a professional tipster is taxed under Schedule D, Case II (*Graham v Arnott (1941) 24 TC 157*).

Garnishee. A person who is *garnished* or warned. The word is especially applied in law to a debtor who is *warned* by the order of a court to pay his debt, not to his immediate creditor, but to a person who has obtained a final judgment against such creditor. The order is called a *garnishee order.*

Gazette. The official publication of the Government, also called the *London Gazette*. It is evidence of Acts of State, and of everything done by the Queen in her political capacity. Orders of adjudication in bankruptcy are required to be published in it; and the production of a copy of the *Gazette*, containing a copy of the order of adjudication, is conclusive evidence of the fact, and of the date of it.

General agent. An agent empowered to act *generally* in the affairs of the principal, or at least to act for him *generally* in some particular capacity; as opposed to one authorised to act for him in a particular manner.
See SPECIAL AGENT.

General Commissioners. General Commissioners known in statute as 'Commissioners for the general purposes of the income tax', provide a forum for an appeal against an assessment, a Revenue notice or certain other acts relating to income tax, capital gains tax and corporation tax. General Commissioners are appointed by the Lord Chancellor and are not remunerated.
See APPEAL.

General lien. The right of certain agents, eg solicitors, insurance brokers, to detain an article from its owner until payment is made, not only in respect of that particular article, but of any balance that may be due on a general account between the parties.
See BAILMENT.

General partner. A member of a limited partnership who is liable for all debts and obligations of the firm (Limited Partnerships Act 1907, s 4(2)).
See LIMITED PARTNERSHIP.

Geographical segment. A geographical area comprising an individual country or group of countries in which an entity operates, or to which it supplies products or services. [SSAP 25 – Segmental reporting]

Ghost. A person with taxable income who does not make tax returns, or otherwise subject himself to the tax paying process.

Gift. A conveyance or transfer which passes either land or goods, gratuitously, ie not in fulfilment of an obligation under a contract or on sale. Gifts may be between living persons, or *inter vivos*, or testamentary, occurring by the execution of the will of a deceased. As to things immovable, 'gift' was once said to be applicable only to lands and tenements given in tail. This limitation of the word is, however, quite obsolete. Blackstone distinguishes a *gift* from a *grant* in that a gift is always gratuitous, without binding consideration, and therefore void in certain cases, whereas a grant is made on some consideration or equivalent, though *grant* is better used to indicate a transfer of property (in particular, land) which is effected by a written instrument.

Gift with reservation. An asset that has been the subject of a gift with reservation is treated as remaining in the estate of the donor at his death, if the reservation continues until the death (FA 1986, s 102(3)). A gift with reservation is made when an individual disposes of property and either (*a*) possession and enjoyment of the property is not bona fide assumed by the donee at or before the beginning of the relevant period, or (*b*) at any time in the relevant period, the property is not enjoyed to the entire exclusion, or virtually the entire exclusion, of the donor and of any benefit to him by contract or otherwise (FA 1986, s 102). The relevant period is the seven-year period ending with the donor's death.

If the gift is to escape IHT on the ground that it was made outside the statutory period, the first essential is that possession or enjoyment must have been assumed to the exclusion of the donor before the start of the period of seven years up to the donor's death. The donee's possession and enjoyment must then satisfy rule (*b*) which contains two distinct limbs, there must be both (i) the entire exclusion of the donor and (ii) the entire exclusion of any benefit to him by contract or otherwise.

Gilt edged. United Kingdom Government stocks.

Gilt strip. The stripping of a gilt causes the entitlement to interest to be held separately from the entitlement to capital repayment. The two separate interests in such a stripped gilt can be reconstituted into a normal gilt holding. Under the loan relationships legislation for corporation tax, where a gilt is stripped, the gilt is treated as if it had been redeemed for its market value (FA 1996, s 95(2)). Where the two separate interests are amalgamated into a single holding, the treatment is repeated, each separate interest being subjected to the loan relationship regime as if there had been a disposal of each of the separate interests, each for its market value (FA 1996, s 95(3)).

Going concern concept. A fundamental basis on which the accounts of an enterprise are drawn up. The concept assumes that the enterprise will continue in operational existence for the foreseeable future. This means in particular that the profit and loss account and balance sheet assume no intention or necessity to liquidate or curtail significantly the scale of operation. Inherent in the 'going concern' concept are: (i) the 'accruals' concept: revenue and costs are accrued (that is, recognised as they are earned or incurred, not as money is received or paid); matched with one another so far as their relationship can be established or justifiably assumed, and dealt with in the profit and loss account of the period to which they relate; provided that where the accruals concept is inconsistent with the 'prudence' concept, the latter prevails. The accruals concept implies that the profit and loss account reflects changes in the amount of net assets that arise out of the transactions of the relevant period (other than distributions or subscriptions of capital and unrealised surpluses arising on revaluation of fixed assets). Revenue and profits dealt with in the profit and loss account are matched with associated costs and expenses by including in the same account the costs incurred in earning them (so far as these are material and identifiable);

(ii) the 'consistency concept': there is consistency of accounting treatment of like items within each accounting period and from one period to the next;

(iii) the concept of 'prudence': revenue and profits are not anticipated, but are recognised by inclusion in the profit and loss account only when realised in the form either of cash or of other assets the ultimate cash realisation of which can be assessed with reasonable certainty; provision is made for all known liabilities (expenses and losses) whether the amount of these is known with certainty or is a best estimate in the light of the information available. [SSAP 2 – Disclosure of accounting policies]

Good consideration. A consideration founded on relationship or natural love and affection. It is not a *valuable* consideration, and will not 'sustain a promise', ie whereas in certain cases a 'consideration' is necessary to give legal validity to a promise, so that an action may be brought for breach of the same, a merely 'good' consideration will not be sufficient for this purpose.

See CONSIDERATION; CONTRACT.

Good faith. The Vienna Convention on the Law of Treaties 1969 has a concept of 'good faith'. In *Sportsman v IRC [1998] STC (SCD) 289* the Special Commissioners have invoked the concept of 'good faith', giving it its ordinary meaning and purpose, and thus have held that the purpose of a tax treaty was not only to prevent double taxation but also to prevent illegitimate tax evasion. This was concluded despite the absence of the second phrase from the list of statutory purposes in TA 1988, s 788(3), which is the authority under which tax treaties are entered into. They then held that the treaty should not be interpreted so as to allow a taxpayer to pay no tax in either country and so concluded that the taxpayer was not entitled to credit for tax which had not been paid in the other country; the taxpayer had argued that credit relief should be given on the basis that the tax was payable in the foreign country.

Goods and chattels. (1) In the widest sense, this expression includes any kind of property which, regard being had either to the subject-matter, or to the quantity of interest in it, is not freehold. But in practice, the expression is most frequently limited to things movable, especially things movable in possession.

(2) Under the VAT Acts, the following supplies amount to supplies of goods unless they are specifically excluded from this category and treated as either a supply of services or neither a supply of goods nor a supply of services:

(1) Any transfer of the whole property in goods.

(2) The transfer of possession in goods under either an agreement for the sale of goods or an agreement which expressly contemplates that the property in goods will pass at a future time specified in the agreement, eg a hire purchase agreement.

(3) The supply of any form of power, heat, refrigeration or ventilation.

(4) The granting, assignment or surrender of a major interest in land.

(5) A transfer or disposal of business assets. This includes any transfer or disposal in favour of a sole proprietor.

(6) Removing goods from one EU member state to another. There are a number of exceptions to this rule.

(7) The supply of water.

(8) The transfer of an undivided share in eligible goods under a non-retail supply while the goods are either subject to a fiscal warehousing regime at the time of supply or subsequently become so subject before they are supplied.

(VATA 1994, Sch 4, paras 1(1), 3, 4, 5(1), (6), 6(1)).

Goodwill. The *goodwill* of a trade or business comprises every advantage which has been acquired by carrying on the business, whether connected with the premises in which the business has been carried on, or with the name of the firm by whom it has been conducted. 'Probability that the old customers will resort to the old place' (Lord Eldon in *Cruttwell v Lye (1810) 17 Ves 346*).

Gourley Principle. When damages are awarded by a court to a claimant in respect of lost earnings, or lost profits, tax which would have been payable on the lost income is to be taken into account in assessing the damages. This principle was established by the House of Lords in *Gourley v British Transport Commission [1955] 3 All ER 396, HL.* By contrast, no deduction should be made if the court award may be liable to tax (*Stoke on Trent City Council v Wood Mitchell and Co Limited [1979] STC 197*).

Government grants. Assistance by government in the form of cash or transfers of assets to an enterprise in return for past or future compliance with certain conditions relating to the operating activities of the enterprise. [SSAP 4 – Accounting for government grants]

Grant. (1) The transfer of property by an instrument in writing without the delivery or the possession of any subject-matter thereof. This may happen: (*a*) where there is no subject-matter capable of delivery, eg in the case of an advowson, patent right, or title of honour (see PATENT); (*b*) where the subject-matter is not capable of *immediate* delivery, in the case of a reversion or remainder (see REVERSION; REMAINDER); (*c*) where, by reason of the subject-matter of the property being in the custody of another, or for any other cause, it is impracticable or undesirable to transfer the immediate possession.

The person making the grant is called the *grantor*; the person to whom it is made the *grantee*. Where the grantor transfers his whole interest in any subject-matter, the grant is generally called an *assignment*.

A grant has always been the regular method of transferring incorporeal hereditaments; eg an advowson, etc, and estates in expectancy, because no 'livery', ie, physical delivery, could be made of such estates. For this reason they were said to *lie in grant*; while corporeal hereditaments in possession were formerly said to *lie in livery.* By the Law of Property Act 1925, s 59 the word 'grant' is not to imply any covenant in law except where otherwise provided by statute. Nor is the word 'grant'

necessary to convey land or to create any interest in it. Nevertheless all lands and all interests lie 'in grant' and are no longer capable of being conveyed by livery (see ibid, s 51).

See INCORPOREAL HEREDITAMENT.

(2) The word *grant* is also frequently used in reference to public money devoted by Parliament for special purposes.

Gratuitous. Made without consideration or equivalent.

See GIFT; CONSIDERATION.

Gratuitous transfers of value. Capital gains tax legislation treats as a 'disposal' three separate types of transaction. In the market value which would be payable by the acquirer under a bargain at arm's length is to be taken as the consideration (TCGA 1992, s 29).

The first of these transactions is where a person has control of a company and exercises that control so that value passes out of shares in the company owned by him, or by a person with whom he is connected, and passes into other shares in or rights over the company. A controlling shareholder using his voting power to pass a resolution increasing the rights of a particular type of share at the expense of his own is clearly shifting value to the other shareholders, although no particular piece of property has been disposed of. Despite the fact that the singular 'person' is referred to, it has been held that the section applies where two or more persons control the company (*Floor v Davis [1979] STC 379*). In *W T Ramsay Ltd v IRC [1981] STC 174* it has also been held that control was exercised when under a pre-arranged scheme a winding-up resolution was passed even though the taxpayer himself did not vote on the motion. Unless there is a scheme, the taxpayer must presumably vote in order to exercise control.

The second type of transaction caught is where, after a transaction whereby the owner of any property has become the lessee of the property, there is an adjustment of the rights and liabilities of the lease which, taken as a whole, favour the lessor.

The third is where there is an asset which is subject to a right or restriction and there is a transaction whereby that right or restriction is extinguished or abrogated in whole or in part. Here the figure to be taken is the value accruing to the owner of the property from which the restriction falls.

Great Britain. England, Scotland, and Wales: Union with Scotland Act 1706, preamble, art 1; Interpretation Act 1978, s 22(1).

Gross earnings. The lessor's gross finance income over the lease term, representing the difference between his gross investment in the lease (as defined above) and the cost of the leased asset less any grants receivable towards the purchase or use of the asset. [SSAP 21 – Accounting for leases and hire purchase contracts]

Gross equity method. A form of equity method under which the investor's share of the aggregate gross assets and liabilities underlying the net amount included for the investment is shown on the face of the balance sheet and, in the profit and loss account, the investor's share of the investee's turnover is noted. [FRS 9 – Associates and joint ventures]

Gross investment in a lease. The total of the minimum lease payments and any unguaranteed residual value accruing to the lessor, calculated at a point in time. [SSAP 21 – Accounting for leases and hire purchase contracts]

Group. (1) A parent undertaking and its subsidiary undertakings. [FRS 2 – Accounting for subsidiary undertakings]

(2) A group for the purpose of relief from corporation tax on an intra-group transfer of an asset consists of a principal company and all its 75% subsidiaries. The 75% is applied to the beneficial ownership of shares. A company owns shares beneficially if it is free to dispose of them as it wishes (TCGA 1992, s 170(2)). There are further rules on the definition of a group to counter the use of 'bridge' companies. The group is still made up of the principal company and its 75% subsidiaries, including 75% subsidiaries of those subsidiaries and so on. However, a subsidiary which is not an effective 51% subsidiary is excluded (TCGA 1992, s 170(3)). A company is an effective 51% subsidiary only if the parent is beneficially entitled to more than 50% of any profits available for distribution or of any assets on a winding-up (TCGA 1992, s 170(7)).

Group reconstruction. Any of the following arrangements:
(*a*) the transfer of a shareholding in a subsidiary undertaking from one group company to another;
(*b*) the addition of a new parent company to a group;
(*c*) the transfer of shares in one or more subsidiary undertakings of a group to a new company that is not a group company but whose shareholders are the same as those of the group's parent;
(*d*) the combination into a group of two or more companies that before the combination had the same shareholders.
[FRS 6 – Acquisitions and mergers]

Group registration. Two or more companies that 'belong' in the UK, are eligible to be treated as members of a VAT group if one company controls the others, or if one person (which can be a company, an individual or a partnership) controls all the companies (VATA 1994, s 43A(1)). It should be noted that control can be by a partnership but the group registration can only apply to companies; the controlling partnership cannot be part of the group registration. A person is held to control a company, for this purpose, if he holds the majority of the voting rights or he controls the composition of the board of directors or is empowered by statute to control that company's activities (VATA 1994, s 43A(2) & (3)). The effects of a group registration are:
(1) The VAT affairs of the group are vested in a group company known as the representative member.
(2) A supply between group companies is normally disregarded (so that no VAT is charged on it and no liability to registration arises in respect of it) but it is not wholly devoid of VAT consequences (eg in relation to attribution of input tax).
(3) Group companies are jointly and severally liable for tax due from the representative member.

(4) A liability to output tax or entitlement to input tax is fixed by reference to the statutory description of the relevant group company rather than that of the representative member.

(VATA 1994, s 43(1), (1AA), (1AB), (2)). See *Customs and Excise Comrs v Svenska International plc [1999] STC 406, HL* for the treatment of input tax incurred before joining a VAT group and *J P Morgan Trading and Finance v Customs and Excise Comrs [1998] V & DR 161* for the treatment of input tax incurred after leaving a VAT group.

Group relief. Group relief for corporation tax enables current trading losses, capital allowances, a non-trading deficit on loan relationships, excess management expenses of investment companies and excess charges on income to be surrendered by one company (the surrendering company) to another (the claimant company) enabling the latter to put the other company's loss etc against its total profits (TA 1988, s 402). Both companies must satisfy the group or consortium tests throughout their respective accounting period but need not be members of the same group or consortium when the claim is made (*A W Chapman Ltd v Hennessey [1982] STC 214*).

If Company A makes a loss and surrenders that relief to Company B, Company A may insist upon receiving some payment. This will be particularly so if it is not a wholly owned subsidiary so that there will be different minority interests as well as different creditors. If the amount paid is due under a legally enforceable agreement and does not exceed the amount surrendered the payment is ignored in computing the profits and losses of either company and is treated neither as a distribution nor as a charge on income (*Haddock v Wilmot Breeden Ltd [1975] STC 255*).

Guarantee. In the strict sense, where one person contracts as surety on behalf of another an obligation to which the latter is also liable as the primary party. A promise to answer for the debt, default or miscarriage of another, which to be enforceable must be evidenced in writing under the Statute of Frauds 1677.

H

HL. House of Lords.

Head lease. A lease created out of a free-hold, being the main lease. Sub-leases may be created out of a head lease. For example, freeholder A may grant a 99-year lease to B and B in turn grants a 25-year lease of the same property to C: the 99-year lease is the head lease and the 25-year lease is a sub-lease (which may, in turn, have sub-sub-leases granted out of it).

Heldover gain. When a claim for holdover relief is made, capital gains tax is not charged on the gain arising on the disposal. Instead, the gain is held over into the purchase of a new asset, thereby reducing the CGT base cost for that purchase and, hence, causing a higher charge to capital gains tax on the ultimate disposal of the new asset (TCGA 1992, s 154(1)(a)).
See HOLDOVER RELIEF.

Herd basis. The normal treatment of animals kept by a farmer is to recognise the animals as trading stock. As an alternative, a farmer can elect for all production herds of any particular class he specifies to be treated under the 'herd basis' (TA 1988, Sch 5, para 2(1)). Where an election for the herd basis has been made, the value of animals in the herd is not taken into account in computing trading profits, the cost of adding animals to the herd is not deductible and the proceeds of the sale of a herd are not brought into assessment.

Higher rate. *See* RATE OF TAX.

Hire-purchase agreement. An agreement, other than a conditional sales agreement under which (*a*) goods are bailed in return for periodical payments by the person to whom they are bailed, and (*b*) the property in the goods will pass to that person if the terms of that agreement are complied with and one or more of the following occurs: (i) the exercise of an option to purchase by that person, (ii) the doing of any other

specified act by any party to the agreement, (iii) the happening of any other specified event (see Consumer Credit Act 1974, s 189(1)).

Hire-purchase contract. A contract for the hire of an asset which contains a provision giving the hirer an option to acquire legal title to the asset upon the fulfilment of certain conditions stated in the contract. [SSAP 21 – Accounting for leases and hire purchase contracts]

Hire-purchase system. Under this system the person who hires the goods becomes, on payment of the last instalment of the amount fixed, the owner of them. The hirer is given certain rights although he defaults in his payments (see the Consumer Credit Act 1974, which controls the extension of credit to individuals, including 'consumer hire agreements').

Hiring. A contract which differs from borrowing only in that hiring is always for a price, stipend, or additional recompense; whereas borrowing is merely gratuitous. It is a bailment for reward whereby the possession of goods, with a transient property in them, is transferred for a particular time or use, on condition that the hirer is to restore the goods so hired as soon as the time has expired or use performed. It is of four kinds. The hiring (1) of a thing for use; (2) of work and labour; (3) of services to be performed on the thing delivered; (4) of the carriage of goods.
See BAILMENT.

Historical cost convention. The accounting policy adopted when assets appear on the balance sheet at the cost, and are not revalued.

Holding, in the Agricultural Holdings Act 1986, means the aggregate of the land (whether agricultural land or not) comprised in a contract of tenancy (see Agricultural Holdings Act 1986, s 1(1)).

Holding company. The top (or principal) company in a group; ie the company that 'holds' the shares of the subsidiary. In many large groups, the function of the holding company is limited to the holding of shares. The function of such a company is purely to act as a holding company, so that the group relationship exists between the various trading companies. In some group structures, the top company employs the directors and, perhaps, provides other head office services to members of the group. In this alternative arrangement, the top company acts as a holding company, but also carries on a trade in its own right, being the trade of providing management services.

Holding out. Inducing other persons to believe in the existence of an authority which does not exist in fact. The party so holding out may afterwards be estopped from denying the supposed authority. As to holding oneself out as a partner, see the Partnership Act 1890, s 3.

See ESTOPPEL.

Holdover relief. The effect of a claim of holdover relief on a gift is that the gain that would otherwise be chargeable to tax is held over so that the gain crystallised by the donor is reduced to £nil. The amount by which the gain for the donor is reduced, also reduces the acquisition cost that the donee is subsequently able to put against the disposal he ultimately makes on the asset for which the holdover relief election has been made.

There are currently two types of holdover relief:
(1) where the capital gains tax disposal is also a chargeable transfer for inheritance tax purposes, a claim can be made under TCGA 1992, s 260;
(2) where the disposal is of an asset within the categories specified below, a claim can be made under TCGA 1992, s 165.

Holdover relief is available not only on gifts; it is available whenever there is 'a disposal otherwise than under a bargain at arm's length'.

Holdover relief is only available under TCGA 1992, s 165 if the asset is within one of the following categories:

(a) an asset used for the purposes of a trade carried on by the transferor or by his personal company;
(b) property that qualifies for agricultural property relief for inheritance tax purposes.

In addition, holdover relief can be claimed on the gift of shares and securities in the categories specified below where the gift is to an individual or a trustee, but not where the recipient is a company.

(c) unquoted shares or securities in a trading company;
(d) shares or securities in a trading company which is the transferor's personal company.

Honorarium. A gratuity given for professional services.

Horizontal integration. The linking of two or more commercial enterprises that carry out the same business, perhaps in different geographical areas. The rationale behind horizontal integration is often to gain economies of scale by minimising administration and other central costs. Thus, a car dealership in south east England that purchases dealerships in other regions of Britain is engaging in horizontal integration.

Contrast: VERTICAL INTEGRATION.

Hotchpot. Literally, a pudding mixed with divers ingredients. But, by a metaphor, it means a commixture or putting together of lands of several tenures, for the equal division of them. The word is frequently applied with reference to settlements which give a power to a parent of appointing a fund among his or her children, in which it is provided that no child, taking a share of the fund under any appointment, is to be entitled to any share in the unappointed part without bringing his or her share into 'hotchpot' and accounting for it accordingly. The effect of such a clause would be to prevent a child who takes under an appointment from claiming his full share in the unappointed part, in addition to his appointed share (see also the Administration of Estates Act 1925, s 47).

See SETTLEMENT; POWER.

Hotel. Hotels attract a capital allowance,

being an annual writing-down allowance of 4% on a straight-line basis (CAA 2001, s 310(1)). The hotel must be a 'qualifying hotel', which is defined by CAA 2001, s 279(1) & (9) as one that fulfils the following conditions:

(a) the building is permanent;

(b) the hotel is open for at least four months during the period from April to October;

(c) when the hotel is open during that period:

 (i) it has ten, or more, letting bedrooms,

 (ii) the sleeping accommodation consists wholly or mainly of sleeping bedrooms,

 (iii) the services provided for guests normally include breakfast, an evening meal, bed-making and cleaning rooms.

The hotel may be outside the UK but the trade must be taxed under Schedule D, Case I.

House of Lords. The upper House of the legislature, consisting of the Lords Spiritual and the Lords Temporal. The Lords Spiritual consist of the archbishops of Canterbury and York; of the bishops of London, Durham, and Winchester; and of twenty-one other bishops. The Lords Temporal are the hereditary peers of England, Scotland, Great Britain and the United Kingdom who have not disclaimed their peerages under the Peerages Act 1963; life peers created under the Life Peerages Act 1958; and Lords of Appeal in Ordinary created under the Appellate Jurisdiction Act 1876. A certain number of peers are elected, under the Act of Union with Scotland, to represent in the House of Lords the body of the Scottish nobility; but it was held in *Petition of the Earl of Antrim [1967] 1 AC 691*, that the right to elect Irish representative peers no longer exists. The aggregate number of the Lords Temporal is not fixed, and may be increased at will by the Crown. By the House of Lords Act 1999 hereditary peers were excluded from the House of Lords save for 90 who, under current standing orders of the House, were elected by the body of hereditary peers. The House of

Lords is also the court of final appeal in all cases, assigning this business by constitutional convention to its Appellate Committee, made up of the Law Lords sitting in panels of five and occasionally seven, except from certain Commonwealth courts, appeals from which are heard by the Judicial Committee of the Privy Council as a court of final appeal. In addition to its appellate jurisdiction, the House of Lords has jurisdiction in impeachment and over peerage claims, and also over any breach of its privileges.

Housing association. A society, body of trustees or company

(a) which is established for the purpose of providing, constructing, improving or managing the construction or improvement of housing accommodation, and

(b) which does not trade for profit (Housing Act 1985, s 5(1)).

Housing trust. A corporation or body which is required by the terms of its constituent instrument (i) to use the whole of its funds for the purpose of providing housing accommodation; or (ii) to devote the whole, or substantially the whole, of its funds for charitable purposes, and, in fact, uses them for the purpose of providing housing accommodation (Housing Act 1985, s 6).

Human rights. The Strasbourg Court on the European Convention on Human Rights has had quite a lot to say about tax procedures in other countries. These may be broken down into three main areas. First, in *Funke v France (1993) 16 EHRR 297* the court used Article 8 of the Convention on protection of a person's private and family life, home and correspondence to examine a search with warrant under French law, French law at that time not requiring a warrant; the court placed considerable emphasis on the types of interference permitted by Article 8(2). Second, they have looked at Article 6 (the right to a fair trial) and held that although, at present at least, their jurisprudence suggests that the determination of a tax liability itself may not be a matter of determining a person's 'civil rights and obligations', nonetheless the imposition of a tax penalty can be treated as a 'criminal charge', and so within the article. In *JJ v Netherlands (1998) 28 EHRR 168* the court looked at a 100% tax penalty (and awarded damages) and rejected a state's right to claim a penalty for a tax fraud committed by someone else (*AP, MP and TP v Switzerland (1997) 26 EHRR 541, EC of HR*). They have also considered whether a tax investigation for tax fraud which took 8½ years was too long and so a breach of Article 6 (*Hozee v Netherlands (1998) unreported*). Third, and in the same vein, the court has held that a right which originates in a tax matter, such as a right to repayment of tax or of indemnity against another person, may be a 'civil right or obligation'. A recent decision by the President of the VAT Tribunals reinforces the view that Article 6 can apply to those tax matters which can be viewed as something other than simply the determination of a tax liability.

Among the issues which have been suggested for consideration in the UK are:

(1) whether the Commissioners may continue to sit in private;

(2) whether points may be taken to the Commissioners by the Revenue when the taxpayer has no equivalent rights;

(3) the highly selective number of cases chosen for criminal prosecution;

(4) the right of the Crown to prosecute after a tax settlement has been reached (*R v W [1998] STC 550*);

(5) whether a taxpayer is given an effective right of appeal if the only remedy in a case is judicial review;

(6) the insistence of Customs and Excise on having disputed VAT paid before an appeal can be begun;

(7) the refusal of a court to allow a taxpayer accused of fraud to summon and cross-examine the informer;

(8) the fundamental principle behind stamp duty enforcement that a document must be stamped if it is to be admissible; and

(9) whether and when Customs and Excise may insist on group treatment for VAT.

This list suggests that the UK tax system may find many human rights issues taken over the next few years. Two contradictory points should be borne in mind.

The first is that although many tax issues have been raised in the Strasbourg jurisprudence not many have succeeded, not least because that court likes to leave a margin of appreciation to the member state. The other is that while the Strasbourg Court may, for sensible political reasons, wish to leave a margin of appreciation to the member state there is no reason why a court of that member state should. Given the enthusiasm with which the UK courts adapted themselves to EC law there is every reason to expect a similar enthusiasm for human rights. Indeed some think the question is how far some judges will incorporate human rights jurisprudence into the UK legal system before the official date for the coming into force of the Human Rights Act 1998. In this connection the fact that human rights is part of EC law and so already part of VAT law should not be forgotten.

Human Rights Act 1998. An Act providing for the implementation by courts in the United Kingdom of those protocols of the European Convention on Human Rights to which the United Kingdom is a signatory.

See HUMAN RIGHTS, EUROPEAN CONVENTION ON.

Human Rights, European Commission of. A commission whose function is to receive from States or individuals petitions claiming to be victims of a violation of a right set out in the European Convention on Human Rights.

See HUMAN RIGHTS, EUROPEAN CONVENTION ON.

The commission must attempt to effect a friendly settlement; it must draw up a report and send it to the Committee of Ministers of the Council of Europe and to the State concerned.

In certain circumstances the matter may be referred to the European Court of Human Rights.

See HUMAN RIGHTS, EUROPEAN COURT OF.

Human Rights, European Convention on. A convention signed at Rome on 4 November 1950.

Its principal provisions relate to (i) the right to life (art 2); (ii) the prohibition of torture, degrading treatment and punishment (art 3); (iii) the prohibition of slavery and forced labour (art 4); (iv) the right to liberty (art 5); (v) the right to a fair trial and a public hearing of the proceedings (art 6); (vi) the right to private life and correspondence (art 8); and (vii) freedom of thought, conscience, religion and association (art 9).

See HUMAN RIGHTS ACT 1998.

Human Rights, European Court of. The Court's function is to hear cases submitted to it by the Committee of Ministers of the Council of Europe concerning the interpretation of the European Convention on Human Rights.

See HUMAN RIGHTS, EUROPEAN CONVENTION ON.

The Court's judgment is final.

I

IHT. Inheritance tax.

ICAEW. Institute of Chartered Accountants in England and Wales.

ICAI. Institute of Chartered Accountants in Ireland.

ICAS. Institute of Chartered Accountants of Scotland.

ISA. Individual savings account (ISA).

IOU (I owe you). A written acknowledgment of a debt. It operates merely as evidence of a debt due by virtue of an antecedent contract. It does not require to be stamped.

Identifiable assets and liabilities. The assets and liabilities of the acquired entity that are capable of being disposed of or settled separately, without disposing of a business of the entity. [FRS 7 – Fair values in acquisition accounting & FRS 10 – Goodwill and intangible assets]

Ill-health. Statute provides for retirement relief where there is a material disposal of business assets made by an individual who at the time of disposal has retired on ill-health grounds below the age of 50 (TCGA 1992, s 163(4)(c)).

In order to qualify for retirement relief on the grounds of ill-health, a claim must be made. The conditions for making the claim are slightly different, according to the status of the individual claiming retirement relief.

If the individual was a sole trader or partner:
(1) He must have ceased to be engaged in work of the kind previously undertaken.
(2) He must be incapable of such work by reason of ill-health.
(3) He must be likely to remain permanently incapable of such work (TCGA 1992, Sch 6, para 3(1)).

If the individual was a full-time working officer or employee of his personal trading company (or holding company of a trading group):
(1) He must have ceased to serve the company in a technical or managerial capacity.
(2) He must be incapable by reason of ill-health of serving the company in such a capacity.
(3) It must be likely that he will remain permanently incapable of serving that company or any company engaged in a similar business in the same capacity.

If the individual was an employee or full-time working officer of his personal trading company:
(1) He must have ceased to exercise the employment.
(2) He must be incapable of exercising it by reason of ill-health.
(3) It must be likely that he will remain permanently incapable of exercising it (TCGA 1992, Sch 6, para 3(4)).

It should be noted that the requirement is for the taxpayer to demonstrate that he is incapable of engaging in a particular work he has undertaken in connection with the particular business concerned. Certain types of business require specific attributes. It could be that the particular medical condition makes it impossible to continue in the particular business, although the particular individual concerned may be able to continue undertaking another type of work. If these are the facts, retirement relief can be claimed in respect of his retirement from the business for which his medical condition makes it impossible for him to continue.

Immovable. A thing which can be touched but which cannot be moved and includes a chattel real (*see* CHATTELS). The general rule as to the law governing immovables is that all rights over, or in relation to them, are governed by the law of the country where the immovable is situated (the *lex situs*).

Impairment. A reduction in the recoverable amount of a fixed asset or goodwill below its carrying value. [FRS 10 – Goodwill and intangible assets, FRS 11 – Impairment of fixed assets and goodwill & FRS 15 – Tangible fixed assets]

Implied. This term can only be properly used to mean 'established by indirect or circumstantial evidence' or, which comes to the same thing, 'presumed in certain circumstances to exist, in the absence of evidence to the contrary', especially with reference to inward intentions or motives as inferred from overt acts.

Thus an *implied trust* has been defined as 'a trust which is founded in an unexpressed but presumable intention', as contrasted with a *constructive trust*, which is one raised by construction of a court of equity without reference to the presumed intention of any party; in this it differs both from an *implied* trust and from an *express* trust.

But the general use of the word 'implied' is wider. The phrase 'implied contract' is often applied to all those events which in law are treated as contracts, whether they arise from a presumed mutual consent or not, provided only that they are not express contracts.

Thus, the phrase is used to mean *sometimes* a genuine consensual contract not expressed in words, or in signs which usage has rendered equivalent to words; *sometimes* an event to which, although not a consensual contract, the law annexes most or all of the incidents of a contract as against any person or persons.

The implied contract is frequently spoken of as a *tacit* contract. It may be defined, in opposition to an express contract, as 'a contract not expressed in words, or in signs which usage had rendered equivalent to words', eg if I order a suit from a tailor, without saying anything as to the price or quality. The tailor, in undertaking the order, tacitly promises me that the suit shall be reasonably fit for wear. I tacitly promise him to pay a reasonable price for it. In implied contracts of this class there is no agreement as to the precise terms and conditions, but there *is* an agreement, though of a general character.

The expression 'implied request' is used in a manner analogous to 'implied contract'. A request is said to be 'implied by law' sometimes when it has been, in fact, made, though not in express words: sometimes when it has never been made.

Improvement. Improvements are capital expenditure and not a revenue expense. TA 1988, s 74 expressly disqualifies in para (d): 'any sums expended for repairs of premises occupied . . . for the purposes of the trade beyond the sum actually expended for the purpose', a provision which restricts deductions to sums actually spent and therefore prohibits the deduction of sums set aside by way of reserve for future expenditure; while para (g) prohibits the deduction of any capital employed in improvements of premises occupied for the purposes of the trade, profession or vocation.

Improving the building of a factory is a capital cost because it is a material improvement of the land. Money spent on the replacement of one kind of rail by a superior kind is not deductible, since it increases the value of the railway line (*Highland Rly Co v Balderston (1889) 2 TC 485* and *LCC v Edwards (1909) 5 TC 383*). Expense incurred in increasing the number of sleepers under each rail was admitted to be capital expense in *Rhodesia Railways Ltd v Bechuanaland Protectorate IT Collector [1933] AC 368 at 372*, but the railway company was allowed to deduct as repairs the cost of works in renewing 74 miles of railway track by replacing rails and sleepers. This was not an improvement since it only restored the worn track to its normal condition and did not increase the capacity of the line in any way. Money spent on pulling down a chimney and building a new bigger and better chimney (*O'Grady v Bullcroft Main Collieries Ltd (1932) 17 TC 93*) or on renovating a factory with a higher roof line and so more space is not deductible (*Thomas Wilson (Keighley) Ltd v Emmerson (1960) 39 TC 360*; *Lawrie v IRC (1952) 34 TC 20*; *Mann Crossman and Paulin Ltd v IRC [1947] 1 All ER 742, 28 TC 410*). The question whether work is a repair or an improvement is one of fact (*Conn v Robins Bros Ltd (1966) 43 TC 266 at 274*).

Where an improvement is carried out no deduction may be claimed for such part of the expenditure as would have been needed to pay for mere repair. In *Thomas Wilson (Keighley) Ltd v Emmerson (1960) 39 TC 360 at 366*, Danckwerts J commented, 'It seems to me to be a hardship and something which is calculated to discourage manufacturers from making the best use of their property'. On the other hand if the work consists of a number of separate jobs it may be possible to distinguish between the different items thus allowing some of the expense, so in *Conn v Robins Bros Ltd (1966) 43 TC 266* the construction of 'a ladies toilet' was held to be an improvement but the insertion of steel joists a repair.

These rules are not confined to physical assets. Sums spent on training courses for proprietors are regarded as capital if intended to give them new expertise, knowledge or skill as distinct from mere updating.

Inadequacy of consideration does not affect the validity of a contract.
See CONSIDERATION.

Inception. Inception of a lease is the earlier of the time the asset is brought into use and the date from which rentals first accrue. [SSAP 21 – Accounting for leases and hire purchase contracts]

Incidental overnight expenses. FA 1995, s 200A(4)–(6) provides statutory exclusion for certain incidental overnight expenses.

The broad effect of the new provisions is to exclude these charges where the overnight accommodation costs associated with them would be allowable deductions under the various travel rules. There is a maximum of £5 per night for expenses in the UK and £10 elsewhere but these limits may be varied by statutory instrument.

An allowable incidental overnight expense is one which is paid wholly and exclusively for the purpose of defraying, or of being used for defraying, any expense which is incidental to that person's being away from his usual place of abode during a qualifying absence from home. An absence from home qualifies if it is a continuous period throughout which that person is obliged to stay away from his usual place of abode and during which he has at least one overnight stay away from that place. In addition, there must be no overnight stay at a place other than a place the expenses of travelling to which are deductible expenses which would be deductible if they had been incurred (FA 1995, s 200A(1)–(3)).

Income arising. Where the settlor has an interest in a settlement (which is widely defined), he is charged to income tax on all income arising. 'Income arising under a settlement' includes any income chargeable to income tax, whether by deduction or otherwise (TA 1988, s 660I(3)). It thus makes no allowance for any trust management expenses. The phrase also includes any income which would have been so chargeable if it had been received in the UK by a person domiciled, resident and ordinarily resident in the UK. This creates a hypothetical remittance to a hypothetical resident and so catches all income wherever it arises.

Income-generating unit. A group of assets, liabilities and associated goodwill that generates income that is largely independent of the reporting entity's other income streams. The assets and liabilities include those directly involved in generating the income and an appropriate portion of those used to generate more than one income stream. [FRS 11 – Impairment of fixed assets and goodwill]

Income tax. Income tax is charged on the taxable income of the year of assessment. This raises the question what is income?

There is no statutory definition of income, beyond the statement that income is taxable if it falls within one or other of the Schedules. The schedular system was created in Henry Addington's Act of 1803, under which income that was to suffer taxation was classified into five Schedules: Schedule A (income from land and buildings), Schedule B (farming profit), Schedule C (public annuities), Schedule D (self-employment and other items not covered by the other Schedules) and Schedule

E (salaries, annuities and pensions). Tax was charged at 5% (which rose to 10% in 1806) and the words 'income tax' were deliberately avoided, the Act being styled as a 'contribution of the profits arising from property, professions, trades and offices'. Practitioners will recognise that the specification of the schedules by Addington in 1803 is substantially the same as the specification today, there having being remarkably little change over the intervening 199 years. Although income tax was repealed after the defeat of Napoleon in 1815 and the belief that the demand on the Parliamentary purse could be satisfied without a tax on incomes, the reintroduction of income tax by Sir Robert Peel in 1842 was effected by a reintroduction of Henry Addington's Schedules, although Sir Robert Peel, in opposition, had argued against the schedular system.

Prior to 1952, income subject to tax was defined in separate Schedules, attached to the Act. In the consolidating statute, Income Taxes Act 1952, the definition of income under the schedular system was moved into the body of the Act, to become part of the text, where it now remains. Income tax is imposed by TA 1988, s 1(1) on the Schedules that are defined in sections 15–20. TA 1988 does not, in terms, impose a charge to income tax, it merely provides the schedular system under which income tax will be administered, if Parliament chooses to impose a charge for the year. In every year since 1842, Parliament has chosen to impose a charge to income tax, although, technically each year's charge is imposed as a temporary measure: ie a charge only lasts for a single fiscal year. Income tax for 2001–02 is imposed by the Finance Act 2001, s 50.

Where income falls within a Schedule it falls to be computed in accordance with the rules in that Schedule and no other. As Lord Radcliffe has said in *Mitchell and Edon v Ross (1961) 40 TC 11 at 61*:

'Before you can assess a profit to tax you must be sure that you have properly identified its source or other description according to the correct Schedule; but once you have done that, it is obligatory that it should be charged, if at all, under that Schedule and strictly in accordance with the Rules that are there laid down for assessments under it. It is a necessary consequence of this conception that the sources of profit in the different Schedules are mutually exclusive.'

In *Fry v Salisbury House Estate Ltd [1930] 15 TC 266*, the company received rents from unfurnished offices in a building. The company also provided services for the offices such as heating and cleaning at an additional charge. The rents were chargeable under Schedule A, although the basis of assessment at that time was not simply the rents minus costs of maintenance but the annual value of the premises, which were revalued every five years, minus a statutory allowance for running costs. The company agreed that its profits from the ancillary services fell within Schedule D, Case I, but resisted the Revenue's argument that it was liable to tax on the actual rent received under Schedule D, Case I rather than the notional rent under Schedule A. The Revenue conceded that it would have to make an allowance in computing tax under Schedule D, Case I for the tax due under Schedule A. The House of Lords found for the company. Although the company could be said to be carrying on a trade and therefore fall within Schedule D, Case I, the Schedules were mutually exclusive and each Schedule was dominant over its own subject matter. The charge under Schedule A therefore excluded the charge under Schedule D, Case I.

Income Tax Acts. All enactments relating to income tax, including any provisions of the Corporation Tax Acts which relate to income tax (Interpretation Act 1978, Sch 1).

Income tax month. Also called the fiscal month, the income tax month runs from 6th of one month to 5th of the following month. An employer is required to account to the Inland Revenue, within 14 days of the end of an income tax month, for all PAYE and national insurance contributions on payments that he has made to employees during the income tax month.

Incoming partner. A partner joining an existing partnership.

A person who is admitted as a partner into an existing firm does not thereby become liable to the creditors of the firm for anything done before he became a partner (Partnership Act 1890, s 17(1)).

Incorporate. (1) To declare in writing in a document that another document shall be taken as part of the document, as if it were set out at length in it.

(2) To establish as a corporation.

(3) To transfer a trade that has been carried on by a sole trader or partnership, etc, into a company created for the purpose of carrying on the trade in future.

See INCORPORATION; INCORPORATION RELIEF.

Incorporation. The creation of a company. A company can be created in the United Kingdom by registration with the Registrar of Companies, or by an Act of Parliament, or by Royal Charter. The company may be created to carry on a new trade, or may continue a trade that had previously been carried on by a sole trader, or a partnership.

See INCORPORATION; INCORPORATION RELIEF.

Incorporation relief. A CGT relief that is given when there is a disposal by an individual or a partnership of the assets of a business, caused by the incorporation of that business so that the business is henceforth carried on by a company (TCGA 1992, s 142). As long as the conditions of s 142 are fulfilled, incorporation relief is given automatically; no claim is necessary and it cannot be disclaimed.

Incorporeal chattels. Personal rights and interests which are not of a tangible nature, eg annuities, stocks and shares, patents and copyrights. A rather rare usage of 'chattels' to mean 'personal property' in its entire extension; 'chattels' is normally restricted to tangible objects, such as chairs, books, etc, and 'incorporeal chattels' referred to as 'intangible personal property'.

See PERSONAL PROPERTY.

Incorporeal hereditament. Intangible rights or interests in land, thus any possession or subject of property which, before 1926, was capable of being transmitted to heirs, and is not the object of the bodily senses. It is, in general, a right annexed to, or issuing out of, or exercisable within, a corporeal hereditament; eg a right of common of pasture, a right of way over land, or an annuity payable out of land. The provisions of Part I of the Law of Property Act 1925 relating to freehold land apply also to incorporeal hereditaments (see s 201 of the Act).

Indefinite payment. Where a debtor owes several debts to the same creditor, and makes a payment without specifying to which of the debts the payment is to be applied.

Indemnity. Compensation for a wrong done, or trouble, expense, or loss incurred. An undertaking, usually by deed, to indemnify another.

Indenture. A deed made by more than one party; so called because there ought regularly to be as many copies of it as there are parties, and historically such copies were engrossed on one sheet of parchment and separated by making indented cuts. By the Law of Property Act 1925, s 56(2), a deed purporting to be an indenture has the effect of an indenture, though not actually indented. By s 57 any deed, whether or not being an indenture, may be described simply as a deed or as a conveyance, mortgage, or otherwise according to the nature of the transaction.

See DEED.

Independent financial adviser. A person authorised under Financial Services Act 1986 to carry on investment business in the United Kingdom. Authorisation may be by means of a direct application to the Secretary of State under FSA 1986, s 26, or by membership of a recognised self-regulating organisation, under FSA 1986, s 7.

Indexation allowance. For a disposal by a company, the cost of an asset is increased by indexation allowance, when calculating the capital gain arising on its disposal, before subjecting the gain to corporation tax. For a disposal after 5 April 1998 by an individual, trustees or personal representatives, indexation allowance is calculated to 5 April 1998 only before subjecting the gain to capital gains tax (TCGA 1992, s 53(1A)). Taper relief is then applied to the gain that is computed.

Indexation allowance is calculated by taking the allowable expenditure and multiplying it by the fraction $\frac{RD-RI}{RI}$ where RD is the retail prices index figure for the month in which the disposal occurs and RI that for the month in which the expenditure is incurred. If RI exceeds RD, the indexation allowance is nil.

Indexation loss. An indexation loss is a loss created by applying indexation allowance (ie the allowance for inflation) to the cost of an asset when performing a computation for CGT (FA 1994, Sch 12, para 2(2)). For disposals after 29 November 1993, no relief has been available for an indexation loss, nor for the increase in a loss arising as a result in indexation allowance (other than some transitional relief available up to 5 April 1995).

Individual savings account (ISA). An ISA allows an individual to hold various investments free of income tax and CGT. Although an individual cannot obtain repayment of the tax credit on a UK company dividend, the manager of an ISA can claim repayment of the tax credit of a dividend received into the account before 6 April 2004. An ISA account may be made up of one or more of the following components only:

(1) stocks and shares;
(2) cash;
(3) insurance.

The ISA language also refers to accounts being designated as a maxi-account or a mini-account or a TESSA only account; this designation is made by the account manager.

A maxi-account must contain a stocks and shares component but it may contain other components but it must be the only account (other than a TESSA only account) to which the individual subscribes that year.

The limit that an investor can invest in

an ISA is £7,000, of which a maximum of £3,000 may be a cash account and a maximum of a further £1,000 may be in life assurance.

In contrast to the restriction where a maxi ISA account is opened, where the investor chooses to open a mini-account, he can choose to use up to three separate providers thus, £1,000 cash can be invested with provider A, £1,000 life assurance with provider B and a further provider C can be used for stocks and shares. However, using a mini ISA means that a limit of £3,000 applies to the stocks and shares element of the ISA.

The TESSA-only account is one which has accepted a transfer of funds from a matured TESSA.

An individual not resident in the UK is not permitted to open an ISA, unless the individual is deemed to perform the duties of a Crown appointment within the UK. However, a UK resident who goes abroad can continue to hold the ISA whilst not resident in the UK, without time limit, although he is not permitted to make further subscriptions to the ISA after ceasing to be resident in the UK.

The ISA regulations include a number of voluntary standards designed to make some schemes attractive to savers as distinct from fund managers; these are the CAT standards which set levels for charges, access and terms.

The Individual Savings Account (ISA) has been available since 6 April 1999. During 1999/2000 nine million ISA accounts were opened, into which £28 billion was deposited and a further £9 billion deposited in the first three months of 2000/01.

Indorsement. A writing on the back of a document. Thus, one speaks of an indorsement on a deed, on a bill of exchange, on a writ, etc.

An *indorsement in blank* is where a person, to whom a bill or note is payable, writes his name on the back of it. The effect of such an indorsement is that the right to sue on the bill will be transferred to any person to whom the bill is delivered, ie to any bearer of it.

See BILL OF EXCHANGE.

A *special* indorsement is an indorsement directing payment of the bill to a specified person or his order; such person is called the *indorsee*. In this case the bill or note, in order to become transferable, must be again indorsed by the indorsee. For the requisites of a valid indorsement, see Bills of Exchange Act 1882, s 32.

See SANS RECOURS.

Industrial and Provident Society. A society for carrying on any industries, businesses or trades specified in or authorised by its rules, whether wholesale or retail, and including dealings of any description with land. Such societies are regulated by the Industrial and Provident Societies Act 1965 to 1975.

Industrial building. Industrial buildings allowance can be claimed for the cost of an industrial building or structure (CAA 2001, s 271), which is elaborately defined in CAA 2001, ss 271(1), 274(1), 284 and Tables A & B. The general effect of the definition is to confine allowances to productive, as opposed to distributive, industries. A building in use for the purposes of a trade carried on in a mill, factory or other similar premises is an industrial building as is a building for the purposes of a trade which consists in the taking and catching of fish or shellfish (CAA 2001, s 18(1)). A building is a factory only if something is made there; so a repair depot normally cannot qualify (*Vibroplant Ltd v Holland [1982] STC 164*). However, a building used for the maintenance or repair of goods will qualify if the goods or materials are employed in a trade or undertaking which itself qualifies (CAA 2001, s 274(1)). Other trades specified are the ploughing or cultivating of land (unless the trader occupies the land in which case he qualifies for agricultural allowances), the working of mineral deposits or a foreign plantation, transport, dock, inland navigation, water, electricity or hydraulic power undertaking, a tunnel, any road, a highway concession or bridge undertaking, the manufacturing or processing of goods or materials, or subjecting goods or materials to any process, the storage of goods which are to be so used (see *Dale v Johnson Bros*

(1951) 32 TC 487) or the end product while it awaits delivery to a customer and the storage of goods on arrival by any means of transport in any part of this country from outside. Stockists can claim allowances, provided they carry on the trade of storing goods. The test is whether the building is used for the purposes of a trade which consists in the storage of the qualifying goods and not whether the building is used for the storage of such goods. An allowance can therefore be claimed for a building even though it is in part used for the storage of other goods (*Saxone Lilley and Skinner (Holdings) Ltd v IRC [1967] 1 All ER 756, 44 TC 122*). An allowance is not available if the storage is merely ancillary to a retail shop (CAA 2001, s 277(1) & (5), see *Bestway (Holdings) Ltd v Luff [1998] STC 357*). Whether the storage area is a warehouse in its own right or merely ancillary to a shop, must be decided by consideration of the nature of the activities that take place in the building and the degree to which they are separate to the activities in the shop (*Sarsfield v Dixons Group plc [1998] STC 938*).

It is not necessary that the building be constructed in this country, indeed foreign plantations are expressly mentioned and defined. However the profits or gains of the foreign trade must be assessable under Schedule D, Case I and not Case V (CAA 2001, s 18(13)).

The definition specifically excludes any building used as, or as part of, a dwelling-house, retail shop, showroom, hotel or office and of any building ancillary to the purposes of those excluded (CAA 2001, s 277(1) & (5)).

Infant. Formerly, a person who was under the age of 21 years; an age at which persons were considered competent for all that the law required them to do, and which was, therefore, designated as *full age*. The age of majority was reduced to 18 (with some exceptions) by the Family Law Reform Act 1969, which also provides that any person not of full age may be described as a *minor* instead of an infant.

Inflation accounting. A method of drawing up financial statements that, in contrast to historic cost accounting, recognises the change in the value of money by inflation. No single method has enjoyed wide acceptance, although in the early 1980s, there was widespread use of current cost accounting as a method of inflation accounting.

Inheritance. A perpetuity in lands or tenements to a man and his heirs. The word is mostly confined to the title to lands and tenements by *descent*.
  See ESTATE.

Inheritance tax. Inheritance tax (IHT) is a tax on transfers of capital. It applies to transfers on or after 18 March 1986. Unlike capital transfer tax (CTT) which preceded it, IHT is designed to operate primarily as a tax on transfers which occur on death. In order to prevent too obvious avoidance the tax also charges retrospectively certain gifts made within the previous seven years. Gifts which are potentially liable to IHT if the transferor should die within this period are known as 'potentially exempt transfers'. There is no tax on such transfers when they are made but if the donor dies within seven years the exemption is lost. The scheme of the tax is further strengthened by the inclusion of gifts made outside the seven-year period but from which the deceased has not been entirely excluded for the past seven years, known as gifts with reservation. Most gifts are potentially exempt. However others are not and, as in the days of CTT, these are known as chargeable transfers and are chargeable immediately—whether or not the transferor dies within seven years; one does not wait for the death of the transferor. The 1986 legislation takes the form of extensive amendment of the CTT legislation which had been consolidated in 1984; this explains why the principal legislation is called the Inheritance Tax Act 1984.

Unlike the old estate duty it otherwise so greatly resembles, IHT charges certain transfers *inter vivos* immediately. However, unlike CTT, there is no immediate charge to tax on most types of *inter vivos* transfer and IHT has an unfortunate willingness to determine the tax payable by looking at the moment of the death of the donor, not only to see whether a potentially exempt transfer has become chargeable but also whether

certain conditions for relief are still satisfied. Unlike a true succession duty, and despite its name, it is charged by reference to the circumstances of the transferor and not those of the transferee. IHT is a charge on the reduction in the estate of the transferor. In this, it is in sharp contrast to CGT which is computed on the value of the property disposed of. Some transfers will give rise to both taxes with the liability to IHT only becoming clear on the deceased's death. Unlike a wealth tax it is charged on moving and not on stationary wealth.

IHT is payable on a transfer of value. A transfer of value is any disposition by which the value of a person's estate is reduced. The tax is levied at one of two rates on the transferor, either 0% or 20% in the case of a lifetime transfer (IHTA 1984, s 7(2) & Sch 1). The effect is a mixture of proportional and progressive features, ie the more transfers of value made the higher the average tax liability is likely to be. If the transfer is made on or after 18 March 1986, it is cumulated with all chargeable transfers made in the previous seven years.

A transfer *inter vivos* (eg a gift) will be a transfer of value unless the transfer is exempt or potentially exempt. Where the transfer is for consideration the consideration received will enter into the computation of the value transferred, only the balance being chargeable. However, commercial transactions are not treated as transfers of value, nor are certain other dispositions.

It is necessary to divide transfers of value into those which are immediately chargeable and those which are only potentially chargeable, which the Act chooses to call potentially exempt. Chargeable transfers enter the cumulative total of transfers made by the transferors at once and, if the total goes over the nil rate band, will give a charge to tax straight away. Potentially exempt transfers by contrast do not give rise to a charge straight away and do not enter the transferor's cumulative total of transfers unless and until the donor dies within a period of seven years from the date of the transfer, whereupon they become chargeable as lifetime transfers but at death rates, with reductions if the donor dies more than three years after the gift. Most types of gift are potentially exempt transfers.

Initial direct costs. Those costs incurred by the lessor that are directly associated with negotiating and consummating leasing transactions, such as commissions, legal fees, costs of credit investigations and costs of preparing and processing documents for new leases acquired. [SSAP 21 – Accounting for leases and hire purchase contracts]

Initial repairs. Where a trader acquires an asset which requires extensive repairs before it is in a usable condition, the expenses of those repairs are not deductible since they are as much capital expenditure as the costs of acquiring the asset itself. Were the rule otherwise a trader could convert at least a part of the prospective capital expense into a revenue item by buying the asset in an incomplete state and finishing the work himself, perhaps by employing the person who had worked on it before its acquisition.

In *Law Shipping Co Ltd v IRC (1924), 12 TC 621* a shipping company bought a ship which was at that date ready to sail with freight booked. The Lloyds survey was then overdue but with the consent of the insurers, the ship was allowed to complete the voyage. The ship cost £97,000 and the company had to spend an extra £51,558 on repairs in order for the vessel to pass the survey. Of that sum some £12,000 was in respect of repairs caused by deterioration during the voyage and was allowed by the Revenue, the balance of £39,500 was not, correctly as the Court of Session held. (See also *IRC v Granite City Steamship Co Ltd 1927 SC 705, 13 TC 1* and the expenditure on the branch line in *Highland Rly Co v Balderston (1889) 2 TC 485.*)

Injunction. A writ issuing, prior to the Judicature Acts, only out of Chancery, in the nature of a prohibition or command, by which the party enjoined was commanded to do some act, such as perform his or her contract, or not to do, or to cease from doing, some act, such act not amounting to a crime but rather a breach of an obligation of civil law. Injunctions may now be granted by all Divisions of the High Court and by the Court of Appeal. They are either (1) *interlocutory*, ie provisional or temporary until the hearing of the cause, or (2) *perpetual*.
See MAREVA INJUNCTION.

Inland Revenue. The revenue of the United Kingdom collected or imposed as stamp duties and taxes, and placed under the care and management of the Commissioners of Inland Revenue.

Input tax. When a VAT registered trader accounts for the amount of VAT he is required to pay to HM Customs & Excise, he deducts from the output tax he has charged on supplies he has made the input tax he has paid others on his purchases. 'Input tax', in relation to a taxable person, is defined in statute as:
(*a*) tax on the supply to him of any goods or services; and
(*b*) tax paid or payable by him on the importation of any goods,
being goods or services used for the purpose of any business carried on by him (Value Added Tax Act 1983, s 14(3)).

In re (in the matter of). These words are applied especially (though by no means exclusively) to name a case relating to an estate or a company which is being wound up.

Insider dealing. The taking advantage by a person of knowledge of the affairs of a company enabling him eg to buy or sell its shares at a profit.

There is no civil liability in respect of insider dealing to the detriment of another person (*Percival v Wright [1902] 2 Ch 421*). But, in general, a person who is knowingly connected with a company must not deal on a recognised stock exchange in securities of that company if he has information which (*a*) he holds by virtue of being connected with the company; (*b*) it would be reasonable to expect a person so connected not to disclose except for the proper performance of the functions attaching to the position of which he is so connected; and (*c*) he knows is unpublished price-sensitive information in relation to those securities (see Company Securities (Insider Dealing) Act 1985, s 1(1)). If he does so deal, he is guilty of a criminal offence (see Company Securities (Insider Dealing) Act 1985, s 8).
See RECOGNISED STOCK EXCHANGE; SECURITIES.

Insolvency. Inability to pay debts.

The Act relating to insolvent debtors is now the Insolvency Act 1986.

Insolvency practitioner. A person acting in relation to a company as its liquidator, provisional liquidator, administrator or administrative receiver or as supervisor of a voluntary arrangement approved by the company under Part I of the Insolvency Act 1986 (see Insolvency Act 1986, s 388(1)).

A person acts as an insolvency practitioner in relation to an individual by acting eg as his trustee in bankruptcy or as trustee under a deed of arrangement (see ibid, s 388(2)).

Acting without qualification is an offence (see ibid, s 389). For the required qualification see ibid, ss 390–398.

Insolvent. Under insolvency law, there are two separate tests under which a company can be determined to be insolvent. These are:

(*a*) The company is unable to pay its debts as they fall due; termed the 'commercial insolvency' test (Insolvency Act 1986, s 123(1)(e)).

(*b*) The value of the company's assets is less than the amount of its liabilities, taking into account contingent or prospective liabilities; termed the 'balance sheet' test (Insolvency Act 1986, s 123(2)).

The above are the tests of insolvency; insolvency does not, necessarily, mean that the company must be wound up. A company that is within definition (*b*) is sometimes referred to as 'technically insolvent'. This phrase is used to indicate that the company fulfils the specified criteria but the directors quite properly consider that it has sufficient funds available to continue trading, in the expectation that sufficient profit will be generated so that assets will, in the future, be sufficient to pay liabilities. This is in contrast to 'wrongful trading', which is the situation where directors may be liable for a company's debts if the company continues trading after the point at which it was clear there was no reasonable prospect that the company would avoid going into insolvent liquidation.

See WINDING-UP; WRONGFUL TRADING.

Instalment. (1) A sum of money less than the whole sum due, paid by a debtor in partial payment of the debt, eg the periodic repayments of a mortgage loan under a mortgage agreement.

(2) A sum of money paid eg monthly under a conditional sale agreement or a hire-purchase agreement.

See HIRE-PURCHASE AGREEMENT.

Institute of Chartered Accountants in England and Wales. ICAEW was founded in 1880, being granted its Royal Charter on incorporation. The Institute has 120,000 members. Members use the designatory letters ACA (Associates) and FCA (Fellows). Many members are in practice but a large number of members hold posts in industry. Website: www.icaew.co.uk

Institute of Chartered Accountants in Ireland. ICAI was founded in 1888 and has 12,000 members, who use the designatory letters CA. Website: www.icai.ie

Institute of Chartered Accountants of Scotland. ICAS was founded in 1854 and has 15,000 members. Members use the designation CA. Many members practise outside Scotland. Website: www.icas.org.uk

Instrument. A deed, will, or other formal legal document in writing.

Insurable interest. Insurance cannot be effected unless the insured has 'an insurable interest'; a term to describe the legal or equitable relation in which the insured stands to the subject-matter insured in consequence of which he may benefit by its safety or be prejudiced by its loss (see generally Marine Insurance Act 1906, ss 5–14, and Life Assurance Act 1774, s 1).

Insurance, or **Assurance**, is a contract by which one party, in consideration of a premium, engages to pay money on a given event, eg death, or indemnify another against a contingent loss. The party who pays the premium is called the insured or assured; the party promising to pay is known as the *insurer* or *underwriter* and the instrument is called a policy of insurance.

Insurances are mainly of six kinds:

(1) Marine insurances, which are insurances of ships, goods, and freight, against the perils of the sea, and other dangers mentioned.

(2) Fire insurances, which are insurances of a house or other property, against loss by fire. Losses to property by theft, flood, etc, are of the same type.

(3) Life assurances, which are engagements to pay to the personal representatives of the assured, or to a named third party nominated by him, or into a discretionary trust created under the policy of insurance, for the benefit of relatives of the insured, within a limited period from the date of his death, a specified sum of money. Life assurance contracts are frequently used as investment vehicles. Although a life policy is not a contract of indemnity (as fire and marine policies are), a person can only insure a life in which he or she has an interest, viz, his or her own, his or her debtors', trustees', or spouse.

See INSURABLE INTEREST.

(4) Accident insurances, which are those against personal injuries caused by accidents of all kinds whether to the insured himself or to an employee.

(5) Motor insurances, which are insurances against liability in respect of accidents on the road caused by a motor vehicle and also against loss of or damage to the vehicle belonging to the insured. Compulsory insurance against liability to a third party is required under the Road Traffic Act 1988, Part VI.

(6) Public liability insurances, which are insurances against liability to members of the public, eg in the case of a collapse of a football stand.

Insurance agent. An agent appointed by the insurers, eg to negotiate the terms of the proposal by the insured and to induce him to make a proposal which the insurers are willing to accept (see *Bawden v London, Edinburgh and Glasgow Assurance Co [1982] 2 QB 534 at 539, CA* (per Lord Esher MR)).

Insurance broker. A person acting as an intermediary between the insured and the insurer with a view to the effecting of an insurance policy. The broker is the agent of the insured and not of the insurer. To use the title 'insurance broker' he must be registered under the Insurance Brokers (Registration) Act 1977.

Insurance company. A company to which Part II of the Insurance Companies Act 1982 applies. An insurance group is defined in section 255A of the Companies Act 1985.

Insurance premium tax. The tax is charged on insurance premiums received on or after 1 October 1994, on UK general insurance contracts, other than shipping and aircraft insurance.

The person liable to pay the premium tax is the insurer, provided that he has a business or other establishment in the UK. If the insurer does not have a business or other establishment in the UK, then the tax is payable by the insurer's tax representative. The Insurance Companies Act 1982, s 10 provides that an insurer from outside the UK, which does not have a place of business in the UK, must appoint a UK resident person as its general representative, and that person will normally be the tax representative for the purposes of the insurance premium tax. The tax representation will be responsible for ensuring that the insurer's obligations to comply with the new tax, and his liabilities to account for it, are met. Regulations have been introduced dealing with the appointment and removal of tax representatives.

The tax is under the care and management of Customs and Excise. Insurers who are liable for the tax are required to register with Customs. Regulations deal with the procedural aspects of registration and de-registration. Where a person decides to form an insurance business, and as a result, is likely to be liable for the insurance premium tax, he must notify Customs of that fact.

The tax is equal to 2.5% of the value of premiums received up to 31 March 1997, and 4% thereafter.

There is also a special rate of tax, 17½%, on premiums received on extended maintenance insurance policies, which relate to the sale of goods. This can, however, best be regarded as quasi-VAT, rather than tax on a true insurance premium, designed to attack schemes set up to avoid VAT by labelling a supply as an insurance premium.

Intangible assets. (1) Non-financial fixed assets that do not have physical substance but are identifiable and are controlled by the entity through custody or legal rights.

An identifiable asset is defined by companies legislation as one that can be disposed of separately without disposing of a business of the entity. If an asset can be disposed of only as part of the revenue-earning activity to which it contributes, it is regarded as indistinguishable from the goodwill relating to that activity and is accounted for as such.

In the context of an intangible asset, control is normally secured by legal rights: a franchise or licence grants the entity access to the benefits for a fixed period; a patent or trade mark restricts the access of others. In the absence of legal rights, it is more difficult to demonstrate control. However, control may be obtained through custody. This could be the case where, for example, technical or intellectual knowledge arising from development activity is maintained secretly.

Where it is expected that future benefits will flow to the entity, but those benefits are not controlled through legal rights or custody, the entity does not have sufficient control over the benefits to recognise an intangible asset. For example, an entity may have a portfolio of clients or a team of skilled staff. There may be an expectation that the clients within the portfolio will continue to seek professional services from the entity, or that the team of staff will continue to make their expert skills available to the entity. However, in the absence of custody or legal rights to retain the clients or staff, the entity has insufficient control over the expected future benefits to recognise them as assets.

Software development costs that are directly attributable to bringing a computer system or other computer-operated machinery into working condition for its intended use within the business are treated as part of the cost of the related hardware rather than as a separate intangible asset.

The definition does not encompass assets, such as prepaid expenditure, that are not fixed assets. [FRS 10 – Goodwill and intangible assets & FRS 11 – Impairment of fixed assets and goodwill]

(2) Licences, quotas, patents, copyrights, franchises and trade marks are examples of categories that may be treated as separate classes of intangible assets. Further subdivision may be appropriate, where different types of licence have different functions within the business. Intangible assets that are used within different business segments may be treated as separate classes of intangible assets. [FRS 10 – Goodwill and intangible assets]

Intellectual property. (1) Any patent, trademark, copyright, design right, registered design, technical or commercial information or other intellectual property (Supreme Court Act 1981, s 72).

(2) No stamp duty is chargeable on any contract or transfer relating to the sale or other disposition of intellectual property. This exemption was introduced for documents executed on or after 28 March 2000 (FA 2000, s 129). For the purposes of this exemption 'intellectual property' means patents, trade marks, registered designs, copyrights or design rights, plant breeders' rights and licences or other rights relating to such matters. The sale consideration must be apportioned on a just and reasonable basis where part of the property sold consists of intellectual property (FA 2000, Sch 34, paras 2 & 3). In practice it is understood that the Stamp Office are willing to treat certain types of intellectual property which do not fall within the statutory definition as also exempt and to accept that any goodwill inherent in an item of exempt intellectual property is also exempt.

Intellectual property law. Broadly framed, intellectual property law comprises the law of patents, industrial designs, trade marks and the law of passing off, the law of copyright, and confidential information. Minus copyright, this area of law is sometimes called 'industrial property'. In general, it concerns more or less exclusive rights, ie monopolies, which are regarded as providing a just framework for the exploitation of certain intangible goods in the market place, such as inventions, designs, literary or artistic works, the goodwill associated with a name, and so on. Although by various means the common law and equity provided some protections in respect of these (eg the action for passing off), the protection of trade marks, designs, patents and copyright is generally now by way of statutory regimes.

The three central areas of intellectual property law are the law of trade marks, the law of copyright, and the law of patents. Trade marks are means by which goods or services in the market place are distinguished from others and so are a prime determinant in allowing for the formation and exploitation of goodwill, ie the likelihood that customers will choose to patronise one business over its competitors. By association with a successful product or products, the exclusive right to use a trade mark may itself become an asset of huge value. Trade marks can be seen to have two general functions associated with their association with a product, the 'origin' function, and the 'communication' function. The 'origin' function is their use as a means of indicating the origin of the product involved, therefore allowing consumers who purchase by the trade mark to assume a product of more or less the same quality. More recently, given the nature of modern advertising, the 'communication' function has been stressed: the trade mark is invested in and presented as a symbol of more than a product's origin, but as an image, its merits or qualities, in particular its superiorities vis-à-vis competing products. Clearly, on the latter function, the aesthetic and cultural properties and associations of the trade mark itself are important, as important as its function in merely distinguishing its owner's products from those of competitors, and trade mark law has to some extent been reshaped, both by Parliament and by the courts, in light of these two functions, which clearly do not indicate equivalent regimes of legal protection for trade marks. The best protection for trade marks is acquired upon registration of the trade mark in a public register.

The law of copyright provides creators of aesthetic, cultural, or informational products, with a monopoly on the right to make copies of these products. Historically, for obvious reasons, literary works, 'artistic' works (ie paintings, drawings, and sculptures) and musical compositions were the products protected, but the protection of this area of law has extended to cover films, videos, sound recordings and, more recently, computer programs. Perhaps the most fundamental, though very problematic, distinction in the law of copyright is that between 'expression' and 'idea'. Copyright protects the expression of ideas, not the ideas themselves. The distinction works most well in the case of literary works or pictorial art. Thus copyright protects an historian's book on the second world war, but does not provide him or her with any monopoly on telling about and interpreting the events of the second world war. Similarly, Picasso's *Guernica* is copyright, but not the event it depicts. The distinction becomes much more problematical in the case of musical works, where the 'expression' and the 'idea' are much less distinguishable, and in the case of utilitarian or functional products, such as computer programs whose chief function is to direct the operations of a computer. Copyright 'subsists' in the created work upon its creation, ie the creator (or his or her employer where the work is created under a contract to do so) has copyright from the instant the work comes into being. Registration is not required.

By contrast with copyright, the law of patents provides a monopoly in the use of ideas themselves, in that an inventor may patent a novel and useful invention: for making the invention patent, ie open to all by disclosing the invention in the process of securing the patent, the inventor obtains the exclusive right to work the invention. For several reasons the justification of the law of patents is one of the most contentious areas of dispute in law and legal theory. The technological innovations which patents represent are now typically the result of scientific research, and the award of a patent only to the first inventor (or rather, the first inventor to file for the patent before the invention is published, ie put into the public realm) creates a 'winner takes all' incentive in industrial innovation. Secondly, there is no necessary connection between the effort expended in coming to an invention and the value of the patent that protects it, so that patents can appear to generate huge windfalls out of proportion to any preceding investment. On the other hand, patents may be defended as necessary incentives for the expenditure of money into research and innovation. Patents are granted for a limited time (generally 20 years from date of application), and there is a mass of law governing the scope of the patent monopoly intended to ensure that the monopoly is only so broad as to cover embodiments of the invention but nothing beyond.

The law of intellectual property concerns not only the rules concerning how monopoly rights are acquired, but the scope of such right, ie in which circumstances they are infringed, and much of the law concerns the licensing of such exclusive rights, and the problems to which licensing may give rise.

See TRADE MARK; PATENT.

Intention. (1) In reference to the construction of wills and other documents, the *intention* of a document is the sense and meaning of it as gathered from the words used in it. Parol evidence is not ordinarily admissible to explain it; the main exceptions to the rule being in the case of a latent ambiguity (*see* AMBIGUITY), and in the case of a word or expression having acquired by local custom a sense different from the ordinary sense.

(2) In reference to civil and criminal responsibility, where a person contemplates any result as not unlikely to follow from a deliberate act of his own, he may be said to *intend* that result, whether he desires it or not. Thus, if a man should, for a wager, discharge a gun into a crowd, and any person should be killed, he would be deemed guilty of *intending* the death of such person; for every man is presumed to *intend* the natural consequence of his own actions.

Inter alia. Amongst other things.

Inter vivos. Between living persons; from one living person to another, eg in the case of a gift. Contrasted with a testamentary

gift, one made in a will, or a *donatio mortis causa*, a gift made in anticipation of death.

Interest. (1) The compendious term to describe any right or title to, or estate in, any real or personal property.

(2) Interest. Schedule D, Case III charges income tax on interest. There is no statutory definition of interest. In *Bennett v Ogston (1930) 15 TC 374 at 379*, Rowlatt J defined it as 'payment by time for the use of money'. *Halsbury* defines it as 'the return or compensation for the use or retention by one person of a sum of money belonging to, or owed to, another'. Thus a payment on a loan may be interest but a dividend on a share is not. The use of the word 'interest' is not conclusive; so where the 'interest' was due shortly after the loan and exceeded the principal sum, the court had little difficulty in holding that the payment was not interest (*Ridge Securities Ltd v IRC (1964) 44 TC 373*). The courts have stressed that the payment must be just recompense and so held that an excessive payment could not be interest (*Cairns v MacDiarmid [1982] STC 226*).

Compensation for delay in payment must be distinguished from compensation for delay in performing some other obligation, and payments by time for the use of money from payments by time for non-performance of obligations—the fact that time is used to measure a payment does not suffice to make the payment interest when there is no principal debt (*Re Euro Hotel (Belgravia) Ltd [1975] STC 682, [1975] 3 All ER 1075*). So, suppose that A buys whisky in bond for £100 and A then gives B an option to buy that whisky at any time within six months for £100 plus 'interest' at the rate of 12% per annum from the time A bought the whisky until B exercises the option. If B exercises the option after three months and pays £103 this would be a simple purchase for £103 and not a purchase for £100 plus £3 interest (*Sir Robert Megarry VC in Chevron Petroleum (UK) Ltd v BP Development Ltd [1981] STC 689 at 695j*).

If a lender offers a loan of £90 without interest on condition that the borrower pays £100 in 12 months, the extra £10 will be interest. Moreover if interest is charged but at an unreasonably low rate and the extra sum is geared to the length of the loan, the courts have held the extra sum to be interest even though the parties called it a premium (*IRC v Thomas Nelson & Sons Ltd (1938) 22 TC 175*).

Where normal commercial rates of interest are charged the question whether any 'premium' or discount is taxed as interest is determined according to the following rules laid down in *Lomax v Peter Dixon & Son Ltd [1943] 25 TC 353 at 363*:

(1) if interest is charged at a rate that would be reasonably commercial on a reasonably sound security there is no presumption that a 'discount' or a 'premium' is interest;

(2) the true nature of the payment is a matter of fact rather than of law;

(3) among the factors relevant will be, the contract itself, the term of the loan, the rate of interest expressly stipulated for, the nature of the capital risk, the extent to which, if at all, the parties expressly took or may reasonably be expected to have taken the capital risk into account in fixing the terms of the contract.

The notion that interest is a sort of service charge for the use of money may explain the initial reluctance of the judges to treat as interest for income tax purposes sums awarded by them by way of interest when awarding damages – such sums were treated as extra damages (eg *IRC v Ballantine (1924) 8 TC 595*). In *Riches v Westminster Bank Ltd (1947) 28 TC 159*, however, this approach was held to be wrong. In that case the taxpayer successfully sued a business partner for his share of the profit on a transaction (£36,255) which the partner had concealed. The judge also awarded him £10,028 as interest at 4% since the original deception, exercising his discretion under the Law Reform (Miscellaneous Provisions) Act 1934, s 3. It was held by the House of Lords that the £10,028 was interest. As Lord Simon put it, 'It is not capital. It is rather the accumulated fruit of a tree which the tree produces regularly until payment' (*(1947) 28 TC 159 at 188*).

Interest cost. The expected increase during the period in the present value of the actuarial liability because the benefits are one period closer to settlement. [FRED 20 – Retirement benefits]

Interest held for resale. Interest held exclusively with a view to subsequent resale is one for which a purchaser has been identified or is being sought, and which is reasonably expected to be disposed of within approximately one year of its date of acquisition; or an interest that was acquired as a result of the enforcement of a security, unless the interest has become part of the continuing activities of the group or the holder acts as if it intends the interest to become so. [FRS 2 – Accounting for subsidiary undertakings & FRS 9 – Associates and joint ventures]

Interest held on a long-term basis. An interest that is held other than exclusively with a view to subsequent resale. [FRS 2 – Accounting for subsidiary undertakings]

Interest in land. The general term to describe any right in land itself, from an ownership interest to an incorporeal hereditament of the least kind. The term is especially used to contrast a personal right against an owner of land to enter into, occupy, or use the land in a particular way, which arises from the owner's granting permission, or a 'licence', to do so. Such a right is personal against the owner, and is not an interest in the land itself as would bind a subsequent owner.

See INCORPOREAL HEREDITAMENT.

Interest in possession. The tax statutes do not give a definition for 'interest in possession', however, it has been described by the House of Lords as: 'a present right of present enjoyment' (*Pearson v IRC [1980] STC 318* per Viscount Dilhorn *at 326b*). Where there is an interest in possession, inheritance tax is charged as if the beneficiary with the interest owned the assets in trust. When there is no interest in possession, the property in trust is outside the estate of any one individual and a very different regime applies. The expression is also crucial in that potential exemption may now be given to a trust with an interest in possession but not to one without. In ordinary property law the term is used to distinguish present interests from future interests, such as remainders or reversions. Thus a gift to A for life but with power to pay the income over to someone else is an interest in possession notwithstanding its defeasibility.

In *Pearson v IRC* property was held on trust for specified beneficiaries subject to a power in the trustees to accumulate income for 21 years. The House of Lords held that this power prevented the beneficiaries from having an interest in possession. The basis for the view of the (bare) majority was that an interest in possession was one which gave a present right to present enjoyment; thus, a right to income under the Trustee Act 1925, s 31(1)(ii) suffices for there to be an interest in possession (*Swales v IRC [1984] STC 413*). The beneficiaries had agreed that if there had been a *duty* to accumulate they would not have had a right to present enjoyment. The Revenue argued—successfully—that there was no difference between a duty to accumulate and a power, since the exercise of that power by the trustees would prevent the beneficiaries from having anything to enjoy.

Interest rate in a lease. The interest rate implicit in a lease is the discount rate that, at the inception of the lease, when applied to the amounts which the lessor expects to receive and retain produces an amount (the present value) equal to the fair value of the leased asset. The amounts which the lessor expects to receive and retain comprise (*a*) the minimum lease payments to the lessor, plus (*b*) any unguaranteed residual value, less (*c*) any part of (*a*) and (*b*) for which the lessor will be accountable to the lessee. If the interest rate implicit in the lease is not determinable, it should be estimated by reference to the rate which a lessee would be expected to pay on a similar lease. [SSAP 21 – Accounting for leases and hire purchase contracts]

Interim dividend. A dividend declared at any time between two annual general meetings of a company as distinct from the final dividend (see *Re Jowitt, Jowitt v Keeling [1922] 2 Ch 442*).

See DIVIDEND; FINAL DIVIDEND.

Interpretation of statute. Tax is imposed by statute. The approach to be taken in the interpretation of a tax statute was considered exhaustively in *MacNiven v Westmoreland Investments Ltd [2001] STC 237*. The traditional analysis of the legal function, and especially the judicial function, is in three parts—finding the facts, interpreting the law and applying the law as determined to the facts as discovered. *MacNiven v Westmoreland Investments Ltd* tells us that the authority for tax decisions must be found in the tax legislation and that there is no authority in that tax legislation for depriving a transaction of a particular effect just because of a tax avoidance purpose. *MacNiven v Westmoreland Investments Ltd* establishes two things. The first is that the question whether the court can apply the preordained composite transaction doctrine depends on the particular legislative context; the interpretation of the legislation comes before the characterisation of the facts. The second is that it is not correct simply to talk about a preordained composite transaction doctrine; the doctrine is simply a manifestation of a deeper, and previously unarticulated, view that some terms of the tax legislation must be interpreted in a broad commercial sense rather than in a narrow legalistic or juristic sense. From this it follows that, in applying a concept which is to be interpreted juristically, there is no room for any preordained composite transaction doctrine. If one pushes the case far enough, one can say that there is no room for such a doctrine even when considering a concept which is to be construed commercially since it is simply superfluous.

Intestacy. The rules for the passing of an estate in England and Wales on an intestacy are given in Administration of Estates Act 1925, s 46 and can be summarised as shown in the *table* on *page 136*.

Intra vires (within its powers). The converse of *ultra vires*.

See ULTRA VIRES.

Inventory. (1) A description or list made by an executor or administrator of all the

Intestacy rules. *(see page 135)*

If the intestate	The estate passes
(1) leaves a husband or wife but no issue and no parent, or brother or sister of the whole blood, or issue of a brother or sister of the whole blood	to the surviving husband or wife absolutely

(2) leaves issue	(*a*) personal chattels plus £125,000 to any surviving husband or wife absolutely
	(*b*) one-half remainder to issue
	(*c*) one-half remainder on statutory trust:
	    life tenant: surviving husband or wife
	    remaindermen: issue

(3) leaves a parent, a brother or sister of the whole blood, issue of a brother or sister of the whole blood, but leaves no issue	(*a*) personal chattels plus £200,000 to surviving husband or wife absolutely
	(*b*) one-half remainder to issue
	(*c*) one-half remainder on statutory trust:
	    life tenant: surviving husband or wife
	    remaindermen: parents (or if predeceased, brothers and sisters of the deceased)

(4) leaves issue but no husband or wife	to the issue
(5) leaves both parents but no issue and no husband or wife	to the parents equally
(6) leaves one parent but no issue and no husband or wife	to the surviving parent
(7) leaves no husband or wife, no issue and no parent but leaves another relative	to whichever appears first in the following list: (*a*) brothers and sisters (*b*) half-brothers and half-sisters (*c*) grandparents (*d*) uncles and aunts (*e*) half-uncles and half-aunts
(8) leaves no surviving spouse, no issue and no relative in the categories in (7) above	to the Crown or to the Duchy of Lancaster or to the Duke of Cornwall

goods and chattels of the deceased, which he is bound to deliver to the court if and when lawfully required to do so (see the Administration of Estates Act 1925, s 25).

See ADMINISTRATOR; EXECUTOR.

(2) Any account of goods sold, or exhibited for the purpose of sale.

Investee. An entity in which the investor has invested. [FRS 9 – Associates and joint ventures]

Investment business. The business of engaging in dealing in, or arranging deals in, or managing investments, or giving investment advice (Financial Services Act 1986, s 1(2)).

Investment company. An 'investment company', eligible for relief for its expenses of management, is any company whose business consists wholly or mainly of the making of investments, and the principal part of whose income is derived therefrom (TA 1988, s 130). The term includes savings banks or other banks for savings, investment trusts and unit trusts. In *IRC v Tyre Investment Trust Ltd, KB 1924, 12 TC 646*, the phrase 'the making of investments' was held to mean 'investing'. It is not necessary for an investment company to buy and sell investments regularly, provided that it takes some active interest in the investments which it has made. It follows, therefore, that a holding company formed to hold shares in subsidiary companies will normally qualify as an investment company. On the other hand, a trading company deriving income from the investment of large amounts of surplus cash will not be an investment company until it can establish that the main part of its business consists in the making of investments, and the principal part of its income is derived therefrom.

In 1995 a clutch of appeals on the status of property management companies caused the Special Commissioners to demonstrate the principles to be applied in judging whether a company is an investment company. The test involves considering four points. First, was the company incorporated to acquire assets to turn them to account for the purposes of profit? Second, what are the activities of the company? Third, is the purpose of holding investments to make money from them? Fourth, is the main business of the company the making of investments? (This list is, effectively, a shortened version of the decision of the Special Commissioner in *100 Palace Gardens Terrace v Winter [1995] STC (SCD) 126 at 129f*, in which it was held that the company under consideration, which was set up to manage a block of flats, was not an investment company and, hence, its management expenses are not deductible.)

Investment fund. An entity:

(a) whose business consists of investing its funds mainly in securities, with the aim of spreading investment risk and giving members the benefit of the results of the management of its funds;

(b) none of whose holdings in other entities (except those in other investment funds) represents more than 15% by

value of the investing entity's investments; and

(c) that has not retained more than 15% of the income it derives from securities.

(This definition is based on three of the four conditions defining an investment company in companies legislation – in Great Britain, section 266 of the Companies Act 1985; in Northern Ireland, Article 274 of the Companies (Northern Ireland) Order 1986; and in the Republic of Ireland, section 47 of the Companies (Amendment) Act 1983. Under the definition above, investment companies as defined in companies legislation will qualify as investment funds but so should certain investment entities that are not companies or do not qualify under the companies legislation because they distribute capital.) [FRS 1 – Cash flow statements]

Investment income. Investment income is income which is not earned income.
See EARNED INCOME.

Investment property. An investment property is an interest in land and/or buildings:

(a) in respect of which construction work and development have been completed; and

(b) which is held for its investment potential, any rental income being negotiated at arm's length.

The following are exceptions from the definition:

(a) A property which is owned and occupied by a company for its own purposes is not an investment property.

(b) A property let to and occupied by another group company is not an investment property for the purposes of its own accounts or the group accounts. [SSAP 19/IAS 40 – Accounting for investment properties]

Investment trust. An investment trust is an investment company which by complying with TA 1988, s 842 is exempt from tax on its chargeable gains. This exemption enables the company to switch investments tax-free. All other income of the company, however, is taxed in the usual way. The exemption for CGT does not extend to shareholders. To obtain relief, the company must comply with the conditions in TA 1988, s 842 for, that is throughout, its accounting period although there are extra-statutory concessions for the first accounting period of a new investment trust and for the accounting period in which an investment trust is wound up. The conditions in TA 1988, s 842 are as follows:

(1) The company must be UK resident; it must not be a 'close' company; and every class of its ordinary share capital must be quoted on a recognised stock exchange.

(2) The company's income must be derived wholly or mainly from shares or securities. The Revenue regard this condition as satisfied if 70% of gross income, before expenses, is so derived.

(3) The company's Memorandum and Articles of Association must prohibit the distribution by way of dividend of surpluses arising on the realisation of investments.

(4) The company must not retain, for any accounting period, more than 15% of the income it derives from shares and securities. With effect from 26 July 1990, this rule does not apply to income which cannot be distributed because of a legal restriction. Where the retention exceeds 15% of income, or, if greater, the amounts which cannot be distributed because of a legal restriction, s 842(1)(e) will not be regarded as infringed if the excess does not exceed £10,000.

(5) No holding of shares and securities in a company must represent more than 15% by value of the investing company's investments. This condition does not apply:

 (a) where a holding, when it was acquired, was worth no more than 15% of the then value of the investing company's investments; and

 (b) to shares held in a company which is itself an investment trust, or would be an investment trust if its ordinary share capital was quoted on a stock exchange. Where an investment trust adds to an existing holding by acquiring other shares or securities for a consideration, the entire holding must be revalued at the date of the latest acquisition, to see whether the 15% test is satisfied. The word 'holding' means all the shares and securities in one company. Where an investment trust has two or more subsidiary companies, all its subsidiaries are treated as a single company.

Invoice. A list of goods which have been sold by one person to another, stating the particulars and prices. The invoice is sent by the seller to the buyer, either with the goods or separately by post.

Irrevocable. That which cannot be revoked. Powers of appointment are sometimes executed so as to be irrevocable. A will is never irrevocable.

See POWER; TRUST.

IR35. In the building industry and in the computer industry, it has been common practice for an individual to establish a company to receive fees for work undertaken by that individual alone. With effect from 6 April 2000, the imposition of PAYE and Class 1 NIC is achieved by what has become known as 'the IR35 rules' enacted as FA 2000, s 60 and Sch 12. The essence of these rules is to extract PAYE and NIC from the intermediate company. (The rules also impose a similar liability where the intermediary is a partnership, although this is likely to be rare in practice.) The onus is on the intermediary company to consider the relationship that would have arisen had the individual supplied by the intermediate company received directly from its customer the payments that the customer makes for those services. If the relationship between the customer and the individual undertaking the work would have been one of employer–employee, the intermediate company is obliged to operate PAYE and charge Class 1 NIC on the payments it receives from the customer, subject to specified deductions.

Issue. (1) The children of a man and his wife. (2) Descendants generally (see the Wills Act 1837, s 33).

Issue at a discount. An issue of shares or of debentures at less than their nominal value, eg an issue of shares with a nominal value of £1 at a price of 75p.

Shares must not be issued at a discount (see Companies Act 1985, s 100(1)). Because they do not form part of the capital of the company, debentures may be issued at a discount (see *Re Regent's Canal Ironworks Co (1876) 3 Ch D 43*).

See SHARE; DEBENTURE.

Issue at a premium. An issue of shares at more than their nominal value, eg an issue of shares with a nominal value of £1 at a price of £1.25.

See SHARE PREMIUM ACCOUNT.

Issue costs. The costs that are incurred directly in connection with the issue of a capital instrument, that is, those costs that would not have been incurred had the specific instrument in question not been issued. [FRS 4 – Capital instruments]

Issued share capital. The nominal value of the shares of a company actually issued.

J

Joint account clause. Where two or more persons advance money and take a mortgage to themselves jointly, the rule in equity is that they are tenants in common, and, therefore, the survivor is a trustee for the personal representatives of the deceased mortgagee. (*See* COMMON, TENANCY IN). To avoid this it became usual, where trustees lend money on mortgage, to insert what is known as a joint account clause in the mortgage deed declaring that on the death of one of the mortgagees the receipt of the survivor shall be a sufficient discharge for the money, and that the survivor shall be able to re-convey the land without the concurrence of the personal representatives of the deceased trustee. The Law of Property Act 1925, s 111, provides that where the sum advanced on mortgage is expressly stated to be lent on a joint account or the mortgage is made to the mortgagees jointly, the money lent shall be deemed to belong to the mortgagees on a joint account, and the survivor shall be able to give a complete discharge for the money.

See MORTGAGE.

Joint and several liability. When two or more persons declare themselves jointly and severally bound, this means that they render themselves liable to a joint action against all, as well as to a separate action against each, in case the conditions of the bond or agreement are not complied with. This means that each may be sued for the entire amount of a claim. The party to whom they are so jointly and severally bound is called a joint and several creditor. Where two or more persons whose negligence has together caused a person injury, they are generally jointly and severally liable to such person. An individual who, as one jointly and severally liable, has paid the entirety of the claim, may bring an action for contribution from the others jointly and severally liable.

Joint arrangement. A contractual arrangement under which the participants engage in joint activities that do not create an entity because it would not be carrying on a trade or business of its own. A contractual arrangement where all significant matters of operating and financial policy are predetermined does not create an entity because the policies are those of its participants not of a separate entity. [FRS 9 – Associates and joint ventures]

Joint control. A reporting entity jointly controls a venture with one or more other entities if none of the entities alone can control that entity but all together can do so and decisions on financial and operating policy essential to the activities, economic performance and financial position of that venture require each venturer's consent. [FRS 9 – Associates and joint ventures]

Joint stock bank. The name given to banking companies other than the Bank of England.

Joint tenancy. Where an estate is acquired by two or more persons in the same land, by the same title, not being a title by descent, and at the same period; and (if created by a written instrument) without any words importing that the parties are to take in distinct shares. The principal feature of this tenancy is that on the death of one of the parties his share accrues to the others by survivorship. Joint tenants are said to be seised *per my et per tout*. In joint tenancy there are four unities, viz, of possession, interest, title and time. By the Law of Property Act 1925, s 36, it is provided that where a legal estate (not being settled land) is beneficially limited to or held in trust for any persons as joint tenants, it shall be held on trust for sale, but not so as to sever their joint tenancy in equity. And see Part IV of Sch 1 to that Act.

A joint tenancy is distinguished from a tenancy in common.

See COMMON, TENANCY IN.

The phrase is also applied to the holding of personal property under the like conditions.

Joint venture. An entity in which the reporting entity holds an interest on a long-term basis and is jointly controlled by the reporting entity and one or more other venturers under a contractual arrangement. [FRS 9 – Associates and joint ventures]

Judgment. The sentence or order of the court in a civil or criminal proceeding.

Judgment creditor. A creditor by virtue of a judgment, eg a plaintiff (or claimant) who has successfully sued a defendant and received an award of damages is a judgment creditor of the defendant, who is a judgment debtor; ie a party entitled to enforce execution under a judgment.

Judgment debt. A debt due under a judgment.

Judgment debtor. A person against whom a judgment ordering him to pay a sum of money stands unsatisfied, and who is liable therefore to have his property taken in execution under the judgment.

Judgment summons. A summons issued on the application of a person entitled to enforce a judgment or order under the Debtors Act 1869, s 5 requiring a person, or where two or more persons are liable under the judgment or order, requiring any one or more of them, to appear and be examined on oath as to his or their means (see County Courts Act 1984, s 147(1)).

Judicial review. A procedure used for certain forms of relief:
(i)   an order of *mandamus*, prohibition or *certiorari*;
(ii)   an injunction to restrain persons from acting in offices in which they are not

entitled to act (see Supreme Court Act 1981, s 31).

A way of challenging a decision of the Revenue is by judicial review, a remedy equally applicable to a challenge to the procedure adopted by Commissioners. The most usual obstacle is that the court will not allow an applicant to use judicial review where the point should be dealt with by appeal. In *R v IRC, ex p Preston [1985] STC 282, HL*, Lord Scarman said: 'a remedy by way of judicial review is not to be made available where an alternative remedy exists . . . Where parliament has provided by statute an appeal procedure, as in the taxes statutes, it will only be very rarely that the courts will allow the collateral process of judicial review to be used to attack an appealable decision' (see also *Re McGuichion [2000] STC 65 CA (NI)*). Conversely, allegations of unfairness in the conduct of the appeal by the General Commissioners are matters for judicial review and not for appeal (*Mellor v Gurney [1994] STC 1025*). When judicial review is sought the rules of judicial review must be followed; so where review is sought for a Revenue failure to decide between two courses of action with regard to an assessment the remedy is an order of *mandamus* to compel the Revenue to decide and not an order quashing the original assessment (*Wang v Commissioner of Inland Revenue [1994] STC 753, PC*). The second is by arguing that the assessment is *ultra vires* (*IRC v Aken [1990] STC 497, CA*). This line of argument has been used—unsuccessfully—to argue that the profits of prostitution could not be taxable since, as a matter of law, the profits of an illegal activity cannot be subject to tax. An inspector does not act *ultra vires* merely because he makes a mistake of law.

K

Key management. Those persons in senior positions having authority or responsibility for directing or controlling the major activities and resources of the reporting entity. [FRS 8 – Related party disclosures]

Know-how. Any industrial information and techniques likely to assist in the manufacture or processing of goods or materials, or in the working of a mine, oil well, etc, or in the carrying out of any agricultural, forestry or fishing operations (Income and Corporation Taxes Act 1988, s 533(7)).

L

LCJ. Lord Chief Justice.

LIBOR. London Inter Bank Offered Rate.

LIFO. Last in first out.

LJ. Lord Justice of Appeal.

Land. (1) Generally not only arable ground, meadow, pasture, woods, moors, waters, etc, but also messuages (*see* MESSUAGE) and houses; including everything of a permanent and substantial nature. Thus, an action to recover possession of a pool must be brought for so much land covered with water, etc. The word 'land' is used in a wide sense in the Law of Property Act 1925. It includes 'land of any tenure, and mines and minerals, whether or not held apart from the surface, buildings or parts of buildings (whether the division is horizontal, vertical or made in any other way) and other corporeal hereditaments; also a manor, an advowson, and a rent (*see* RENT) and other incorporeal hereditaments and an easement (*see* EASEMENT), right, privilege, or benefit in, over, or derived from land; but not an undivided share in land' (see s 205(1)(ix)).

See REAL AND PERSONAL PROPERTY; PROPERTY.

(2) The provisions under the Capital Gains Tax Acts do not customarily refer to 'land' but to 'an interest in land'. 'Land' includes 'messuages, tenements and hereditaments, housings and buildings of any tenure' (TCGA 1992, s 288(1)) and any 'right in or over land' (Interpretation Act 1978, Sch 1). Hence, any reference in the Capital Gains Tax Acts to 'land' includes an interest in a building, even though the land underneath may be in separate ownership.

Unsurprisingly, in determining whether an asset is located in the UK or elsewhere, any interest in land is to be treated as situated where the land is situated, except for an interest that is solely in the land acting as security (TCGA 1992, s 275(1)). A debt secured on land is located where the creditor is resident (TCGA 1992, s 275(1) & (2)).

Freehold land is never a wasting asset, whatever its nature and whatever the nature of the buildings and works on it. A lease with 50 or fewer years to run is a wasting asset (TCGA 1992, s 44(1)(a)).

As a result of the wide definition of 'land', the Revenue consider that rollover relief is potentially available on the grant of an option over land, despite the treatment in TCGA 1992, s 144 where an option is regarded as separate from the asset itself.

In *Faulks v Faulks [1982] 15 EG 15* a milk quota was treated as an interest in the land to which it related. In a press release, the Inland Revenue stated that this case was not a tax case and does not affect the CGT treatment; the Revenue maintaining that a quota is an asset separable from land. The practical effect of the distinction is, however, made of less importance by FA 1988, s 112 and FA 1993, s 86 which provide that rollover relief is available for milk quotas, potato quotas and suckler cow premium quotas.

Landfill tax. Landfill tax is a tax on the disposal of waste in landfill sites such as tips and disused quarries. Site operators are accountable for the tax which applies to disposals on or after 1 October 1996 (FA 1996, s 40). All waste disposed of by a landfill at licensed sites is liable to tax whether or not a charge is made for its disposal.

The stated objective of tax is, at least in part, to act as an incentive to reduce waste and to encourage other means of waste disposal less damaging to the environment than landfill disposal.

The tax is administered by Customs and Excise.

Landlord. A person of whom lands and tenements are leased; a lessor; who has a right to distrain for rent in arrears, etc, the *tenant* being the person in possession of the lands by the lease.

Lands Tribunal. A tribunal with powers to determine questions relating to the compulsory acquisition of land, etc. Constituted under the Lands Tribunals Act 1949.

See APPEAL.

Lapse. (1) The failure of a testamentary disposition in favour of any person, by reason of the death of the intended beneficiary in the lifetime of the testator. In two cases, however, of the intended beneficiary dying in the testator's lifetime, there is no lapse. The first case is that of a devise of real estate to any person for an *estate tail* (*see* ESTATE), where any issue who would inherit under such entail are living at the testator's death. The second case is that of a devise or bequest to a *child* or *other issue* of the testator, leaving issue, any of whom are living at the testator's death (see the Wills Act 1837, ss 32, 33).

(2) The lapse of an insurance policy occurs when it is not renewed at or before the expiration of the current period of insurance or of the days of grace, if any. The insured cannot enforce it in respect of any claim arising afterwards (see *Webb and Hughes v Bracey [1964] 1 Lloyd's Rep 465*).

Last in first out. LIFO is one of the two basic methods of valuing stocks, or finished goods. The value of goods in stock is calculated on the assumption that the withdrawals from stock represent items most recently added to stock.

Lease. A grant of land, giving possession of the land, but not a grant of a freehold estate. Also called a demise or letting of lands or tenements. The grantor is called the *lessor*, the grantee the *lessee*. Leases may be granted for a term of years (ie a defined period) or for life, or at will (ie for no certain time, but merely until the lessor demands the giving up of the land), and usually a rent is demanded. The interest created by the lease must be *less* than the lessor has in the premises, or it is not a *lease* but an *assignment*. By the Law of Property Act 1925, ss 53, 54 all leases except those not exceeding three years and with a rent of not less than two-thirds of the improved annual value must be by deed.

In accounting standards, a lease is defined as:

A lease is a contract between a lessor and a lessee for the hire of a specific asset. The lessor retains ownership of the asset but conveys the right to use of the asset to the lessee for an agreed period of time in return for the payment of specified rentals. The term 'lease' as used in this statement also applies to other arrangements in which one party retains ownership of an asset but conveys the right to the use of the asset to another party for an agreed period of time for specified payments. [SSAP 21 – Accounting for leases and hire purchase contracts]

Lease term. The lease term is the period for which the lessee has contracted to lease the asset and any further terms for which the lessee has the option to continue to lease the asset, with or without further payment, which option it is reasonably certain at the inception of the lease that the lessee will exercise. [SSAP 21 – Accounting for leases and hire purchase contracts]

Leasehold. Any interest in land less than freehold. But, in practice, the word is generally applied to an estate for a fixed term of years.

Ledger. Traditionally, a ledger was a large book, with a separate page for each account required for the enterprise. Normally, every enterprise required a nominal ledger containing the accounts required to bring together the accounting system, a sales ledger, containing the accounts for the individual customers of the enterprise, and a purchase ledger, containing the accounts for the suppliers to the enterprise. With computerisation, the sales and purchases ledgers have continued, albeit computerised, but the nominal ledger has effectively been replaced by an electronically based double entry system, often run on a bespoke accounting package or, alternatively, using an extended trial balance (ETB).

Legacy. A bequest or gift of goods and chattels by will. A legacy may be either specific, demonstrative, or general:

(1) A *specific legacy* is a bequest of a specific part of the testator's personal estate.

(2) A *demonstrative legacy* is a gift by will of a certain sum directed to be paid out of a specific fund.

(3) A *general legacy* is one payable out of the general assets of the testator.
See ADEMPTION OF A LEGACY.

Legal estate. An estate in land, fully recognised as such in a court of Common Law, has been hitherto called the 'legal estate'.

Legal obligation. An obligation that derives from:

(a) a contract (through its explicit or implicit terms);

(b) legislation; or

(c) other operation of law.

[FRS 12 – Provisions, contingent liabilities and contingent assets]

Lessee. A person to whom a lease is granted. See LEASE.

Lessor. A person by whom a lease is granted.

Letter of comfort. When a bank lends money to a subsidiary company, it is usual for the bank to request a letter of comfort from the parent company, in which that company records that it is aware of the subsidiary's borrowing, it supports the borrowing application and the intention of the parent is for the subsidiary to remain in business. There are often specific assurances, and, frequently, guarantees required by a bank, which may be appended to a letter of comfort.

Letter of credit. A letter written by one person (usually a merchant or bank) to another, requesting him to advance money, or entrust goods to the bearer, or to a particular person by name, and for which the writer's credit is pledged. It may be either *general*, addressed to all merchants or other persons, or *special*, addressed to a particular person by name. It is not negotiable.

Letter of engagement. See ENGAGEMENT LETTER.

Letter of representation. Before an Auditors' Report is signed, it is normal for the auditor to require from the directors of the company concerned (or their equivalent in the case of a non-corporate body) a letter in which the directors give the factual information on which the accounts are based. A letter of representation will always include confirmation that the auditor has had access to all relevant books and records required for the construction of the accounts; the letter may also specify any legal claims against the enterprise of which the directors are aware and any post-Balance Sheet events that have arisen that are material to the accounts.

Liabilities. An entity's obligations to transfer economic benefits as a result of past transactions or events. [FRS 5 – Substance of transactions, FRS 12 – Provisions, contingent liabilities and contingent assets]

Liability method. The method of computing deferred tax whereby it is calculated at the rate of tax that it is estimated will be applicable when the timing differences reverse. Under the liability method deferred tax not provided is calculated at the expected long-term tax rate. [SSAP 15 – Accounting for deferred tax]

Licence. In real property law, an authority to do an act which would otherwise be a trespass. A licence to enter or occupy land passes no interest (*see* INTEREST IN LAND), and, therefore, if A grants to B the right to fasten boats to moorings in a river, this does not amount to a demise, nor does it give the licensee an exclusive right to the use of the moorings.

Licensee. A person who enters premises with the permission of the occupier, granted either GRATUITOUSLY or for CONSIDERATION.

Lien. (1) As applied to personalty (*see* PERSONALTY), a lien is the right of an agent or a bailee to retain the possession of a chattel entrusted to him until his claim upon it is satisfied.
See BAILMENT; GENERAL LIEN.

(2) As applied to realty, a *vendor's lien* for unpaid purchase-money is his right to enforce his claim on the land sold; a right which is recognised in a court of equity,

subject to the doctrines of that court for the protection of *bona fide* purchasers for valuable consideration without notice.

See VENDOR'S LIEN.

(3) As applied to the sale of goods, the unpaid seller has a lien under the Sale of Goods Act 1979, ss 41–43.

(4) Accountants' lien: Until a client has paid the fee for the preparation of his accounts, it is said that the accountant who has prepared the accounts and has not been paid has a lien over the client's books from which the accounts have been prepared. The Institute of Chartered Accountants in England & Wales advises members that they should not assume that such a right will be upheld by the Court.

Life annuity. *See* ANNUITY.

Life assurance. A transaction whereby in consideration of a single or periodical payment of premium a sum of money is secured to be paid on the death of the person whose life is assured or on his reaching a specified age.

See INSURANCE, QUALIFYING POLICY.

Lifting the veil is where the court ignores the principle of corporate personality (*see* CORPORATE PERSONALITY, PRINCIPLE OF) and looks at the economic reality of the situation, eg where (i) the membership of the company falls below two, as required by the Companies Act 1985, s 1(1); (ii) an officer of the company signs a bill of exchange on behalf of the company without any mention of the company's name on it contrary to the Companies Act 1985, s 349(4); (iii) there has been fraudulent trading (*see* FRAUDULENT TRADING); (iv) the company is a 'sham'; (v) it is believed in time of war that the company is controlled by alien enemies (see *Daimler Co Ltd v Continental Tyre & Rubber Co Ltd [1916] 2 AC 307, HL*).

See COMPANY LAW.

Limitation of actions. *See* LIMITATION, STATUTES OF.

Limitation of liability. The limitation of liability of members of a company according to their shareholdings.

See COMPANY; COMPANY LAW.

Limitation, statutes of. A statute of limitation is one which provides that no court shall entertain proceedings for the enforcement of certain rights if such proceedings were set on foot after the lapse of a definite period of time, reckoned as a rule from the date of the violation of the right. Various statutes have been passed with this object; they were consolidated with amendments by the Limitation Act 1980. The Act provides, *inter alia*, that actions founded on simple contract and tort should not be brought after the expiration of six years from the date on which the cause of action accrued; that an action on a specialty may not be brought after the expiration of twelve years; that, in general, no action may be brought to recover land after the expiration of twelve years from the date when the right of action accrued.

Limited company. A company in which the liability of each shareholder is limited by the number of shares which he has taken or by guarantee, so that he cannot be called on to contribute beyond the amount of his shares or guarantee (see generally the Companies Act 1985).

See COMPANY; COMPANY LAW.

Limited executor. An executor of a deceased person for certain limited purposes, or for a certain limited time.

See EXECUTOR.

Limited interest. The charge to income tax on income arising from a beneficiary's entitlement to an estate of a deceased person depends on whether the beneficiary's interest is absolute or limited (TA 1988, s 696 cf s 695). A beneficiary has a limited interest if he does not have an absolute interest but would have a right to income if administration were complete (TA 1988, s 701(3)).

Limited liability. *See* LIMITED COMPANY; COMPANY LAW.

Limited liability partnership. A limited liability partnership is treated in law as a 'body corporate' and is subject to aspects of company law (Limited Liability Partnership Act 2000, s 1; TA 1988, s 118ZA). However, for tax purposes, the same treatment is applied to the assessment of the profits enjoyed by individual partners as would be applied if the partnership were not a limited liability partnership (Limited Liability Partnership Act 2000, s 10). That is, a limited liability partnership is treated as transparent for tax purposes and each partner is assessed to tax on his individual share of the limited liability partnership's income (TA 1988, ss 111 & 114). An individual who is a partner in a limited liability partnership is entitled to claim interest relief on a loan raised in order to provide capital for the partnership (TA 1988, s 362(1)). However, a partner's undrawn profits in a limited liability partnership are a debt of that entity and are not part of the individual partner's capital, unless there is an agreement between the partners to override the general provision. Consequently, when calculating any loss relief available to an individual partner, the ceiling is applied without reference to the individual partner's undrawn profits (TA 1988, ss 117 & 118ZA–118ZD).

Where there is a liability to negligence, for which an individual partner takes personal responsibility, the capital contribution made by that individual partner to the limited liability partnership is treated as an addition of capital subscribed for the purpose of computing loss relief (TA 1988, s 63A and FA 1994, Sch 20, para 4).

Where an ordinary partnership converts to a limited liability partnership, the conversion is ignored for tax purposes. Hence, the individual partners' overlap profit relief continues, unaffected by the change of legal liability. If, conversely, a limited liability partnership is created to take over only a part of a former partnership's trade, which is not recognisably 'the business' that was previously carried on by the unlimited partnership, the cessation provisions are triggered, including the triggering of overlap profit relief against the profits brought into assessment (see TA 1988, ss 63 & 63A(3)).
See PARTNERSHIP.

Limited owner. A tenant for life, in tail or by curtesy, or other person not having a fee simple in his absolute disposition (see the Settled Land Act 1925, s 20).
See SETTLED LAND.

Limited partner. A member of a limited partnership who at the time of entering into it contributes to it a sum or sums as capital or property valued at a stated amount, and who is not liable for the debts or obligations of the firm beyond the amount so contributed (Limited Partnerships Act 1907, s 4(2)).
See LIMITED PARTNERSHIP.

Limited partnership. A partnership consisting of one or more persons called 'general partners', who are liable for all the debts and obligations of the firm, and one or more persons called 'limited partners' who at the time of entering into the partnership contribute a stated amount of capital, and are not liable for the obligations of the firm beyond that amount (see the Limited Partnerships Act 1907).
See PARTNERSHIP.

Lineal descendant. *See* DESCENDANT.

Liquid assets. Cash and assets that can readily be turned into cash, such as trade debts. (Whether marketable investments are regarded as liquid assets depends on the view taken by the enterprise as to the ease with which they can be encashed.) The ratio liquid assets: current liabilities is an indication of the liquidity of the enterprise.

Liquid resources. Current asset investments held as readily disposable stores of value. A readily disposable investment is one that:
(*a*) is disposable by the reporting entity without curtailing or disrupting its business; and
(*b*) is either:
  (i) readily convertible into known amounts of cash at or close to its carrying amount, or
  (ii) traded in an active market.
[FRS 1 – Cash flow statements]

Liquidated damages. An ascertained amount, expressed in pounds and pence, which an injured party has sustained, or is taken to have sustained. A term in a contract may specify an amount of liquidated damages for a breach of which the breaching party is bound to pay; the purpose of such a clause is to avoid the necessity of proving the extent of loss, and thus damages, at trial. The term is used in contradistinction to a penalty. Terms in contracts imposing penalties for breach are not generally enforceable at law.

See CONTRACT LAW.

Liquidation. The winding-up of a company.

See LIQUIDATOR.

Liquidation committee. A committee appointed by the creditors and members of a company in liquidation to exercise the functions conferred on the committee by the Insolvency Act 1986 (see Insolvency Act 1986, ss 101, 141).

Liquidator. An officer appointed to conduct the winding-up of a company; to bring and defend actions and suits in its name, and to do all necessary acts on behalf of the company. He may be appointed either by resolution of the shareholders in a voluntary winding-up, or by the Court in a compulsory winding-up (see the Insolvency Act 1986, ss 91, 135–140).

See OFFICIAL LIQUIDATOR.

Liquidity. The extent to which the liquid assets of the enterprise enable it to satisfy the current liabilities.

Listed building. A building which is included in a list compiled or approved by the Secretary of State under the Planning (Listed Buildings and Conservation Areas) Act 1990, s 1 (Planning (Listed Buildings and Conservation Areas) Act 1990, s 1(5)).

Works affecting such buildings are restricted: ibid, ss 7–22.

Listed security. A security that is quoted on a recognised Stock Exchange. For the London Stock Exchange, a listed security is one with a quotation on the Official List of Securities.

Listing requirements. The conditions to be satisfied before a security can be traded on a Stock Exchange. For the London Stock Exchange, these are specified in the Yellow Book.

Livestock. Cattle (bulls, cows, oxen, heifers or calves), sheep, goats, swine, horses (including asses and mules), or poultry (domestic fowls, turkeys, geese or ducks) (see Dogs (Protection of Livestock) Act 1953, s 3). In Part I of the Agriculture Act 1967, the term is limited to cattle, sheep and pigs; whereas under the Agriculture Act 1947, s 109, it includes any creature kept for the production of food, wool, skins or furs, or for the purpose of its use in the farming of land.

By the Animals Act 1971, s 11 the word 'livestock' means cattle, horses, asses, mules, hinnies, sheep, pigs, goats and poultry and also deer not in the wild state, and, in cases where dogs cause injury or death to them, pheasants, partridges and grouse in captivity.

Living together. Where a husband and wife are living together, any transfer of assets from one to the other is treated as a disposal without a chargeable gain arising (TCGA 1992, s 58(1)). Statute states that a husband and wife shall be treated as living together unless (*a*) they are separated under an order of a Court of Competent Jurisdiction, or by a Deed of Separation, or (*b*) they are in fact separated in such circumstances that the separation is likely to be permanent (TA 1988, s 282 applied to CGT by TCGA 1992, s 288(3)).

From the start of the fiscal year following a year in which the couple cease to live together, any transfer of assets is treated as giving rise to a CGT disposal. If the transfer is then in consideration of divorce or otherwise in recognition of a liability that one has to the other, holdover relief is not available. In the House of Lords, Lord Brightman described these provisions by saying that on looking to this section for guidance, 'the answer was Delphic' (*Gubay v Kington [1984] STC 99 at 115b*). In that case, the House of Lords ruled that, whatever the meaning of 'living together' when applied to CGT, it cannot cause a gain made by a non-resident wife to be charged on a UK resident husband.

Lloyd's. An association in the City of London regulated by Lloyd's Act 1982. Its members are (i) underwriters who undertake liability on contracts of insurance; and (ii) brokers who act as intermediaries between underwriters and persons wishing to effect insurances with them.

Loan note. A document entitling the owner to repayment of a loan. Many loan notes are tradeable; some are listed on a stock market.

Loan relationship. For corporation tax but not for income tax, all income from corporate and government debt is subject to a single regime called 'loan relationships'. The regime brings together interest arising on debt and the gain or loss arising from the holding of a financial instrument. The old distinctions between income and capital are swept away. The loan relationships regime affects not only income received under but also expenditure incurred, eg sums paid out. In the new regime the distinction between yearly interest and short interest remains of importance only in respect of withholding tax, the distinction is abolished for the purpose of establishing deductibility.

Statute defines a 'loan relationship' in one of two separate ways. First, a loan relationship arises where a company is a debtor or a creditor in respect of a money debt which arose as a result of a transaction for the lending of money (FA 1996, s 81(1)), so finance leases and hire-purchase contracts are not loan relationships. Second, it also arises where an instrument is issued for the purpose of representing security for, or the rights of a creditor or in respect of, a debt (FA 1996, s 81(3)). One of the critical words here is 'security'; the issue of an insurance policy is not the issue of a security, nor is the issue of a share (FA 1996, s 81(4)).

For the first alternative definition, a money debt is defined as one which falls to be settled by the payment of money or the transfer of a right to settlement, such as by the issue of a security (FA 1996, s 81(2)).

The second definition is provided to bring loan notes and promissory notes within the legislation. If there is no instrument issued, a debt does not fall within the second definition. In particular, 'it does not extend to invoices or payments under guarantee . . . If there is a loan of money, the promissory note is covered; if there is not, then it is not'.

A guarantee is outside the scope of the provisions since, in order for a loan relationship to exist the company must be a creditor or a debtor (FA 1996, s 81(1)) and a guarantor is not, itself, in that relationship.

Loan societies. Those established for advancing money on loan to the industrial classes (see the Loan Societies Act 1840).

Local currency. The currency of the primary economic environment in which an entity operates and generates net cash flows. [SSAP 20 – Foreign currency translation]. (FRS 13 'Derivatives and other financial instruments' uses the term 'Functional currency' rather than the term 'local currency', although the definitions of the two terms are identical.)

London Inter Bank Offered Rate. LIBOR is the rate at which the clearing banks lend to each other. Unlike bank base rate, LIBOR varies from day to day. Interest on loan by a bank to its customer may be specified as a margin above LIBOR, rather than a margin above base rate, but this is less frequently found than previously.

London Stock Exchange. This is now a colloquial term for the International Stock Exchange of the UK and Republic of Ireland, which took over the business of the London Stock Exchange on 27 October 1986 ('the big bang'). The London Stock Exchange runs two markets: the main market (which has its origins in the 17th century) for listed companies and the alternative investment market (AIM), created in 1995 to provide a market for certain unlisted companies.

Long life asset. The rationale for capital allowances being given to a trader in computing the profits charged to income tax, or corporation tax, is that the allowance is a substitute for depreciation that is charged in the financial accounts of the enterprise. For the majority of items of machinery and plant, the writing-down allowance at 25% per annum on a reducing balance basis is likely to give a tax allowance that is of the same order as the depreciation charged in the financial accounts. This is not the case where the asset is an electricity generating station or an aircraft with a useful life of 30 years. The privatisation of the utility companies and the transport companies threw a spotlight on the difference between the tax treatment and the accounting treatment of such long life assets. For expenditure after 25 November 1996, the capital allowance for machinery and plant is at 6% per annum (instead of 25% pa) when the asset purchased is a 'long life asset'. (Subject to *de minimis* provisions.)

A 'long life asset' is defined in CAA 2001, s 91 as: 'plant or machinery which . . . can reasonably be expected to have a useful economic life of at least 25 years'. The test is applied when the item is new, even when the trader purchases it second-hand. 'Useful economic life' is defined, in turn, as starting when first brought into use by any person for any purpose and ending when it is no longer likely to be used by anyone as a fixed asset.

The Revenue have published their view as to what constitutes a long life asset. The Revenue accept as not long life assets not only assets that are expected to be worn out within 25 years but also assets purchased for a specific production run that is not likely to last for 25 years, or where the product is likely to be obsolete within that period, as long as the asset is not expected to be readily saleable at the end of that period. Where the asset is purchased to serve a specific contract that is likely not to be renewed to run over the 25-year period, the Revenue accept that the asset is not a long life asset. Different treatment can be applied to different entities that operate together. The example is given of jets for long haul flights depreciated over 20 years but, based on past experience of similar aircraft, it is likely that the planes will continue in service for more than 25 years, perhaps with non-UK airlines. Such jets would be considered to be long life assets. However, if the engines for these jets are depreciated over fifteen years (being the projected life of the engine in flying hours divided by the planned use per annum) these engines would be accepted as not being long life assets.

Long-term contract. A contract entered into for the design, manufacture or con-struction of a single substantial asset or the provision of a service (or a combination of assets or services which together constitute a single project) where the time taken substantially to complete the contract is such that the contract activity falls into different accounting periods. A contract that is required to be accounted for as long-term by this accounting standard will usually extend for a period exceeding one year. However, a duration exceeding one year is not an essential feature of a long-term contract. Some contracts with a shorter duration than one year should be accounted for as long-term contracts if they are sufficiently material to the activity of the period that not to record turnover and attributable profit would lead to distortion of the period's turnover and results such that the financial statements would not give a true and fair view, provided that the policy is applied consistently within the reporting entity and from year to year. [SSAP 9 – Stocks and long-term contracts]

Loss. (1) Generally, any disadvantage that may be compensated by an award of damages, ie money compensation. It can include, in particular in respect of profits lost due to a breach of contract, a loss by not getting what one might get, as well as a loss by parting with or destruction of what one has.

(2) An excess of expenditure over income in a profit and loss account.

(3) In closely prescribed circumstances a loss may give rise to a relief from tax by being set against an equivalent amount of income and relieving that income from any liability to tax. The following are the major categories of loss relief:

(a) *trading loss: set off against general income of that and the preceding year*
   If one sustains a loss in one's trade, profession or vocation the correct figure for the profits chargeable to income tax for the year is nil. One may then claim relief under TA 1988, s 380.

(b) *trading loss: relief against capital gains*
   Where the person's trading loss cannot be set against general income of that year and relief has not been given in

any other way, it may be set against chargeable capital gains realised in that year under FA 1991, s 72.

(c) *trading loss: rolling forward*
To the extent that relief for the allowable loss has not been given against general income either under TA 1988, s 380 or some other provision the loss may be carried forward and set off, not against the general income of subsequent years, but only against the future profits (if any) of the trade under TA 1988, s 385(1).

(d) *trading loss: incorporation of business*
If the business is transferred to a company and the sole or main consideration is the transfer of shares of the company to the individual, the individual can claim relief against income derived by him from the company, whether by dividend or otherwise, for example under a service agreement, but the loss must be set off against earned income before being set off against distributions. Relief is obtained by a claim under TA 1988, s 386.

(e) *trading loss in early years of trading*
A carry back of a trading loss is allowed where the loss arises in the first four years of business. The loss may be carried back and set off against *general* income for the three years before that in which the loss is sustained by means of a claim under TA 1988, s 381.

(f) *trading loss in the period leading to cessation of a trade*
Once a trade, profession or vocation has been permanently discontinued, a terminal loss may be carried *back* and set off against the profits charged under Schedule D in respect of the trade for the three years last preceding that in which the trade ends, by means of a claim under TA 1988, s 388.

(g) *Schedule E losses*
TA 1988, s 380 purports to give relief for a loss sustained in an employment (although not to offices). However, the Revenue do not accept that a claim can ever arise—even when expenses exceed emoluments. This is because TA 1988, s 198 only allows expenses to be deducted if they are defrayed 'out of' emoluments.

(h) *Schedule D, Case VI loss*
Relief can be claimed under TA 1988, s 392 against other Case VI income of that year and then rolled forward and set against other Case VI income of later years; however, the statutes which place certain types of income in Case VI often restrict their use to absorb losses.

(i) *Schedule D, Case V loss*
A loss arising from a trade or profession carried on wholly overseas can be given relief under TA 1988, ss 380, 385 or 388 but only against other foreign income.

(j) *Schedule A loss*
The general rule is that the rents from all properties in the UK are aggregated and expenditure is deducted from the aggregate. This automatically provides loss relief for a deficit on a single property, where there is other property let to provide a surplus. TA 1988, s 379A(1) provides that any net losses may be rolled forward indefinitely and set off against any profit of a Schedule A business carried on in a subsequent year.

(k) *Losses on unquoted shares in trading companies*
Although capital losses are the province of CGT and may not be set off against income, an exception is made where the loss arises from the disposal of unquoted shares in a trading company or member of a trading group. Relief under TA 1988, s 574 is available in respect of shares for which the individual or his spouse subscribed.

(l) *Capital losses*
The charge to capital gains tax is levied on the aggregate of chargeable gains less allowable losses in a year of assessment (TCGA 1992, s 2(2)(a)). Hence, there is automatic relief for an allowable loss against total chargeable gains for the year.
Any allowable loss that is not relieved by offset against other gains in the year in which it arises is carried forward and set against chargeable gains accruing in the next subsequent year in which they arise (TCGA 1992, s 2(2)(b)).

Where, at death, the deceased has unrelieved losses, any allowable losses on disposals made by the deceased in the fiscal year in which he dies are first set against chargeable gains for that year and then the excess is put against any chargeable gains in the previous three years (TCGA 1992, s 62(2)).

(m) Company losses

A company's trading loss can be put against the total profits of the company for the same accounting period and for the preceding accounting period, by a claim under TA 1988, s 393A.

A company's trading loss not set against its total profits is carried forward and put against future trading profits, under TA 1988, s 393.

A company receives relief for Schedule A losses and capital losses in (broadly) the same way as an individual.

Lower rate. *See* RATE OF TAX.

Lump sum. A lump sum paid on retirement is tax-free for the recipient whether payable as of right, at the discretion of the scheme manager, or at the behest of the recipient (TA 1988, s 189). This exemption applies to a lump sum, whether it arises under an occupational pension scheme (including a non-contributory scheme), a personal pension plan, or a retirement annuity plan. The exemption for a lump sum is also available for an *ex gratia* payment by an employer of up to one-twelfth of the earnings cap, where the employee is not otherwise within a pension scheme, or a larger sum by prior approval of Inland Revenue Pension Schemes Office (see SP13/91).

This exemption is not unrestricted. First, it does not apply to an unjustified payment of compensation for early retirement unless due to ill-health; such a payment is charged to tax by TA 1988, s 148. A payment can only be a tax-free lump sum if it is properly regarded as a benefit earned by past service (TA 1988, s 188(2)). Second, it does not apply to unauthorised payments from a fund nor to a payment after the cessation of tax exemptions (TA 1988, s 600). Third, it does not

apply unless the scheme in question is an approved scheme, a statutory scheme or a foreign government scheme (TA 1988, s 189) or, alternatively, is a funded unapproved retirement benefits scheme and the lump sum is attributable to employer contributions to the scheme on which the employee has been charged to tax (TA 1988, ss 189(b), 595 & 596A(8)).

In the case of an approved occupational defined benefits scheme the maximum lump sum that can be paid in commutation of pension is subject to the rules under which approval is given and normally (but subject to accelerated accrual) must not exceed 3/80ths of final salary for each year of service up to a maximum of 40 years' service.

In the case of a personal pension plan, the tax-free lump sum can be up to 25% of the fund. For a retirement annuity policy, it is actuarially defined, and typically is in the range 25 – 30% of the fund.

Lump sums paid by overseas pension schemes covering employees who were not UK resident when employer contributions were made would normally be subject to UK income tax if the employee was resident in the UK at the time of receipt. This is because the scheme will not normally be a UK approved scheme and the employee will not have been charged to UK income tax on the employer contributions. However, an extra-statutory concession has been issued under which lump sums paid from such unapproved schemes are exempt from UK tax if the employee's overseas service is at least 75% of his total service in the employment in question; or the whole of the last ten years' service; or not less than 50% of that employment, including any ten of the last 20 years.

Other types of lump sum are subject to special rules of taxation. Thus the consideration paid for a restrictive covenant given in connection with an office or employment past or present or future is liable to income tax under Schedule E (TA 1988, s 313). Second, sums payable for termination of the office are chargeable to tax under TA 1988, s 148 to the extent that they exceed £30,000.

M

MR. Master of the Rolls.

Machinery and plant. Capital allowances are available for the purchase costs of machinery or plant used in a trade, profession or vocation. Neither machinery nor plant is defined in the Capital Allowances Act, and the question whether an item is plant or machinery depends on the facts of the case.

Different definitions have been suggested for specific instances. In *Yarmouth v France (1887) 19 QBD 647* a claim was brought by a workman under the Employers' Liability Act 1880 for damages for injuries sustained due to a defect in his employer's plant, in that case a vicious horse. Lindley LJ said (*at 658*):

'in its ordinary sense (plant) includes whatever apparatus is used by a business man for carrying on his business—not his stock-in-trade, which he buys or makes for sale; but all goods and chattels, fixed or movable, live or dead, which he keeps for permanent employment in his business.'

On the authority of this case, the Revenue consider that 'machinery and plant' includes fixtures and fittings of a durable nature. So railway locomotives and carriages (*Caledonian Rly Co v Banks (1880) 1 TC 487*) and tramway rails (*LCC v Edwards (1909) 5 TC 383*) have been held to be plant as have knives and lasts used in the manufacture of shoes (*Hinton v Maden and Ireland Ltd (1959) 38 TC 391*), but not the bed of a harbour (*Dumbarton Harbour Board v Cox (1918) 7 TC 147*), nor stallions for stud purposes (*Earl of Derby v Aylmer (1915) 6 TC 665*), nor an underground electrical substation (*Bradley v London Electricity plc [1996] STC 1054*), nor a car wash (*Attwood v Anduff Car Wash Ltd [1997] STC 1167, CA*).

It is now clear that machinery and plant is not confined to things used physically but extends to the intellectual storehouse of the trade or profession, eg the purchase of law books by a barrister (*Munby v Furlong [1977] STC 232*). The Revenue view is that a thing must have physical manifestation to qualify as plant. It is not, however, necessary that the object be active, although a passive object may be less obviously plant. Computer software is treated as being machinery or plant by CAA 2001, s 71(1).

By concession a caravan on a holiday caravan site, being used mainly for holiday lettings, qualifies for capital allowances as plant.

Plant does not include the place where the business is carried on; 'plant' is that with which the trade is carried on as opposed to the 'setting or premises' in which it is carried on (per Pearson LJ in *Jarrold v John Good & Sons Ltd (1963) 40 TC 681 at 696*).

An item cannot be plant if its use is as the premises or place on which the business is conducted. In *Wimpy v Warland [1989] STC 273 at 279* Fox LJ said:

'There is a well established distinction, in general terms, between the premises in which the business is carried on and the plant with which the business is carried on. The premises are not plant. In its simplest form that is illustrated by [the] example of the creation of atmosphere in a hotel by beautiful buildings and gardens on the one hand and fine china, glass and other tableware on the other. The latter are plant; the former are not. The former are simply the premises in which the business is conducted.'

The distinction between setting and plant depends in part upon the degree of sophistication to be employed in the concept of a setting. The problem is acute when electrical apparatus and wiring are concerned. The matter has to be resolved by the use of the functional test and so, for example, while lighting will not usually be plant it will become so if it is of a specialised nature, as where it is designed to provide a particular atmosphere in a hotel; this must be judged by reference to the intended market (*Cole Bros Ltd v Phillips [1982] STC 307, HL; Hunt v Henry Quick Ltd [1992] STC 633; IRC v Scottish and Newcastle Breweries Ltd [1982] STC 296*). The light fitting was allowed in *Wimpy International Ltd v Warland [1988] STC 149 at 176*.

The case law distinction between buildings and apparatus is indistinct. Relatively recent cases have shown that items which cannot be plant under the case law test include a prefabricated building at a school used to accommodate a chemistry laboratory (*St John's School (Mountford and Knibbs) v Ward [1975] STC 7*), a canopy over a petrol station (*Dixon v Fitch's Garage Ltd [1975] STC 480, [1975] 3 All ER 455*), an inflatable cover over a tennis court (*Thomas v Reynolds [1987] STC 135*), a floating ship used as a restaurant (*Benson v Yard Arm Club Ltd [1979] STC 266*). These failed the business test—they performed no function in the trade. Many of these cases now appear in the statutory list of assets which cannot qualify as plant. Permanent quarantine kennels (*Carr v Sayer [1992] STC 396*), putting greens at a nine-hole golf course (*Family Golf Centres Ltd v Thorne [1998] STC (SCD) 106*) and a car washing facility operated on a conveyor belt system (*Attwood v Anduff Car Wash Ltd [1997] STC 1167, CA*) probably met the business test but certainly failed the premises test.

On the other hand it has been held that a silo used in the trade of grain importing was not simply part of the setting and could not be considered separately from the machinery and other equipment within it (*Schofield v R and H Hall Ltd [1975] STC 353*). Likewise a swimming pool at a caravan site was held to be plant since it was part of the apparatus of the business (*Cooke v Beach Station Caravans Ltd [1974] STC 402*), as were decorative screens placed in the windows of a building society's offices as the screens were not the structure within which the business was carried on (*Leeds Permanent Building Society v Procter [1982] STC 821*), and, perhaps surprisingly, mezzanine platforms installed by a wholesale merchant to increase storage space (*Hunt v Henry Quick Ltd [1992] STC 633 at 644 and 645*: note the doubts of

Vinelott J *at 644*). In the celebrated House of Lords case of *IRC v Scottish and Newcastle Breweries Ltd [1982] STC 296, HL* murals designed to attract customers were held to be plant as was a metal seagull sculpture and other items designed to create 'ambience'.

These cases prove the old adage that an ounce of evidence (before the Commissioners) is worth a ton of law.

The boundary between, on the one hand, machinery and plant and, on the other hand, its setting is now the subject of statutory elaboration in CAA 1990, Sch AA1.

CAA 1990, Sch AA1 excludes from the category of 'machinery or plant' any expenditure on the provision of a building. It defines building as including any asset in the building which is incorporated into the building, or which, by reason of being moveable or otherwise, is not so incorporated, but is of a kind normally incorporated into buildings (CAA 2001, ss 21(3) & 23(3)). This abstract statement is supplemented by a table with two columns of items; all items are then swept into the definition of buildings. Items in the first column cannot be machinery or plant; items in the second column may (CAA 2001, s 23(3), List C, items 18–21; on scope see *Family Golf Centres Ltd v Thorne [1998] STC (SCD) 106*). Cold stores, caravans provided mainly for holiday lettings and any moveable building intended to be moved in the course of the trade may also be plant. It is provided that an asset cannot come within column 2 if its principal purpose is to insulate or enclose the interior of the building or provide an interior wall, a floor or a ceiling which (in each case) is intended to remain permanently in place (CAA 2001, s 22(3)). Examples of items in column 1 are walls, floors, ceilings, doors, gates, shutters, windows and stairs and in column 2 electrical, cold water, gas and sewerage systems provided mainly to meet the particular requirements of the trade, or provided mainly to serve particular machinery or plant used for the purposes of the trade.

A structure is defined as a fixed structure of any kind, other than a building. Again there is a table with two columns and items in the first column cannot qualify whereas items in the second may do so. Examples from the first column include any dam, reservoir or barrage (including any sluices, gates, generators and other equipment associated with it), any dock and any dyke, sea wall, weir or drainage ditch; the column ends ominously with any structure not within any other item in this column. The second column includes expenditure on the provision of towers used to support floodlights, of any reservoir incorporated into a water treatment works, of silos used for temporary storage or on the provision of storage tanks, of swimming pools, including diving boards, slides and any structure supporting them and of fish tanks or fish ponds. This second column had to be substantially widened in the course of debate.

CAA 1990, Sch AA1 provides that expenditure on the acquisition of any interest in land cannot qualify as plant. This bar also extends to any asset which is so installed or otherwise fixed in or to any description of land as to become, in law, part of that land (CAA 2001, s 24). The definition of land in the Interpretation Act 1978 is modified—see CAA 2001, s 22(3)(b).

CAA 1990, Sch AA1 does not affect a number of special provisions which treat specified expenditure as if it were machinery or plant—thermal insulation, computer software, films, tapes and discs, fire safety, sports grounds and security (CAA 2001, s 23(1), (2)). It is also provided that nothing in the Schedule is to affect the question whether expenditure on the provision of any glasshouse which is constructed so that the required environment (ie air, heat, light, irrigation and temperature) for growing plants is provided automatically by means of devices which are an integral part of its structure is, for the purposes of this Act, expenditure on the provision of machinery or plant (CAA 2001, s 23, List C, item 17).

The stated purpose of the enactment of CAA 1990, Sch AA1 is to provide that buildings and structures cannot qualify as plant (although it is also stated that the broad aim is that expenditure on buildings and structures which already qualify as plant should continue to do so). Of the twelve cases reported between 1975 and 1997 seven were cases in which the Revenue successfully appealed against a Commissioners' determination that the items were plant, one was a successful appeal by a taxpayer against a Commissioners' decision in favour of the Revenue, in two the court agreed with the Commissioners that the items were plant and in two the Commissioners had decided that some items were plant but the court decided that more items were plant. Of those items which the court decided were plant one or two have now been taken into the non-plant category by the statutory list (eg the windows in *Leeds Permanent Building Society v Procter [1982] STC 821*). However, for the most part the list may be taken to reflect what the courts have achieved. The effect of the change is partly to provide detailed guidance and partly simply to prevent the judges from changing the law themselves.

'Main objects' rule. A rule that where the 'objects' clause of a company's memorandum of association sets out the company's main object, and also lists other objects, those other objects are to be construed as being merely incidental to the main object (see *Stephens v Mysore Reefs (Kangundy) Mining Co Ltd [1902] 1 Ch 745*). If a company's 'main object' has gone, the company may be wound up (see *Re Amalgamated Syndicate [1897] 2 Ch 600*). Modern practice is to exclude the rule by making all the objects of the company independent objects (see *Cotman v Brougham [1918] AC 514*).

Maintenance. Providing children, or other persons in a position of dependence, with food, clothing, and other necessaries.

Maintenance, power of. A power, provided in a deed or will in which property is conveyed or bequeathed on trust, empowering the trustee or trustees to spend the income of the trust property in the maintenance and education of the children who are to participate in the property when they come of age. The present provisions as to the maintenance and education of children are contained in the Trustee Act 1925, s 31.

See TRUST.

Major interest. The supply of a 'major interest' in land is a supply of goods for VAT purposes (VATA 1994, Sch 4, para 4). The supply of an interest in land that is not a major interest, is treated for VAT purposes as a supply of services (VATA 1994, s 5(2)(b)). Statute defines 'a major interest' as a freehold or as a tenancy for a term exceeding 21 years (VATA 1994, s 96(1)).

Majority. Full age. Reduced to 18 from 21 by the Family Law Reform Act 1969.

Malfeasance. The commission of some act which is in itself unlawful, as opposed to *non-feasance*, which is the omission of an act which a man is bound by law to do; and to *misfeasance*, which is the improper performance of some lawful act.

Managed on a unified basis. Two or more undertakings are managed on a unified basis if the whole of the operations of the undertakings are integrated and they are managed as a single unit. Unified management does not arise solely because one undertaking manages another. [FRS 2 – Accounting for subsidiary undertakings]

Management expenses. An investment company is able to deduct its management expenses from its investment income, in computing its liability to corporation tax (TA 1988, s 75).

Viscount Simonds has said in *Sun Life Assurance Society v Davidson (1958) 37 TC 330 at 354* that the term 'expenses of management' is 'insusceptible of precise definition'. It is clearly wider than the expenses to which the managers are put, but does not extend to all expenses incurred by the company. In *Sun Life*, the House of Lords held that all revenue expenses incurred by a company in managing its business qualify for relief. Relief is given for revenue expenses incurred in managing the investment business as is illustrated by *Holdings Ltd v IRC [1997] STC (SCD) 144*, where relief was allowed for fees levied by accountants and solicitors in respect of any company investigation and enforceability of letters of assurance, respectively.

Management expenses include:

(1) staff costs, including wages, salaries, pension contributions, and the cost of staff training and welfare;
(2) other indirect costs, including stationery, printing, advertising, repairs to equipment, legal and other professional fees, and unrelieved VAT; and
(3) property maintenance costs, including rents, rates, maintenance and repairs of premises occupied for business purposes.

Stamp duty and brokerage on the acquisition or sale of investments are not management expenses, and likewise legal expenses incurred in the acquisition of property as an investment are not deductible. Relief is available, however, for expenditure incurred in evaluating an investment, such as the legal costs of investigating title, as well as for expenditure on an abortive investment.

Management letter. After a firm of accountants has completed its construction of the accounts of an enterprise (whether with or without an audit being undertaken), it is good practice for the firm to send a management letter to the directors of the enterprise (or their equivalent). The purpose of the letter is to suggest possible improvements that could be made to the company's accounting and internal control system or to pass on other items of information obtained during the audit that are believed to be of benefit to the client.

Manager. *See* RECEIVER.

Managing director. One of the directors of a company appointed to deal with the day-to-day management. The duration of his appointment, his remuneration and powers are defined by the directors. He is usually appointed under a service contract.

Mandamus. The writ of mandamus is a command issued in the Queen's name, and directed to any person, corporation, or inferior court, requiring them to do some particular thing which appertains to their office and duty. In its application, it may be considered as confined to cases where relief is required in respect of the infringement of some *public* right or duty, and where no effective relief can be obtained in the ordinary course of an action.

Mandate. A direction or request, which may be provided for by a contract, but which is itself complied with for no (further) consideration. Thus a cheque is a mandate by the drawer to his banker (the drawee) to pay the amount to the payee. The issuer of a mandate may be called the mandator, and the person to whom the direction is addressed, the mandatory.

Manufactured dividends. These are payments due under a contract or other arrangements for the transfer of shares and may represent either a dividend or interest but where an arrangement has been made so that there would be no charge to tax on the effective income received. The tax rules now found in TA 1988, Sch 23A are an updated version of a provision first introduced in 1960. At that time it was described as dealing with something 'which the ordinary layman could fairly describe as a swindle at the expense of the honest taxpayer—not a criminal conspiracy but a racket' (HC Official Report 1960, Vol 624, col 451 (Sir Edward Boyle)). Briefly, a vendor (V) would sell a stock on The Stock Exchange 'cum div' but would not buy the stock until later, when it had gone ex div. V would then hand over to the purchaser (P) the stock together with a net amount of the dividend and a voucher showing the tax deducted. Thus P would receive the dividend net of income tax which he might be able to reclaim. Yet no tax would have reached the Treasury since the operator was not required to account for the tax and he would make a profit since the difference between the price cum div and price ex div would be more than the net amount of dividend after tax had been deducted.

The dividend manufacturing rules in TA 1988, Sch 23A operate so that tax is charged as if X, the person from whom T buys back the securities, was to pay T an amount representative of the dividend. Where the repurchase price is reduced to compensate for the loss of the dividend the

amount is the real dividend (TA 1988, s 737C(2)). There are further rules for interest (TA 1988, s 737C(7) & (8)) and for overseas securities (TA 1988, s 737C(10) & (11)) and further adjustments to take account of sums treated as falling under the deemed manufacture rules (TA 1988, s 737C(3), (4), (9) & (11)). There are separate rules for:

(1) UK equities: the amount representing the dividends is treated as a dividend if the manufacturer of the payment is a company resident in the UK (TA 1988, Sch 23A, para 2(2)).

(2) Interest on UK securities: the amount is treated as an annual payment (TA 1988, Sch 23A, para 3(2)(a) & (3)).

(3) Overseas dividends: the payment made by the manufacturer is treated as an annual payment (TA 1988, Sch 23A, para 4).

(4) Irregular payments: there is also a catch-all provision to sweep up any sums which exceed the amount of the real dividend. The excess is treated as a separate fee received for entering into the contract (TA 1988, Sch 23A, para 7).

(5) Sale and repurchase of securities: the person who would have received any dividend payable during the period between sale and repurchase is taxed as if he had actually received that dividend (TA 1988, s 737A(1)).

Mareva injunction. An injunction (which takes its name from *Mareva Compania Naviera SA v International Bulkcarriers SA [1980] 1 All ER 213n, CA*) which may be granted to restrain a defendant from transferring abroad any of his assets which are within the jurisdiction. Mareva injunctions are now called 'freezing orders' after the usage in the Civil Procedure Rules 1998.

Margin. (1) The difference between sales revenue and cost of goods, usually expressed as a percentage.

(2) The difference between the buying price quoted for shares by a market maker and the selling price.

(3) The amount above base rate at which a bank charges interest.

Marginal cost. In cost accounting, the marginal cost of manufacturing is the additional cost that arises by virtue of one extra unit being manufactured.

Marginal rate of tax. The percentage that is charged in tax of an increase in income (or profits or gains) of £1. Thus, corporation tax is charged at 20% up to the lower limit and at 30% above the upper limit, this gives a marginal rate of tax of 32½% for profits between those two limits (ie for each extra £1 of profit 32.5p corporation tax is payable).

Market maker. A dealer in securities (such as on the London Stock Exchange) who undertakes to buy and sell listed securities, acting as principal. Hence, a market maker must always have a buying and selling price for each particular security for which he provides a market (although the price is always shown as applicable up to a certain size of trade). Prior to 27 October 1986, market makers were jobbers.

Market value. (1) FRS 10 & 11 define readily ascertainable market value as:

The value of an intangible asset that is established by reference to a market where:
(*a*) the asset belongs to a homogeneous population of assets that are equivalent in all material respects; and
(*b*) an active market, evidenced by frequent transactions, exists for that population of assets.

Intangible assets that meet those conditions might include certain operating licences, franchises and quotas. Other intangible assets are by their nature unique: although there may be similar assets, they are not equivalent in all material respects and so do not have readily ascertainable market values. Examples of such assets include brands, publishing titles, patented drugs and engineering design patents. [FRS 10 – Goodwill and intangible assets & FRS 11 – Impairment of fixed assets and goodwill]

(2) Where property has to be valued for either IHT or for CGT the general rule is that the value is the price which it might reasonably be expected to fetch if sold on the open market at the relevant time (IHTA 1984, s 160 & TCGA 1992, s 272(2)); the costs of such a sale are ignored. The price is not to be reduced on the ground that the whole property is placed on the market at the same time. While this exercise presupposes a hypothetical value of hypothetical property between hypothetical parties, evidence of actual transactions is admissible, the question of what weight should be attached to those transactions is one of fact (*IRC v Stenhouses's Trustees [1992] STC 103, CS*).

The whole process was summarised by Hoffmann LJ in *IRC v Gray [1994] STC 360 at 371–2, CA* as follows:

'Certain things are necessarily entailed by the statutory hypothesis [of sale at market value]. The property must be assumed to have been capable of sale in the open market, even if in fact it was inherently unassignable or held subject to restrictions on sale. The question is what a purchaser in the open market would have paid to enjoy whatever rights attached to the property at the relevant date (see *IRC v Crossman [1937] AC 26*). Furthermore, the hypothesis must be applied to the property as it actually existed and not to some other property, even if in real life a vendor would have been likely to make some changes or improvements before putting it on the market (see *Duke of Buccleuch v IRC [1967] 1 AC 506 at 525*). To this extent, but only to this extent, the express terms of the statute may introduce an element of artificiality into the hypothesis.

In all other respects, the theme which runs through the authorities is that one assumes that the hypothetical vendor and purchaser did whatever reasonable people buying and selling such property would be likely to have done in real life. The hypothetical vendor is an anonymous but reasonable vendor, who goes about the sale as a prudent man of business, negotiating seriously without giving the impression of being either over-anxious or unduly reluctant. The hypothetical buyer is slightly less anonymous. He too is assumed to have behaved reasonably, making proper inquiries about the property and not appearing too eager to buy. But he also reflects reality in that he embodies whatever was actually the demand for that property at the relevant time. It cannot be too strongly emphasised that although the sale is hypothetical, there is nothing hypothetical about the open market in which is it supposed to have taken place. The concept of the open market involves assuming that the whole world was free to bid, and then forming a view about what in those circumstances would in real life have been the best price reasonably obtainable. The practical nature of this exercise will usually mean that although in principle no one is excluded from consideration, most of the world will usually play no part in the calculation. The inquiry will often focus on what a relatively small number of people would be likely to have paid. It may have to arrive at a figure within a range of prices which the evidence shows that various people would have been likely to pay, reflecting, for example, the fact that one person had a particular reason for paying a higher price than others, but taking into account, if appropriate, the possibility that through accident or whim he might not actually have bought. The valuation is thus a retrospective exercise in probabilities, wholly derived from the real world but rarely committed to the proposition that a sale to a particular purchaser would definitely have happened.

It is often said that the hypothetical vendor and purchaser must be assumed to have been "willing", but I doubt whether this adds anything to the assumption that they must have behaved as one would reasonably expect of prudent parties who had in fact agreed a sale on the relevant date. It certainly does not mean that having calculated the price which the property might reasonably have been expected to fetch in the way I have described, one then asks whether the hypothetical parties would have been pleased or disappointed with the result; for example, by reference to what the property might have been worth at a different time or in different circumstances. Such considerations are irrelevant.'

To perform a fiscal valuation is to follow statutory fiction. In *IRC v Crossman [1937] AC 26*, Lord Russell said:

'It is not a question of ascertaining their actual value, or their true value, or their intrinsic value, or their value in some particular person's ownership, the value to be ascertained is their statutory value.'

On which, in *Holt v IRC [1953] 2 All ER 1499*, Danckwerts J commented:

'The result is that I must enter into a dim world peopled by the indeterminate spirits of fictitious or unborn sales.'

In the real world, there may be restrictions on a sale taking place. These restrictions may be legal, administrative, or purely practical. In judging the market value for statutory purposes, all restrictions must be assumed to be removed. Any person who would have to give consent to a sale is assumed to have given that consent. In *Re Aschrott, Clifton v Strauss [1927] 1 Ch 313*, the shares were held by an enemy alien in time of war. Any sale would have been illegal. The court ruled that the illegality of a sale was to be ignored in judging the market value of the shares.

All possible purchasers must be considered (*A-G v Jameson [1905] 2 IR 218*).

If a higher price is to be obtained by dividing up an asset, such as a shareholding, it is this higher price that is to be taken (*Smyth v Revenue Comrs [1931] IR 643*).

Different assets can be assumed to be amalgamated in order to get a higher price. In *IRC v Gray [1994] STC 360*, the value of the freehold of agricultural land encumbered by a lease was adjudged on the assumption that the sale of the land would take place along with the sale of the deceased's 98% interest in the partnership which was entitled to the tenancy under the lease.

Events after valuation date are ignored, except insofar as they could have been foreseen (*Holt v IRC [1953] 2 All ER 1499*).

No regard is had to the expenses that would arise on an actual sale (*Duke of Buccleuch v IRC [1966] 1 QB 851*).

Where the value is of shares in a private company, the statutory fiction is that the hypothetical purchaser will be entered onto the company register, but he has then acquired shares which are subject to the restrictions in the articles on any subsequent sale he wishes to make (*A-G v Jameson [1905] 2 IR 218*).

If an actual sale from an estate would trigger a tax liability, the valuation is, first, undertaken without regard to the consequence of this deemed disposal. The liability thus triggered is, then, treated as a liability of the estate (*Alexander v IRC [1991] STC 112, CA*).

Marriage settlement. A settlement of property between an intended husband and wife, made in consideration of their marriage.

Marriage value. The amount by which the value of two enterprises, if merged, is greater than the sum of their two separate values. (The same concept is applied to merging two landholdings, either two physically separate holdings or the merger of a freehold and the leasehold interest in a single holding.)

Master of the Rolls was one of the Judges of the Court of Chancery, and keeper of the rolls of all patents and grants which pass the Great Seal, and of all records of the Court of Chancery. He was formerly one of the Masters in Chancery, and his earliest judicial attendances seem to have been merely as assessor to the Chancellor, with the other Masters. His character as an independent Judge was fully established in the reign of George II. The title now names the president of the Civil Division of the Court of Appeal (see the Supreme Court Act 1981, s 3(2)), thus the most senior judge of civil law matters except for the Law Lords.

Matching concept. One of the fundamental concepts in accounting, under which all revenue for the period relating to the period of account is brought into the financial statements for that period and is matched by bringing in all expenditure relating to that revenue.

Material interest. Certain charge provisions only apply if an individual has a material interest in a company; thus, for example, a director who does not have a material interest in a company and receives emoluments of less than £8,500 a year is not subject to an income tax charge on certain benefits in kind, such as the provision of a company car.

Statute states that a person is treated as having a material interest in a company if he, either on his own or with one or more associates, or if any associate of his with or without such associates:

(1) is the beneficial owner of, or able, directly or through the medium of other companies, or by any other indirect means, to control more than 5% of the ordinary share capital of the company, or

(2) in the case of a close company, possesses, or is entitled to acquire, such rights as would, in the event of the winding-up of the company or in any other circumstances, give an entitlement to receive more than 5% of the assets which would then be available for distribution among the participators (TA 1988, s 168(11)).

Materiality. The extent to which a particular figure is relevant in considering whether it affects a true and fair view being given by a set of financial statements. Thus, a provision of £100,000 for obsolescence of stock in a large multi-national company is unlikely to be material; a provision of £100,000 in valuing the stock of a corner shop is almost certainly material. When drawing up an audit programme to be used to audit a set of financial statements, the programme should test all entries that are material to the true and fair view to be given by the financial statements. Matters that are not material can be regarded as outside the audit opinion.

Matrimonial home. The Matrimonial Homes Act 1983 gives no rights to a wife who already has a proprietary, contractual or statutory right to occupy the home, but a wife who has none of these rights has: (*a*) if in occupation, a right not to be evicted or excluded from the dwelling-house or any part of it by the other spouse, except by court order; (*b*) if not in occupation, a right, by court order, to enter and occupy the dwelling-house.

Maturity. A bill of exchange or note is said to be at *maturity* when the time arrives at which it is payable.

See BILL OF EXCHANGE.

Measurement bases. Those monetary attributes of the elements of financial statements—assets, liabilities, gains, losses and changes to shareholders' funds—that are reflected in financial statements. Where a business holds an asset, purchased at some point in the past, that asset will have a number of different 'values'. It will have a historical cost, being the amount for which it was originally acquired. In addition it will have a current net realisable value and, if it is capable of being replaced, it will have a current replacement cost. These different 'values' are examples of monetary attributes of the asset. Other examples arise when different attributes are combined in a formula. For example, in a historical cost system, stocks are stated at the lower of historical cost and net realisable value. Similarly, in a current cost measurement system, the current value of an asset, using the value to the business rule, is the lower of replacement cost and recoverable amount. Some monetary attributes will be suitable for use in financial statements only in conjunction with others. A monetary attribute, or combination of attributes, that may be reflected in financial statements is called a measurement basis. Measurement bases fall into two broad categories—those that reflect current values and those that reflect historical values. (Value in use is unlikely to be appropriate for use in financial statements by itself. It will generally be used in conjunction with other monetary attributes, as in the value to the business rule.) [FRED 21 – Accounting policies]

Meeting. A gathering or assembly of persons, convened for the conducting of business eg, of a company, or relating to the affairs of a bankrupt.

Provisions as to meetings of companies are contained in the Companies Act 1985, ss 366 *et seq*. Such meetings include (*a*) *annual general meeting*, which must be held each year and at an interval of not more than fifteen months after the preceding annual general meeting; (*b*) *extraordinary general meeting*, which may be convened on the requisition of members holding not less than one-tenth of the paid-up capital of the company.

Members' voluntary winding-up. A winding-up in the case of which a declaration of solvency has been made in accordance with the Insolvency Act 1986, s 89 (see Insolvency Act 1986, s 90).

See DECLARATION OF SOLVENCY.

Memorandum of association. A document to be subscribed by two or more persons for a lawful purpose, by subscribing which, and otherwise complying with the requirements of the Companies Act in respect of registration, they may form themselves into an incorporated company, with or without limited liability. It states the company's name, particulars of capital, objects, etc. Its objects cannot be varied even by the whole body of shareholders except under the special provisions of the Companies Act 1985, ss 4, 5 and 6.

Merger. (1) The combining of two or more enterprises. In order to ascertain the correct tax treatment of a merger of partnerships, it is necessary to ascertain whether one has continued its trade and been joined by the other, which ceased its old trade, or whether the trade of the merged partnership is a new trade commenced at the date of the merger, the separate trades of the partnerships prior to that date having ceased. For incorporated bodies, what is referred to as a 'merger' is often a reorganisation whereby shares are exchanged (and, perhaps, issued) in order to create a group under common ownership, while the trading activities remain in their separate companies.

(2) In accounting standards, a merger is defined as:

A business combination that results in the creation of a new reporting entity formed from the combining parties, in which the shareholders of the combining entities come together in a partnership for the mutual sharing of the risks and benefits of the combined entity, and in which no party to the combination in substance obtains control over any other, or is otherwise seen to be dominant, whether by virtue of the proportion of its shareholders' rights in the combined entity, the influence of its directors or otherwise. [FRS 6 – Acquisitions and mergers]

(3) When a leasehold interest in land is acquired by the freeholder, the acquisition causes the lease to be cancelled, by the merger of the two interests. (Law of Property Act 1925, s 185 provides that there is no merger by operation of law only of any estate the beneficial interest in which would not be deemed to be merged or extinguished in equity.)

Messuage. A house comprising the outbuildings, the orchard, and curtilage or courtyard and, according to the better opinion, the garden also.

Mileage allowance. From 6 April 2002 the extra-statutory administrative arrangements of the fixed profit car scheme are replaced by the new statutory regime of TA 1988, ss 197AD–AH & Sch 12AA. These provisions provide a new statutory 'mileage allowance'. This is a fixed sum that applies irrespective of the size of the car and, thus, reflects environmental concerns by a deliberate use of the tax system to disadvantage the user of a larger car. Where an employee uses his private car for travel on his employer's business, the employer can pay the employee a mileage allowance of any sum up to the statutory mileage allowance, without the receipt being treated as a taxable emolument. This scheme covers only sums paid for business travel. Where the payment by the employer exceeds the statutory mileage allowance, only the excess is treated as a taxable emolument. Where the payment made by the employer is less than the statutory mileage allowance, the employee can claim the shortfall as a tax-deductible cost. Whereas the previous FPCS table gives mileage rates that are higher for larger cars, the new statutory 'mileage allowance' is a fixed sum that applies irrespective of the size of the car and, thus, reflects environmental concerns by a deliberate use of the tax system to disadvantage the user of a larger car.

See QUALIFYING TRAVELLING EXPENSE.

Minimum lease payments. The minimum payments over the remaining part of the lease term (excluding charges for services and taxes to be paid by the lessor) and:

(a) in the case of the lessee, any residual amounts guaranteed by him or by a party related to him; or

(b) in the case of the lessor, any residual amounts guaranteed by the lessee or by an independent third party.

[SSAP 21 – Accounting for leases and hire purchase contracts]

Minor. A person under the age of 18 years (see the Family Law Reform Act 1969).

See GUARDIAN; INFANT.

Minor interests. A term introduced under the REGISTERED LAND regime; major interests are those such as legal freehold or leasehold titles to land, whose registration forms the basis of the system; minor interests are lesser interests in land that may be protected by being registered against the title to the land to which the minor interest relates. The expression is defined by the Land Registration Act 1925, s 3 as 'the interests not capable of being disposed of or created by registered dispositions and capable of being overridden (whether or not a purchaser has notice thereof) by the proprietors unless protected as provided by this Act, and all rights and interests which are not registered or protected on the register and are not overriding interests, and include:

(a) in the case of land held on trust for sale, all interests and powers which are under the Law of Property Act 1925 capable of being overridden by the trustees for sale, whether or not such interests and powers are so protected; and

(b) in the case of settled land, all interests and powers which are under the Settled Land Act 1925, and the Law of Property Act 1925, or either of them, capable of being overridden by the tenant for life or statutory owner, whether or not such interests and powers are so protected as aforesaid.'

Minority interest in a subsidiary undertaking. The interest in a subsidiary undertaking included in the consolidation that is attributable to the shares held by or on behalf of persons other than the parent undertaking and its subsidiary undertakings. [FRS 2 – Accounting for subsidiary undertakings]

Minutes. The record kept of a meeting.

Mischief. The problem or situation to which a statute is addressed; thus to attend to the mischief of a statute is to attend to its object or purpose.

Mistake. (1) In civil cases at Common Law, mistake is admitted as a foundation of relief in three cases only: (i) in actions 'for money had and received' to recover money paid under a mistake of fact (*see* UNJUST ENRICHMENT); (ii) in actions of deceit to recover damages in respect of a mistake induced by fraudulent misrepresentation; and (iii) as a defence in actions of contract where the mistake of fact was of such a nature as to preclude the formation of any contract in law, eg where there was a mutual mistake as to the subject-matter of the contract, and therefore, no consensus *ad idem* by the parties, or where the mistake was made as to the identity of one of the parties where such identity was an inducement to the other to enter into the contract, or where the mistake related to the nature of the contract under such circumstances as would, if the contract were embodied in a deed, justify a plea of *non est factum*.

(2) In equity, mistake gives relief in a much wider range of cases than at Common Law, though it must be borne in mind that 'mistake', as a legal term on which a right to relief may be founded, has a much narrower meaning than as a popular expression. The relationship between the parties to a transaction may impose a duty on one party to inform the mind of the other party of all the material facts, and if, in such a case, the party owing such duty enters into a transaction with the party to whom the duty is owed, without informing him of all the material facts, the latter is entitled to relief on the ground of breach of duty.

Clearly proved and obvious mistakes in written instruments, etc, will also be relieved against by the court. The rectification (*see* RECTIFICATION), setting aside, etc, of written instruments is part of the business assigned to the Chancery Division of the High Court.

(3) Relief for a mistake made in a return of income, profits or gains may be available under TMA 1970, s 33.

Mitigation. 'The hallmark of tax mitigation . . . is that the taxpayer takes advantage of a fiscally attractive option afforded to him by the tax legislation, and genuinely suffers the economic consequences that Parliament intended to be suffered by those taking advantage of the option' (per Lord Nolan in *IRC v Willoughby [1997] STC 995 at 1003–1004* considering the application of TA 1988, s 741 which provides an exemption from s 739 if avoiding a liability to tax is not one of the purposes of the transaction). *See*, by contrast, AVOIDANCE.

Mixed fund. A fund consisting of the proceeds of both real and personal property. *See* REAL AND PERSONAL PROPERTY.

Mixed questions of law and fact. Cases in which a jury finds the facts and the Court decides, by the aid of established rules of law, what is the legal result of those facts.

Moiety. One-half.

Monetary items. Money held and amounts to be received or paid in money and, where a company is not an exempt company, should be categorised as either short-term or long-term. Short-term monetary items are those which fall due within one year of the balance sheet date. [SSAP 20 – Foreign currency translation]

Money. A store of value and a medium of exchange which exists in units, or is denominated in units, which are units of account.

Money bill. A bill for granting aids and supplies to the Crown. It is defined in the Parliament Act 1911 as a public bill which in the opinion of the Speaker of the House of Commons contains only provisions dealing with finance and taxation.

Money laundering. Converting 'dirty money' into 'clean money'. Thus, the proceeds of crime may be paid into the account of a respected organisation, so that withdrawals from that account have the appearance of money raised by legitimate activity.

Money market. The market for short-term loans, typically one week or one month fixed interest deposits. For an individual to place funds on the money market, his clearing bank will usually require a deposit of at least £25,000.

Monopolies and Mergers Commission. A commission whose duty it is to investigate and report on any question referred to it with respect to (*a*) the existence of a monopoly situation; (*b*) a newspaper merger; or (*c*) the creation of a merger situation (Fair Trading Act 1973, s 5(1)). A monopoly reference may be made to the Commission by the Director General of Fair Trading (ibid, s 50) or by the Secretary of State or by him and any Minister acting jointly (ibid, s 51). Such a reference may be limited to the facts (ibid, s 48), or not so limited (ibid, s 49). If the reference was made by the Director General of Fair Trading, the Commission must make a report to the Secretary of State (ibid, s 54(1)). If the reference was made by a Minister, the report must be made to that Minister (ibid, s 54(1)). The report must be laid before Parliament (ibid, s 83). It may be published in such manner as appears to the Minister to be appropriate (ibid, s 83).

Monopoly. A licence or privilege allowed by the Sovereign for the buying and selling, making, working, or using of anything to be enjoyed exclusively by the grantee. Monopolies were, by the Statute of Monopolies 1623, declared to be illegal and void, subject to certain exceptions specified in it, including patents in favour of the authors of new inventions.

The question whether a monopoly situation exists may be referred to the Monopolies and Mergers Commission.

Monopoly situation. A situation existing in the supply of goods or services (Fair Trading Act 1973, ss 6 and 7). It exists in the case of the supply of goods where eg at least one-quarter of all the goods of any description are supplied in the United Kingdom by one person (ibid, s 6(1)(a)). It exists in the case of the supply of services where eg at least one-quarter of that supply is made by one person (ibid, s 7(1)(a)).

Month. At Common Law the meaning of the term 'month' is 28 days, otherwise called a *lunar month*. But, in ecclesiastical and commercial matters, a month is interpreted to mean a calendar month; also, by the Interpretation Act 1978, in an Act of Parliament it is to mean a calendar month. Also by the Law of Property Act 1925, s 61 the word 'month' in all deeds, contracts, wills, orders, and other instruments executed, made, or coming into operation after 1925, means a calendar month, unless the context otherwise requires.

Moral rights, in relation to copyright consist of (*a*) a right of the author of a copyright literary, dramatic, musical or artistic work, and of the director of a copyright film, to be identified as such when the work is performed in public or broadcast or when the film is shown in public or broadcast (Copyright, Designs and Patents Act 1988, s 77); (*b*) the right of the author of such works to object to derogatory treatment of them (ibid, s 80). ('Derogatory treatment' means distortion or mutilation of the work prejudicial to the honour or reputation of the author or director (ibid, s 80(2)(b)).) The moral rights continue to subsist as long as copyright subsists in the work (ibid, s 86(1)); and (*c*) the right of a person not to have a literary, dramatic, musical work or artistic work falsely attributed to him as author, and not to have a film falsely attributed to him as director (ibid, s 84). (The right as to false attribution continues to subsist until 20 years after a person's death: ibid, s 86(1).)

Mortgage (Lat *Mortuum vadium*, ie dead pledge). A conveyance, assignment, or demise of real or personal estate as security for the repayment of money borrowed.

If the conveyance, assignment, or demise is of land or any estate in it, the transaction is called a mortgage, notwithstanding that the creditor enters into possession. But the transfer of the possession of a movable chattel to secure the repayment of a debt is called not a *mortgage*, but a *pledge*. Mortgages are either (*a*) legal, including statutory; or (*b*) equitable.

The term 'mortgage' is applied: (1) to the mortgage transaction; (2) to the mortgage deed; and (3) to the rights conferred by it on the mortgagee. By the Law of Property Act 1925, s 85, a mortgage of an estate in fee simple is only capable of being effected at law either by a demise for a term of years absolute, subject to a provision for cesser on redemption, or by a charge by deed expressed to be by way of legal mortgage. Any purported conveyance of an estate in fee simple by way of mortgage made after 1925 will operate as a demise to the mortgagee, in the case of a first mortgage, for a term of 3,000 years; and in the case of a second or subsequent mortgage for a term one day longer than the term vested in the first or other mortgagee.

See CHARGE BY WAY OF LEGAL MORTGAGE.

Under s 86 a legal mortgage of leaseholds can now only be made by a sub-demise for a term of years absolute, less by one day than the term vested in the mortgagor, or by a charge by deed expressed to be by way of legal mortgage. The right to create equitable charges by deposit of documents or otherwise is, however, preserved.

Mortgagee. The creditor in whose favour a mortgage is created.

See MORTGAGE.

Mortgagor. The debtor who creates a mortgage.

See MORTGAGE.

Movables. Goods, furniture etc, which may be moved from place to place.

Mutual business. It is necessary to distinguish a profit from a trade from an excess of contribution over expenditure. If I allow myself £10 a week for housekeeping but spend only £9, no one would contend that the £1 saved was taxable profit. The immunity of the £1 from tax rests on two principles, either of which is sufficient; the one is that no man can trade with himself and the other is that the sum does not represent a profit.

This immunity has been applied to groups of people who combine for a purpose and contribute towards expenses, as in the case of a golf club whose members pay a club subscription. Here too any excess of income from subscriptions over expenses is free from tax (*Carlisle and Silloth Golf Club v Smith (1913) 6 TC 48 and 198*). Each member is entitled to a share of the surplus and it is irrelevant that there is only a limited liability to contribute to any deficiency (*Faulconbridge v National Employers Mutual General Insurance Association Ltd (1952) 33 TC 103*). Wherever therefore there is identity of contributors to the fund and the recipients from the fund, it is impossible that the contributors should derive profits from contributions made by themselves to a fund which could only be expended or returned to themselves (see per Lord Normand in *English and Scottish Joint Co-operative Wholesale Society Ltd v Assam Agricultural IT Comr [1948] 2 All ER 395 at 400; IRC v Eccentric Club Ltd (1924) 12 TC 657* and Finlay J in *National Association of Local Government Officers v Watkins (1934) 18 TC 499 at 506*). Even if the club had a bar at which drinks were served at prices which yielded a profit there is no liability to tax since the bar is merely a part of the club, and is open only to members who thus make certain additional contributions to the fund.

The mutuality principle has been used to exempt a local authority from liability to tax on its rates but today its scope is limited to farmers' co-operatives, mutual insurance companies, institutions like the BBC, clubs and societies.

The principle of mutuality applies even though the contributions are made to a separate legal entity (see Rowlatt J in *Thomas v Richard Evans & Co Ltd (1927) 11 TC 790 at 823*), such as a company, so long as the company exists as an instrument obedient to their mandate as is the case with members of a mutual insurance company (see Lord Cave in *IRC v Cornish Mutual Assurance Co Ltd (1926) 12 TC 841 at 866–7*). Income from investments is taxable in the usual way. Any excess of premium income over liabilities will also be the income of the company. However, so long as such income is returnable to the members either in the form of bonuses or by way of reduction of premiums, that income is exempt from tax since although the company is trading this sum is not a profit to its members (see eg Lord Macmillan in *Municipal Mutual Insurance Ltd v Hills (1932) 16 TC 430 at 448*).

An attempt was made in FA 1933, s 31 to tax the profits arising to mutual companies from dealings with members. Since it was the mutuality of the transaction rather than the fact that it was with a member which gave immunity from taxation, the House of Lords, in a somewhat unimaginative construction of the statute, ruled that even if the transactions had been with non-members they would be exempt from tax and thus deprived the statute of any force

(*Ayrshire Employers Mutual Insurance Association Ltd v IRC (1946) 27 TC 331 at 347*). The section remained on the statute book unamended until the pre-consolidation changes of 1987. When such companies became the subject of profits tax in 1937 the legislature was more direct and simply taxed the profits of the trade of mutual companies. This more direct approach succeeded until the abolition of profits tax in 1958. Since 1958, the surplus arising from mutual trading has not been subjected to tax.

Mutual debts. Debts due on both sides, as between two persons.
See SET-OFF.

Mutual wills. Wills made by two persons who leave their estate reciprocally to the survivor.

Mutuality. Reciprocity of obligation, two persons being mutually bound.

N

NAO. National Audit Office.

NASDAQ. National Association of Securities Dealers Automated Quotation System.

NAV. Net Asset Value.

NBV. Net Book Value.

NIC. National insurance contributions.

'Names'. The members of a syndicate of underwriters who do not take any active part in the business, but authorise one of the members to do so, and to underwrite policies in their names (see *Thompson v Adams (1889) 23 QBD 361 at 362* (per Mathew J)). *See* SYNDICATE; UNDERWRITER.

National Association of Securities Dealers Automated Quotation System. A US computerised market providing quoted prices for smaller companies, many of which are in the field of high technology.

National Audit Office. The UK Government office charged with examining the economy, efficiency and effectiveness with which Government departments, and local authorities, use their resources. Much of the work of the NAO is concerned with effectiveness and not simply financial efficiency.

National Insurance Contributions. National Insurance Contributions are classified in the following classes:
Class 1
These are due in respect of the earnings of 'employed earners' as defined which are broadly employees and office holders:
1 *Primary contributions.* These are due (normally by deduction under the PAYE system) from the employed earner. From 6 April 2000, they are payable on earnings between the primary earnings threshold and the upper earnings limit. From 6 April 2001, the primary threshold is the same as the secondary threshold, and both are the same (within the odd pound or two) as the personal tax allowance. For 1999/2000, they were payable on earnings between the lower and upper earnings limits. Prior to that, they were payable on total earnings if they reached the lower earnings limit but only on earnings up to the upper earnings limit and, as now, were not due on the excess.
2 *Secondary contributions.* These are due from the 'secondary contributor', ie the employer or government department, public authority etc paying the office holder. They are payable on all those earnings of the employed earner which exceed the secondary earnings threshold. Prior to 6 April 1999 they were payable at a multiplicity of rates on all earnings, if earnings exceeded the lower earnings limit. Since 6 October 1985 there has been no ceiling on secondary contributions.
Class 1A
These are yearly contributions payable by employers in respect of taxable benefits in kind provided to their employees. They are payable at the not contracted-out rate for Class 1 secondary contributions and are calculated on amounts parallel to those used under the income tax rules for taxing benefits provided to directors and higher-paid employees. Until 6 April 2000, Class 1A contributions were payable only in respect of the provision of cars and private use petrol.
Class 1A contributions secure no benefits for employees under the contributory scheme.
Class 1B
These are yearly contributions payable by employers in respect of PAYE Settlement Agreements. They are payable at 12.2% for 1999/2000 (the first year of the charge) and 2000/01: 11.9% for 2001/02.
Like Class 1A contributions, the Class

1B charge secures no benefits for employees under the contributory scheme.

Class 2

These are modest flat rate contributions payable by all self-employed earners. They secure incapacity, maternity and long-term benefits, mainly retirement pension and bereavement benefits.

Class 3

These are voluntary contributions which can only be paid by those not otherwise securing benefits through contributions and secure only the long-term benefits.

Class 4

These are payable on business profits between a lower and upper threshold which are immediately derived by an individual from carrying on a trade, profession or vocation. They are thus payable by the majority of self-employed earners who also pay Class 2 contributions.

Business profits for this purpose are ascertained as for income tax and collection is through the income tax system, ie the Class 4 contributions are treated as amounts payable under the Schedule D, Case I or Case II self-assessment.

National Savings. Government investments organised by the Department for National Savings (prior to 1969 known as the Post Office Savings Department). Products currently available are:

Cash Mini ISA
TESSA Only ISA
Premium Bonds
5-Year Index Linked Savings Certificate
2-Year Index Linked Savings Certificate
5-Year Fixed Interest Savings Certificate
2-Year Fixed Interest Savings Certificate
Children's Bonus Bonds
Fixed Rate Savings Bonds (6 month, 1 year and 2 year)
Capital Bonds
Pensioners' Bonds (1 year, 2 year and 5 year)
Income Bonds
Investment Account
Treasurers' Account

Natural persons. Persons in the ordinary sense of the word, as opposed to *artificial* persons or corporations.

See PERSON.

Necessaries. Goods suitable in life of a minor or other person concerned and to his actual requirements at the time of sale and delivery (Sale of Goods Act 1979, s 3(3)). Where necessaries are sold and delivered to a minor or to a person who by reason of mental incapacity or drunkenness is incompetent to contract, he must pay a reasonable price for them (ibid, s 3(2)).

Negative goodwill on consolidation. Where an acquisition is made and the consideration paid is less than the value of the net tangible asset acquired, the difference creates negative goodwill. Under FRS 10, negative goodwill is required to be recognised and disclosed on the balance sheet below goodwill. Negative goodwill should be written back in the profit and loss account over the period that the enterprise is expected to benefit from the negative goodwill.

Negligence. The tortious failing to take adequate care so as to cause injury or loss to another, and which exposes the negligent party to an action for damages. In order to establish liability for negligence, it must be shown that the defendant owed a duty of care to the plaintiff (claimant), that the defendant fell below the standard of care appropriate to the circumstances in which the duty was owed, and that the plaintiff's injury or loss was caused by the defendant's breach of the standard of care, ie the injury was not too 'remote' in terms of causation.

Negligible value. Where a taxpayer has invested money in shares which later become valueless, it is clear that the person has suffered a commercial loss. However, the scheme of the capital gains tax legislation is that a gain or loss is only crystallised when there is a 'disposal'. Relief is provided in this scenario by allowing the taxpayer to make a negligible value claim, the making of the claim being treated as a disposal for capital gains tax purposes (TCGA 1992, s 24).

The Revenue have expressed the view that 5% of original value is 'small' and that 'negligible' should be considerably less. The Revenue release lists of quoted securities which it accepts have become of negligible value for the purposes of TCGA 1992, s 24. Inland Revenue Capital Gains Manual para CG 13131 instructs inspectors to accept a negligible value claim where the loss is less than £10,000, where the company is registered in the UK, is not a plc and is in liquidation or has ceased trading. Inland Revenue internal instructions also require inspectors to accept a negligible value claim where an asset is still in existence with its value unchanged, but the owner no longer has an interest in that asset because, for example, the asset has been stolen (CG 13139–13146).

Negotiable instruments. Instruments purporting to represent so much money, in which the property passes by mere delivery, eg bills of exchange, promissory notes, etc (see the Bills of Exchange Act 1882, ss 31, 32). Such instruments constitute an exception to the general rule that a man cannot give a better title than he has himself.

See BILL OF EXCHANGE; PROMISSORY NOTE.

Negotiate. To transfer for value a negotiable instrument.

See NEGOTIABLE INSTRUMENTS.

Net asset value. The sum calculated by dividing the value of net assets in a company by the number of shares in issue. The calculation can be performed in three ways, depending on the numerator. NAV can reflect the asset value as shown in the company's accounts (ie depreciative historic cost); NAV can show current market value of assets; NAV can recognise liabilities that would arise on the break-up of a company.

Net cash investment. The net cash investment in a lease at a point in time is the amount of funds invested in a lease by a lessor, and comprises the cost of the asset plus or minus the following related payments or receipts:

government or other grants receivable towards the purchase or use of the asset;
rentals received;
taxation payments and receipts, including the effect of capital allowances;

residual values, if any, at the end of the lease term;
interest payments (where applicable);
interest received on cash surplus;
profit taken out of the lease.
[SSAP 21 – Accounting for leases and hire purchase contracts]

Net debt. The borrowings of the reporting entity (comprising debt as defined in FRS 4 'Capital Instruments' (paragraph 6), together with related derivatives, and obligations under finance leases) less cash and liquid resources. Where cash and liquid resources exceed the borrowings of the entity reference should be to 'net funds' rather than to 'net debt'. [FRS 1 – Cash flow statements]

Net dividend. A dividend excluding the tax credit enjoyed by shareholders.

Net investment. (1) The net investment which a company has in a foreign enterprise is its effective equity stake and comprises its proportion of such foreign enterprise's net assets; in appropriate circumstances, intra-group loans and other deferred balances may be regarded as part of the effective equity stake. [SSAP 20 – Foreign currency translation]
(2) The net investment in a lease at a point in time comprises:
the gross investment in a lease; less
gross earnings allocated to future periods.
[SSAP 21 – Accounting for leases and hire purchase contracts]

Net present value. The sum calculated by reducing a projected future cash flow by a discount factor to reflect the cost of borrowing, or the return required on an investment.

Net proceeds. The fair value of the consideration received on the issue of a capital instrument after deduction of issue costs. [FRS 4 – Capital instruments]

Net profit. The profit for a period of account produced by an enterprise after deducting all expenses but before distributions. Net profit can be pre-tax profit or post-tax profit.

Net realisable value. (1) The actual or estimated selling price (net of trade but before settlement discounts) less:
all further costs to completion; and
all costs to be incurred in marketing, selling and distributing.
[SSAP 9 – Stocks and long-term contracts]
(2) The amount at which an asset could be disposed of, less any direct selling costs. [FRS 10 – Goodwill and intangible assets & FRS 11 – Impairment of fixed assets and goodwill]

Net relevant earnings. Any individual who is not a member of an employer's occupational pension scheme, is entitled to pay a sum each year into a personal pension plan. The sum is then treated as net of basic rate tax and eligible for further relief, if the individual is a higher rate taxpayer. The maximum contribution into a personal pension plan is calculated by applying the percentage relevant for the individual's age (17½% if under aged 36, rising to 40% for those aged 61 plus) applied to the higher of £3,600 and the 'net relevant earnings' of the year of contribution or any of the five preceding years. The definition of net relevant earnings given in TA 1988, s 644 is exceedingly complex. Broadly, net relevant earnings are:

(a) emoluments under Schedule E, including benefits in kind,
(b) income chargeable under Schedule D and immediately derived by the individual from the carrying on or exercise by him of his trade, profession or vocation,
(c) profits from the commercial lettings of furnished holiday accommodation in the UK (TA 1988, s 503(2)(b)).

The following are not treated as relevant earnings:

(a) Schedule E benefits arising from the acquisition or disposal of shares,
(b) amounts taxable under TA 1988, s 148 (termination etc payments),
(c) emoluments from an investment company that the individual (or with connected persons) controls.

The net relevant earnings cannot exceed the earnings cap given by TA 1988, s 640A.

New York Stock Exchange. The NYSE was founded in 1792 and moved to Wall Street a year later. Renamed New York Stock Exchange in 1983, it is the largest exchange in North America.

Next of kin. An expression generally used for the persons who, by reason of kindred were on the death of a person intestate, before 1926, entitled to his personal estate and effects under the Statute of Distributions. For the rules of succession on intestacy, *see* INTESTACY.

Nikkei Index. The index of prices of shares listed on the Tokyo Stock Exchange. It is calculated as a price weighted index of 225 Japanese equities.

Nominal share capital. The nominal value of the shares which a company is authorised by its memorandum of association to issue.

Nominee shareholder. A person who is registered as the owner of shares in a company but who, in fact, holds them on behalf of and to the order of another person. *See* BARE TRUST; TRUST.

Non-adjusting events. Non-adjusting events are post balance sheet events which concern conditions which did not exist at the balance sheet date. [SSAP 17 – Accounting for post balance sheet events]

Non-beneficial occupation. No income tax charge arises on accommodation provided for an employee when the employee's occupation is 'non-beneficial'. This is when the taxpayer comes within any of three situations. These are: (a) where it is necessary for the proper performance of the employee's duties that he should reside in the accommodation (TA 1988, s 145(4)(a)); (b) where the employment is one of the kinds of employment in which it is customary to provide living accommodation and the accommodation is provided for the better performance of the duties of the employment (TA 1988, s 145(4)(b)); (c) where, there being a special threat to his security, special security arrangements are in force and he resides in the accommodation as part of those arrangements (TA 1988, s 145(4)(c)).

Non-cumulative preference share. A share that receives a dividend in preference to ordinary shares but has no right to a dividend that was not paid in a previous year. *Contrast:* CUMULATIVE PREFERENCE SHARES.

Non-equity dividends. Dividends relating to non-equity shares. [FRS 4 – Capital Instruments & FRS 1 – Cash flow statements]

Non-equity shares. Shares possessing any of the following characteristics:
(*a*) any of the rights of the shares to receive payments (whether in respect of dividends, in respect of redemption or otherwise) are for a limited amount that is not calculated by reference to the company's assets or profits or the dividends on any class of equity share.
(*b*) any of their rights to participate in a surplus in a winding-up are limited to a specific amount that is not calculated by reference to the company s assets or profits and such limitation had a commercial effect in practice at the time the shares were issued or, if later, at the time the limitation was introduced.
(*c*) the shares are redeemable either according to their terms, or because the holder, or any party other than the issuer, can require their redemption.
[FRS 4 – Capital instruments, FRS 6 – Acquisitions and mergers & FRS 13 – Derivatives and other financial instruments]

Non-executive director. A director of a company who is not involved in the day-to-day management of the business. The Cadbury report in 1992 recommended that all UK listed companies should appoint non-executive directors to provide independent judgement on issues of strategy, performance and standards of conduct.

Non-participating preference share. The most frequently found type of preference share and does not carry a right to participate in profits above a stated percentage return on the nominal value.

Non-trading partnership. A partnership not engaged in the buying and selling of goods, such as a partnership created to hold property and collect rents (*Higgins v Beauchamp [1914–1915] All ER Rep 937*).

Not negotiable. If a cheque is crossed with these words, the person taking it has not and is not capable of giving a better title to the cheque than that which the person from whom he took it had (see the Bills of Exchange Act 1882, s 8).
See CHEQUE; BILL OF EXCHANGE; NEGOTIABLE INSTRUMENTS.

Notary, or **Notary public.** One who attests deeds or writings to make them authentic in another country. He is generally a solicitor, who has taken examination that tests knowledge of the form of documentation required in foreign jurisdictions.

Notice. A word which sometimes means knowledge, either actual, or imputed by construction of law; sometimes a formal notification of some fact, or some intention of the party giving the notice; sometimes the expression of a demand or requisition.

Novation. The substitution of a new obligation for an old one, or of a new debtor for an old one, with the consent of the creditor.

O

OECD. ORGANISATION FOR ECONOMIC CO-OPERATION AND DEVELOPMENT.

Obiter dictum. A dictum, ie statement, of a Judge on a point not directly relevant to deciding the case before him.

Objects clause. A clause in the memorandum of association setting out the objects of the company.

The memorandum of every company must state the objects of the company (see Companies Act 1985, s 2(1)(c)). The company has power to alter the objects clause by special resolution (see ibid, s 4).

See MEMORANDUM OF ASSOCIATION.

Objects of a power, objects of a trust. Where property is settled on trust and a power under the terms of the trust is given to any person or persons to appoint property among a limited class, the members of the class are called the *objects of the power*. Thus, if a parent has a power to appoint a fund among his children, the children are called the objects of the power. Similarly, those persons who are entitled to receive property under the terms of the trust are called the *objects of the trust*.

See POWER; TRUST.

Obligating event. An event that creates a legal or constructive obligation that results in an entity having no realistic alternative to settling that obligation. [FRS 12 – Provisions, contingent liabilities and contingent assets]

Obligation. (1) Legal or moral duty as opposed to physical compulsion. Legal obligations may exist by virtue of law, eg the obligation to take care so as not to negligently injure others, or may be voluntarily undertaken, as with contractual obligations.

(2) A bond containing a penalty, with a condition annexed, for the payment of money, performance of covenants, or the like.

See BOND.

Obligor. The person bound by an obligation to another person called the *obligee*, who is entitled to the benefit of the bond or obligation.

See BOND.

Obsolescence. When a change in technology, or customer demand, makes stock items unsaleable, obsolete stock should be valued at no more than its scrap value in the financial statements of the enterprise.

Occupational pension scheme. The modern approved occupational scheme owes a great deal to the Civil Service schemes which were established during the 19th century. This is in part because the railway companies and certain other large commercial concerns of the time modelled their own arrangements on those of the Civil Service but more importantly because when the 'old code' of approval was brought in by FA 1921 the Revenue in exercising their discretionary power to approve schemes looked to the rules of the state schemes in deciding what could be accepted: hence such rules as the maximum pension payable being 40/60ths of final salary became part of the code.

The 'old code' remained in being until 1970 but did not cover all forms of occupational scheme. As a result there were inconsistencies between the tax treatments applying to different kinds of scheme. Certain staff assurance schemes, for example, did not qualify for tax exemption of the income generated by the amounts subscribed. Again under 'old code' approved schemes it was not possible for the member to commute part of his pension into a tax-free lump sum whereas this had long been allowed under statutory schemes and certain other arrangements requiring a more limited form of approval.

The 'new code' of approval was established in 1970 to replace the 'old code': it provides a simple and uniform framework of rules and practices applying to all occupational pension schemes. The relevant legislation is TA 1988, ss 590–612, Schs 22, 23.

The main consequences of obtaining exempt approval under the new code are:

(1) employer contributions are allowable tax deductions to the extent that they are ordinary annual contributions;

(2) employee contributions are deductible from earnings subject to an overall limit of 15% of annual remuneration;

(3) the employer's contributions are not taxable emoluments of the employee;

(4) the income and capital gains arising on fund investments are exempt from tax;

(5) pensions paid during retirement are taxable on the members as earned income under Schedule E.

Occupier. The person residing or having the right to reside in or on any house, land or place.

Occupier's liability. The liability of occupiers to third parties entering their premises, eg for injuries suffered due to accidents caused by the premises' disrepair; see the Occupiers' Liability Act 1957 and the Occupiers' Liability Act 1984.

Offer. (1) One of the conditions for a valid contract: An expression of readiness to do something (eg to purchase or sell), which, if followed by the unconditional acceptance of another person, results in a contract.

See CONTRACT LAW.

(2) Offer of shares or debentures in a company (see Companies Act 1985, s 45).

See SHARE; DEBENTURE.

Offer of settlement. An offer made by one party to a legal proceeding to another to settle the case on particular terms. The offer is made by way of notice to the other side and, if accepted, concludes the legal proceeding. If the offer is not accepted, the court may take into consideration the offer in its award of costs. See Civil Procedure Rules 1998, Part 36.

Office. An office denotes 'a subsisting, permanent, substantive position which has an existence independent of the person who fills it, and which is filled in succession by successive holders' (Rowlatt J in *Great Western Rly Co v Bater [1920] 3 KB 266 at 274, 8 TC 231 at 235*). Examples include a director of a company (*Lee v Lee's Air Farming Ltd [1961] AC 12*), even if he has a contract of employment and owns all the shares, a trustee or executor (*Dale v IRC (1951) 34 TC 468*; *A-G v Eyres [1909] 1 KB 723*), a company auditor (*Ellis v Lucas [1966] 43 TC 276*), a National Health service consultant (*Mitchell and Edon v Ross (1961) 40 TC 11*) and a local land charges registrar (*Ministry of Housing and Local Government v Sharp [1970] 2 QB 223*). By contrast in *Edwards v Clinch ([1981] STC 617*) a person appointed to act as an inspector at a public inquiry did not hold an office since the post had no existence independent of him; there was neither continuity nor permanence. It thus seems that the essence of an office is the independence of its existence from the identity of the present holder.

Official custodian for charities. An officer appointed under the Charities Act 1960, s 3 to act as a trustee for charities in the cases provided for by the Act.

Official liquidator. The Official Receiver, or one of them nominated by the Secretary of State for Trade and Industry, in case of an order for the compulsory winding-up of a company, is to bring and defend suits and actions in the name of the company, and generally to do all things necessary for the winding-up of the affairs of the company, until he or any other person on the application of the creditors or contributories is appointed by the court as liquidator. If he is appointed he is then called Official Receiver and Liquidator (see the Insolvency Act 1986, s 136).

See LIQUIDATOR.

Official list. The daily list of share prices issued by the Council of the London Stock Exchange, showing all transactions in listed securities that have been marked.

Official rate of interest. An employee earning more than £8,500 a year, or any director, who receives a loan from his employer is, in general, subject to an income tax charge on the benefit of any low interest rate applied to the loan (TA 1988, s 160). The benefit is calculated as the difference between the amount of interest that would have been paid at an official rate of interest and any interest actually paid (TA 1988, s 160(1)).

The official rate is determined by reference to commercial mortgage rates (SI 1989/1297) and is fixed at the start of a fiscal year. Special regulations provide for the calculation of the official rate of interest where the loan is made in the currency of a foreign country. For this rule to apply the employee must normally live in that country and have done so at some time within the period of six years ending with the year of assessment. Where these conditions are satisfied, regulations apply (TA 1988, s 161(2)). Regulations have been made for loans in Japanese Yen and Swiss francs (Taxes (Interest Rate) (Amendment) Regulations 1994, SI 1994/1307 and Taxes (Interest Rate) (Amendment No. 2) Regulations 1994, SI 1994/1567).

Official receivers. Officials appointed by the Secretary of State, who act as interim receivers and managers of bankrupts' estates (see the Insolvency Act 1986, ss 399–401).

Official Solicitor. An officer of the Supreme Court who acts for persons suffering under disability, etc (see the Supreme Court Act 1981, s 90).

Onerous contract. A contract in which the unavoidable costs of meeting the obligations under it exceed the economic benefits expected to be received under it. [FRS 12 – Provisions, contingent liabilities and contingent assets]

Ongoing actuarial valuation. An ongoing actuarial valuation is a valuation in which it is assumed that the pension scheme will continue in existence and (where appropriate) that new members will be admitted. The liabilities allow for expected increases in earnings. [SSAP 24 – Accounting for pension costs]

Open contract. A contract of which not all the terms are expressly mentioned. The expression is used especially of a contract for sale of land in which there is no express condition as to title and in which the law makes certain presumptions.

Open ended investment company. A collective investment scheme under which: (*a*) the investment portfolio belongs beneficially to, and is managed by, a company having as its purpose the investment of its funds with the aim of spreading investment risk and giving its members the benefit of the results of the management of those funds, and (*b*) the rights of the participants are represented by shares in or securities of that body which: (i) the participants are entitled to have redeemed or repurchased, or (ii) the body ensures can be sold by the participants to an investment exchange at a price related to the value of the property to which they relate (Financial Services Act 1986, s 75(8)).

Opening accounts. The commencement of dealings in account. When an account has been settled and its correctness is afterwards impugned, it is said to be re-opened. *See* ACCOUNT.

Operating lease. An operating lease is a lease other than a finance lease. [SSAP 21 – Accounting for leases and hire purchase contracts]

Operation of law. When a legal right, duty, or liability comes into existence not by an individual's exercise of a legal power, it comes into existence by operation of law. Thus, when a party agrees a contract and in consequence has contractual rights and duties he or she did not have before, these rights and duties arise in virtue of his or her exercise of a power to make contracts, so these rights and obligations do not arise by operation of law. Where, however, A tortiously injures B, A is now legally liable to compensate B, and this liability arises by operation of law; A has not exercised any legal right or power to make himself liable to B by tortiously injuring B; A has no such legal right or power, indeed, A is under a legal duty not to injure B tortiously.

Operative part of a deed is that part whereby the object of the deed is effected, as opposed to the recitals, etc.
See RECITAL.

Option. (1) The word is used on the Stock Exchange to express a right to take or sell stock on a future day.
See TIME BARGAIN.

(2) An option of purchase in a lease is the right given to the lessee to purchase, during the term, the reversion.
See REVERSION.

As to options to purchase land, and registration thereof, see ss 2, 3 of the Land Charges Act 1972. As to the powers of a tenant for life to grant options, see the Settled Land Act 1925, s 51.

Order. (1) Any command of a court of justice which follows the rendering of a decision, either where the decision does not dispose of the merits of the case before them, eg in interlocutory proceedings, or where it does, in which case the order will normally be one which provides a successful plaintiff with a remedy, eg an order to the defendant to pay damages.

(2) Some Statutory Instruments are called Orders.
See STATUTORY INSTRUMENT.

Order, payable to. A bill of exchange or promissory note payable to order is a bill or note payable to a given person, or as he shall direct by any indorsement he may make on it. Until he has so indorsed it, no one else can maintain an action on it; and in this respect it differs from a bill or note *payable to bearer*.
See BILL OF EXCHANGE; PROMISSORY NOTE.

Order of discharge. An order obtainable by a bankrupt; made by a court of bankruptcy, which has the effect of releasing the bankrupt from his debts, except such as have been incurred by fraud and certain other debts (see the Insolvency Act 1986, ss 280, 281).

Ordinarily resident. Capital gains tax is stated to be charged 'in respect of chargeable gains accruing to [a person] in a year of assessment during any part of which he is resident in the United Kingdom, or during which he is ordinarily resident in the United Kingdom' (TCGA 1992, s 2(1)). Common sense would suggest that ordinary residence is narrower than residence. In *IRC v Lysaght [1928] 13 TC 511 at 528*, Viscount Sumner said, 'I think the converse to ordinarily is extraordinarily and that part of the regular order of a man's life, adopted voluntarily and for settled purposes, is not extraordinary.' A person is ordinarily resident in the UK if he habitually and normally resided lawfully in the UK from choice and for a settled purpose throughout the relevant period apart from temporary or occasional absences. A specific limited purpose, such as education, can be a settled purpose; it is irrelevant that his real house was outside the UK or that his future intention and occupation might be to him outside the UK (*Shah v Barnet London Borough Council [1983] 1 All ER 226*).

The Revenue view ordinarily resident as 'broadly equivalent to habitually resident'. It would appear that presence, although necessary for residence is not necessary for ordinary residence. It may also be that ordinary residence, unlike residence, at least for an adult, is a voluntary matter (see *Miesagaes v IRC (1957) 37 TC 493*).

It has been argued, on the authority of *Shah v Barnet London Borough Council [1983] 1 All ER 226* and *IRC v Lysaght [1928] 13 TC 511*, that an individual's ordinary residence is nearly always the same as his residence. Certainly, an individual who buys or rents a house in France and moves there, having sold or let his house in England, has made a change in the ordinary pattern of his life and can be viewed as having become ordinarily resident in France, even if subsequent events are such that his time in France is relatively short. On this view, the only individuals who are not resident in the UK for a particular year but, nevertheless, are ordinarily resident in the UK for that year are those who have adopted a totally peripatetic lifestyle, or whose presence in another country is enforced on them: a gap year student who has spent the year backpacking across several continents or an unfortunate individual who has spent the year imprisoned in a foreign country yearning for home.

The notes to the residence pages of the self-assessment tax return take a pragmatic approach; on the basis of the notes, any individual who is not resident in the UK is, treated as not ordinarily resident.

Where an individual comes to the UK for the purpose of employment here but does not acquire accommodation on a lease of more than three years, ordinary residence is treated by the Revenue as beginning at the start of the tax year following the third anniversary of the arrival. Individuals arriving in the UK for other purposes are now treated the same way. In the Revenue view, the purchase of accommodation outright for a lease longer than three years (or a change of intention with regard to the length of stay) causes ordinary residence to begin with the start of the year of arrival or, if later, the year of the purchase or change of mind (Statement of Practice SP 17/91).

Ordinary activities. Any activities which are undertaken by a reporting entity as part of its business and such related activities in which the reporting entity engages a furtherance of, incidental to, or arising from, these activities. Ordinary activities include the effects on the reporting entity of any event in the various environments in which it operates, including the political, regulatory, economic and geographical environments, irrespective of the frequency or unusual nature of the events. [FRS 3 – Reporting financial performance]

Ordinary resolution. A resolution passed by a majority of the shareholders in a company (see *Bushell v Faith [1970] 1 All ER 53, HL at 56* (per Lord Upjohn)).

Ordinary share. Ordinary shares participate in the net profit for the period only after any other types of shares such as preference shares. An entity may have more than one class of ordinary shares. Ordinary shares of the same class will have the same rights to receive dividends. [FRS 14 – Earnings per share]

See DIVIDEND; PREFERENCE SHARES.

Organisation for Economic Co-operation and Development. An organisation established by a Convention signed in Paris in December 1960 between the United Kingdom and various foreign powers. A support fund, to assist members who are in balance of payments difficulties, became available to United Kingdom participation by the OECD Support Fund Act 1975.

Origin of turnover. Origin of turnover is the geographical segment from which products or services are supplied to a third party or to another segment. [SSAP 25 – Segmental reporting]

Ostensible or **nominal partner.** A person who allows his credit to be pledged as a partner; eg where a person's name appears in a firm, or where he interferes in the management of the business, so as to produce in strangers a reasonable belief that he is a partner. The person so acting is answerable as a partner to all who deal with the firm without having notice at the time that he is unconnected with it.

See FIRM; PARTNERSHIP.

Outgoings. A term often found in connection with the sale of land. The liability to outgoings, eg rates and taxes, is co-terminous with the right to receive the rents and profits of the land, and, therefore, where a time for completion is fixed by the contract for sale, as from which the purchaser is to be let into possession, or into receipt of the rents and profits, it is presumed that the vendor is liable to outgoings up to that date only.

See COMPLETION.

Where no time for completion is fixed, then, in the absence of express stipulation, the outgoings must be borne by the vendor up to the time when the purchaser could prudently have taken possession of the premises sold. Usually, however, the conditions of sale provide that, on completion, all rents, profits, rates, taxes and other outgoings are to be apportioned, if necessary, as from the date fixed for completion; so that where apportioned outgoings have been paid in advance by the vendor, as rates and taxes often are, he will require to be repaid the proportion due to be paid by the purchaser. As to apportioned outgoings not paid in advance, eg ground rent, the purchaser is allowed to deduct from the purchase-money the proportion payable by the vendor.

Output tax, in relation to a taxable person, means tax on supplies which he makes (Value Added Tax Act 1983, s 14(3)).

Over. In conveyancing, a gift or limitation *over* means one which is to come into existence on the determination of a particular estate. Thus in a gift of Blackacre (*see* BLACKACRE) to A for life, but if he marries, then to B for life, the gift to B is a gift over. *See* ESTATE.

Overdraft. A borrowing facility repayable on demand that is used by drawing on a current account with a qualifying financial institution. [FRS 1 – Cash flow statements]

Overdue bill or note. A bill of exchange or promissory note is said to be *overdue* so long as it remains unpaid after the time for payment is past.
See BILL OF EXCHANGE; PROMISSORY NOTE.

Ownership. The right to the exclusive enjoyment of things which can be owned, ie things which can be property. It may be *absolute*, in which case the owner may freely use or dispose of his property, or *restricted*, as in the case of co-ownership, where the general rule is that co-owners must act unanimously in the exercise of any powers incidental to ownership, such as the power to give the property away. *Beneficial* ownership is the right of enjoyment of property; the legal owner of property has the beneficial ownership where there are no trust or equitable obligations binding the property; where the property is subject to a trust, the beneficiaries of the trust who have the equitable title enjoy the beneficial ownership, for the legal owner must act towards the property so as to benefit them.

Ownership is the largest interest in property, its unlimited and undefined scope deriving from the right to exclude others. There are however myriad other sorts of lesser interests in property, in particular land, such as security interests, easements over land, and so on. The chief distinguishing feature is that these interests can more or less be precisely defined. Thus an easement is a right of way across the land of another. *See* PROPERTY.

P

P & L Account. Profit and loss account.

PAYE. *See* PAY-AS-YOU-EARN.

PC. Privy Council; Privy Councillor.

P/E. Price earnings ratio.

PEP. Personal equity plan.

PET. Potentially exempt transfer.

PILON. Pay in lieu of notice.

Panel on Take-overs and Mergers. *See* CITY CODE ON TAKE-OVERS AND MERGERS.

Par value. The nominal price of a share or other security. The term is commonly applied to government stock, where repayment is specified as 'at par': ie on the specified maturity date, the holder of government gilt edged stock receives from the Bank of England £100 for each £100 nominal value of stock registered in his name.

Parent undertaking. An undertaking is the parent undertaking of another undertaking (a subsidiary undertaking) if any of the following apply:
(a) It holds a majority of the voting rights in the undertaking.
(b) It is a member of the undertaking and has the right to appoint or remove directors holding a majority of the voting rights at meetings of the board on all, or substantially all, matters.
(c) It has the right to exercise a dominant influence over the undertaking:
  (i) by virtue of provisions contained in the undertaking's memorandum or articles; or
  (ii) by virtue of a control contract. The control contract must be in writing and be of a kind authorised by the memorandum or articles of the controlled undertaking. It must also be permitted by the law under which that undertaking is established.
(d) It is a member of the undertaking and controls alone, pursuant to an agreement with other shareholders or members, a majority of the voting rights in the undertaking.
(e) It has a participating interest in the undertaking and:
  (i) it actually exercises a dominant influence over the undertaking, or
  (ii) it and the undertaking are managed on a unified basis.

A parent undertaking is also treated as the parent undertaking of the subsidiary undertakings of its subsidiary undertakings. [FRS 2 – Accounting for subsidiary undertakings]

Part disposal. If there is a part disposal, the proportion of the acquisition cost attributable to the part disposal to compute the capital gain arising is A/(A+B), where A is the consideration for the disposal and B is the market value of the remainder (TCGA 1992, s 42). Statute states:

'There is a part disposal of an asset where an interest or right in or over the asset is created by the disposal, as well as where it subsists before the disposal, and generally, there is a part disposal of an asset where, on a person making a disposal, any description of property derived from the asset remains undisposed of' (TCGA 1992, s 21(2)(a)).

Thus, there is a part disposal when either: (a) there is a disposal of a physical part of an asset or (b) rights are created out of an asset. An example of (b) is the granting of a lease by the freeholder.

What is the disposal of an asset and what is a part disposal out of an asset? There is very little authority to guide one. In *Cottle v Coldicott [1995] STC (SCD) 239* the Revenue successfully argued that the sale of a milk quota without any land was the sale of a separate asset and not a part disposal of the land. In *Berry v Warnett [1982] STC 396* S transferred shares to a nominee trustee and a few weeks later assigned his beneficial interest to a Jersey company in return for money and a life interest. The House of Lords held that the sale was a disposal of S's entire beneficial interest in the shares and not a part disposal of the holding. There is also *Zim Properties Ltd v Procter [1985] STC 90* in which the court held that a sum received on the settlement of a negligence action against solicitors arose from the right to sue which was an asset quite separate from the property to which the claim related.

While robust common sense can solve a number of these problems one also has to reconcile one's conclusions with the words of the statute. Common sense tells one that there are disposals of an entire asset when an asset is transferred to a company in return for new shares issued by the company and where there is a sale of a business for unascertained consideration (*Marren v Ingles [1980] STC 500*). On the other hand, part disposals arise from the grant of a lease out of a freehold, the sale of shares where shares of the same category in the vendor's pool remain in his ownership and the sale of land forming part of a larger holding. It has been suggested that a possible test is that in the first two cases the person making the disposal is left with an item of property which did not exist before the disposal; whereas in the last three there is an asset which can be identified as being undisposed of throughout. However, the legislation talks of there being a part disposal when the taxpayer holds 'any description of property derived from the asset' (TCGA 1992, s 22(2)(b)). This suggests that some disposals are part disposals even where there is not an asset remaining in the vendor's ownership throughout the transaction. Thus, a sale of land subject to a leaseback is generally treated as a part disposal, even though there is an instant during the transaction at which the person making the disposal has no interest in the land at all.

Part of a business. Retirement relief is available on the disposal of a part of a business. A distinction must be drawn between the disposal of an asset and the disposal of 'a part of a business'. In *Atkinson v Dancer [1988] STC 758 at 764c, f & 770c*, Gibson J said:

'Has there been a disposal by sale of a business or a part of a business? ... A business is, in ordinary language, not the same as an asset used in the business ... Thus, the fact that a farmer sells some land of his own which he has been using for farming business, prima facie, will not amount to the sale of his farming business or any part thereof because it is only the sale of a business asset and not in itself the sale of a business or any part of it. This is notwithstanding that it would be virtually inevitable that the sale of land on which the business has been conducted will reduce the activity of the farmer and probably his profits ... It cannot be said that the nature and extent of the activities after each sale were wholly or substantially different from what they were before the sale. Again, it seems to me that the only true and reasonable conclusion to the facts is that there was no disposal of a part of the business but merely the disposal of a chargeable asset.'

The judgment of Gibson J has been termed 'the interference test'. The test is applied by looking from the vendor's point of view; the question is whether the business (or part of it) has been disposed of, not whether any business has been acquired by a purchaser; there need be no acquisition.

In *Barrett v Powell [1998] STC 283* a tenant farmer received £120,000 for surrendering the tenancy of approximately one third of the total area he farmed. However, the landlord granted him a temporary licence for a further eighteen months which enabled him to continue harvesting the same area. The taxpayer ceased all farming activities three years after the surrender of the tenancy. The court, overturning the Commissioners' decision, held that the nature of the business carried on after the receipt of £120,000 was the same as prior to that date. Hence, there was no 'interference'.

Participating dividend. A dividend (or part of a dividend) on a non-equity share that, in accordance with a company's memorandum and articles of association, is always equivalent to a fixed multiple of the dividend payable on an equity share. [FRS 4 – Capital instruments]

Participating interest. (1) An interest held by an undertaking in the shares of another undertaking which it holds on a long-term basis for the purpose of securing a contribution to its activities by the exercise of control or influence arising from or related to that interest. A holding of 20% or more of the shares of an undertaking shall be presumed to be a participating interest unless the contrary is shown. An interest in shares includes an interest which is convertible into an interest in shares, and includes an option to acquire shares or any interest which is convertible into shares. An interest held on behalf of an undertaking shall be treated as held by that undertaking. [FRS 2 – Accounting for subsidiary undertakings]

(2) An interest held in the shares of another entity on a long-term basis for the purpose of securing a contribution to the investor's activities by the exercise of control or influence arising from or related to that interest. The investor's interest must, therefore, be a beneficial one and the benefits expected to arise must be linked to the exercise of its significant influence over the investee's operating and financial policies. An interest in the shares of another entity includes an interest convertible into an interest in shares or an option to acquire shares. [FRS 9 – Associates and joint ventures]

(3) Companies Act 1985, s 260 provides that a holding of 20% or more of the shares of an entity is to be presumed to be a participating interest unless the contrary is shown. The presumption is rebutted if the interest is either not long-term or not beneficial.

Participator. A participator is a person having a share or interest in the capital or income of the company, and, without prejudice to the generality of the preceding words, includes:

(*a*) any person who possesses, or is entitled to acquire, share capital or voting rights in the company;

(*b*) any loan creditor of the company;

(*c*) any person who possesses, or is entitled to acquire a right to receive or participate in distributions of the company or any amounts payable by the company to loan creditors by way of premium on redemption; and

(*d*) any person who is entitled to secure that income or assets (whether present or future) of the company will be applied directly or indirectly for his benefit.

(TA 1988, s 417(1)).

Parties. (1) Persons who voluntarily take part in anything, in person or by attorney; eg the parties to a deed.

(2) Persons required to take part in any proceedings, and bound by them, whether they do so or not; eg the defendants in a suit or action. *See further* the Civil Procedure Rules 1998.

Partition. A dividing of land held in joint tenancy or by tenancy in common, ie in one of the forms of co-ownership, between the co-owners, so that the estate in joint tenancy or tenancy in common is destroyed, and each party has henceforth an undivided share. This may be done by agreement, by deed of partition, or compulsorily by an action in the Chancery Division.

See JOINT TENANCY; COMMON, TENANCY IN.

Under the Supreme Court Act 1981, s 61(1), Sch 1 the partition of real estates is assigned to the Chancery Division of the High Court.

Partner, continuing. *See* CONTINUING PARTNERS.

Partner, general. *See* GENERAL PARTNER.

Partner, incoming. *See* INCOMING PARTNER.

Partner, limited. *See* LIMITED PARTNER.

Partner, outgoing. *See* RETIRING PARTNER.

Partner, retiring. *See* RETIRING PARTNER.

Partner, sleeping. *See* SLEEPING PARTNER.

Partner's lien. A right vested in a partner to hold the whole or part of the partnership assets until certain payments are made to him. (See Partnership Act 1890, s 41(a).)

Partnership, as defined by the Partnership Act 1890, s 1 is: Partnership is the relation which subsists between persons carrying on a business in common with a view of profit.

In contrast to a company, which is a corporate body having its own legal personality (*see* COMPANY LAW), a partnership has no legal personality; vis-à-vis dealings with third parties, partners are essentially agents for each other, so that each partner is liable for the acts of each other undertaken in the course of the business of the partnership; partners are also fiduciaries in respect of each other, in that they must act so as to serve the interests of the partnership as a whole in the course of business of the partnership, not to benefit their own individual interests.

It is a question of fact whether a particular person is a partner in an enterprise or merely a senior employee. In so far as this involves a question of construing a document, it will raise questions of law. Although the receipt by a person of a share of the profits is *prima facie* evidence that he is a partner further evidence may be needed to establish exactly when the partnership begins to trade (*Saywell v Pope [1979] STC 824*). In *Fenston v Johnstone Saywell v Pope (1940) 23 TC 29* the appellant wished to buy some land but lacked finance. He therefore agreed with another person to share the profits and losses and to assist in the development of the land. The document said that there was no partnership and described the appellant's share of the profits as a fee for introducing the other person to the vendor. It was held that there was a partnership. On the other hand in *Pratt v Strick Saywell v Pope (1932) 17 TC 459* there was held to be no partnership where a doctor sold his practice to another but agreed as part of the sale to stay in his house with the purchaser for some three months introducing the purchaser to the patients and sharing receipts and expenses over that period. In both these cases the decisions of the Commissioners were reversed.

Partnership articles. The contract between partners setting out the details of the relationship between them.

Partnership at will. A partnership containing no fixed term for its duration. Where no fixed term has been agreed on, any partner may determine the partnership on giving notice of his intention to do so to all the other partners (Partnership Act 1890, s 26(1)).

Partnership deed. The document that records the terms under which the partners in a partnership have agreed to carry on the business of the partnership, the way in which profits are to be shared and the ownership of partnership assets. Clauses commonly found in a partnership deed include matters such as the payment required for goodwill on entering or leaving a partnership, the expulsion of a bankrupt partner and voluntary limitations of actions of a partner, for example hiring staff. Where there is no provision in the partnership deed for a particular circumstance, and previous actions of the partners have not demonstrated any verbal agreement on the point, the relationship between partners and the rights of individual partners is determined in accordance with the provisions of Partnership Act 1890.

Partnership, dissolution of. The bringing of a partnership to an end.

A partnership may be dissolved (i) by the expiration of the period for which it is to last or by notice of dissolution; (ii) by the death or bankruptcy of a partner or a charge on his share; (iii) under a clause in the partnership agreement giving a right to claim dissolution if a specified event occurs; (iv) by illegality; (v) by an order of the Court; (vi) by an order of an arbitrator.

Partnership, limited. *See* LIMITED PARTNERSHIP.

Partnership property. All property and rights and interests in property originally brought into the partnership stock or acquired, whether by purchase or otherwise, on account of the firm, or for the purposes and in the course of the partnership business (Partnership Act 1890, s 20(1)).

Past service. (1) Service before a given date.

(2) Service before entry into the pension scheme. [SSAP 24 – Accounting for pension costs]

Past service cost. The increase in the actuarial liability related to employee service in prior periods arising in the current period as a result of the introduction of, or improvement to, retirement benefits. [FRED 20 – Retirement benefits]

Patent. A privilege granted to the first inventor of an invention.

Patents are the subject of the Patents Act 1977 (as amended by the Copyright, Designs and Patents Act 1988).

The Act relates principally to (i) patentability (*see* PATENTABLE INVENTION) (ss 1–6); (ii) the right to apply for a patent (ss 7–13); (iii) the application for a patent (ss 14–16); (iv) examination and search to see whether the application complies with requirements of the Act (ss 17–21); (v) the grant of a patent and its duration (ss 24, 25); (vi) registration (ss 32–34); (vii) licences of right and compulsory licences (ss 46–54); (viii) infringement (ss 60–71); (ix) revocation of patents (ss 72, 73); and (x) European, European Community and international protection of patents (ss 77–95).

A patent can be granted only if the invention is patentable: ibid, s 1 (*see* PATENTABLE INVENTION). Any person is allowed to apply for a patent (Patents Act 1977, s 7). An application must be made in the prescribed form and must be filed at the Patent Office (*see* PATENT OFFICE): ibid, s 14(1). The application must then be published by the Registrar: ibid, s 16(1). He must then refer it to an examiner for preliminary examination and search: ibid, s 17. The term of a patent which is granted is 20 years: ibid, s 25. The Registrar must keep a register of patents: ibid, s 32.

An invention by an employee belongs to his employer if it was made in the course of the employee's normal duties: ibid,

s 39(1). If it was not so made, it belongs to the employee: ibid, s 39(2).

The patentee may apply for an entry to be made in the register that licences under the patent are to be available as of right: ibid, s 46. After three years from the date of the grant of the patent a person may apply for a licence on the ground that eg it is not being commercially worked in the United Kingdom: ibid, ss 48–50.

A patent is infringed if (*a*) where the invention is a product, a person makes or disposes of it; or (*b*) where the invention is a process, he uses it: ibid, s 60(1). A patentee may bring proceedings for infringement: ibid, ss 61–71.

A patent may be revoked: ibid, ss 72, 73.

A patentee may apply for a European patent, a European patent (UK), and an international patent (*see* PATENT CO-OPERATION TREATY): ibid, ss 77–95.

See INTELLECTUAL PROPERTY LAW.

Patent Co-operation Treaty. A treaty signed at Washington on 19 June 1970, giving the protection of a patent in all countries which are parties to it (Patents Act 1977, s 130(1)).

Patent Office. An office established in 1853. Applications for patents are made to it.

See PATENT.

Patentable invention. An invention which is (*a*) new; (*b*) involves an inventive step; and (*c*) is capable of industrial application (Patents Act 1977, s 1(1)). An invention is 'new' if it does not form part of the state of the art: ibid, s 2(1). It involves an 'inventive step' if it is not obvious to a person skilled in the art: ibid, s 3.

See PATENT.

Patentee. A person to whom a patent is granted.

Pay and file. The system of reporting a UK corporation tax liability and paying the tax due that operated for accounting periods ending after 30 September 1993 and before 1 July 1999. Under pay and file, a company had an obligation to calculate the corporation tax payable, but it was necessary for the Inland Revenue to raise an assessment in the sum calculated by the taxpayer company in order to create a legally collectable liability. For accounting periods ending after 1 July 1999, self-assessment has replaced pay and file.

Pay in lieu of notice. Pay in lieu of notice may either be a particular form of compensation for breach of contract by the employer or it may be compensation provided under the terms of the employment.

When under the contract of employment the employer is required to give say three months' notice but does not do so, the employee could claim for breach of contract and accordingly 'pay in lieu of notice' if this situation falls into the former category and is not earnings for national insurance contribution purposes. But where the contract allows the employer either to give three months' notice or to give pay in lieu, or where under a fixed term contract the balance of remuneration becomes payable on premature termination these payments are contractual and so earnings for contribution purposes. Likewise, the pay in lieu of notice will be contractual if the employer gives the required period of notice but does not require the employee to work during the notice period or if the contract provides for this possibility.

Similar considerations affect Schedule E liability. In *EMI Group Electronics Ltd v Coldicott [1999] STC 803, CA at 820* Chadwick LJ said:

'Notice of intention to terminate—or a payment in lieu of notice—is something to which the employee is entitled in addition to a redundancy payment—as the present case itself illustrates. Notice of intention to terminate—or a payment in lieu of notice—gives recognition to the obvious fact that it is likely to take time to find other employment; and that a prudent employee enters into employment on terms that, when the time comes for that employment to end, he will have the security of a continued right to receive his salary (or a payment in lieu) while he finds other employment.

I am satisfied, therefore, that . . . a payment in lieu of notice, made in pursuance of a contractual provision, agreed at the outset of the employment, which enables the taxpayer company to terminate the employment on making that payment, is . . . properly to be regarded as an emolument *from* that employment. In my view, for the reasons which I have set out, such a payment is an emolument from the employment. That was the view reached by the commissioners and by the judge. I am satisfied that they were correct.'

Pay-as-you-earn. The system of tax collection under Schedule E to the Income and Corporation Taxes Act 1988, whereby the person chargeable has tax deducted by instalments from his salary by his employer, who is then accountable to the Commissioners of Inland Revenue for the payment of the sums so deducted. See TA 1988, s 203.

Payee. A person to whom, or to whose order, a bill of exchange, cheque, or promissory note is expressed to be payable.
See BILL OF EXCHANGE; CHEQUE; PROMISSORY NOTE.

Payments on account. (1) All amounts received and receivable at the accounting date in respect of contracts in progress. [SSAP 9 – Stocks and long-term contracts]

(2) A payment of income tax required on 31 January during the tax year and 31 July following the tax year in respect of that year (see TMA 1970, s 59A).

Penalties. Statute provides for a penalty to be imposed on a taxpayer in various circumstances.

UK statute treats the imposition of a tax penalty as a civil matter. However, The Strasbourg Court on the European Convention on Human Rights ruled in *JJ v Netherlands (1998) 28 EHRR 168* that the imposition of a tax penalty can be treated as a 'criminal charge', and so within Article 6 of the European Convention (the right to a fair trial). In that case, the European Court ruled that the Dutch Revenue was to pay damages to the taxpayer for having imposed a penalty without having satisfied the conditions for a fair trial that are stated in the Convention. It may follow that the procedures currently adopted in the UK are in contravention of the Convention. In some respects, the UK statutory code may require amendment as a consequence of the UK having brought the European Convention into UK law by the passing of Human Rights Act 1998. In *AP, MP and TP v Switzerland (1997) 26 EHRR 541, EC of HR*, the Court rejected a state's claim for a penalty for a tax fraud committed by someone else.

See HUMAN RIGHTS ACT.

(1) For the direct taxes (income tax, corporation tax and CGT), the penalty most frequently applied is a tax-geared penalty. This is 100% of the tax lost (TMA 1970, s 95). Statute gives the Revenue discretion to reduce the penalty (TMA 1970, s 102). This power is routinely used by the Revenue to provide a 'tariff' of penalties, rewarding taxpayers who co-operate in an investigation.

In addition to tax-geared penalties, statute provides fixed penalties, which include:

(*a*) failure to make a return by the due date—£100 (TMA 1970, s 93(1)(a));

(*b*) continuing failure to make a return— £60 per day (TMA 1970, s 93(1)(b));

(*c*) failure to produce documents—£50 (TMA 1970, s 97AA);

(*d*) failure to supply information on 'special return'—£300 (TMA 1970, s 98(1)(i));

(*e*) continuing failure to supply information on a 'special return'—£60 per day (TMA 1970, s 98(1)(ii));

(*f*) supply of incorrect information on a 'special return'—£3,000 (TMA 1970, s 98(2));

(*g*) failure to make a sub-contractor's return—£100 per 50 sub-contractors (TMA 1970, s 98A(3));

(*h*) assisting in the preparation of an incorrect return—£3,000 (TMA 1970, s 99);

All penalties attract interest in the case of late payment (TMA 1970, s 103A).

Where an employer has not accounted to the Revenue for PAYE, the inspector may determine the amount of PAYE due using the authority of IT (Employments) Regulations 1993, SI 1993/744, reg 49(2).

This has the effect that penalties are payable (see Regulation 49(7)).

(2) For inheritance tax, penalties may be incurred for failing to deliver an account, failing to make a return, failing to comply with a notice seeking information and any fraud or negligence in connection with the supply of accounts or information. There may also be criminal liability. The penalty for fraud by an accountable person is £50 plus twice the amount of tax that would have been lost—this is in addition to a liability for the tax (IHTA 1984, ss 247, 249–253). There are also penalties for failing to comply with a notice issued by the Special Commissioners or to appear before them (IHTA 1984, ss 245 & 246).

(3) Most National Insurance contributions are collected through the PAYE system or in the case of Class 4 contributions through Schedule D, Case I or Case II assessments. Where, following inspection visits, irregularities come to light, the Revenue will require recovery of arrears. This approach to recovery treats the unpaid contributions in the same way as unpaid PAYE (Social Security (Contributions) Regulations 1979, SI 1979/591, reg 46; Sch 1, para 28(1)). Hence, the same penalties are applied as for the direct taxes.

(4) For Stamp Duty, there is, normally, no penalty for the failure to stamp a document. Instead, the sanction is that the document is not admissible in legal proceedings. However, there is a £300 penalty if the taxpayer fails to stamp a document that has been adjudicated (SA 1891, s 12A(2)). There are also penalties for failure to provide information, refusal to allow the inspection of documents, fraudulent acts and omissions. The penalty is usually £30 (or the amount of the stamp duty, if lower), but rises to £3,000 where fraud is involved (eg SA 1891, s 5).

(5) For VAT, a person is liable to a penalty for serious misrepresentation on a VAT return. The prescribed penalty is 15% of the tax lost for the prescribed accounting period concerned (VATA 1994, s 63(1)). A trader is not liable to a penalty if he has a reasonable excuse for his conduct (VATA 1994, s 63(10)(a)).

Pension. The payment of a sum of money; especially a periodical payment for past services.

Pension scheme. A pension scheme is an arrangement (other than accident insurance) to provide pension and/or other benefits for members on leaving service or retiring and, after a member's death, for his/her dependants. [SSAP 24 – Accounting for pension costs]

Pensionable payroll/earnings. Pensionable payroll/earnings are the earnings on which benefits and/or contributions are calculated. One or more elements of earnings (eg overtime) may be excluded, and/or there may be a reduction to take account of all or part of the state scheme benefits which the member is deemed to receive. [SSAP 24 – Accounting for pension costs]

Pensions Ombudsman. A commissioner whose duty it is to investigate and determine complaints by persons alleging that they have sustained injustice in consequence of maladministration by the trustees or managers of an occupational personal pension scheme (Social Security Pensions Act 1975, s 59B).
See OCCUPATIONAL PENSION SCHEME.

Peppercorn rent. A rent of a peppercorn, that is, a nominal rent. Although of very little value, the payment of a peppercorn does count as the transfer of valuable consideration, and so a peppercorn rent is good consideration for the grant of a lease.
See CONSIDERATION.

Per capita. *See* CAPITA, DISTRIBUTION PER.

Per stirpes. *See* STIRPES, DISTRIBUTION PER.

Perfect trust. An executed trust.

Performance. The doing wholly or in part of a thing agreed to be done, usually under a contract.

Period of absence. For the purpose of the CGT exemption on the taxpayer's principal private residence, certain periods of non-occupation are deemed to be periods of residence. First, the period of 36 months immediately before disposal is treated as a period of owner occupation (TCGA 1992, s 223(1)). This may benefit owners who move elsewhere but experience difficulty in selling the house. Second, by Revenue concession, a period of up to 12 months before occupation is also treated as owner occupation if the owner cannot take up residence because the house is being built or repaired. Third, certain other periods are treated as periods of residence, provided they are both preceded and followed by periods of occupation and no other residence is eligible for relief during the period of absence. These periods are:

(1) any period of up to three years;
(2) any period of overseas employment; and
(3) any period not exceeding four years during which the owner could not occupy the house by reason of his place of work or a reasonable condition imposed by his employer that he should reside elsewhere

(TCGA 1992, s 223(3) & (7)).

Where the period of absence under (1) or (2) is exceeded, only the excess (not the whole period) is treated as giving rise to a chargeable gain.

Fourth, where a person (either an employee or a self-employed person) lives in job related accommodation, he may claim another house as his residence, provided he intends in due course to occupy it as his only or main residence (TCGA 1992, s 222(8) & (9)).

Period of account. A period of account is simply the period for which a company (or other enterprise) makes up its accounts. The choice of the period of account is entirely a matter for the directors of the company, the partners of a partnership or the sole trader. For a company, the choice of a period of account will determine the accounting period(s) for which profits are assessed under the rules in TA 1988, s 12(2) & (3). For an unincorporated business, the choice of a period of account will determine the fiscal year in which profits are assessed under the rules in TA 1988, ss 60–63, it may create overlap profit relief, or use relief previously created under the rules in TA 1988, ss 63 & 63A.

See ACCOUNTING PERIOD.

Permanent differences. Differences between an entity's taxable profits and its results as stated in the financial statements that arise because certain types of income and expenditure are non-taxable or disallowable, or because certain tax charges or allowances have no corresponding amount in the financial statements. [FRED 19 – Deferred tax]. In the UK, the cost of business entertainment is shown as an expense in the financial statements but is not allowable as a deduction for tax purposes; hence it is a permanent difference.

See DEFERRED TAX. *Contrast:* TIMING DIFFERENCES.

Permanent establishment. Most tax treaties operate so that business profits are taxed in the country of the taxpayer's residence, unless the taxpayer has a permanent establishment in the other territory. If there is a permanent establishment it is then necessary to compute the profits of that permanent establishment and those profits will often be subjected to taxation in the other territory.

In the OECD Model Double Tax Agreement, a permanent establishment is defined generally as 'a fixed place of business through which the business of an enterprise is wholly or partly carried on'. This requires the existence of an identifiable place of business, which has some degree of permanence (so that, for example, a hotel room where an individual stayed for one night could not be a permanent establishment). It is also necessary that the business of the enterprise in question should be at least partly carried on through the place of business. This requires a close connection between the enterprise and place of business: it is not, for example, sufficient if goods produced by the enterprise are sold at the place of business by an independent third party acting as principal. According to the official commentary to the OECD model, however, it is not necessary for the place of business to contribute to the profits of the enterprise. This is significant, because certain categories of income and gains will not be exempt if they are connected with a permanent establishment.

The model agreement goes on to state specifically that the term 'permanent establishment' includes a place of management, branch, office, factory, workshop, mine, oil or gas well and a quarry or any other place of extraction of natural resources. It should be noted that there is no reference to *exploration* for natural resources so that, if a person undertaking exploration activities does not otherwise have a permanent establishment, there will be no permanent establishment unless the agreement specifically covers exploration activities.

Furthermore, the model agreement specifically provides that, as a general rule, where an enterprise has an agent who has and habitually exercises an authority to conclude contracts in the name of the enterprise, the enterprise is deemed to have a permanent establishment through which the activities undertaken by the agent are carried on. Of course, where an agent constitutes a permanent establishment on general principles, the fact that he does not habitually conclude contracts in the name of the enterprise does not prevent his being a permanent establishment.

There are two important exceptions to the agency rule. First, the existence of an agent will not be treated as giving rise to a permanent establishment if the activities of the agent are limited to those which, as explained below, are not of themselves treated as giving rise to a permanent establishment. Secondly, an enterprise is not treated as having a permanent establishment merely because it carries on business through a broker, general commission agent or other independent agent, provided he is acting in the ordinary course of his business.

The model agreement contains a list of activities which are deemed not, of themselves, to constitute a permanent establishment. These are largely cost-centre activities which are remote from the actual realisation of profits, such as the maintenance of a purchasing or information-gathering office or the storage, display or delivery of goods. A building site or construction or installation project constitutes a permanent establishment only if it lasts for more than 12 months.

The model agreement also provides that a subsidiary which resides or trades in the country in question is not of itself a permanent establishment of its parent company. Of course, if the subsidiary acted as agent for the parent it would constitute a permanent establishment, unless the circumstances were such that it fell within the independent-agent category: the provision is inserted merely to confirm the principle that a subsidiary company is a separate legal entity from its parent.

Perpetuity. The attempt, by deed, will, or other instrument, to control the devolution of an estate beyond the period allowed by law, is spoken of as an attempt to create a *perpetuity*, and the disposition so attempted to be made is void. The modern (post-17th century) common law rule required that interests in property given by *inter vivos* grant or trust, or by a will or testamentary trust, must vest in interest absolutely, ie the intended recipients must have the absolute right to an interest in the property (*see* VEST *et seq.*), within a certain period from the time the grant or will or trust came into effect. Thus it prevented persons from controlling the distribution of their property long after they were dead by imposing restrictions upon it far into the future.

The rule was logically straight-forward, but in practice was often very difficult to apply and it created various traps for inexperienced conveyancers and draughtsmen, both because of the way the time limit was calculated, and because of the way it took into account the possibility of events occurring which might make a gift fail. The time period of the rule was framed to allow testators to make gifts to their grandchildren that would not vest until the children reached the age of majority, which was 21 when the rule was devised. The rule was devised to make that possible, but also to make sure that this was the limit of what a testator could do to extend the time before his gifts actually vested; in consequence, the allowable time period was framed in a particular way, in reference to 'lives in being' plus a further period of 21 years. The way in which this limit worked is best

explained by an example. If I leave property in my will to be divided equally between all my grandchildren who attain the age of 21, under the rule we calculate the time period within which the donees will become entitled to their shares of the property as follows: If I have any living grandchildren when I die their shares will vest when they each turn 21, and so, being alive at my death, they must turn 21 within 21 years following my death. But more children may be born to my living children. My own children who are alive at my death are lives in being for the purpose of the rule. (If I am a man and my wife is pregnant with my child, a child *en ventre sa mere*, as the expression goes, that child counts as a child living at my death, thus a life in being for the purpose of the rule.) The rule now works as follows: obviously, any child born to my children must be conceived before my children die; therefore, the last grandchild of mine which could possibly be born will be conceived no later than the death of my last living child; therefore that last grandchild will turn 21 (ignoring periods of gestation) no later than 21 years after the death of the last life in being. Thus a gift to any or all of my grandchildren who attain their age of majority, 21, must vest, if it vests at all (all of my grandchildren may, as it turns out, die before 21—that makes the gift fail, but not for perpetuity), within the period determined by the lifetime of the last surviving life in being plus 21 years. Thus the rule can be stated as follows: a gift is valid if the interests in the property of those who are intended to benefit must vest, if they vest at all, within 21 years following the death of the last surviving life in being.

The famous trap of the 'unborn widow' shows the complexities of applying the rule. Consider this testamentary gift: 'Blackacre to my son A for life, then to A's widow for life, then to A's eldest child then living absolutely'. A is already alive, so is a life in being for the purpose of the rule. The problem is that A might marry someone who is not alive at the testator's death. After growing up and marrying A, she might outlive A (and anyone else alive at my death) by more that 21 years. So the gift to A's eldest son might vest more than

21 years after the death of the last life in being, so the gift is void from the outset.

The rule was modified by the Perpetuities and Accumulations Act 1964, which prevents gifts from failing for perpetuity at the outset of the gift because the gift might vest outside the perpetuity period. The Act takes a 'wait and see' approach, and in general any gifts which in fact vest within the perpetuity period (or a specified period of 80 years) will be good.

See WILL; ESTATE; TRUST; VEST.

Person. (1) A human being capable of rights, also called a *natural* person.

(2) A corporation or legal person, ie an *artificial* person (see the Interpretation Act 1978, s 5, Sch 1).

Personal allowances. Personal allowances are generally fixed sums, which are deductible from total income in calculating taxable income before income tax is imposed (TA 1988, s 256). Being personal allowances they can be claimed only by individuals as opposed to, for example, trusts, and therefore are distinguishable from other deductions such as interest payments. Further they may generally be claimed only by UK residents, citizens of Commonwealth countries, most EC residents and anyone entitled under a tax treaty. Allowances are available only for the year of assessment; allowances which are not used in one year cannot be rolled forward (or backwards) to another year. Most allowances may not be assigned directly; some may be assigned indirectly if one person can provide income for another to absorb that other's allowance.

The value of personal allowances increases each year by the increase in the retail prices index, but it is open to Parliament to specify a different amount (TA 1988, s 257C).

In the past, personal allowances have been used to provide relief for the cost of children and dependent relatives, as well as providing a small monetary advantage enjoyed by the married couple that has not been available to the unmarried. In the UK, these are now largely treated within the social security system and not the income tax system. In contrast to the tax systems in most other European countries, the UK now has only the following categories of personal allowance:

(a) The principal allowance (TA 1988, s 257(1)).

(b) Age allowance: An individual who is aged 65 or more at the end of the fiscal year may claim an increased personal allowance (TA 1988, s 257(2)). This is increased further from age 75 (TA 1988, s 257(3)). However, where the individual's total income for that year exceeds a specified limit, the additional allowance given on account of age is reduced by one-half of the excess of total income over the specified limit (TA 1988, s 257(5)).

(c) Married couple's allowance for the over 65s (TA 1988, s 257A).

(d) Blind person's allowance (TA 1988, s 265).

Allowances (a) and (b) are an exemption from income tax of the first tranche of income. Allowances (c) and (d) are given by means of a reduction in the income tax liability, the reduction being 10% of the allowance.

Personal chattels. Things movable, as opposed to interests in land.

See CHATTELS.

Personal company. Retirement relief is available on the disposal of shares in a company which is the taxpayer's personal company. An individual's personal company is a company in which he is entitled to exercise 5% or more of the voting rights (TCGA 1992, Sch 6, para 1(2)). It has been held that a voting right which a person chooses not to exercise is still a voting right for this purpose, even if he has contracted with another shareholder not to vote (*Hepworth v William Smith Group [1981] STC 354*). The shares must qualify in their own right and can never qualify by virtue of their being held as an asset of a partnership (*Durrant v IRC [1995] STC (SCD) 145*).

Personal credit agreement. An agreement between an individual ('the debtor') and any other person ('the creditor') by which the creditor provides the debtor with credit of any amount (Consumer Credit Act 1974, s 8(1)).

See CREDIT.

Personal equity plan. A personal equity plan (PEP) is a portfolio of shares held by an approved plan manager on behalf of an individual investor. Provided the conditions of the scheme are satisfied, gains from the sale of shares within a plan, and withdrawal of capital from a plan are free of CGT. Dividends, and interest from cash holdings in the plan, are exempt from income tax if they are reinvested in the plan (Personal Equity Plan Regulations 1989, SI 1989/469, reg 17, issued under the authority of TA 1988, s 333). The 10% tax credit on a dividend received by a plan manager is repayable where the dividend is declared before 6 April 2004 (FA 1998, s 76). A plan cannot be opened after 5 April 1999, nor can further funds be added to the plan after that date. However, a plan that is in existence at that date continues to enjoy the tax advantages offered (FA 1998, s 76(1)).

Personal pension scheme. A scheme or arrangement providing benefits, in the form of pensions or otherwise payable on death or retirement to employed earners who are members of the scheme (Social Security Act 1986, s 84(1)). Personal pensions have been made available from 1 July 1988 for both self-employed persons and employees who are not members of their employer's occupational scheme. Employees can no longer be compelled by their terms of employment to belong to an employer-sponsored scheme and thus if the employee does not in fact participate in the employer's scheme, the earnings from the employment are relevant earnings so allowing a personal pension scheme to be set up (SSA 1986, s 15). The employer may make contributions to the personal pension scheme set up by the employee (TA 1988, s 638(6)). In that case such contributions are not to be treated as taxable emoluments of the employee but they must be aggregated with the employee's contributions in applying the relevant percentage of net relevant earnings limit (TA 1988, ss 643 & 640(4)). Personal pension schemes can be contracted out of SERPS. In this case the employer and employee will continue to pay national insurance contributions on the same basis as if the employee was contracted in but the DSS will pay the contracted-out rebate directly into the personal pension scheme. The part of the contracted-out rebate attributable to the employee's contributions are grossed up at the basic rate of income tax (TA 1988, s 649(1)).

Pension providers are not confined to life assurance companies and friendly societies. Other financial institutions, eg banks and their subsidiaries, authorised building societies and their associated pension companies and authorised unit trusts, may also operate personal pension schemes (TA 1988, s 632).

There is free transferability of other kinds of retirement schemes into personal pension schemes.

Personal property. *See* REAL AND PERSONAL PROPERTY.

Personal representative. An executor or administrator, whose duty it is to settle the affairs and dispose of the property of a deceased person.

Personalty. Personal property. Personalty is either *pure* or *mixed*. Pure personalty is personalty unconnected with land; mixed personalty is a personal interest in land, or connected with it.

See PROPERTY; REAL AND PERSONAL PROPERTY; CHATTELS.

Persons acting in concert. Persons who, pursuant to an agreement or understanding (whether formal or informal), actively cooperate, whether by the ownership by any of them of shares in an undertaking or otherwise, to exercise control or influence over that undertaking. [FRS 8 – Related party disclosures]

Petitioning creditor. A creditor who petitions that his debtor may be adjudicated bankrupt. The creditor's debt must be a liquidated one of not less than £750, and is one which the debtor appears either unable to pay or to have no reasonable prospect of being able to pay, and there is no outstanding application to set aside a statutory demand in respect of the debt (see the Insolvency Act 1986, s 267).

See STATUTORY DEMAND.

Petroleum Revenue Tax. Petroleum Revenue Tax is charged on the profits from oil obtained by a participator in an oil field who operates under the authority of a licence granted under the Petroleum Act 1998 (or its Northern Ireland equivalent). Tax is charged at a percentage of the profit made in the exploitation of the oil field. Detailed and specialist provisions for the computation of a profit for the purpose of PRT are specified in Oil Taxation Act 1975, as amended by Petroleum Revenue Tax Act 1980, and subsequent Finance Acts.

The administration of Petroleum Revenue Tax is by the Inland Revenue.

Place of trade. A UK resident is assessed to income tax under Schedule D, Case I on the profits of a trade carried on in the UK, but under Schedule D, Case V on the profits of a trade carried on outside the UK. A non-resident is taxable under Schedule D, Case I on his profits from a trade carried on in the UK (TA 1988, s 18(1)(a)(iii)). It was decided in 1860 that the mere purchase of goods in this country for export and resale abroad was not enough to amount to trading in the UK (*Sulley v AG (1860) 5 H & N 711, 2 TC 149n*). In *Erichsen v Last (1881) 8 QBD 414, 4 TC 422 at 425* trading in the UK was defined by Brett LJ:

'Wherever profitable contracts are habitually made in England by or for a foreigner with persons in England because those persons are in England, to do something for or to supply something to those persons, such foreigners are exercising a profitable trade in England even though everything done or supplied by those persons in order to fulfil the contract is done abroad.'

Most of the cases have been concerned with the sale of goods by a non-resident to someone in the UK, and the basic test has been that the trade is carried on where the contracts of sale are made (eg *Maclaine & Co v Eccott [1926] AC 424, 10 TC 481*). The place of a contract is determined according to English domestic law and this is the place at which the acceptance of an offer is communicated. It follows that an acceptance by post completes the contract at the place of posting whereas an acceptance by telex completes the contract at the place of receipt. This principle is comparatively simple to apply when the foreigner deals directly with the customer but difficult questions of fact arise when an intermediary is employed. The fact that the foreigner uses an agent or stations an employee in England is not sufficient to create a trade within as distinct from with the UK (as in *Greenwood v F L Smidth & Co [1922] 1 AC 417, 8 TC 205*).

The notion that the place of the contract determines the place of the trade is a very English notion since it combines the obsession with sale as the paradigm contract with the doctrine of the source. In *Maclaine & Co v Eccott [1926] AC 424 at 432* while describing the place of the contract as the most important and indeed the crucial question, Lord Cave listed other factors such as the place where payment is to be made for the goods sold, and the place where the goods are to be delivered, and disclaimed any exhaustive test. The place of contract has been further downgraded by Lord Radcliffe in *Firestone Tyre and Rubber Co v Lewellin (1957) 37 TC 111 at 142*: 'It cannot mean more than that the law requires that great importance should be attached to the place of sale. It follows that the place of sale will not be the determining factor if there are other circumstances present that outweigh its importance.' The formulation generally preferred is that of Atkin LJ: 'Where do the operations take place from which the profits in substance arise?' (*F L Smidth & Co v Greenwood (1921) 8 TC 193*). So in *IRC v Brackett [1986] STC 521* a non-resident company was held to be trading in the UK where its agent carried on its activities in the UK, these being the essential operations of the company's trade.

Placing. The sale of newly issued shares to a group of investors chosen by a company, or, more frequently, by its broker. Placings are favoured as minimising the cost of raising capital from a stock market. A placing may also provide an opportunity to determine the shareholders and, in particular, the size of shareholdings.

Planning permission. Permission to carry out development of land. Such permission must be sought from the local planning authority under the Town and Country Planning Act 1971.

Plant and machinery. Capital allowances are given for machinery and plant used for the purpose of a trade and, in certain circumstances, in connection with the letting of land and buildings.

For a full discussion of the definition of assets that attract capital allowances, *see* MACHINERY AND PLANT.

Pooled car. No car benefit is charged on any individual when a car is owned by an enterprise and is treated as a pooled car. A car is treated as a pooled car for a tax year if:

(*a*) in that year it was made available to, and actually used by, more than one of those employees, and in the case of each of them, it was made available to him by reason of his employment but it was not in that year ordinarily used by one of them to the exclusion of the others; and

(*b*) in the case of each of them any private use of the car made by him in that year was merely incidental to his other use of it in the year; and

(*c*) it was in that year not normally kept overnight on or in the vicinity of any residential premises where any of the employees was residing, except while being kept overnight on premises occupied by the person making the car available to them.

Portion. A part of a person's estate which is given or left to a child or person to whom another stands in *loco parentis*. The word is specially applied to payments made to younger children out of the funds comprised in their parents' marriage settlement, and in pursuance of the trusts of it.

Possession. (1) When a man actually enters into lands and tenements. This is called actual possession.

(2) When lands and tenements descend to a man, and he has not yet entered into them. This is called possession in law. Thus, there are estates in possession as opposed to estates in remainder or reversion. Into the former a man has a right to enter at once; of the latter the enjoyment is delayed.

See ESTATE.

(3) The exercise of the right of ownership, whether rightfully or wrongfully. This has been defined as 'physical detention, coupled with the intention to use the thing detained as one's own'.

See OWNERSHIP.

(4) As used in the Law of Property Act 1925, possession includes receipt of rents and profits or the right to receive the same, if any (see s 205(1)(xix)).

Post balance sheet events. Those events, both favourable and unfavourable, which occur between the balance sheet date and the date on which the financial statements are approved by the board of directors. [SSAP 17 – Accounting for post balance sheet events]

Post-dating an instrument. The dating of an instrument as of a date after that on which it is executed. A bill of exchange, note or cheque may be post-dated (see the Bills of Exchange Act 1882, s 13).

See BILL OF EXCHANGE; PROMISSORY NOTE; CHEQUE.

Post-nuptial. After marriage; thus, a post-nuptial settlement is a settlement made after marriage, and, not being made in consideration of marriage, it is, in general, considered as *voluntary*, that is, as having been made on no valuable consideration.

See CONSIDERATION.

Potential ordinary share. A financial instrument or a right that may entitle its holder to ordinary shares. Examples of potential ordinary shares are:

(*a*) debt or equity instruments, including preference shares, that are convertible into ordinary shares;

(*b*) share warrants and options;

(*c*) rights granted under employee share plans that may entitle employees to receive ordinary shares as part of their remuneration and similar rights granted under other share purchase plans; and

(d) rights to ordinary shares that are contingent upon the satisfaction of certain conditions resulting from contractual arrangements, such as the purchase of a business or other assets, ie contingently issuable shares.

[FRS 14 – Earnings per share]

Potentially exempt transfer. A key concept for inheritance tax is the concept of the potentially exempt transfer. A potentially exempt transfer is exempt after the passage of seven years without the transferor dying; if the transferor dies in that period, it becomes chargeable (IHTA 1984, s 3A(4)). If the transferor dies within the seven-year period, the transfer has its potentially exempt status retrospectively removed and it falls to be taxed as if it had been a chargeable transfer when made. The amount of tax payable on the potentially exempt transfer that has become chargeable is determined by reference to the cumulative total of chargeable transfers in the previous seven years prior to the date of the potentially exempt transfer—not the date of the death.

There are three elements. First, the transfer must be a transfer of value made by an individual. Second, it must (apart from this provision) be a chargeable transfer, and not an exempt transfer. Third, it must, in broad terms, be either a gift to another individual (including a settled gift under which the individual has an interest in possession) or a gift into an accumulation and maintenance trust (IHTA 1984, s 3A).

A transfer of value by or to a close company is not a potentially exempt transfer. However, the termination of an interest in possession in settled property can be an exempt transfer (IHTA 1984, s 3A(7)).

Power. A capacity at law to alter the rights, duties, or powers of oneself or others. Thus a person possessed of property has the power to transfer it by gift, thus altering the rights of the donee and his or her own, as each now stands in a different legal relationship to the property following the gift; a person has a power to give his property at death by will; and so on. The most common use of the term is in respect of powers of appointment, powers often given by will or under the terms of a trust to appoint, ie give, real or personal property independently of the other terms of the will or trust and often in defeasance of other estates or interests otherwise given under the will or trust. The person entitled to exercise the power (who is called the *donee of the power*) may have no interest in the property in question, in which case the power is called a power *collateral*, or *in gross*; or he may himself have an interest in the property, and the power is then called a power *coupled with an interest*, or a power *appendant* or *appurtenant*, eg in case of a parent having a life interest in property, with power to appoint the property (either by deed or will) to his children after his death. The exercise of the power is called an *appointment*; and the persons taking the property under such an appointment are called *appointees*, and not grantees or assigns.

Powers may be *general*, giving a right to appoint as the donee may think fit, even to him or herself, or *special* only in favour of some or all of certain persons or classes of persons. Also they may be powers of *revocation*, eg in voluntary settlements, or of *revocation and new appointment*, eg in marriage settlements to enable shares of children to be rearranged. After 1925 powers of appointment, with certain exceptions, will operate only in equity (see the Law of Property Act 1925, s 1(7)).

Power of attorney. An authority given by one person to another to act for him in his absence, eg to convey land, receive debts, sue, etc. The party so authorised to act is called the *attorney* of the party giving the authority. See the Powers of Attorney Act 1971, which provides that a power of attorney must be made by DEED. A form of general power of attorney is printed in Sch 1 to the Act. Some powers of attorney are not revoked by the mental incapacity of the donor and are known as enduring powers.

See ENDURING POWER OF ATTORNEY.

Power to enjoy. The taxation of residents coupled with the non-taxation of non-residents might encourage residents to arrange for income which would otherwise come to them to be held by non-residents and especially by such artificial entities as trusts and companies. TA 1988, s 739 operates to treat as income of a UK resident income arising to a non-resident when the resident individual has 'power to enjoy' that income.

TA 1988, s 739(2) applies where there has been a transfer of assets, and charges any individual who has, by virtue of the transfer or any associated operations, the power to enjoy income which in consequence of the transfer becomes that of a person resident or domiciled outside the UK. Such income is deemed to be that of the person with the power to enjoy and is taxed under Schedule D, Case VI. The concept of income becoming payable to a non-resident is wide enough to include the profits of a non-resident trader (*IRC v Brackett [1986] STC 521*).

TA 1988, s 739(3) applies where there is a transfer of assets and whether before or after the transfer an individual ordinarily resident in the UK receives a capital sum. This sum must be connected with the transfer and be either

(a) a sum paid or payable by way of loan, or

(b) any other sum paid or payable otherwise than as income and which is not paid or payable for full consideration in money or money's worth.

Thus this does not apply where a resident simply sells assets for full market value to a non-resident.

Neither of these provisions will apply if the individual shows to the satisfaction of the Board that (a) the purpose of avoiding tax liability was not the purpose or one of the purposes for which the transfer or associated operations were made, or (b) that the transfer was a bona fide commercial transaction and not designed for the purpose of avoiding liability to taxation (TA 1988, s 741).

Six points can be noted:

(1) For both provisions there must be a transfer of assets or operations associated with the transfer. Further the income accruing to the non-resident must accrue by virtue of or in consequence of that transfer or those operations. It is not necessary that the income should come from the transferred assets. The situs of the assets is unimportant. The term asset is defined to include property or rights of any kind and has been construed in a way similar to that for CGT. It therefore includes rights under a contract of employment. The term transfer is defined to include the creation of rights or property.

(2) For both provisions the transferee must be either not resident or not domiciled in the UK when the income accrues, regardless of his residence when the transfer is made. Whether they apply if the transferor becomes ordinarily resident only after the transfer is not completely clear, but it is unlikely that they apply.

(3) For both provisions the associated operations may be by the transferor or the transferee or any other person. The scope of an 'associated operation' is very widely defined in s 742(1), as operations of any kind effected by any person in relation to any of the assets, or income or assets representing those assets or that income. Thus the transfer of shares or a partnership to a company, taking up residence or domicile overseas, an exchange of debentures and the making of a will have all been held to be associated operations, but not the death of a testator.

(4) For s 739(2) there has to be a power to enjoy income. This requirement is satisfied if any of the following sets of circumstances exist:

(a) The income is in fact so dealt with by any person as to be calculated, at some point of time and whether in the form of income or not, to enure for the benefit of the individual.

(b) The receipt or accrual of the income operates to increase the value to the individual of assets held by him or for his benefit.

(c) The individual receives or is entitled to receive, at any time any benefit provided or to be provided out of that income or out of moneys that are or will be available for the purpose by reason of the effect or successive effects of the associated operations on that income and on any assets which directly or indirectly represent that income.

(*d*) The individual may, in the event of the exercise or successive exercise of one or more powers by whomsoever exercisable and whether with or without the consent of any other persons, become entitled to the beneficial enjoyment of the income.

(*e*) The individual is able in any manner whatsoever, and whether directly or indirectly, to control the application of the income.

(5) The fact that the resident has no power to enjoy the income of the transferee is not conclusive; the section asks whether he has the power to enjoy any income of any person; so control over the transferee is sufficient.

(6) The Board has the most extensive power to demand information in applying this section both from the transferor and any other person. There is some protection for solicitors and bankers.

Practice. The procedure in a court of justice, through the various stages of any matter, civil or criminal, pending in it. The practice in the Supreme Court was formerly regulated by the Supreme Court Act 1981, and the Rules of the Supreme Court 1965, and amending rules, which may be found in the 'Supreme Court Practice'. The practice in the county courts was regulated by the County Courts Act 1984, and the County Court Rules 1981. Both have been replaced save for minor reservations by the Civil Procedure Rules 1998 made under the Civil Procedure Act 1997.

Precatory words. Words in a will or settlement 'praying' or 'desiring' that a thing shall be done. In some cases such words have created a trust; and such a trust is sometimes called a *precatory trust*.

See TRUST.

Precedent condition. *See* CONDITIONS PRECEDENT AND SUBSEQUENT.

Precedents. Examples which may be followed. The word is used principally, though by no means exclusively, to indicate one of the two following things:

(1) A decision in a court of justice cited in support of any proposition for which it is desired to contend. A prior decision of the House of Lords is binding on all inferior courts, though no longer necessarily upon the House of Lords itself, and nothing except an Act of Parliament can alter it.

(2) Drafts of deeds, wills, mortgages, pleadings, etc, which may serve as patterns for future draftsmen and conveyancers.

Pre-emption. A right to purchase before another person.

(1) In general, when a company issues new shares, it is required to offer the shares to its existing shareholders in the proportion in which existing shares are held; that is, in proportion with their existing pre-emption rights (Companies Act 1985, s 89). A private company may, however, in its articles exclude shareholders' pre-emption rights (Companies Act 1985, s 91).

(2) A right given to the owner from whom lands have been acquired by compulsory powers in case they should become *superfluous* for the undertaking for which they were acquired (see the Lands Clauses Consolidation Act 1845, ss 127–129). As to registration of rights of pre-emption, see the Land Charges Act 1972, s 2(4)(iv); and as to releases of such rights, see the Law of Property Act 1925, s 186 which provides that if not released, they remain in force as equitable interests only.

Preference, fraudulent. A term used in connection with payments, transfers, conveyances, etc, made by a company or person unable to pay his debts by way of preference to some of his creditors over others (see the Insolvency Act 1986, s 239 (company) and s 340 (individual)). Where there has been a fraudulent preference, the court may make such order as it thinks fit for restoring the position to what it would have been if the preference had not been given (see ibid, ss 239, 340).

Preference shares in a company are shares entitling their holders to a preferential dividend; so that a holder of preference shares is entitled to have the whole of his dividend (or so much of it as represents the extent to which his shares are, by the constitution of the company, to be deemed preference shares) paid before any dividend is paid to the ordinary shareholders. Sometimes such shares have preference also in regard to capital in the event of winding-up.

See SHARE.

Preferential debts. Payments that are made in preference to the right of others in bankruptcy, the winding-up of companies, or the administration of estates of persons dying insolvent. On a winding-up one year's rates and taxes, sums due for value added tax for the last six months, four months' remuneration owed to an employee not exceeding a sum prescribed by order made by the Secretary of State in each case, and certain amounts under the Social Security Act 1975, are payable in priority to all other debts (see the Insolvency Act 1986, s 386, Sch 6).

See PREFERENCE, FRAUDULENT.

Pre-incorporation contract. A contract purporting to be made by a company or by a person acting as its agent before the company has been incorporated.

Subject to any agreement to the contrary, such a contract has effect as one entered into by the person purporting to act for the company or as agent for it, and he is personally liable on the contract accordingly (see the Companies Act 1985, s 36(4)).

Prejudice, without. Phrase often used in a solicitor's letter for the purpose of guarding himself as to anything contained in it being construed as an admission of liability.

Premises. (1) The commencement of a deed, setting out the number and names of the parties, with their additions or titles, and the recital, if any, of such deeds and matters of fact as are necessary to explain the reasons on which the deed is founded; the consideration upon which it is made; and,

if the deed is a disposition of property, the particulars of the property intended to be transferred by it; also the operative words, with the exceptions and reservations (if any).

See DEED; RECITAL; OPERATIVE PART OF A DEED.

(2) Hence it has come to mean the lands granted; and hence any specified houses or lands.

(3) Propositions antecedently supposed or proved.

Premium. (1) A lump sum paid for the granting of a lease. When a premium is paid on the issue of a lease for less than 50 years, a proportion of the premium paid is treated as income subject to income tax under Schedule A (TA 1988, ss 34–39). The proportion subjected to income tax is greater, the shorter the period of the lease. The part of the premium not subject to income tax is then subject to CGT as a part disposal. A premium is defined as 'including any like sum whether payable to the immediate or superior landlord or to a person connected with such landlord' (TA 1988, s 24(1)). It is likely that a payment to a third party other than a connected person is a premium; such a payment is a premium for the Landlord and Tenant (Rent Control) Act 1949 (see *Elmdene Estates Ltd v White [1960] AC 528, [1960] 1 All ER 306*). A premium in non-monetary form is caught (TA 1988, s 24(4)).Thus a payment required by a landlord on the grant of a lease to a tenant would fall within this rule but a payment required by the tenant on the assignment of his interest would not. A payment exacted by the tenant on the grant of a sub-lease would be caught.

A 'premium' is defined by TCGA 1992, Sch 8, para 10(2) as including 'any like sum, whether payable to an intermediate or a superior landlord'; presumably this means any sum like a premium, a term usually meaning a sum paid by the tenant to the landlord for the lease. A 'premium' includes any sum (other than rent) paid on or in connection with the granting of a tenancy, except in so far as other sufficient consideration for the payment is shown to have been given (TCGA 1992, Sch 8, para 10(2)). In *Clarke v United Real (Moorgate)*

Ltd [1988] STC 273 at 299/300 Walton J said:

'Now what is a premium? Having in mind the dictum of Lord Goddard CJ in *R v Birmingham (West) Rent Tribunal [1951] 2 KB 54 at 57, [1951] 1 All ER 198 at 201*, that "The whole conception of the term is a sum of money paid to a landlord as consideration for the grant of a lease", I ventured to define a premium as any sum paid by the tenant to the landlord in consideration of the grant of the lease.... "Key money" was a premium, and hence, in any event, available to be caught as such under that description.'

The following payments are treated as lease premiums:

(1) Payment in lieu of rent.
(2) Consideration for the surrender of a lease.
(3) Consideration for the variation of a lease (TCGA 1992, Sch 8, para 3).

(2) An amount paid to a company for the issue of a share, insofar as the payment exceeds the nominal value of the share. The sums so received create the company's share premium account, which is a non-distributable reserve (Companies Act 1985, s 130). Companies Act 1985, s 131 provides relief from the requirement to create a share premium account in certain circumstances ('merger relief').

Presumption. That which comes near, in greater or less degree, to the proof of a fact. It is called violent, probable, or light, according to the degree of its cogency. Presumptions are also divided into (1) *præsumptiones juris et de jure*, otherwise called irrebuttable presumptions (often, but not necessarily, fictitious), which the law will not suffer to be rebutted by any counter-evidence; eg that an infant under ten years is not responsible for his actions; (2) *præsumptiones juris tantum*, which hold good in the absence of counter-evidence, but against which counter-evidence may be admitted; and (3) *præsumptiones hominis*, which are not necessarily conclusive, though no proof to the contrary is adduced.

Price earnings ratio (P/E). The market price of a company's share divided by the earnings per share of the company. (Sometimes called the company's 'multiple'.)

Prima facie case. A litigating party is said to have a *prima facie* case when the evidence in his favour is sufficiently strong for his opponent to be called on to answer it. A *prima facie* case, then, is one which is established by sufficient evidence, and can be overthrown only by rebutting evidence adduced on the other side.

Prime cost. The sum calculated by adding the cost of direct materials, direct labour and direct expenses.

Principal. (1) The amount of money which has been borrowed, as opposed to the interest payable thereon.

See INTEREST (2).

(2) A person who employs an agent.

(3) The general or compendious term for the person(s) to whom a fiduciary owes his fiduciary duties.

See AGENT; FIDUCIARY.

Principal company. For the purpose of relief for the capital gain arising on the transfer of an asset between two companies that are members of the same group, a group consists of a principal company and all its 75% subsidiaries. The 75% is applied to the beneficial ownership of shares. A company owns shares beneficially if it is free to dispose of them as it wishes; it is irrelevant that the shares may not be owned very long (*Burman v Hedges and Butler Ltd [1979] STC 136*). A company can only be a principal company if it is at the head of the corporate chain. So a company cannot be a principal company if it is a 75% subsidiary of another company. (There is an exception if the company does not form part of a group because it is not an effective 51% subsidiary: TCGA 1992, s 170(5).)

Principal private residence relief. Any gain is wholly or partly exempt if it is attributable to the disposal of or of an interest in a dwelling-house which is or has been the owner's only or main residence (TCGA 1992, s 222). It is sufficient that the house was the owner's residence at any time during the period of ownership, however long ago the period of owner-occupation ended.

There is no requirement that the residence should be in the UK. It is, however, necessary that it is a dwelling-house which has been used as the taxpayer's residence; this is a question of fact— a caravan can qualify (*Makins v Elson [1977] STC 46*); but a merely transitory occupation of a house does not qualify (*Goodwin v Curtis [1998] STC 475*). It has also been held that a separate bungalow adjacent to but within the curtilage of a dwelling-house was part of the dwelling-house even though the bungalow was occupied by a part-time caretaker (*Batey v Wakefield [1981] STC 521*). In *Lewis v Lady Rook [1992] STC 171, CA*, the Court of Appeal considered that separate buildings were only included if they were within the curtilage of, and appurtenant to, the main house.

As well as the actual site of the dwelling-house, land is included in the exemption if the owner has it as the garden or grounds of the dwelling-house, for his own occupation and enjoyment. If the garden or grounds exceed 0.5 hectare, the exemption applies only if the Commissioners are satisfied that the larger area was, having regard to the size and character of the house, required for the reasonable enjoyment as a residence.

To determine what larger area is 'required' in any particular case, Evans-Lombe J in *Longson v Baker [2001] STC 6 at 15* adopted the formulation made in the judgment in a 1938 compulsory purchase case (per Parcq J in the case of *Re Newhill Compulsory Purchase Order 1937, Payne's Application [1938] 2 All ER 163*, a case decided on 9 March 1938 under the provisions of s 75 of the Housing Act 1936):

"'Required', I think, in this section does not mean merely that the occupiers of the house would like to have it, or that they would miss it if they lost it, or that anyone proposing to buy the house would think less of the house without it than he would if it was preserved to it. 'Required' means, I suppose, that without it there would be such a substantial deprivation of amenities or convenience that a real injury will be done to the property owner, and a question like that is obviously a question of fact.'

The test is whether the house requires the larger grounds 'not the wishes, desires or intentions of any particular owner of the house' (per THK Everett, Special Commissioner, in *Longson v Baker [2000] STC (SCD) 244 at 248d*. In the High Court, Evans-Lombe J said: 'the Commissioners approach . . . cannot be faulted under the statutory provisions', *[2001] STC 6 at 14j*).

The exemption is lost if the acquisition of the house was wholly or partly for the purpose of making a gain from its disposal (TCGA 1992, s 224(3)). Likewise where expenditure is incurred in carrying out improvements or in acquiring additional land with the purpose of gain, then there will be a charge on the proportion of the gain attributable to that expenditure. A mere hope of making a gain is probably insufficient to lose the exemption.

Prior period adjustments. Material adjustments applicable to prior periods arising from changes in accounting policies or from the correction of fundamental errors. They do not include normal recurring adjustments or corrections of accounting estimates made in prior periods [FRS 3 – Reporting financial performance]. When an enterprise makes a change in its accounting policy, FRS 3 requires that the financial results of the current year be reported using the new policy, after restating opening values. The comparative figures for the previous year are then restated from the previous report, by applying the new accounting policy. The net total of the adjustment to the accumulated reserves that arises from the change in accounting policy is known as the prior year adjustment. A prior year adjustment may also arise on the correction of a fundamental error. The correction of an estimate is not, however, grounds for a prior year adjustment. For tax purposes, it is normally necessary to bring the prior year adjustment into the current year when calculating the liability to income tax (or corporation tax).

Priority. Any legal precedence or preference; eg when one says that certain debts are paid in *priority* to others; or that certain incumbrancers of an estate are allowed *priority* over others, ie are to be allowed to satisfy their claims out of the estate before the others can be admitted to any share in it, etc.

See PREFERENTIAL DEBTS.

Private Law. The law governing the relations between individuals, not individuals and the state, except in so far as the state's rights are akin to those of private parties (ie as a tortfeasor, as a contracting party, as an owner of property, and as one able unjustly to enrich another or be unjustly enriched), thus the law of torts, contract, property, and unjust enrichment.

Private limited company. A limited company that has a restriction on offering shares to the public at large. In general, a private limited company is subject to fewer constraints on its activities and fewer reporting requirements than a public company.

Privity of contract. The relation subsisting between the parties to the same contract. Thus if A, B and C mutually contract, there is privity of contract between them. But if A contracts with B, and B makes an independent contract with C on that same subject matter, there is no privity of contract between A and C.

Those not privy to a contract are normally neither liable under it nor entitled to bring an action for any benefit under it. Now, however, by the Contract (Rights of Third Parties) Act 1999, third parties in certain circumstances may enforce a contract to obtain a benefit under it.

See CONTRACT LAW.

Pro rata. Proportionately.

Probate. The exhibiting and proving wills by executors in the High Court on which the original is deposited in the registry of the court, and a copy, called the *probate copy*, is made out under the seal of the court, and delivered to the executor, together with a certificate of its having been proved.

It may be either *in common form* or *in solemn form per testes*, where the will is disputed or irregular. For the procedure in regard to the granting of probate, see Part V of the Supreme Court Act 1981. Contentious business is dealt with in the Chancery Division of the High Court; non-contentious business has been assigned to the Family Division.

Procedure. The steps taken in an action or other legal proceeding.

Product liability insurance. Insurance taken out by persons liable for damage caused by a product.

Production overheads. Overheads incurred in respect of materials, labour or services for production, based on the normal level of activity, taking one year with another. For this purpose each overhead should be classified according to function (eg production, selling or administration) so as to ensure the inclusion, in cost of conversion, of those overheads (including depreciation) which relate to production, notwithstanding that these may accrue wholly or partly on a time basis. [SSAP 9 – Stocks and long-term contracts]

Profession. The term profession involves the idea of an occupation requiring either purely intellectual skill, or of manual skill controlled, as in painting and sculpture or surgery, by the intellectual skill of the operator; such an occupation is distinct from one which is substantially the production or sale or arrangements for the production or sale of commodities (*IRC v Maxse (1919), 12 TC 41 at 61*). So a journalist and editor carry on a profession but a newspaper reporter carries on a trade (*(1919) 12 TC 41 at 61*). The question is one of fact and degree and the crux is the degree of intellectual skill involved. So one who ran a service for taxpayers seeking to recover overpaid tax or to reduce assessments was held by the Commissioners to be carrying on a trade and the Court of Appeal felt there was no error of law (*Currie v IRC (1921) 12 TC 245*). Other traders include a stockbroker (*Christopher Barker & Sons v IRC [1919] 2 KB 222*) and a photographer (*Cecil v IRC (1919) 36 TLR 164*). In *Salt v Fernandez [1997] STC (SCD) 271*, the Special Commissioner distinguished between the profession being carried on by Dr Salt as an author and the trade of publishing, which was also carried on by Dr Salt. Cash accounts were accepted for the former but earnings accounts required for the latter.

Professional indemnity insurance. A type of insurance effected by various persons, eg solicitors, accountants, brokers, architects, against their liability to pay damages to their clients by reason of their negligence in the performance of their professional duties.

Profits. Income Tax under Schedule D, Cases I and II is charged on 'profits' (TA 1988, s 60(1)). The measure of income assessable under Schedule A is, similarly, defined by reference to 'profits' (TA 1988, s 21A). For a company, corporation tax is chargeable on the 'total profits' (TA 1988, s 6(1)). In contrast to the approach taken in a number of continental countries, the UK Taxes Acts do not provide a formulation of the measure of profit. Some provisions, most notoriously TA 1988, s 74, list items that are not to be included as expenses and other provisions possible for specified deductions (such as capital allowances), but no attempt is made to formulate either income or expenditure. This is in contrast to the approach in, for example, Germany where the fiscal code enumerates the categories into which a receipt must fall if it is to be recognised as a taxable credit and the categories within which a payment must fall if it is to be recognised as a tax-deductible debit.

The earliest judicial formulation as to what constitutes 'profit', as a measure on which a tax liability is to be charged, was given in 1888 by Lord Herschell:

'The profit of a trade or business is the surplus by which the receipts from the trade or business exceed the expenditure' (*Russell v Aberdeen Town and County Bank (1888) 2 TC 321 at 327*).

For Hicks, an economist writing in 1946, an attempt to define 'income' is 'chasing a will-o'-the-wisp'. McDonald comments:

'Profit is an abstraction; it is not something given in nature ... Profit

measurement is a purposive activity, the measurement, whilst being a measure of something, is determined not by what is measured but by the purpose for which the measurement is undertaken' (*[1995] BTR 484*).

Every enterprise has to choose an appropriate set of accounting policies. Different accounting policies will give different measures of profit and, hence, different amounts of tax payable. The extent to which tax law determines taxable profit and the extent to which taxable profit is a function of chosen accounting policies is a question that has been at the heart of a series of court decisions.

In recent years courts have tended to avoid constructing rules for tax computations that differ from the approach taken for commercial accounts. In *Herbert Smith v Honour [1999] STC 173 at 204d*, Lloyd J gave an extensive review of the case law on provisions and concluded:

'While I would not say that the judge-made rule as to the relevance of accounts prepared in accordance with generally accepted principles of commercial accounting does not permit non-statutory exceptions beyond those already recognised in decided cases, I am not able to hold that the relevance of such accounts is subject to a general exception prohibiting the deduction of sums entered in the debit side of the accounts by way of a provision in accordance with the prudence concept as set out in para 14(d) of SSAP 2.'

The court upheld the similar approach adopted by Special Commissioners who allowed a deduction for the provision for the cost of repairs that were necessary to be undertaken in the future (*Jenners Princes Street Edinburgh Ltd v IRC [1998] STC (SCD) 196*). Similarly, in *Tapemaze v Mellurish [2000] STC 189* accounts were drawn up in accordance with FRS 3 so that the write-back of a provision for rentals paid in advance and a provision for deferred maintenance, a total of £5,189,609, was treated in the accounts as an increase in the profit of the final year of trading. The court upheld the Special Commissioners' decision to reject the taxpayer's application that this sum should be treated for tax purposes as income of the company that accrued over a series of later years and not as income of the single year in which it was recognised for accounting purposes.

Profits à prendre. Rights exercised by one person in the soil of another, accompanied with participation in the profits of the soil, eg rights of pasture, or digging sand. *Profits à prendre* differ from easements in that the former are rights of profit, and the latter are mere rights of convenience without profit.

See EASEMENT.

Profit-sharing schemes. (1) Until 2000, an employer was able to register a profit related pay scheme under which employees could receive a tax-free profit related bonus. The last period for which such a scheme has been available is a period of account that begins before 1 January 2000.

(2) Privileged tax treatment is afforded to shares appropriated to approved profit-sharing schemes. A trust is essential. The company provides the trustees with money with which they acquire shares from the company which they then appropriate to particular individuals (TA 1988, s 186 and Schs 9 & 10). The treatment ensures that no income tax is paid when the shares are set aside for the employee. Further there is a charge to CGT, and not to income tax, on the value of the shares when they are sold provided, in general, that they are not sold for five years. No new schemes will be approved unless the application for approval is received by the Revenue before 6 April 2001; further, appropriations to such schemes will cease to have beneficial tax treatment unless completed before 5 April 2002.

Projected unit method. An accrued benefits valuation method in which the actuarial liability makes allowance for projected earnings. An accrued benefits valuation method is a valuation method in which the actuarial liability at the valuation date relates to:

(a) the benefits for pensioners and deferred pensioners (ie individuals who have ceased to be active members but are entitled to benefits payable at a later date) and their dependants, allowing where appropriate for future increases; and

(b) the accrued benefits for members in service on the valuation date. The accrued benefits are the benefits for service up to a given point in time, whether vested rights or not.

[FRED 20 – Retirement benefits]

Promise. A voluntary engagement by one person to another for the performance or non-performance of some particular thing. It differs from a contract, in that a contract involves the idea of mutuality, which a promise does not.

See CONTRACT; COVENANT.

Promissory note, otherwise called a *note of hand,* is defined by the Bills of Exchange Act 1882, s 83 as an unconditional promise in writing, made by one person to another, signed by the maker, engaging to pay on demand or at a fixed or determinable future time, a sum certain in money, to or to the order of a specified person or to bearer. The person who makes the note is called the maker, and the person to whom it is payable is called the payee. It differs from a bill of exchange, in that the maker stands in the place of drawer and acceptor.

See BILL OF EXCHANGE.

Promoter. Person who assists in the establishment of a company (see the Companies Act 1985, s 67).

Promotion money. Money paid to the promoters of a company for their services in launching the concern.

Property. The concept of property in any legal system dictates how valuable parts of the world can be made the subject matter of rights, rights which may be distributed by various modes, such as gift, contract, or the command of law.

The subject matter of property consists of the different sorts of things which can be owned. The sorts of property in the law are traditionally divided into two classes, real property and personal property, which roughly corresponds to the civil law distinction between *immovables* and *movables,* the former term in each case referring to land, and the latter to things other than land, in particular tangible objects like furniture, books, clothing, etc. Tangible objects of this latter kind are called 'chattels' in English law. Unfortunately, the traditional division between real 'estate' and personal property in English law is hampered by the fact that leasehold interests, ie the right of a lessee or tenant in the land leased to him, was regarded as personal property rather than real property because originally a lessee out of possession could not get the assistance of the courts of common law in a 'real' action to be put in possession of the land, ie get the real thing. As a consequence, leasehold interests in land were treated as personal property; land being tangible, a kind of chattel, but nevertheless an interest in land, the odd hybrid 'chattels real' was used to designate leasehold interests. Following the reorganisation of property law by the property legislation of 1925, leasehold interests are now regarded as property in land as much as any other kind of right in land. The great development of types of property has occurred on the personal side, for it is into that category that new forms of intangible property, ie property with no physically possessible subject-matter, has been placed. Thus personal property can be divided into the tangible, chattels, and the intangible. The traditional terms for marking this distinction are choses in possession, and choses in action, the former being things ownership of which is secured by possession, thus material chattels, the latter being abstract *rights* the value of which lies in *action*, ie the legal process. Thus debts are choses in action because one is secured the value of a debt (being paid the certain sum of money one is owed) by the power to proceed at law against the debtor. The same goes, eg, for bank balances (the debt one is owed by one's bank). Certain abstract rights of this kind can be reduced to 'documentary intangibles', that is, the rights become embodied in paper, and the title to these rights can be transferred by the proper transfer of the paper. An important class of these is NEGOTIABLE INSTRUMENTS, which are subject to

particular rules of title. A different kind of personal property entirely is the right to a monopoly constituted by a patent or copyright, ie intellectual property rights. While again these are abstract, and may be enforced by legal process, the monopoly itself is not secured by legal process; rather, violations of the monopoly are enjoined or compensated, and in this way intellectual property rights are more like rights in tangible property than choses in action.

Property Acts 1925, Property Legislation of 1925. A major legislative reorganisation and reform of property law, in particular of land law, comprised of six Acts of 1925, plus further supplementary provisions and amendments passed in 1926. The six Acts comprising the legislation were the Law of Property Act, The Land Registration Act, The Land Charges Act, The Settled Land Act, The Trustee Act, and The Administration of Estates Act.

Prospective benefits. A prospective benefits method of valuation is a valuation method in which the actuarial value of liabilities relates to:

(*a*) the benefits for current and deferred pensioners and their dependants, allowing where appropriate for future pension increases; and

(*b*) the benefits that active members will receive in respect of both past and future service; allowing for future increases in earnings up to their assumed exit dates, and where appropriate for pension increases thereafter. [SSAP 24 – Accounting for pension costs]

Protective trust. Trusts giving a 'protected' interest for life or any less period to a beneficiary, to ensure that the interest shall not be lost to the beneficiary's creditors. On the happening of the beneficiary's bankruptcy, or upon his attempting to assign his interest to another and other similar events, the protected life interest 'determines', ie is extinguished, and the interest is henceforward held under a DISCRETIONARY TRUST whereby the trustees may, in their absolute discretion, apply the income of the fund, usually for the beneficiary and his or her spouse and children. A statutory form of such trusts is provided by the Trustee Act 1925, s 33.

Prove. (1) To establish by evidence.

(2) To establish a debt due from an insolvent estate, and to receive a dividend on it.

(3) To prove a will.

Provision. A liability of uncertain timing or amount. [FRS 12 – Provisions, contingent liabilities and contingent assets]

Proxy. A person deputed to vote in the place or stead of the party so deputing him, eg in the House of Lords; at meetings of creditors of a bankrupt; at meetings of the shareholders of a company; and on various other occasions.

Prudence. A fundamental basis of accounting. Revenue and profits are not anticipated, but are recognised by inclusion in the profit and loss account only when realised in the form either of cash or of other assets the ultimate cash realisation of which can be assessed with reasonable certainty; provision is made for all known liabilities (expenses and losses) whether the amount of these is known with certainty or is a best estimate in the light of the information available. [SSAP 2 – Disclosure of accounting policies]

Public company. A company limited by shares or limited by guarantee and having a share capital, being a company

(*a*) the memorandum of which states that the company is to be a public company; and

(*b*) in relation to which the provisions of the Act as to the registration or re-registration of a company as a public company have been complied with (see the Companies Act 1985, s 1(3)).

Constraints on the PLC that are not applied to a private limited company include a requirement that the Company Secretary be professionally qualified (or qualified by experience), that the company has an authorised share capital of at least £50,000, one-quarter of which must be paid up, and that its memorandum follows the specification given in Table F of Company

Regulations 1985 (SIs 1985/854 and 1985/1052).

Public liability insurance. A type of insurance protecting the insured against liabilities to third parties other than his employees arising out of the condition or management of his property or the conduct of his business.

Public trustee. An official appointed pursuant to the Public Trustee Act 1906 as a corporation sole to deal with trusts where there is a difficulty in finding someone to serve as a trustee, thus in a sense, a trustee of last resort.

Pur autre vie. For another's life; eg a tenant *pur autre vie* is a tenant whose estate is to last during another person's life.

See ESTATE.

Purchased goodwill. The difference between the cost of an acquired entity and the aggregate of the fair values of that entity's identifiable assets and liabilities. Positive goodwill arises when the acquisition cost exceeds the aggregate fair values of the identifiable assets and liabilities. Negative goodwill arises when the aggregate fair values of the identifiable assets and liabilities of the entity exceed the acquisition cost. [FRS 10 – Goodwill and intangible assets & FRS 11 – Impairment of fixed assets and goodwill]

Purchaser. (1) One who acquires real or personal estate by gift or contract.

(2) Under the Law of Property Act 1925 the word means a purchaser in good faith for valuable consideration, and includes a lessee, mortgagee, or other person who for valuable consideration acquires an interest in property, except that in Part I of that Act and elsewhere as expressly provided, the word only means a person who acquires an interest in or charge on property for money or money's worth; and in reference to a legal estate includes a chargee by way of legal mortgage. See s 205(1)(xxi).

Purpose trust. A trust to carry out a purpose, as opposed to a trust for the distribution of the trust property to persons.

Public, or charitable, purpose trusts are allowed by law and enforced by the Attorney-General or the Charity Commissioners. Purpose trusts not of a charitable nature are generally void, save for a few exceptions, trusts 'of imperfect obligation', ie testamentary trusts for the maintenance of animals, for the upkeep of graves, or for the saying of private masses for the better repose of the testator's soul.

Q

QB. Queen's Bench.

QBD. Queen's Bench Division.
See QUEEN'S BENCH DIVISION.

QC. Queen's Counsel.

Qualification share. A share which a director of a company must hold in order to be appointed or to continue as such. Where a qualification is fixed, it must be disclosed in the prospectus (see the Companies Act 1985, Sch 3, Part I, para 1(b)).

Qualified report. Where an audit is required, whether by company law or by other controlling regulations, the auditor is required to report as to whether, in his opinion, the financial statements give a true and fair view of the profits and loss and state of affairs of the accounting entity for the period stated. Auditing standards require the auditor to give one of three types of report. An 'unqualified report' (colloquially referred to as 'A clean report') is given if the auditor considers that the financial statements give a true and fair view and that the accounts have been drawn up in accordance with applicable accounting standards. An 'adverse report' is given if the auditor considers that the financial statements do not give a true and fair view. A 'qualified report' is given in two situations: (*a*) the auditor considers that the financial statements give a true and fair view but the accounts have not been drawn up in accordance with an accounting standard that is appropriate to the accounts, and (*b*) the auditor considers that the financial statements give a true and fair view of the books of record and other information that have been provided to him, but he considers that he requires further information to satisfy himself of the veracity of the financial statements and this further information has not been made available to him.

Where a qualified report is given, this is shown by the auditor's report stating: 'In my opinion, the accounts give a true and fair view . . . *except that . . .*'
See ADVERSE OPINION; AUDITORS' REPORT.

Qualifying donation. A taxpayer making a qualifying donation to a charity is entitled to deduct the amount of the donation from his income (or from profits, in the case of a company), when calculating the income tax (or corporation tax) liability. A donation is treated as a qualifying donation if it meets the following conditions:

(*a*) The payment must be made during the fiscal year for which relief is claimed (TA 1988, s 399(7AA)).

(*b*) The donor is resident in the UK or, if not, is making the donation out of income subject to UK tax (FA 1990, s 25(2)).

(*c*) The payment is not already relieved under the payroll deduction scheme (FA 1990, s 25(2)(d)).

(*d*) The payment is not the conversion of a loan previously made (*Battle Baptist Church v IRC and Woodham [1995] STC (SCD) 176n*).

(*e*) The payment is not subject to repayment (FA 1990, s 25(2)(b)).

(*f*) The payment must not be associated with the acquisition of property by the charity from the donor or a person connected with him (FA 1990, s 25(2)(f)).

(*g*) Neither the donor nor any person connected with him may receive a benefit in consequence of making it, other than the right to admit to view property or wildlife where the preservation of property or conservation of wildlife is the sole or main purpose of the charity (FA 1990, s 25(5E)–(5G)). (Specified de minimis exemptions for benefits provided by other charities are also ignored: FA 1990, s 25(2)(e).)

(*h*) The donor gives an appropriate declaration in relation to it to the charity (FA 1990, s 25(1)(c)).

As from 2000/01 there is no minimum amount of a qualifying donation. From 6

April 2000, a covenanted payment to charity is a qualifying donation. The long-standing machinery requiring a four-year commitment no longer applies.

Qualifying financial institution. An entity that as part of its business receives deposits or other repayable funds and grants credits for its own account.
[FRS 1 – Cash flow statements]

Qualifying policy. When a taxpayer takes out a qualifying life assurance policy, the assurance company is exempt from tax on the income and gains arising in the policy fund (TA 1988, s 592(2)). No tax liability arises on the policyholder when a payment is made from the policy (TA 1988, s 539(2)). In the case of a policy created before 14 March 1984, tax relief is given on the premiums paid (TA 1988, s 266). Relief is given only if the policy is a 'qualifying policy'; that is, a policy that satisfies the conditions in TA 1988, Sch 15. For whole life or endowment assurances the term must be at least ten years. The premiums must be payable at yearly or shorter intervals for at least ten years or until the event specified, whether death or disability. The total premiums payable under the policy in any period of 12 months must not exceed twice the amount payable in any other 12-month period or one-eighth of the total premiums payable if the policy were to run for the specified term. The policy must guarantee that the sum payable on death will be at least 75% of the total premiums payable if the policy were to run its term.

Qualifying travelling expenses. TA 1988, s 198, as rewritten in 1998, allows holders of offices or employments to deduct expenses which they are obliged to incur and defray out of the emoluments if those expenses are either:
(a) qualifying travelling expenses, or
(b) 'any amount (other than qualifying travelling expenses) expended wholly exclusively and necessarily in the performance of the duties of the office or employment.'
Qualifying travelling expenses fall into two categories.

(a) The first category consists of amounts necessarily expended on travelling in the performance of the duties of the office or employment. (Two employments, where the employers are members of the same group of companies are treated as if they were one employment.)
(b) The second category of qualifying expenses consists of expenses of travelling which (i) are attributable to the necessary attendance at any place of the holder of the office or employment in the performance of the duties of the office or employment, but (ii) which are not expenses of ordinary commuting or private travel.
(TA 1988, s 198(1B)).

Relief is also provided for five categories of expenses related to travel that are considered to be environmentally sensible ideas on the part of employers:
(a) A works bus service (TA 1988, s 197AA). The service must be one for conveying employees on qualifying journeys. Journeys qualify not only if they are between one workplace and another but also, and in complete contrast to the rules in s 198A, between home and workplace. In either case the journey must be in connection with the performance of the duties of the office or employment. In addition the service must be available to employees generally and the main use of the service must be for qualifying journeys by those employees (TA 1988, s 197AA(4) & (7)). In an unusual—and hideous—legislative form of words, the exemption is 'subject to substantial compliance with the condition that the service must be used only by the employees for whom it is provided *or* their children (defined widely but excluding those aged 18 or over)' (TA 1988, s 197AA(4)).
(b) Where an employer provides financial or other support for a public transport road service (TA 1988, s 197AB). Again, the service must be for qualifying journeys. The terms on which the employees travel must not be more favourable than to other passengers and the service must be available to employees generally.

(c) Spaces for parking motor cycles and facilities for parking cycles (TA 1988, s 49). Quite why cycles need facilities and motor cycles only need spaces is unclear. Presumably this wording is intended to cover facilities for locking bicycles up.

(d) The provision by an employer to an employee of a cycle or a cyclist's safety equipment (TA 1988, s 197AC). The benefit or facility must be available to employees generally. The employee must use it mainly for qualifying journeys (TA 1988, s 197AC(4)).

(e) Capital allowances are extended to employees who provide their own bicycles for qualifying journeys (CAA 2001, s 80(1)) or, as an alternative, the employer can pay to an employee a tax-free business allowance of 12p per business mile cycled by the employee.

See FIXED PROFIT CAR SCHEME; MILEAGE ALLOWANCE.

Quarter days are, in England, the four following days:

(1) The 25th March, being the Feast of the Annunciation of the Blessed Virgin Mary, commonly called Lady Day.

(2) The 24th June, being the Feast of St John the Baptist, otherwise called Midsummer Day.

(3) The 29th September, being the Feast of St Michael and All Angels, commonly called Michaelmas Day.

(4) The 25th December, being the Feast of the Nativity of Christ, commonly called Christmas Day.

Quasi-contract. An act or event from which, though not a consensual contract, an obligation arises *as if* from a contract (*quasi ex contractu*), eg an executor or administrator is bound to satisfy the liabilities of the deceased to the extent of his assets received, *as if* he had contracted to do so.

Quasi-distribution. A loan by a company to a shareholder can be referred to as a 'quasi-distribution'. This was a device that was widely used prior to the enactment of what is now TA 1988, s 419 to avoid the tax charges that arose for both the company and for the shareholder when an actual distribution was made. Now, when a loan is made by a close company to a participator a sum equal to corporation tax at 25% is due from the company to the Revenue by way of corporation tax when the loan is made (TA 1988, s 419(1)). This advance payment cannot be set off against the company's own liability to CT on its profits. This payment is additional to any other liability. If the loan is at a low rate of interest, the borrower may incur liability under TA 1988, s 160.

Quasi-subsidiary. A quasi-subsidiary of a reporting entity is a company, trust, partnership or other vehicle that, though not fulfilling the definition of a subsidiary, is directly or indirectly controlled by the reporting entity and gives rise to benefits for that entity that are in substance no different from those that would arise were the vehicle a subsidiary. [FRS 5 – Substance of transactions]

Queen's Bench Division. The jurisdiction of the former Court of Queen's Bench was assigned in 1873 to the then newly-constituted Queen's Bench Division of the High Court of Justice. This Division is still one of three which together form the High Court, the others being the Chancery Division and the Family Division.

The Queen's Bench Division consists of the Lord Chief Justice, who is the president of it, and Puisne Judges, the numbers of which are laid down by Orders in Council made under the Supreme Court Act 1981, s 4(4). As to the assignment of business to the Queen's Bench Division, see the Supreme Court Act 1981, s 61(1), Sch 1.

Quid pro quo. A compensation, or the giving of one thing of value for another thing of like value.

See CONSIDERATION.

Quorum. The *minimum* number of persons necessarily present for a meeting, eg the annual general meeting of a company.

R

R. *Rex* or *regina,* as in the Queen's signature, Elizabeth R.

RSC. Rules of the Supreme Court made by a Rule Committee of judges and lawyers under the authority of the Supreme Court Act 1981. The rules were revised in 1965, and might be found in 'The Supreme Court Practice'; these rules have largely been superseded by the Civil Procedure Rules 1998, made under the Civil Procedure Act 1997.

Rack-rent. Rent of the full annual value of the tenement on which it is charged, or as near to it as possible.

Ramsay principle. The courts have the power to ignore the steps inserted for no commercial purpose and to levy tax on the basis that the end result had been achieved without the intermediate result. In order to ignore a step in a transaction: 'First, there must be a preordained series of transactions; or, if one likes, a single composite transaction. This composite transaction may or may not include the achievement of a legitimate commercial (ie business) end . . . Secondly, there must be steps inserted which have no commercial (business) purpose apart from the avoidance of a liability to tax—not "no business effect"' (per Lord Brightman in *Furniss v Dawson [1984] STC 153*). The scope of the principle has been substantially reduced by the decisions of the House of Lords in *MacNiven v Westmoreland Investments Ltd [2001] STC 237.*

Rate. A tax levied by local authorities on the occupation of hereditaments, irrespective of a person's income generally, and irrespective of whether the ratepayer was, in fact, deriving profits or gain from such occupation. Rates are payable in respect of business premises only. The Act relating to rates with regard to business premises is the General Rate Act 1967. The tax in respect of domestic property is now the Council Tax.

Rate of return. The income generated by an enterprise expressed as a percentage of the sum invested to generate the income.

Rate of tax. (1) Income Tax: The scheme of the rate structure is that there are four rates used to tax income:

Starting rate: An individual (but not any other person who is charged to income tax) is subject to the starting rate on the first tranche of all types of income above the personal allowance.

Basic rate: Income tax at basic rate is charged on all income that is not subject to starting rate, lower rate or higher rate. For an individual, this means that the basic rate is charged on income (other than savings income) within the 'basic rate band'. The basic rate band extends to a figure that is approximately twice the national average income; hence, over 90% of individuals pay tax at basic rate only. Basic rate is applied to the income of all persons who are subject to income tax. As well as applying to individuals, the basic rate of tax is applied to the income of personal representatives, trustees and the UK income of certain foreign companies. For persons other than individuals, starting rate and higher rate are not applied; hence, the charge is at basic rate irrespective of the amount of the income.

Lower rate: Income assessed under Schedule F (ie UK dividends) and equivalent foreign income is charged to income tax at the 'lower Schedule F rate' which is equal to the starting rate. Other savings income is charged to income tax at the lower rate. For an individual, the charge at either of these lower rates extends in so far as the income is within the basic rate band.

Higher rate: All income arising to an individual that is above the basic rate band is charged at higher rate. For income assessed under Schedule F and equivalent for income, the charge is at the Schedule F higher rate.

Trustees of certain trusts are subject to 'the rate of the trust' on income that is accumulated or paid at the trustees' discretion.

(2) Capital Gains Tax: The scheme of the rate structure for CGT is that there are three rates used to tax capital gains:

Starting rate: An individual (but not any other person who is charged to CGT) is subject to the starting rate on the first tranche of capital gains.

Lower rate: CGT at lower rate is charged on all chargeable capital gains that are not subject to starting rate, or higher rate.

Higher rate: All chargeable gains arising to an individual that are above the basic rate band is charged at higher rate.

Trustees of most trusts are subject to 'the rate of the trust' on all capital gains, irrespective of the size of gain.

(3) Corporation Tax: The scheme of the rate structure for corporation tax is that there are three rates used to tax the profits of a company:

Starting rate: The starting rate of tax is applied to the first tranche of all types of income of a company (TA 1988, s 13AA). For the purposes of this relief 'profits' includes income, capital gains and franked investment income but not group income (TA 1988, s 13(7)). This rate applies to companies resident in the UK (other than close investment holding companies) but not to non-resident companies with a UK branch. The Revenue, however, interpret a non-discrimination clause in an applicable double tax agreement as entitling the non-resident company to this rate. The decision of the European Court in *R v IRC, ex p Commerzbank AG (Case C-330/91) [1993] STC 605, CJEC* seems to give branches of companies of another member state a right to use that rate.

Small companies' rate: The small companies' rate is applied to profits of a company that are above the limit for starting rate but do not exceed the specified upper limit for the financial year.

Full rate: The full rate of corporation tax is applied to profit above the small companies' upper limit.

A tapering charge applies between starting rate and small companies' rate and, again, between small companies' rate and full rate. This operates so that the effect of the lower rate is progressively removed as profits increase.

(4) Stamp Duty: In stamping a share transfer document (or when Stamp Duty Reserve Tax is applied in situations where there is no document), the rate of tax is a specified percentage of the consideration. The percentage is fixed and does not vary according to the quantum of the consideration. In stamping any other document subject to *ad valorem* duty, the amount of stamp duty payable is computed by reference to a table which gives progressively increasing rates for increasing quantum of consideration.

(5) Value Added Tax: The scheme of the rate structure for VAT is that there are three rates applied to supplies:

Zero rate: Supplies specified in VATA 1994, Sch 8 are charged at 0%.

Reduced rate: Supplies specified in VATA 1994, Sch A1 are charged at reduced rate.

Full rate: All supplies not otherwise specified, and not exempted from VAT, are charged at full rate.

(6) National Insurance Contributions: The different classes of NIC are subject to different rates, which are specified for each separate fiscal year.

Re Petitt. The rule in *Re Petitt* applies when an agreement states that P is to pay Q £100 'free of tax', P is then required to make a payment to Q of £100; this is equivalent to £128.20 gross and Q's income is therefore taken to include not £100 but £128.20.

If Q has no other income he will be able to reclaim £29.87 from the Revenue on account of his personal reliefs. If he were allowed to keep the sum, he would have benefited to the tune of £128.20 and not £100 as undertaken by P; Q is therefore directed by the rule in *Re Pettit, Le Fevre v Pettit [1922] 2 Ch 765* to hold the sum recovered from the Revenue on trust for P. Q is therefore under an obligation to make the repayment claim (*Kingcome, Hickley v Kingcome [1936] 1 All ER 173, [1936] Ch 566*).

The rule in *Re Pettit* is one of trust law and applies whenever the construction of the agreement, trust or will requires it. There is a clear distinction between £100 'free of tax' to which the rule applies and 'such sum as after deducting tax at the current rate shall leave £100'—known as a formula deduction covenant—to which the rule does not apply; the former indicates the extent to which Q is to benefit while the latter does not.

The rule applies to agreements, estates and trusts. However, its status in Scotland is unclear. Illogically the rule does not apply to court orders (see *Jefferson v Jefferson [1956] 1 All ER 31*) with the result that the same words will have one effect in an agreement and a different one in an order.

Real, besides its ordinary meaning, has two special meanings:

First, as being applicable to a thing in contradistinction to a person.

Secondly, as applicable to land, and especially freehold interests in it, as opposed to other rights and interests.

Real and personal property. Real property is not synonymous with property in land, nor is personal property synonymous with movable property. Thus, a title of honour, though annexed to the person of its owner, is real property, because in ancient times such titles were annexed to the ownership of various lands. On the other hand, shares in companies are personal property. A lease for years is also personal property, because in ancient times an ejected lessee could not recover his lease by a real action; but he could bring a personal action for damages against his landlord, who was bound to warrant him possession.

The code of succession on intestacy which was enacted by Part IV of the Administration of Estates Act 1925 applies alike to real and personal property.
See PROPERTY.

Realty. Real estate, ie freehold interests in land; or, in a larger sense (so as to include chattels real), things substantial and immovable, and the rights and profits annexed to or issuing out of them.
See CHATTELS.

Receipt. A written acknowledgment of the payment of money. A receipt for the purchase-money of land may be embodied in the purchase-deed (see the Law of Property Act 1925, ss 67, 68).

Receiver. (1) An officer appointed to receive the rents and profits of property, and account for them to the court, eg in actions for dissolution of partnership or for the administration of an estate. If there is a business to be carried on temporarily, the receiver may also be appointed *manager*. A receiver may be appointed by an interlocutory order of the court in all cases in which it appears to be just or convenient. As to the power of a mortgagee to appoint a receiver, see the Law of Property Act 1925, s 101.

(2) Under the Insolvency Act 1986, s 287 the Official Receiver may be appointed to act as interim receiver of the debtor's property.

(3) Under the Mental Health Act 1983, s 99 a Judge may by order appoint a receiver for a mentally disordered person.

Recital. That part of a deed which recites the deeds, agreements, and other matters of fact, which may be necessary to explain the reasons on which it is founded.

Recitals are not essential to the validity of a deed, and are often dispensed with.
See DEED; PREMISES; OPERATIVE PART OF A DEED.

Reckonable date. The date from which interest is calculated on late payment of income tax and capital gains tax. This is normally:
(*a*) Unpaid/underpaid balancing payment: 31 January following the fiscal year.
(*b*) Unpaid/underpaid payment on the first payment on account: 31 January during the fiscal year.
(*c*) Unpaid/underpaid payment on the second payment on account: 31 July following the fiscal year.
(TMA 1970, ss 86(2), 59A(2) and 59B(3), (4)).

Recognised stock sxchange. Statute states that the market value of a share is the price quoted where the share is listed on a recognised Stock Exchange. Various provisions apply to shares that are not listed on a recognised Stock Exchange; for example, where such an unlisted share has been subscribed for and is then sold at a loss, income tax relief is available for the loss (TA 1988, ss 573, 574). A recognised Stock Exchange is the London Stock Exchange and designated Stock Exchanges in the following countries: Australia, Austria, Belgium, Brazil, Canada, China, Denmark, Finland, France, Germany, Greece, Irish Republic, Italy, Japan, Korea, Luxembourg, Malaysia, Mexico, Netherlands, New Zealand, Norway, Portugal, Singapore, South Africa, Spain, Sri Lanka, Sweden, Switzerland, Thailand, United Kingdom, United States (TA 1988, s 841).

Recognition. The process of incorporating an item into the primary financial statements under the appropriate heading. It involves depiction of the item in words and by a monetary amount and inclusion of that amount in the statement totals. [FRS 5 – Substance of transactions]

Reconstruction occurs when a company transfers the whole of its undertaking and property to a new company under an arrangement by which the shareholders of the old company are entitled to receive shares or other similar interests in the new company.

Recoverable amount. The greater of the net realisable value of an asset and, where appropriate, the value in use. [FRS 7 – Fair values in acquisition accounting, FRS 10 – Goodwill and intangible assets & FRS 11 – Impairment of fixed assets and goodwill]

Rectification. The correction of an instrument in writing so as to express the true intention of the parties. Actions for this purpose are assigned to the Chancery Division (see the Supreme Court Act 1981, s 61(1), Sch 1).

Redemption. The buying back of a mortgaged estate by payment of the sum due on the mortgage.

Reduced rate. *See* RATES OF TAX.

Reduction of capital. As to the cases in which a company may reduce its capital, see the Companies Act 1985, s 135. In all cases a special resolution must be passed, and in most cases an application to the court is necessary. The words 'and reduced' may be ordered to be added to the name of the company.

Redundancy pay. National insurance contributions are not charged on redundancy pay (Social Security (Contributions) Regulations 2001, SI 2001/1004, Sch 3, Part X, para 6, see SSCBA 1992, s 3(3)(a)).

The term 'redundancy payment' is not defined for this purpose and the question therefore arises whether it is confined to statutory redundancy pay under the employment protection legislation or can include additional payments on account of redundancy. This issue was considered in *Mairs v Haughey [1992] STC 495* where the view was upheld that so far as taxability is concerned there is 'no difference in principle between statutory redundancy payments and payments of the same character made in genuine redundancy circumstances under consensual arrangement' (*at 542*). According to Lord Hutton CJ, the enhanced redundancy payment would not have been made to the employee 'in return for acting as or being an employee' (alluding to the test in *Hochstrasser v Mayes*) but 'because he was ceasing to be an employee and to cushion him against the hardship of losing his employment' (*at 519*).

It will be noted that the essence of redundancy as so defined is that the job is no longer required, not that the job holder is no longer wanted.

Registered auditor. When a company is required by Companies Act 1985, s 384 to appoint an auditor, the appointment must be of a registered auditor. A registered auditor can be an individual or a firm (Companies Act 1989, s 25(2)). In the UK, a registered auditor must be a member of a recognised supervisory body (Companies Act 1989, s 25(2)), the supervisory body having been granted a Recognition Order by the Secretary of State in accordance with Companies Act 1989, s 11.

Registered land. Land or any estate or interest in land the title to which is registered under the Land Registration Act

1925, including any easement, right, privilege, or benefit which is appurtenant or appendant to it, and any mines and minerals within or under it (Land Registration Act 1925, s 3). The system of registered land is governed by the Land Registration Acts 1925 to 1986. Land may be registered with:
(i)   an absolute title;
(ii) a possessory title; or
(iii) a qualified title.

A register of title to freehold land must be kept by the Chief Land Registrar (Land Registration Act 1925, s 1).

There is power to make orders rendering registration compulsory in certain areas: ibid, s 120.

Registered office. An office of the company to which all communications and notices may be addressed.

A company must at all times have a registered office (see the Companies Act 1985, s 287(1)).

Registered office clause. A clause in the memorandum of association stating whether the company's registered office is to be situate in England or Scotland, and thus fixing the nationality of the company. *See* REGISTERED OFFICE.

Regular cost. The consistent ongoing cost recognised under the actuarial method used. [SSAP 24 – Accounting for pension costs]

Regulation. (1) As opposed to a statutory provision or law, a regulation is a rule made by Order In Council as authorised by statute.

(2) In European Union law, a form of legislation.

See EUROPEAN UNION.

Related parties. For Financial Reporting Standard 8, 'related parties' are defined as:
(*a*) Two or more parties are related parties when at any time during the financial period:
(i)   one party has direct or indirect control of the other party; or
(ii) the parties are subject to common control from the same source; or
(iii) one party has influence over the financial and operating policies of

the other party to an extent that that other party might be inhibited from pursuing at all times its own separate interests; or
(iv) the parties, in entering a transaction, are subject to influence from the same source to such an extent that one of the parties to the transaction has subordinated its own separate interests.
(*b*) For the avoidance of doubt, the following are related parties of the reporting entity:
(i)   its ultimate and intermediate parent undertakings, subsidiary undertakings, and fellow subsidiary undertakings;
(ii) its associates and joint ventures;
(iii) the investor or venturer in respect of which the reporting entity is an associate or a joint venture;
(iv) directors (including shadow directors) of the reporting entity and the directors of its ultimate and intermediate parent undertakings; and
(v)   pension funds for the benefit of employees of the reporting entity or of any entity that is a related party of the reporting entity.
(*c*) The following are presumed to be related parties of the reporting entity unless it can be demonstrated that neither party has influenced the financial and operating policies of the other in such a way as to inhibit the pursuit of separate interests:
(i)   the key management of the reporting entity and the key management of its parent undertaking or undertakings;
(ii) a person owning or able to exercise control over 26% or more of the voting rights of the reporting entity, whether directly or through nominees;
(iii) each person acting in concert in such a way as to be able to exercise control or influence (in terms of 'Related party disclosures') over the reporting entity; and
(iv) an entity managing or managed by the reporting entity under a management contract.

(*d*) Additionally, because of their relationship with certain parties that are, or are presumed to be, related parties of the reporting entity, the following are also presumed to be related parties of the reporting entity:

  (i) Members of the close family of any individual falling under parties mentioned in (*a*)-(*c*) above; and

  (ii) partnerships, companies, trusts or other entities in which any individual or member of the close family in (*a*)-(*c*) above has a controlling interest.

Sub-paragraphs (*b*), (c) and (*d*) are not intended to be an exhaustive list of related parties. [FRS 8 – Related party disclosures]

Related party transaction. The transfer of assets or liabilities or the performance of services by, to or for a related party irrespective of whether a price is charged. [FRS 8 – Related party disclosures]

Related property. For inheritance tax purposes, where (*a*) there is a transfer of property, and (*b*) other property is related to it, and (*c*) the value of the property transferred is less than the value of the 'appropriate portion' of that plus the related property, the value of the property transferred is that portion (IHTA 1984, s 161). In determining the appropriate portion, the general rule is that the value of each property is taken as if it did not form part of the aggregate; however, this rule does not affect the calculation of the aggregate value (IHTA 1984, s 161(3)). Where shares of the same class are concerned, the appropriate proportion will be found by taking simply the number of shares (IHTA 1984, s 161(4)).

Relative. In relation to a child, 'relative' means a grandparent, brother, sister, uncle or aunt, whether of the full blood, of the half-blood or by affinity (see the Adoption Act 1976, s 72(1)).

Remainder. Where any estate or interest in land is granted out of a larger one, and an ulterior estate expectant on that which is so granted is at the same time conveyed away by the original owner. The first estate is called the *particular estate*, and the ulterior one the *remainder*, or the *estate in remainder*. Thus, if land is conveyed to A for life, and after his death to B, A's interest is called a *particular* estate, and B's a *remainder*. The word, though properly applied to estates in land, is also applicable to personalty. After 1925 remainders subsist only as equitable interests. See Part I of the Law of Property Act 1925.

See REVERSION.

Remainderman. A fixed interest trust (that is, a trust that is not a discretionary trust) has two categories of beneficiary, with two separate interests. The life tenant has an interest in the income generated from the trust fund, being entitled to receive the income as it arises for the period specified in the trust deed. (Which is, typically, for the lifetime of the named life tenant.) At the end of the period for which the life tenant is entitled to income, the trust fund passes to the beneficiary (or beneficiaries) named as the remainderman. Thus, a will trust for surviving spouse will typically instruct the trustees to pay income from the trust fund to the surviving spouse and, on the death of the surviving spouse, the fund then passes to the children, who are, thus, the remaindermen.

Remedy. The means given by law for the recovery of a right, or of compensation for its infringement, to be distinguished from punishments or penalties, which are not remedies for the victim whose rights were violated, but harms or disadvantages levied in the name of the public upon those guilty of committing an offence. The law has remedies of various kinds, which can be distinguished in different ways. A first distinction is that between a *personal* and a *proprietary* remedy. A personal remedy is one which binds only the defendant against whom it is awarded, the most typical example being an award of DAMAGES, ie a money payment in compensation for an injury or loss. The defendant subject to an order to pay damages has an obligation to do so, but only he or she is bound. If he or she is bankrupt, or dies and his or her estate is insufficient to provide for the payment, the plaintiff will not recover. Impecunious defendants subject only to a remedy of damages are for this reason sometimes said to be 'judgment proof'. Proprietary remedies are orders in respect of specific property; thus, for example, a successful action establishing title to land will result in the award of a right to the immediate possession of the land, and an order for the eviction of a wrongful possessor if necessary. Certain remedies, in particular pecuniary remedies, may also be characterised on the basis of whether they are *compensatory, restitutionary*, or effect *disgorgement*. A compensatory remedy compensates a plaintiff for a loss or injury suffered; a restitutionary remedy is one which restores value received by the defendant to the plaintiff; a disgorgement remedy (which is sometimes included under the rubric 'restitutionary') is one which by which the defendant must provide value to the plaintiff measured not by the plaintiff's loss, nor by an amount of value received by the defendant from him or her, but by the value the defendant acquired in the course of some breach of the plaintiff's rights, as, for example, where a fiduciary makes a profit from his or her principal in breach of the obligation of loyalty and good faith.

See UNJUST ENRICHMENT.

Generally, where a plaintiff has suffered a loss, an award will be compensatory. However, the law occasionally gives *exemplary* or *punitive* damages, damages which are more than compensatory, to make an example of or punish the defendant where his or her violation of the plaintiff's right has been particularly egregious, or perhaps as a means of effecting disgorgement so as to prevent the defendant profiting from his or her wrong.

Besides the foregoing remedies, the court may *enjoin* the parties in various ways, ie issue an injunction to a party to do something (a positive or mandatory injunction) or refrain from doing something (a negative injunction). An example of a negative injunction is the court's enjoining a defendant from continuing to commit a nuisance, eg by ordering him or her to cease industrial operations creating excessive noise. An example of a positive injunction is a court's order to a seller of land to convey the land to the buyer upon payment of the price. A positive injunction in this context is called an order for the specific performance of the contract of sale. Injunctions originally developed in the court of EQUITY, as did the court's power to rescind or rectify documents, and a rescission or rectification of a document may similarly dispose of a dispute.

The court may also make declarations, ie the court may declare what the rights of the parties are. While not a remedy, strictly speaking, declarations of this kind may serve to resolve a dispute, and in that respect may be considered a remedy.

See also ADMINISTRATIVE LAW.

Remittance. An individual who has his domicile outside the UK is subject to UK income tax on income from a foreign source in so far as he has remitted that income during the tax year. Such an individual is subject to UK capital gains tax on gains made on the disposal of foreign assets in so far as those gains have been remitted to the UK.

There is no uniform definition of a remittance. Where the remittance basis applies, income tax is levied under Schedule D, Case IV, on the full amount of the sums received in the UK (TA 1988, s 65(5)(a)).

Where the remittance basis applies and tax is levied under Schedule D, Case V, tax is levied not only on actual sums received from remittances payable in the UK but also actual sums received from property imported or from money or value arising from property not imported or from money or value so received on credit or on account in respect of any such remittances, property, money or value brought or to be brought into the UK. These instances are illustrations and are *not* exhaustive (per Lord Radcliffe in *Thomson v Moyse (1960) 39 TC 291 at 335*). Like Case IV, Case V requires that actual sums be received in the UK (TA 1988, s 65(5)(b)). It follows that if foreign income were converted into a car which was then brought into the UK, no liability would arise under the remittance basis. If, however, the car were then sold, the proceeds might be taxable in the year in which the car was sold (see *Scottish*

Provident Institution v Farmer (1912), 6 TC 34). If by that time the source has been extinguished, or he had given the car to someone else, the proceeds will not be taxable *(Bray v Best [1989] STC 159, HL).*

For income falling within Schedule E, Case III, it is provided that emoluments shall be treated as received in the UK if they are paid, used or enjoyed in or in any manner or form transmitted or brought to the UK (TA 1988, s 132(5)). It is clearly contemplated that this would be parallel to TA 1988, s 65(5) since TA 1988, s 123(5) also provides that s 65(6)–(9) shall apply to s 123(5) as it applies for the purposes of s 65(5). However, the wording is much wider and s 123(5) clearly contemplates the possibility of transmission in kind while s 65(5) does not. Nor can s 123(5) be confined to emoluments received in kind but which have not altered their form. The point remains untested by litigation. The current position under Schedule E, Case III is that the ending of the source will not preclude liability (FA 1989 s 36(3)).

Remuneration. Payment for services. Can include reasonable allowances in respect of expenses properly incurred in the pursuance of the duties of any office.

Renewal expenditure. *See* REPAIRS AND RENEWALS.

Renewal of lease. A re-grant of an expiring lease for a further term. Leases may be surrendered in order to be renewed without a surrender of under-leases by virtue of the Law of Property Act 1925, s 150. For rules in regard to renewal of leases, see eg the Landlord and Tenant Act 1954, which provides security of tenure for certain tenants occupying residential premises under ground leases, and for occupying tenants of business premises.

Renewals basis. The distinction between repair and renewal is blurred by the Revenue practice of allowing the cost of replacing machinery and plant as a revenue expense. This practice is quite distinct from the capital allowances system. There appear to be two distinct legal bases for this practice. One is the general theory of profit which would equate a renewal with a repair and would regard both as maintaining intact the capital originally invested in the physical assets of the business. The disadvantage of this explanation is that it is quite inconsistent with case law, eg *Odeon Associated Theatres Limited v Jones (1972) 48 TC 257.*

The second explanation rests on TA 1988, s 74(1)(d) which disallows sums spent on the 'supply, repairs or alterations of any implements, utensils or articles employed, for the purposes of a trade, profession or vocation, beyond the sum actually expended for those purposes'. As drafted this simply prohibits the deduction of reserves for future expenditure and so may be taken to allow actual expenditure; further it draws no distinction between initial and replacement utensils. Moreover it would confine the allowance to implements, utensils and articles and thus not necessarily cover all types of machinery and plant (see *IRC v Great Wigston Gas Co (1946) 29 TC 197).* An item may be capital expenditure even though on utensils (see *Hinton v Maden and Ireland Ltd (1959) 38 TC 391).*

It seems best to regard this as an extra-statutory concession dating from the days when there were no capital allowances. This not only avoids the problems mentioned but also justifies the Revenue's insistence that some renewals allowances are to be made only over a period of two or three years.

Where the renewals basis is adopted the allowance given is the cost of the new article (excluding additions or improvements) less the scrap or realised value of the replaced article. The cost of the new article may be greater or less than that of the old.

To claim a renewals allowance is to classify the expenditure as revenue. However, this is not to prevent a later switch to the capital allowance system. The two systems of relief are alternatives.

Renouncing probate, is where a person appointed executor of a will refuses to accept the office.

See EXECUTOR; PROBATE.

Rent. The periodic payment, generally of

money, by a tenant to his or her landlord in consideration of the former's right to possess the land. A rent includes a rent service or a rentcharge, or other rent, toll, duty, royalty or annual or periodical payment in money or money's worth, reserved or issuing out of or charged on land (Law of Property Act 1925, s 205(1)(xxiii)).

Rent a room. The purpose behind this complicated relief is to provide an incentive to those who have spare rooms in their homes to let them out (F(No. 2)A 1992, s 59 and Sch 10, paras 1, 9). An individual who receives relevant sums in respect of a qualifying residence or residences may elect to be exempt from income tax on rent received up to the limit of a gross rent of £4,250. Rent can be exempt if it is a receipt in respect of the use of furnished accommodation in the residence (or residences) or any relevant goods or services (F(No. 2)A 1992, Sch 10, para 2(2)). Goods and services are relevant if they are, or are similar in nature to, meals, cleaning and laundry (F(No. 2)A 1992, Sch 10, para 8). The Revenue view is that this relief does not extend to income from uses other than as furnished living accommodation.

If the gross rent received exceeds £4,250, the taxpayer may choose between being taxed on the whole *profit* in the usual way and an alternative basis consisting of being taxed on the gross receipts so far as they exceed £4,250 (F(No. 2)A 1992, Sch 10, para 11).

Rentcharge. Any annual or other periodic sum charged or issuing out of land except (a) rent reserved by a lease or tenancy; or (b) any sum payable by way of interest (Rentcharges Act 1977, s 1). A rentcharge in possession issuing out of or charged on land being either perpetual or for a term of years is a legal estate (Law of Property Act 1925, s 1(2)). No rentcharge may be created after 22 August 1977 (Rentcharges Act 1977, s 2(1)).

Reorganisation. A reorganisation is not treated as a disposal of a shareholding (TCGA 1992, s 127). There is a reorganisation if there is a reorganisation or reduction of share capital; this is stated to include (a) the allotment of shares or debentures in proportion to shareholdings and (b) any alteration of share rights—assuming that there are at least two classes (TCGA 1992, s 126). An allotment to debenture-holders does not qualify. The guiding principle appears to be that there is continued identity of the shareholders, holding their shares in the same proportions (*Dunstan v Young Austen Young Ltd [1989] STC 69*). Although a reduction in share capital is a reorganisation, both the paying off of redeemable share capital and the redemption of shares other than by the issue of new shares or debentures are excluded (TCGA 1992, s 126(3)). The reorganisation rules do not apply to the extent that the shareholder receives consideration other than the new holding (such as a cash payment) from the company, or any consideration from the other shareholders (TCGA 1992, s 128(3)).

Repairs and renewals. Expenditure on a repair is revenue expenditure, as is renewal expenditure. Buckley LJ said in *Lurcott v Wakely and Wheeler [1911] 1 KB 905 at 923, 924*:

"'repair' and 'renew' are not words expressive of clear contrast . . . repair is restoration by renewal or replacement of subsidiary parts of a whole. Renewal, as distinguished from repair, is reconstruction of the entirety, meaning by the entirety not necessarily the whole but substantially the whole subject matter under discussion.'

Thus the replacement of a slate on a roof would be a repair (per Rowlatt J in *O'Grady v Bullcroft Main Collieries Ltd (1932) 17 TC 93 at 101*), but the rebuilding of a retort house in a gas works would be a renewal (per Donovan J in *Phillips v Whieldon Sanitary Potteries Ltd (1952) 33 TC 213 at 219*).

This test presupposes a satisfactory definition of the unit repaired or renewed. In *O'Grady v Bullcroft Main Collieries Ltd (1932) 17 TC 93* a chimney used to carry away fumes from a furnace had become unsafe and so the company built a new one. Rowlatt J said that in his view the chimney was not a part of the factory but an entirety.

Similarly, in *Margrett v Lowestoft Water and Gas Co (1935) 19 TC 481* the replacement of a reservoir by a new one was a renewal, not a repair. On the other hand in *Samuel Jones & Co (Devonvale) Ltd v IRC (1951) 32 TC 513* the costs of replacing an unsafe chimney at a factory were held deductible. In the Court of Session which reversed the Special Commissioners Lord Cooper said that the factory was the entirety, the chimney therefore only a part of the entirety. The court also stressed the low cost of the replacement of the chimney relative to the insured value of the factory, a point not taken in *O'Grady v Bullcroft Main Collieries Ltd*. The distinction between a part and the entirety thus appears to be a convenient method of describing a conclusion rather than a helpful test.

The question seems to be one of the size and importance of the work. One big job may be capital whereas a combination of small jobs may be revenue. In *Phillips v Whieldon Sanitary Potteries Ltd (1952) 33 TC 213* the replacement of a barrier protecting a factory from water in a canal was held to be a renewal and so capital expenditure, the court taking into account the extent of the work, the permanent nature of the new barrier and the enduring benefit it would confer on the business by preserving a part of the fixed capital. In that case Donovan J followed the *Bullcroft* case and reversed the Commissioners.

An expenditure may be in respect of a repair as opposed to a renewal even though it is carried out some time after the need has first arisen. Thus the costs of keeping a channel dredged would be income expenditure even though the dredging was done only once every three years or so (per Rowlatt J in *Ounsworth v Vickers Ltd (1915) 6 TC 671*). There is no need to take away every grain of sand as it comes.

Contrast CAPITAL EXPENDITURE.

Repeal (Fr *Rappel*). A calling back. The revocation of one statute, or a part of it, by another (see the Interpretation Act 1978, s 17).

Reporting accountant. An individual or firm appointed by an enterprise to report on the financial statements. Typically, reporting accountants are appointed when there is not a statutory requirement to appoint an auditor as the enterprise is not incorporated or is a small or medium-sized company exempt from the audit requirement. Reporting accountants are not required to be registered auditors.

Reports. The following is a list of the principal law reports used for tax and accounting cases and the abbreviations by which they are known: *(see table page 217)*

Representative occupation. CGT rollover relief on the sale of land and/or buildings is not available unless the land is occupied by the taxpayer claiming rollover relief. Similarly, retirement relief can be given for the sale of land used as an asset of the trade. Where an employee has lived in a house owned by the taxpayer, these reliefs can be available if the occupation by the employee is representative occupation. The leading case on the nature of occupation is *Northern Ireland Comr of Valuation v Fermanagh Protestant Board of Education HL, [1969] WLR 1709* where Lord Upjohn said:

'The result of the authorities on this question of occupation seems to me quite clearly to be as follows. First, if it is essential to the performance of the duties of the occupying servant that he should occupy the particular house, or it may be a house within a closely defined perimeter, then, it being established that this is the mutual understanding of the master and the servant, the occupation for rating and other ancillary purposes is that of the master and not of the servant . . .'

A distinction can be drawn between a person who receives from his employer a right to live in the property (which is beneficial occupation by the employee) and an employee who is paid to live in the premises (which is representative occupation). It is only when occupation is in the second category that rollover relief and/or retirement relief can be available (*Langley v Appleby [1976] STC 368*).

Occupation of a farmhouse is rarely representative occupation. In *Anderton v Lamb [1981] STC 43* rollover relief was claimed for houses occupied by junior partners of a partnership. The claim failed.

Reports. *(see page 216)*

Abbreviation	Report
AC	Appeal Cases
All ER	All England Law Reports
BCLC	Butterworths Company Law Cases
B & CR	Bankruptcy and Companies Winding-up
Ch	Chancery
Ch App	Chancery Appeal Cases
Ch D	Chancery Division
CLR	Common Law Reports
CMLR	Common Market Law Reports
Court Sess Ca	Court of Session Cases
ECJ	European Court of Justice
ECR	European Court Reports
EG	Estates Gazette
EGLR	Estates Gazette Law Reports
EHRR	European Human Rights Reports
Ex D	Exchequer Division
Exch	Exchequer Reports
HL Cas	House of Lords' Cases
ICLR	Irish Reports Common Law
IR	Irish Reports
LJ	Law Journal
NLJR	New Law Journal Reports
QB	Queen's Bench Reports
QBD	Queen's Bench Division
STC	Simon's Tax Cases
TR	Taxation Reports
TC	Tax Cases
TLR	Times Law Reports
VATTR	Value Added Tax Tribunal Reports
WLR	Weekly Law Reports

Repudiation. A rejection or disclaimer; especially of a person's disclaiming a share in a transaction to which he might otherwise be bound by tacit acquiescence.

Research and development expenditure. (1) Expenditure falling into one or more of the following broad categories (except to the extent that it relates to locating or exploiting oil, gas or mineral deposits or is reimbursable by third parties either directly or under the terms of a firm contract to develop and manufacture at an agreed price calculated to reimburse both elements of expenditure):

(*a*) pure (or basic) research: Experimental or theoretical work undertaken primarily to acquire new scientific or technical knowledge for its own sake rather than directed towards any specific aim or application;

(*b*) applied research: Original or critical investigation undertaken in order to gain new scientific or technical knowledge and directed towards a specific practical aim or objective;

(*c*) development: Use of scientific or technical knowledge in order to produce new or substantially improved materials, devices, products or services, to install new processes or systems prior to the commencement of commercial production or commercial applications, or to improving substantially those already produced or installed.

[SSAP 13 – Accounting for research and development]

(2) Finance Act 2000 provides two separate tax reliefs to encourage research and development. Firstly, it provides some new definitions and procedures, outlined below, for the long established scientific research allowances, now renamed research and development allowances. Secondly, it provides a new tax credit for expenditure on research and development by small and medium-sized companies. These new credit rules give a credit for 150% of the expenditure but do not apply if the expenditure is capital in nature (FA 2000, Sch 21, para 3(2)).

Research and development allowances, previously called scientific research allowances, are available for capital expenditure on scientific research, provided it is related to the trade carried on (or to be carried on). The research may be carried on by someone other than the trader provided it is on behalf of the trader, an expression which requires something close to agency (CAA 2001, ss 439–447). The allowance does not extend to the costs of creating a training centre since research is confined to natural or applied science for the advancement of knowledge (CAA 2001, ss 438(3)–(6) & 440). Costs in acquiring rights in scientific research are not allowed.

Research and development is defined, by TA 1988, s 837A, by reference to accounting practice (TA 1988, s 837A(2)–(5)), which brings in SSAP 13.

Reservation. A keeping back, eg when a person lets his land, *reserving* a rent. Sometimes it means an exception; eg when a person lets a house, and *reserves* to himself one room. And see the Law of Property Act 1925, s 65, which provides that a reservation of a legal estate operates at law without any execution of the conveyance by the grantee of the legal estate out of which the reservation is made.

Resident. In general, a person who is resident in the UK for a tax year is subject to UK income tax and UK capital gains tax on his worldwide income (although, if not domiciled within the UK, this may be on the basis of sums remitted to the UK in the tax year). By contrast, a person not resident in the UK for a tax year is subject to UK income tax on income arising in the UK only and is not subject to UK capital gains tax, even on disposals of assets in the UK.

There is no statutory definition of residence although in practice much turns on the Revenue code in Inland Revenue leaflet IR 20. The basis for this code is uncertain since the cases on which they rest are for the most part illustrations of the principle that since residence is a question of fact the courts cannot reverse a finding by the Commissioners simply because they would not reach the same conclusion. The Revenue practice is based on decisions in favour of the Revenue and conveniently ignores those in favour of the taxpayer.

The Revenue code has three rules:

Revenue rule 1: 183 days actual residence

One who has actually resided in the UK, a confusing statutory phrase, for a period equal in the whole to six months in any year of assessment is treated as resident.

The word 'months' is ambiguous. In *Wilkie v IRC [1952] 32 TC 495* the respondent arrived in the UK at 2 pm on 2 June 1947 intending to leave at the end of November. Events conspired against him and not only did he have to undergo an operation which compelled him to select a flight out of the UK at the last possible moment, but his arrangement to fly on 30 November was cancelled by the airline. He finally left at 10 am on 2 December, 182 days and 20 hours after his arrival. The court rejected the idea that 'months' meant lunar months not calendar months, and the respondent escaped a tax charge of £6,000. The court also held that parts of a day (20 hours) could be taken into account although a part of a day does not count as a whole day.

The six months must be in the year of assessment but need not be continuous. Under the code six months is equated with 183 days ignoring the days of arrival and departure, and whether or not it is a leap year (TA 1988, s 336(1)). However, it is presumably open to one who is present for six of the months of 31 days (with intervals abroad during the short months) to argue that he was present for only six months even though his actual presence was 186 days.

Revenue rule 2: habitual and substantial visits
A person intending to live in the UK permanently or to come and remain for three years or more is treated as resident and ordinarily resident from the date of arrival.

A visitor is normally regarded as resident here if he visits the UK regularly, ie his visits after four years average 91 days or more in the tax year; such a visitor becomes resident as from the fifth year. If he intends to follow this pattern from the beginning he is treated as resident from the beginning. Equally a decision say in year 3 that the visits will follow this pattern will cause him to be resident as from 6 April of year 3. The role of intention is of great importance in such cases. In calculating the periods of 91 days over four years the Inland Revenue will not take into account days spent in the UK because of exceptional circumstances, eg illness.

The bases for this rule are the decisions of the House of Lords in *Levene v IRC* *[1928] 13 TC 486* and *IRC v Lysaght [1928] 13 TC 511*, each of which concerns a claim by a resident to have given up residence.

In *Levene v IRC* the taxpayer had been resident in this country in previous years but had left the country in 1919. He did not set up a place of abode overseas. From 1919 to 1925 he spent about five months in each year in the UK but had no fixed abode in this country. He was 'a bird of passage of almost mechanical regularity' (per Viscount Sumner, *at 501*). The reasons for his visits were the obtaining of medical advice, visiting his relatives, taking part in certain religious observances and dealing with his income tax affairs. The Commissioners held that he was resident here, a decision not reversed by the House of Lords.

In *IRC v Lysaght* the taxpayer had resided in England where he lived with his family and was managing director of the family business. In 1919 he went to live permanently in Ireland and set up a home there. He retained a seat on the board of the company, visited England once a month for meetings but for no other purposes. On such visits he was not accompanied by his

wife and he usually stayed at a hotel. The Commissioners held that he was still resident in the UK. The House of Lords could find no reason for holding that there was no evidence to support that finding and therefore dismissed the appeal. For Viscount Sumner the crucial point appeared to be that the taxpayer was obliged to come to this country, that that obligation was continuous and the sequence of the visits excluded the element of chance and occasion (*at 529*). For Lord Buckmaster with whom Lord Atkinson agreed the matter was one of fact and degree and so pre-eminently one of fact (*at 534*). Lord Warrington was not sure that he would have taken the same view as the Commissioners (*at 537*). Viscount Cave dissented, arguing that the matter was one of mixed fact and law and so could be interfered with and, if it was a matter of fact, that there was no evidence to support the conclusion reached by the Commissioners (*at 533*).

IRC v Lysaght has generally been looked upon as marking the most extreme frontier of residence. However, the case concerned the two years immediately after the move to Ireland. The taxpayer was still involved in the running of the English business and he had no business interests in Ireland. He remained a member of a London club and had a bank account in Bristol. Moreover his visits, although only for company meetings once a month, lasted on average a week and meant that he was physically present in England for 94 days in the one year and 101 days in the other. The fact that he had found a permanent home outside the jurisdiction is only one factor to be weighed against these.

The importance of recognising that in *IRC v Lysaght* the House of Lords merely declined to interfere with a finding of fact by the Commissioners is shown by a comparison of that case with *IRC v Brown (1926) 11 TC 292* where the taxpayer's usual habit was to spend seven months in Mentone, two months in Switzerland or at the Italian lakes and three months in the UK. The Special Commissioners held that he was not resident. Rowlatt J held that he could not interfere with that finding. The same judge later held that he could not interfere with the finding of fact by the

Commissioners in *IRC v Lysaght*. Yet it is the *Lysaght* case, despite the doubts on the facts expressed in the House of Lords, which is taken as the basis of current Revenue practice under the code.

Revenue rule 3: coming to the UK

A person coming to the UK for a purpose, eg employment, and intending to stay for at least two years will be treated as resident from the day of arrival until the date of departure. A person coming for a purpose lasting less than two years or not knowing how long the stay will be will only be treated as resident here if he spends 183 days or more in the UK in the tax year (ie he comes within rule 1). A person coming to the UK for purposes other than work may also now be treated as resident as from the date of his arrival.

Residual value. The net realisable value of an asset at the end of its useful economic life. Residual values are based on prices prevailing at the date of acquisition (or revaluation) of the asset and do not take account of expected future price changes. [FRS 10 – Goodwill and intangible assets]

Residuary devisee. A person entitled under a will to the *residue* of the testator's lands; ie to such as are not specifically devised by the testator's will. By the Wills Act 1837, s 25 it is provided that, unless a contrary intention appears by the will, such real estate or interest as is comprised, or intended to be comprised in any devise in such will contained, which fails or is void by reason of the death of the devisee in the lifetime of the testator, or by reason of the devise being contrary to law, or otherwise incapable of taking effect, is included in the residuary devise (if any) contained in the will.

Residuary estate. A testator's property not specifically devised or bequeathed (see the Administration of Estates Act 1925, s 33(4)).

Residuary legatee. A person to whom the residue or a proportionate share in the residue of a testator's personal property is left, after debts, funeral expenses, and specific and pecuniary legacies have been satisfied.

Residue. The residue of the personal estate of a deceased person after payment of the debts and specific and pecuniary legacies.

Resolution. Any matter resolved upon, especially at a public meeting.

(1) *Resolutions of creditors*. These are resolutions passed at meetings of the creditors of a bankrupt. Resolutions thus passed are of three kinds:

1. An *ordinary resolution*, which is decided by a majority in value of the creditors present personally or by proxy at the meeting and voting on such resolution.
2. A *special resolution*, which is decided by a majority in number and three-fourths in value of the creditors present personally or by proxy at the meeting and voting on such resolution.
3. A resolution which is required for the approval of a debtor's composition or scheme (see the Insolvency Act 1986, Part VIII).

(2) *Resolutions of companies*. An extraordinary resolution is defined to be a resolution passed by a majority of not less than three-fourths of the members of the company present in person or by proxy at a general meeting of which notice specifying the intention to propose the extraordinary resolution has been duly given (see the Companies Act 1985, s 378(1)).

A special resolution is defined as one which has been (*a*) passed in the manner required for an extraordinary resolution, and (*b*) confirmed by a majority of such members as may be present at a subsequent meeting of which not less than 21 days' notice has been given (see the Companies Act 1985, s 378(2)).

(3) *Resolutions in Parliament*. In Parliament, every question, when agreed to, assumes the form of an *order*, or a *resolution* of the House. By its *orders*, the House directs its committees, its members, its officers, the order of its own proceedings and the acts of all persons whom they concern. By its *resolutions*, the House declares its own opinions and purposes.

Resolution for voluntary winding-up. A resolution under any of the provisions of the Insolvency Act 1986, s 84(1), which provides that a company may be wound up voluntarily

(a) when the period (if any) fixed for the duration of the company by the articles expires, or the event (if any) occurs, on the occurrence of which the articles provide that the company is to be dissolved, and the company in general meeting has passed a resolution requiring the company to be wound up voluntarily;

(b) if the company resolves by special resolution to be wound up voluntarily;

(c) if the company resolves by extraordinary resolution to the effect that it cannot by reason of its liabilities continue its business, and that it is advisable to wind up (see the Insolvency Act 1986, s 84(2)).

Resort, court of last. A court from which there is no appeal.

Respondent. A party called on to *answer* a petition or an appeal.

Restraint of trade. Contracts in general restraint of trade, ie unlimited as to time or area, are void. Contracts in partial restraint may, however, be upheld.

Restrictive covenant. An interest in the land of another, first recognised in equity. An owner of one piece of land may hold a restrictive covenant over the land of another; such a covenant restricts the second owner in the use of his property. A typical restrictive covenant prevents the owner bound from using his land for industrial purposes. Such covenants were a means by which developers of land could maintain the amenities of a neighbourhood before the advent of public planning law.

Restrictive indorsement. An indorsement on a bill of exchange or promissory note which restricts the negotiability of the bill or note to a particular person, or a particular purpose; as 'pay to I.S. only', or 'pay John Holloway for my use'. It is to be distinguished from a *blank indorsement*, which consists merely of the signature of the indorser; from a *full indorsement*, which makes the bill or note payable to a

given person or his order; and from a *qualified indorsement*, which qualifies the liability of the indorser (see the Bills of Exchange Act 1882, s 35).
See BILL OF EXCHANGE; PROMISSORY NOTE; INDORSEMENT.

Restructuring. A programme that is planned and controlled by management, and materially changes either:

(a) the scope of a business undertaken by an entity; or

(b) the manner in which that business is conducted.

[FRS 12 – Provisions, contingent liabilities and contingent assets]

Rests. Periodical balancings of an account made for the purpose of converting interest into principal, and charging the party liable with compound interest.

Resulting trust. A trust whereby the beneficial interest in the trust property 'results' or jumps back to the settlor. Presumed intention resulting trusts are informal trusts where the beneficial interest results to the settlor on the basis of an evidentiary presumption, thus, eg, where there is no evidence of X's intentions when X gratuitously transferred property to Y, Y will generally hold the property on bare trust for X (*see* BARE TRUST). Automatic resulting trusts arise on the failure of an intended gift on trust, thus, eg, where X transfers property to Y on trust for A for life and then to A's children in equal shares, and A dies childless, following A's death Y will hold the property on bare trust for X (or X's successor in title).
See TRUST.

Retirement benefits. All forms of consideration (except equity compensation benefits) given by an employer in exchange for services rendered by employees that are payable after the completion of employment.

Retirement benefits do not include termination benefits because these are not given in exchange for services rendered by employees. [FRED 20 – Retirement benefits]

Retirement relief. Retirement relief has been available since the introduction of capital gains tax in 1965. It has always been a valuable relief; between 1993 and 1998, it was particularly generous. Retirement relief continues to be available on disposals made up to 5 April 2003, but the limits are progressively reduced after 5 April 1999. Retirement relief is given on a 'material disposal'.

The disposal of a business or part of it is a material disposal if the business is owned by an individual for at least one year ending with the date of the disposal and on or before the date the business ceased the individual has reached age 50 or retired through ill-health (TCGA 1992, s 163(3) & (4)). The rules relating to businesses owned by an individual extend to partnerships (TCGA 1992, s 163(8)).

Relief is also available when the disposal is of shares in a company owning the business and the company is a trading company which is either:

(1) that individual's personal company; or
(2) a member of a trading group of which the holding company is that individual's personal company

(TCGA 1992, s 163(2)(c)).

An individual's personal company is a company in which he is entitled to exercise 5% or more of the voting rights. The individual must be a full-time working officer or employee of the company or, if the company is a member of a group or commercial association of companies, a full-time working officer or employee of one or more companies in that group or association.

Statute provides for retirement relief where there is a material disposal of business assets made by an individual who at the time of disposal has retired on ill-health grounds below the age of 50 (TCGA 1992, s 163(4)(c)).

Retiring partner. A partner who leaves a partnership.

A partner who retires from a firm does not thereby cease to be liable for partnership debts or obligations incurred before his retirement (Partnership Act 1890, s 17(2)). A retiring partner may be discharged from any existing liabilities by an agreement to that effect between himself and the members of the firm as newly constituted and the creditors: ibid, s 17(3).

Revaluation of assets. Where assets, typically land and buildings, have a current value that is substantially in excess of the historic cost, the enterprise may choose to restate the value in its financial statements, using the current market value. The revaluation thus undertaken creates a surplus that, in the case of a company, is required to be displayed as a non-distributable revaluation reserve. Companies Act 1985, Sch 7, para 1(2) requires the directors to make a statement in the directors' report whenever the current market value of the company's land and buildings differs substantially from the amount at which the assets are shown in the company's balance sheet.

Revenue. The yearly rent that accrues to every man from his lands and possessions. But it is applied especially to the general income received by the State in taxes, etc, and to the hereditary revenues of the Crown.

Revenue expenditure. Revenue expenditure is a deduction in computing profits on which income tax or corporation tax is charged. Capital expenditure is not deductible in computing profits, although such expenditure may qualify for relief under the capital allowance system.

For a discussion of the distinction between revenue expenditure and capital expenditure, *see* CAPITAL EXPENDITURE.

Reverse charge. Under UK value added tax law, services are supplied in the country where the supplier belongs. Partly exempt traders could reduce their irrecoverable input tax by obtaining services from overseas traders (who would not charge tax on the supply) rather than UK traders (who would). This would both cause distortions in trading patterns and result in a reduction in VAT revenues. These consequences are avoided by making the recipient liable to account for the tax chargeable if he is a taxable person. The value of supplies received by a non-taxable person are taken into account in determining whether he is liable to registration.

A person belonging in the UK who receives a relevant supply of services is treated as if *he* had supplied them in the

UK in the course or furtherance of his business if both of the following conditions are met:

(1) The services are supplied by a person who belongs in a country other than the UK.

(2) The recipient uses the services for the purposes of his business.

(VATA 1994, s 8(1)).

The supply is deemed to be made in the UK in order to bring it within the charge to tax in VATA 1994, s 4(1) and the supply is deemed to be made in the course or furtherance of business in order to bring it within the charge to tax.

The supply is treated as taking place on either the date when the supply is paid for (where there is a consideration in money) or the last day of the prescribed accounting period in which the services were performed (where the consideration is not in money) (VAT Regulations, SI 1995/2518, reg 82).

The value of the supply for tax purposes is the money consideration for which it is made (if there is one) or such amount in money as is equivalent to that amount (in other cases) (VATA 1994, Sch 6, para 8).

Reverse premiums. Reverse premiums are sums paid by a landlord to a tenant at the start of a lease. In Canada they are known by the more informative name of lease inducement payments. In the 1998 Privy Council decision on the New Zealand appeal in *IRC v Wattie [1998] STC 1160*, reverse premiums were held to be capital receipts, and so non-taxable. This produced a lack of symmetry in that the payment would often be made by a property developer so that the sums paid would be deductible while the sum received was not taxable. The decision has now been superseded by FA 1999, Sch 6. Such payments are now taxable—regardless of their treatment in the hands of the person making the payment.

The Revenue view on the operation of FA 1999, s 54 and Sch 6 is that all cash payments are 'caught', as are taxable inducements such as contributions towards specified tenant's costs, for example fitting out, start up or relocation. Sums paid to third parties to meet obligations of the tenant, such as rent to a landlord under an old lease, or a capital sum to terminate such a lease, are also within the terms of the provisions, as is the effective payment of cash by other means, eg the landlord's writing off a sum which the tenant owes. However, an inducement is not caught where it does not represent actual outlay. In the Revenue guidance, the following examples are given of inducements that do not give rise to a tax charge:

(1) The grant of a rent free period of occupation and replacement by agreement of an existing lease at a rent which a change in market conditions has made onerous by a new lease at a lower rent.

(2) Replacement by agreement of an existing lease containing some other provision the tenant has found onerous by a new lease without the onerous condition.

Reversion. The residue of an estate in land *left in the grantor* to commence in possession after the determination of some particular estate granted by him; eg where X, the owner of Blackacre, grants Blackacre to A for life, X has the reversion, ie the right to take back the property upon A's death. Similarly, a landlord has the reversion in the estate in land he has leased for the land will return to him at the end of the lease.

Reversionary interest. An interest in real or personal property in remainder or reversion.

Revocation. The reversal by any one of a thing done by himself, eg when it is provided in a marriage settlement or other instrument, that an appointment may be made 'with or without power of revocation', it is implied that the party making the appointment may, if he thinks fit, reserve the power of annulling what he has done. A power granted or reserved in a deed or other instrument to revoke an appointment already made, and to make a fresh one, is called a *power of revocation and new appointment*. Any act or instrument which is capable of being annulled by its author is said to be *revocable*.

Some instruments are in their nature

revocable, eg wills. Deeds under seal are not, in general, revocable, unless a power to revoke is expressly reserved. A will may be revoked (1) by marriage (unless it is expressed to have been made in contemplation of marriage); (2) by the execution of another will or codicil or by some writing of revocation executed as a will; (3) by the burning, tearing or other destruction of the original will (*animo revocandi*) by the testator, or by some other person in his presence and by his direction (see the Wills Act 1837, ss 19, 20). Where the whole property is disposed of during the testator's lifetime, the will ceases to have effect.

Revocation of probate. Where probate of a will, having been granted, is afterwards recalled by the court on proof of a subsequent will, or other sufficient cause.

See PROBATE.

Right. A lawful title or claim to anything. Rights, along with duties (or obligations) and powers, are the basic elements which determine a person's legal position. *General* rights are those which apply to all persons, simply in virtue of their being full subjects of the law, eg the right to assemble, the right not to be assaulted. *Special* rights are those which arise by the exercise of powers, eg the rights of the parties under a contract having exercised their power to make a contract, or by operation of law on the occurrence of certain events, such as the right to bring a claim for damages against one who has negligently caused one loss or injury.

See POWER; and the entries which follow.

Rights issue. A right given to a shareholder to subscribe for further shares in the company usually at a price lower than the market price of the existing shares, the number usually being in proportion to the shareholder's present shareholding, eg a right to subscribe for one new share for every five which he holds.

Risk. Uncertainty as to the amount of benefits. The term includes both potential for gain and exposure to loss. [FRS 5 – Substance of transactions]

Rollover relief. Rollover relief enables a charge to capital gains tax to be deferred until the subsequent sale of the asset into which the gain has been rolled (TCGA 1992, ss 152–159). Rollover relief is only available where the claimant carries on a trade and both the old and the new assets are used in a trade carried on by the taxpayer.

If the relief is claimed, the disposal is treated as reduced by the lower of: (*a*) the amount spent on the new asset, and (*b*) the gain that would otherwise arise on the disposal. The same sum is then deducted from the base cost of the new assets. Full rollover is available provided that the acquisition cost of the new assets equals or exceeds the actual disposal proceeds of the old asset.

The relief is available only for the following types of asset specified in TCGA 1992, ss 152(1) & 155:

(*a*) any building or part of a building and any permanent or semi-permanent structure in the nature of a building, occupied (as well as used) only for the purposes of the trade;

(*b*) any land occupied (as well as used) only for the purposes of the trade;

(*c*) fixed plant or machinery which does not form part of a building or of a permanent or semi-permanent structure in the nature of a building;

(*d*) ships, aircraft and hovercraft ('hovercraft' having the same meaning as in the Hovercraft Act 1968);

(*e*) goodwill;

(*f*) satellites, space stations and space vehicles (including launch vehicles);

(*g*) milk quotas and potato quotas;

(*h*) ewe and suckler cow premium quotas;

(*i*) fish quotas (as from 29 March 1999) (FA 1993, s 86(2));

(*j*) rights of a member of a Lloyds Syndicate;

(*k*) oil licences (FA 1999, s 103).

Romalpa clause. In *Aluminium Industrie Vasseen BV v Romalpa Aluminium Ltd [1976] 2 All ER 577, CA*, the court upheld a clause in the sale contract by which the seller retained the ownership of goods until the buyer had paid for the goods. Thus, when the buyer went into liquidation before paying for the goods, the seller was able to enforce the return of the goods, rather than be listed as simply an unsecured creditor.

Royal Assent (Lat *Regius assensus*). The assent given by the Sovereign to a bill passed in both Houses of Parliament. The royal assent to a bill had formerly to be given either in person, or by commission by letters patent under the Great Seal, signed with the Sovereign's hand, and notified to both Houses assembled together in the upper House. The procedure has been modified by the Royal Assent Act 1967. A bill, on receiving the royal assent, becomes an Act of Parliament.

Rule. (1) A regulation for the government of a society, eg a club or trade union, agreed to by its members.

(2) A rule of procedure made by a lawful judicial authority for some court or courts of justice, eg the Rules of the Supreme Court 1965. See also the Supreme Court Act 1981, s 84.

(3) An order made by a superior court on motion in some matter over which it has summary jurisdiction.

(4) A point of law settled by authority.

Rule against perpetuities. *See* PERPETUITY.

Rule of court. (1) An order made on motion, generally in open court, or else made generally to regulate the practice of the court.

(2) A submission to arbitration, or the award of an arbitrator, is said to be made a *rule of court*, when the court makes a rule that such submission or award is to be conclusive (see the Arbitration Act 1950, ss 1, 26).

Rule of law. The doctrine that all men are equal before the law, and that acts of officials in carrying out government orders are cognisable in the ordinary courts of law.

S

S. Section (of an Act).

SERPS. State Earnings Related Pension Scheme.

SI. Statutory instrument. *See* STATUTORY INSTRUMENT.

SORP. Statement of Recommended Practice.

SSAP. Statement of Standard Accounting Practice.

STEP. Society of Trust and Estate Practitioners.

Sale. A transfer of property from one person to another in consideration of a price paid in money.

Sale of goods, contract for. A contract by which the seller transfers or agrees to transfer the property in goods to the buyer for a money consideration, called the price (Sale of Goods Act 1979, s 2(1)). The contract may be absolute or conditional (ibid, s 2(3)).

There are implied conditions that the seller has a good title to the goods (ibid, s 12); that the goods will comply with their description (ibid, s 13); and that, in a contract for sale by sample, the bulk will correspond with the sample in quality, the buyer will have a reasonable opportunity of comparing the bulk with the sample, and the goods will be free from any defect, rendering them unmerchantable, which would not be apparent on reasonable examination of the sample (ibid, s 15(2)).

There is an implied warranty that (i) the goods are free, and will remain free until the time when the property is to pass, from any charge or encumbrance not disclosed or known to the buyer before the contract is made; and (ii) the buyer will enjoy quiet possession of the goods except so far as it may be disturbed by the owner or other person entitled to the benefit of any charge or encumbrance so disclosed or known (ibid, s 12(2)).

Where the seller sells goods in the course of a business, there are implied conditions that:

(i) the goods are reasonably fit for the purpose for which they are supplied;

(ii) they are of merchantable quality (ibid, s 14(2), (3)).

As to the extent to which a seller may contract out of the above conditions and warranties, see ibid, s 55.

Sans recours. Without recourse; meaning 'without recourse to me'. These words are appended to an indorsement on a bill of exchange or promissory note to qualify it, so as not to make the indorser responsible for any payment on it. This is the proper mode of indorsing a bill where an agent indorses on behalf of his principal.

See BILL OF EXCHANGE; PROMISSORY NOTE.

Savings income. Since 1996/97 'savings income' been charged at lower tax rates from other income, unless the taxpayer is subject to higher rate. Even a higher rate taxpayer is subject to a lower rate of tax on dividends than on income that is not savings income.

For the bank or other financial institution that pays interest, etc, the rate of withholding tax on savings income is the lower rate, not basic rate (except for dividends, when there is a deemed tax credit at 10%).

'Savings income' is:

(*a*) Any income chargeable under Schedule D, Case III.

(*b*) Any dividend or other distribution from a UK company chargeable under Schedule F.

(c) 'Equivalent foreign income' (TA 1988, s 1A(3)).

'Equivalent foreign income' is equivalent to a description of income falling within subsection (*a*) above but arises from securities or other possessions out of the UK; or consists of any such dividend or other distribution of a company not resident in the UK as would be chargeable under Schedule F if the company were resident in the UK.

However, the following types of income are specifically excluded from the favourable treatment applied to savings income:

(a) Any annuity other than a purchased life annuity.

(b) Any other annual payment that is not interest.

(c) Any rent received in respect of wayleaves or from mines and quarries, which is brought into Schedule D, Case III by TA 1988, s 119 or s 120.

(d) Any overseas income that is assessed on a remittance basis.

(e) Income from a foreign estate (TA 1988, s 1A(2)(a)).

A 'chargeable event' arising when a withdrawal is made from a non-qualifying life assurance policy is not within the definition of 'savings income' (TA 1988, s 540).

Schedular system. Income tax is charged on the taxable income of the year of assessment. This raises the question what is income?

There is no statutory definition of income, beyond the statement that income is taxable if it falls within one or other of the Schedules. The schedular system was created in Henry Addington's Act of 1803, under which income that was to suffer taxation was classified into five Schedules: Schedule A (income from land and buildings), Schedule B (farming profit), Schedule C (public annuities), Schedule D (self-employment and other items not covered by the other Schedules) and Schedule E (salaries, annuities and pensions). Tax was charged at 5% (which rose to 10% in 1806) and the words 'income tax' were deliberately avoided, the Act being styled as a 'contribution of the profits arising from property, professions, trades and offices'. Practitioners will recognise that the specification of the schedules by Addington in 1803 is substantially the same as the specification today, there having been remarkably little change over the intervening 199 years. Although income tax was repealed after the defeat of Napoleon in 1815 and the belief that the demand on the Parliamentary purse could be satisfied without a tax on incomes, the reintroduction of income tax by Sir Robert Peel in 1842 was effected by a reintroduction of Henry Addington's Schedules, although Sir Robert Peel, in opposition, had argued against the schedular system.

Prior to 1952, income subject to tax was defined in separate Schedules, attached to the Act. In the consolidating statute, Income Taxes Act 1952, the definition of income under the schedular system was moved into the body of the Act, to become part of the text, where it now remains. Income tax is imposed by TA 1988, s 1(1) on the Schedules that are defined in sections 15–20. TA 1988 does not, in terms, impose a charge to income tax, it merely provides the schedular system under which income tax will be administered, if Parliament chooses to impose a charge for the year. In every year since 1842, Parliament has chosen to impose a charge to income tax, although, technically each year's charge is imposed as a temporary measure: ie a charge only lasts for a single fiscal year. Income tax for 2001/02 is imposed by the Finance Act 2001, s 50.

Where income falls within a Schedule it falls to be computed in accordance with the rules in that Schedule and no other. In *Mitchell and Edon v Ross (1961) 40 TC 11 at 61* Lord Radcliffe said:

'Before you can assess a profit to tax you must be sure that you have properly identified its source or other description according to the correct Schedule; but once you have done that, it is obligatory that it should be charged, if at all, under that Schedule and strictly in accordance with the Rules that are there laid down for assessments under it. It is a necessary consequence of this conception that the sources of profit in the different Schedules are mutually exclusive.'

The six Schedules are:

Schedule A taxes all rents, premiums and other income arising from land in the UK (TA 1988, s 15).

Schedule B taxed the occupation of woodlands in the UK managed on a commercial basis. The charge to tax under this Schedule was abolished with effect from 6 April 1988.

Schedule C taxed income from public revenue dividends paid in the UK. This Schedule was abolished for 1996/97 and subsequent years.

Schedule D taxes annual profits or gains which fall into one or other of its six Cases:

Case I taxes profits or gains arising from any trade;

Case II taxes the profits or gains arising from a profession or vocation;

Case III taxes interest, annuities and other annual payments together with discounts and dividends from public revenue;

Case IV taxes the profits or gains arising from securities outside the UK;

Case V taxes the profits or gains arising from possessions out of the UK;

Case VI taxes any annual profits or gains not falling under any other Case or Schedule.

(TA 1988, s 18).

Schedule E taxes emoluments from an office or employment (TA 1988, s 19).

Schedule F taxes distributions by companies resident in the UK (TA 1988, s 20).

Scheme of arrangement. An arrangement between a debtor and his creditors whereby it is agreed that the debts are to be paid or partly paid under an agreed scheme, instead of the debtor being adjudged bankrupt.

Scrip. Certificates of shares in a company. A scrip certificate is a certificate entitling the holder to apply for shares in a company, either absolutely or on the fulfilment of specified conditions.

Seal. Wax impressed with a device, and attached as a mark of authenticity to letters and other instruments in writing. A contract under seal is called a *specialty contract* or *covenant*. It needs no valuable consideration to support it, as a contract not under seal does.

See DEED; CONSIDERATION; CONTRACT.

Secret trust. A trust created by a testator who leaves property by his will to a person who has agreed to hold the property on trust for another when he receives it under the distribution of the testator's estate. As such, the trust is a testamentary trust which does comply with the formality requirements of the Wills Act 1837, viz that any testamentary gift must be made in writing signed by the testator and attested by two witnesses, but EQUITY has enforced such trusts, either on the principle that it would be a fraud to allow the legatee to resile from his agreement and take the property for his own benefit, or on the basis that being made between the testator and the legatee while alive, the trust is INTER VIVOS, though 'constituted' at the testator's death, and as such is not testamentary so need not comply with the Wills Act.

A half or semi-secret trust is one in which the trust obligation is made apparent in the will, but the particular OBJECT OF THE TRUST is not disclosed. Such trusts are likewise enforced by EQUITY, though the rules differ slightly, as do the possible rationales for doing so.

See TRUST.

Secured creditor. A creditor who holds some special security for his debt, eg a mortgage or lien.

See SECURITY.

A secured creditor in the liquidation of a company may either give up his security or give credit for its value and prove, ie claim in the liquidation proceedings, for his whole debt, or else realise his security and prove for the balance and receive a dividend *pari passu* with the other creditors (see the Insolvency Act 1986 and Rules made under it).

Securities in the Company Securities (Insider Dealing) Act 1985 means listed securities and, in the case of a company within the meaning of the Companies Act 1985 or a company registered under Chapter II of Part XXII of that Act or an unregistered company, the following securities (whether or not listed), that is to say, any shares, any debentures or any right to subscribe for, call for or make delivery of a share or debenture (see the Company Securities (Insider Dealing) Act 1985, s 12(1)).

See LISTED SECURITY.

Security or **Security Interest.** A kind of interest, or right, in property owned by another. A security interest 'secures' the repayment of a debt by an owner of property, for if the debtor/owner fails to pay the debt according to the terms of the contract for repayment, the creditor with the security interest, called a 'secured creditor', can take action with respect to the secured property, typically by exercising a power to sell the property and take the proceeds of sale as repayment of the debt. Originally at common law, all security interests were effected by way of possession. Thus, under a mortgage, the lender, the mortgagee, secured his loan by taking a conveyance of land from the borrower, the mortgagor. The lender thus became the legal owner of the property with the immediate right to its possession. Under the terms of the mortgage, the mortgagee had the obligation to re-convey the property to the mortgagor on repayment of the mortgage loan, but should the mortgagor fail to meet his repayment obligations, the mortgagee, having ownership and thus the immediate right to take possession of the land, could take possession of the land for his own use, or sell it. Similarly, chattels were pledged. A pledge is a form of BAILMENT, by which the pledgor, the borrower, gives possession of a chattel to his lender, the pledgee, as security for the repayment of his loan. On the pledgor's failure to meet his repayment obligations, the pledgee is entitled to sell the chattel. Many security interests no longer take effect by way of possession, as for example the modern mortgage, but by way of legal rights to sell the property of the lender upon his failure to meet his repayment obligations. Irrespective of how the security interest takes effect, a security interest is a proprietary interest or right in the property of the lender; thus it will (generally) bind third parties who take the property from the lender by way of sale or gift or otherwise, for the right attaches to the property itself. Where the more modern form of security interest is created, ie not by way of the creditor taking possession of the property, it is generally not obvious to third parties whether a particular item of property, whether land or a chattel, is the subject of a security interest, for it remains in the possession of the lender, and therefore Parliament has imposed various registration regimes (eg land registration, Companies Act 1985, s 395) whereby the existence of security interests can be determined by a search of a public register.

Self-assessment. Introduced with effect from fiscal year 1996/97, self-assessment was the most fundamental reform of the administration of personal taxation since the introduction of PAYE in 1944. Nine million individual taxpayers receive a self-assessment tax return each year. Under self-assessment, the responsibility for the management of an individual's tax affairs is placed firmly on that individual with the requirements for the individual to produce an assessment on himself, taking in all his income and capital gains assessable for the particular fiscal year (see TMA 1970, s 9). The liability calculated by the taxpayer himself under self-assessment process is a debt that can be collected, if necessary, by County Court or High Court action, even though the Revenue has taken no action to create the debt. In this respect, self-assessment is a fundamental change from the previous system, under which a debt was created by a Revenue-produced assessment.

Under self-assessment, the requirement to compute taxable income and calculate a capital gain using all the complexity of the Taxes Acts, lies solely with the taxpayer. If a market value is required, the taxpayer must supply it. If information is not available until after the due date for the submission of a tax return (normally 31 January the following fiscal year), the taxpayer must supply an estimate. If the actual value turns out to differ from the estimate, the taxpayer suffers an interest charge on any additional tax that is found to be payable, or receives a repayment supplement where the estimate is found to have lead to an overpayment of tax. The system of self-assessment was a total change to the previous system. As Leonard Beighton, then Deputy Chairman of the Board of Inland Revenue, said at a press conference on 12 January 1994: 'This is a culture change. A change for taxpayers, a change for the Department and a change for all tax agents'. When presenting the case for self-assessment to Government ministers, the Inland Revenue Economics Unit estimated that self-assessment would reduce the current compliance costs by between £125 million and £250 million a year, being a saving of between 1.5% and 2.75% of the tax yield.

Semble. It appears; an expression often used in law reports, to indicate that such was the opinion of the court on a point not directly before it.

Separate maintenance. Maintenance provided by a husband for his wife on the understanding that she is to live separate from him.

Separation. The living apart or separately by a husband and wife often, though not necessarily, with the intention later to divorce. A deed of separation is a deed made between husband and wife, whereby each covenants not to molest the other, and the husband agrees to pay so much to trustees for her separate maintenance, the trustees covenanting to indemnify him against his wife's debts.

See SEPARATE MAINTENANCE.

Though the law allows provision to be made for a separation already determined on, it will not sanction any agreement to provide for the contingency of a future separation.

A *decree* for judicial separation may be granted under the Matrimonial Causes Act 1973, s 17. An *order* for separation (now known as a 'matrimonial order') may be obtained from justices under the Matrimonial Proceedings (Magistrates' Courts) Act 1960, s 2.

Servant. Servants are of three types:
(1) Domestic servants
(2) Employees
(3) Apprentices
Two particular legal consequences flow from the status of servant, of any of the three types:
(1) If a servant by his negligence does any damage to a third party, the master is liable for his negligence, provided the damage is done while the servant is acting in his master's employment.

(2) Whereas it is, in general, prohibited for a person to *maintain*, that is, abet and assist, a claimant in a law suit, a master is entitled to maintain his servant in any action at law against a third party.

Services. VAT is charged on supplies. There are two categories of supply: (*a*) a supply of goods; (*b*) a supply of services.

Anything done for a consideration which is not a supply of goods is a supply of services unless it is specifically treated as neither a supply of goods nor a supply of services (VATA 1994, s 5(2)(b)). 'Anything done' includes, amongst other things, the grant, assignment or surrender of any right. For examples, see *Naturally Yours Cosmetics Ltd v Customs and Excise Comrs (case 230/87) [1988] STC 879, ECJ* (procuring a gathering at which goods are sold); *Customs and Excise Comrs v Tilling Management Services Ltd [1979] STC 365* (procuring a group relief payment); *GUS Merchandise Corpn Ltd v Customs and Excise Comrs [1981] STC 569, CA* (agreeing to act as agent); *Customs and Excise Comrs v Diners Club Ltd [1989] STC 407, CA* (making payments under a credit card scheme); *Customs and Excise Comrs v High Street Vouchers Ltd [1990] STC 575* (redeeming vouchers at a discount); *Customs and Excise Comrs v Battersea Leisure Ltd [1992] STC 213, Ridgeons Bulk Ltd v Customs and Excise Comrs [1994] STC 427* (covenanting to refurbish premises); *Mirror Group Newspapers Ltd v Customs and Excise Comrs [2000] STC 156* (issuing shares); *Neville Russell (a firm) v Customs and Excise Comrs [1987] VATTR 194* and contrast *Iliffe & Holloway v Customs and Excise Comrs [1993] VATTR 439* (accepting a lease); *Cooper Chasney Ltd v Customs and Excise Comrs [1990] 3 CMLR 509* (relinquishing a trade name); *Oxford Film Foundation v Customs and Excise Comrs (1990) VAT decision 5031* (providing publicity benefits for a sponsor). It does not include functions which a trader is obliged to carry out on his own behalf (see *National Coal Board v Customs and Excise Comrs [1982] STC 863*; *British European Breeders' Fund v Customs and Excise Comrs [1985] VATTR*

12). Examples of supplies of services include procuring a gathering at which goods are sold, procuring a group relief payment, agreeing to act as agent, making payments under a credit card scheme, redeeming vouchers at a discount, granting a commodity option, covenanting to refurbish premises, accepting a lease, procuring discounts for members of a buying group, relinquishing a trade name and providing publicity benefits for a sponsor.

The following specific activities amount to a supply of services:

(1) The transfer of any undivided share in the property of goods, eg if A and B jointly own an asset and A sells his share to C.

(2) The transfer of possession of goods, eg the hire, lease, rental or loan of goods.

(3) Using business goods for private or non-business purposes.

(4) Exchanging reconditioned articles for unserviceable articles of a similar kind when carried out by a trader who regularly offers to provide such facilities.

(VATA 1994, Sch 4, paras 1(1)(a), (b) & 5(4), (6)).

Set-off. The merging (wholly or partially) of a claim of one person against another in a counterclaim by the latter against the former. Thus, a plea of set-off is a plea whereby a defendant acknowledges the justice of the plaintiff's demand, but sets up another demand of his own, to counterbalance that of the plaintiff, either in whole or in part.

Where a claim by a defendant to a sum of money is relied on as a defence to the whole or part of a claim made by the plaintiff, it may be included in the defence and set off against the plaintiff's claim, whether or not it is also added as a counterclaim.

Setting. Machinery and plant used by a trader attracts capital allowances. The setting in which it is placed does not attract allowances (unless it qualifies as an industrial building). For a discussion of the distinction between, on the one hand, machinery and plant and, on the other hand, its setting, *see* MACHINERY AND PLANT.

Settled estates. *See* SETTLEMENT; SETTLED LAND.

Settled land. Land limited by *way of succession*, that is, limited to a person other than the person for the time being entitled to the beneficial enjoyment of it; thus land which is held by A for life, and thereafter to B, is limited by way of succession and is settled land. A in this example is called a limited owner (see the Settled Land Act 1925). A is also the tenant for life, and the Settled Land Act 1925 expanded the powers of the tenant for life of settled land to mortgage, lease, sell or otherwise deal with it, the Act providing protections for those with future interests in the land.

See LIMITED OWNER.

Settlement. (1) An alternative word for a trust created by a deliberate act, as opposed to a resulting trust or a trust created by the operation of statute (eg by intestacy). The word 'settlement' is more commonly applied to a trust established by a deed made *inter vivos*, in contrast to a will trust that is created by a testamentary disposition that takes place as a consequence of the death of the testator.

(2) When there is a settlement, the income arising from the property settled is assessed to income tax on the settlor if the settlor or his spouse is able to receive income or capital from the fund settled in any circumstances whatsoever or when a payment is made to any minor unmarried child of the settlor (TA 1988, ss 660A & 660B). The term 'settlement' is stated to include 'any disposition, trust, covenant, agreement, arrangement or transfer of assets' (TA 1988, s 660I(1)).

This definition of settlement repeats the earlier formulation. Under those earlier provisions it was said that the word 'settlement' is not a dominating word which colours the others and that the word 'arrangement' is not a term of art (Greene MR in *IRC v Payne (1940) 23 TC 610 at 626*). Many acts have been held to be settlements, including the setting up of corporate structures (an arrangement) and the disclaimer of an interest by a remainderman (a disposition) as the following cases show. The limiting factor is that a transaction can only be a settlement if it contains an element of bounty (*IRC v Plummer [1979] STC 793, [1979] 3 All ER 775*; *Chinn v Collins [1981] STC 1*).

If there is no element of bounty the transaction is not a settlement; this follows even if the transaction is not carried out for commercial reasons. The test of bounty was applied in *Butler v Wildin [1989] STC 22*. Parents who were architects had worked for a company without fee. They had arranged for shares to be held by their infant children. Vinelott J, reversing the Special Commissioner, held that there was a settlement. The children had contributed nothing of substance and were not exposed to any risk. Income arising from the company in the form of dividends was therefore not the income of the children and the claim for repayment of income tax because they had unused personal allowances failed.

See BARE TRUST.

(3) For inheritance tax, a settlement is defined by IHTA 1984, s 43(1) as:

'Any disposition or dispositions of property, whether effected by instrument, by parol or by operation of law, or partly in one way and partly in another, whereby the property is for the time being:

(*a*) held in trust for persons in succession or for any person subject to a contingency; or

(*b*) held by trustees on trust to accumulate the whole or any part of any income of the property or with power to make payments out of that income at the discretion of the trustees or some other person, with or without power to accumulate surplus income; or

(*c*) charged or burdened (otherwise than for full consideration in money or money's worth paid for his own use or benefit to the person making the disposition), with the payment of an annuity or other periodical payment payable for a life or any other limited or terminable period.'

Property is settled whether or not the settlement was created for value—except for head (*c*).

Head (*a*) is sufficient to cover entailed interests, life interests and contingent interests, but not purely concurrent interests, while head (*b*) catches discretionary and accumulation trusts.

Head (*c*) deals only with annuities or other periodical payments which are charged on property. Annuities payable under a personal obligation only do not create settlements. The phrase 'or other periodical payments' is presumably to be construed *eiusdem generis* with annuity and so does not cover instalments of capital. The obligation must be for life or any other limited or terminable period so that while a rent charge for a limited period will give rise to a settlement unless for full consideration, a perpetual rentcharge will not. When full consideration is in issue, it does not matter who provides it (*A-G v Boden [1912] 1 KB 539*).

(4) A deed whereby property is *settled*, ie subjected to a string of limitations. In this sense one speaks of *marriage settlements* and *family settlements*.

(5) The termination of a disputed matter by the adoption of terms agreeable to the parties to it.

(6) In the context of pensions, the Accounting Standards Board has issued the following definition in a draft statement:

An irrevocable action that relieves the employer (or the defined benefit scheme) of the primary responsibility for a pension obligation and eliminates significant risks relating to the obligation and the assets used to effect the settlement. Settlements include:

(*a*) a lump-sum cash payment to scheme members in exchange for their rights to receive specified pension benefits; and

(*b*) the purchase of an irrevocable annuity contract sufficient to cover vested benefits.

[FRED 20 – Retirement benefits]

Settlor. A settlor is defined as any person by whom the settlement was made (TA 1988, ss 681(4) & 670). In addition a person is deemed to have made a settlement if he has made or entered into a settlement directly or indirectly, a phrase which is then made the subject of a non-exclusive example— by having provided or undertaken to provide funds, directly or indirectly for the purposes of the settlement (TA 1988, s 660I(2)). So in *IRC v Buchanan (1957) 37 TC 365* B made the settlement, and so was a settlor, when she disclaimed her interest. Similarly there was an indirect provision of funds in the case of the film star in *IRC v Mills ([1974] STC 130)*. A person makes a settlement if he carries out any steps of that settlement. So where the taxpayer had carried out one step and later a scheme was devised and carried out by his solicitors and accountants, it was held to be part of his settlement even though he was not consulted or present at any meetings (*Crossland v Hawkins (1961) 39 TC 493*). An infant can make a settlement.

The notion of a settlor is then widened to include one who has made a reciprocal arrangement with another person for that other person to make or enter into the settlement. The purpose here is to catch the obvious device whereby A makes a settlement on B's children and in return B makes a settlement on A's children; in such instances there must be a reciprocal arrangement (eg *Hood Barrs v IRC (1946) 27 TC 385*). However, there is not a reciprocal arrangement if X gives property to Y who then transfers it to a settlement: Y is the settlor and X is not—unless there is some conscious association between X and the proposed settlement (per Lord Keith in *Fitzwilliam v IRC [1993] STC 502, HL, at 516*).

Where funds are provided for a settlement a very strong inference is to be drawn that they are provided for that purpose, an inference which will be rebutted if it is established that they were provided for another purpose. So in *IRC v Mills* the infant provided funds for the purposes of a settlement even if unconsciously.

Seventh directive. A directive of the European Community issued in 1983 specifying the form of consolidated financial statements required of groups of companies. The directive was implemented in the UK by Companies Act 1989.

Shadow ACT. Although ACT is not payable in respect of qualifying distributions on or after 6 April 1999 the legislation makes provision, through regulations, for the treatment of any remaining unrelieved surplus ACT which had not by then been set off against a company's corporation tax liability (FA 1998, s 32).

The company may set such surplus ACT off against corporation tax due for accounting periods beginning on or after 6 April 1999. Shadow ACT arises where a company resident in the UK makes a 'relevant distribution', ie a distribution, made after 5 April 1999. A distribution which would be relevant is excluded if it is within the manufactured dividend rules or is equivalent to what was group income under the pre-1999 rules. Shadow ACT is calculated using the pre-1999 rate of 25% of the amount of the dividend.

Like pre-1999 ACT there are rules reducing the amount of shadow ACT where the company has received franked investment income. No shadow ACT is to be treated as having been paid until the company has distributed more than it has received. For this purpose the FII is treated as being the sum of distributions received multiplied by 9/8ths; there are also rules on surplus FII.

Shadow director. A person in accordance with whose directions or instructions the directors of a company are accustomed to act (see the Companies Act 1985, s 741(2)). But a person is not deemed a shadow director by reason only that the directors act on advice given by him in a professional capacity (see ibid, s 741(2)).

Sham. The acts done are intended to give the appearance of creating legal rights different from those which were actually created. In the case of a sham transaction the parties do not intend to carry the transaction out at all. 'It is of the essence of this type of sham transaction that the parties to a transaction intend to create one set of rights and obligations but do acts or enter into documents which they intend should give third parties, in this case the Revenue, or the court, the appearance of creating different rights and obligations' (per Arden LJ in *Hitch's Executors v Stone [2001] STC 214, CA*).

Share. (1) A share or proportion of the capital of a company, entitling the holder to a share in the profits of the company. Shares may be of different classes, the principal among which are:

(a) *Preference shares*, the holders of which have preference over other classes as regards dividends and the repayment of capital. These may be either *non-cumulative* or *cumulative*, the latter entitling the holders to arrears of dividend, as well as to current dividends, in priority to other shareholders; they may also be *redeemable* at a future date.

(b) *Ordinary shares*, which carry no such special rights or privileges.

(c) *Deferred shares*, the holders of which are entitled to any surplus after payment of dividends to the other classes of shareholders in accordance with the terms laid down in the memorandum and articles of association of the company.

(2) For the specific purpose of Financial Reporting Standard 2, the Accounting Standards Board has issued the following definition of 'shares':

The reference to shares is to allotted shares in an entity with a share capital, to rights to share in the capital in an entity with capital but no share capital, and to interests conferring any right to share in the profits, or imposing a liability to contribute to the losses or giving an obligation to contribute to debts or expenses in a winding-up for an entity without capital. [FRS 2 – Accounting for subsidiary undertakings]

(3) For the specific purpose of Financial Reporting Standard 4, the Accounting Standards Board has issued the following definition of 'a share':

A share in the share capital of the reporting company (or, in the context of consolidated financial statements, the holding company of a group), including stock.

[FRS 4 – Capital instruments]

See DIVIDEND, MEMORANDUM OF ASSOCIATION; ARTICLES OF ASSOCIATION.

Share, forfeiture of. *See* FORFEITURE OF SHARE.

Share, founder's. *See* FOUNDER'S SHARE.

Share, surrender of. *See* SURRENDER OF SHARE.

Share certificate. A certificate specifying the number of shares held by a member of a company. It is *prima facie* evidence of his title to the shares (Companies Act 1985, s 186).

Share dividend. A dividend paid by a company in the form of extra shares instead of in cash.
See DIVIDEND.

Share premium account. Where shares are issued for consideration in excess of the nominal value, the difference between the issue price and the nominal value constitutes a share premium which must be posted to the company's share premium account. The share premium account is a non-distributable reserve, but may be used for any of the following purposes:

(a) the issue of bonus shares,

(b) the writing off of preliminary expenses,

(c) the writing off of underwriting commissions,

(d) the paying of a premium on the redemption of debentures,

(e) the paying of a premium on the purchase by a company of its own shares.
(Companies Act 1985, s 130(1) & (2)).

Share warrant. A warrant stating that its bearer is entitled to the share specified in it (see the Companies Act 1985, s 188(1), (2)). The shares may be transferred by delivery of the warrant (see ibid, s 188(2)).

Shareholders' funds. The aggregate of called-up share capital and all reserves, excluding minority interests. [FRS 4 – Capital instruments]

Shares, consolidation of. *See* CONSOLIDATION OF SHARES.

Shares, sub-division of. *See* SUB-DIVISION OF SHARES.

Sharkey v Wernher. The rule in *Sharkey v Wernher* is that where a trader disposes of trading stock otherwise than in the course of trade, he is deemed to dispose of it at market value and that figure must be entered as a credit in his accounts. This principle applies whether he supplies the goods to himself or to some other person unless the disposal is a genuine commercial transaction. The value entered in the books of the transferor is also entered in the books of any trader acquiring the stock (*Ridge Securities Ltd v IRC (1964) 44 TC 373)*. In *Sharkey v Wernher (1955) 36 TC 275* Lady Zia Wernher carried on the business of a stud farm; she also rode horses for pleasure. She transferred a horse reared at the farm to her personal use and entered the costs incurred in respect of the horse until the date of its transfer as a credit item in the account of the stud farm. There was thus no attempt to take tax advantage of the deductions she had already been allowed. The Revenue successfully contended that the horse should be entered not at cost but at market value.

The rule is subject to two technical objections. First, the profit alleged to be made comes from a course of dealing with oneself; it is precisely because this is alleged to be impossible that no charge to tax arises from mutual dealings. In reply Viscount Simonds said (*at 296*) that 'the true proposition is not that a man cannot make a profit out of himself but that he cannot trade with himself', a principle which was not to apply where trading stock was removed from the trade for a man's own use and enjoyment. However, this is not consistent with other formulations of the mutuality principle.

Second, the decision appears to conflict with the fundamental principle that a person is taxed on what is actually earned and not on what he might have earned. However, in *Sharkey v Wernher* the taxpayer received value; the question therefore is the figure to be entered in the accounts. Lord Radcliffe (*at 307*) rejected the idea of taking the cost figure on the grounds that market value 'gives a fairer measure of assessable trading profit' and was 'better economics'. For a trader who was concerned with the profitability of his trade it would be better book-keeping to include market value. However, the issue is not what is good book-keeping but the correct basis for taxation. In this regard it may be

noted that the cost figure was in conformity with then accepted accountancy practice (see Lord Oaksey's dissenting judgment).

Ship. Ships have for many years been treated specially for capital allowance purposes. If the expenditure qualifies for a first year allowance the allowance may be postponed or reduced in whole or in part (CAA 2001, s 130(1), (3)–(5)); the amount deferred can be claimed as a first year allowance in a later year (CAA 2001, s 131(1), (2), (4)). This freedom to depreciate applies to writing-down allowances also. The writing-down allowance may be deferred in whole or in part in prescribed circumstances (CAA 2001, ss 129–133). Expenditure on ships is not pooled.

There is no statutory definition of a ship but there have been many decisions on its meaning under the Merchant Shipping Acts. So a floating gas container without power and not fitted for navigation was held not to be a ship (*Wells v Gas Float Whitton No 2 (Owners) [1897] AC 337, HL*) but a hopper barge without engine or sail was held to be a ship (*The Mac (1882) 7 PD 126, CA*). There is, however, a statutory definition of qualifying ships for the purpose of the 1995 rules on deferment of balancing charges—the vessel must be of a sea-going kind of at least 100 g.r.t. and meet certain registration requirements and certain vessels (eg hovercraft) are specifically excluded. To be a qualifying ship it must be registered in the UK, a dependent territory, a Crown dependency, the Isle of Man or Channel Islands or another state within the EU or EEA.

FA 1995, ss 94–98 and FA 1996, Sch 35 contain new rules on the treatment of balancing charges, the broad effect of which is to allow such charges arising on the disposal of qualifying ships to be rolled over for a period of up to three years to be set off against subsequent expenditure on new ships within that period (CAA 2001, ss 151 & 146). This treatment is analogous to rollover relief for capital gains tax. The amount that can be rolled forward is that needed to ensure that there is no tax liability in the year. Tax deferred may be recovered if, for example, the new ship is not bought or does not meet the terms of the provisions. The ship may have been owned by the taxpayer previously but there must be a six-year gap (CAA 2001, ss 147(1) & 148).

Since 1 January 2000, a shipping company has been able to elect to compute its corporation tax liability by reference to the tonnage of its fleet, ignoring the profits actually generated (FA 2000, Sch 22, para 3).

Short life assets. The effect of the writing-down allowance for machinery and plant is that about 90% of the cost is written off over eight years. Because some assets have a shorter life expectancy than this, the rules have been amended to allow such short life assets to be kept out of the general pool (CAA 2001, s 86). One advantage is that if the asset is disposed of any balancing allowance is given immediately instead of waiting for the overall effect on a pool—but only if it is disposed of within, approximately, five years.

The short life asset is kept in a pool of its own and the normal 25% writing-down allowance applied on the normal reducing basis (CAA 2001, ss 65(2) & 86(1)). The advantage is, thus, solely in the year of disposal, when the remaining balance of expenditure becomes a balancing allowance. The (irrevocable) election for the treatment of an asset as a short life asset must be made within two years of the year of acquisition (CAA 2001, s 85(1)–(4)).

Shorts. Government stock ('gilts') with a life of less than five years.

Short-term debtors and creditors. Financial assets and financial liabilities that meet all of the following criteria:

(*a*) they would be included under one of the following balance sheet headings if the entity was preparing its financial statements in accordance with Schedule 4 to the Companies Act 1985:

   (i) debtors;

   (ii) prepayments and accrued income;

   (iii) creditors: amounts falling due within one year, other than items that would be included under the 'debenture loans' and 'bank loans and overdrafts' subheadings;

   (iv) provisions for liabilities and charges; or

   (v) accruals and deferred income;

(*b*) they mature or become payable within 12 months of the balance sheet date; and

(*c*) they are not a derivative financial instrument.

[FRS 13 – Derivatives and other financial instruments]

Sight, bills payable at. Are equivalent to bills of exchange payable on demand (see the Bills of Exchange Act 1882, s 10).
See BILL OF EXCHANGE.

Signature. An indication, by sign, mark, or generally by the writing of a name or initials, that a person intends to bind himself to the contents of a document.

Simple contract. A contract, express or implied, which is created by a verbal promise, or by a writing not under seal.
See CONTRACT; DEED.

Simple contract debt. A debt arising out of a simple contract.
See SIMPLE CONTRACT.

Simple trust. A trust which requires no act to be done by the trustee except conveyance or transfer to his *cestui que trust* on request by the latter.

Sleeping partner. A partner taking no active part in the administration of a firm. But as far as creditors are concerned, he is as much a partner and as responsible as such as if he took an equally active part in the administration with the partner or partners who ostensibly carry it on.

Small company. A small company is entitled to file abbreviated accounts with the Registrar of Companies, containing limited information on a balance sheet and no profit and loss account. A small company is one that meets the following criteria:

(*a*) a balance sheet total of £1.4 million or less,

(*b*) a turnover of £2.8 million or less,

(*c*) no more than 50 employees.

(Companies Act 1985, s 247).

A small company is exempt from disclosure with respect to compliance with accounting standards: ibid, s 248.

Small companies' rate. *See* RATE OF TAX.

Small company rate. When a company has profits of less than £300,000 for a 12-month period, corporation tax is levied at the 'small company rate' (TA 1988, s 13(1)). The name is a misnomer, and applies to any size of company, however large, if the profits are in the specified band. For the purposes of this relief 'profits' includes income, capital gains and franked investment income but not group income (TA 1988, s 13(7)). This rate applies to companies resident in the UK (other than close investment holding companies) but not to non-resident companies with a UK branch. The Revenue, however, interpret a non-discrimination clause in an applicable double tax agreement as entitling the non-resident company to this rate. The decision of the European Court in *R v IRC, ex p Commerzbank AG (Case C-330/91) [1993] STC 605, CJEC* seems to give branches of companies of another member state a right to use that rate.

Marginal relief applies when the profits exceed £300,000 but not £1.5m. The corporation tax due at the full rate of 30% is calculated and then reduced by a sum determined by a complex formula. The reduction declines until the figure reaches £1.5m at which point it vanishes; it provides a smooth graduation of liability from the lower rate to the full rate of CT; this gives a marginal tax rate higher than full rate. The figures of £300,000 and £1.5m are not index-linked and were last increased in 1994. But for express provision, it would be easy to exploit these benefits by dividing a business between many companies. It is therefore provided that when the company has one or more associated companies in the accounting period the figures of £300,000 and £1.5m shall be divided by the total number of companies which are associated with each other (TA 1988, s 13(3)). This technique of crude division by the number of companies rather than division according to the size of profits, has the effect that two associated companies each with a profit of £300,000 will together pay less tax than if one had profits of £599,000 and the other of £1,000. For this purpose, overseas companies under common control are treated as 'associated companies', even if the overseas company has no liability to UK tax.

Small disposal. Statute provides that, in four circumstances, there is no immediate charge to capital gains tax in respect of an amount of consideration received that is regarded as 'small'. Instead, the consideration received is treated as reducing the acquisition cost that is put against the ultimate disposal of the asset concerned. The circumstances where this treatment is adopted are a capital distribution (TCGA 1992, s 122(2)), cash received on a share reorganisation (TCGA 1992, s 116(13)), a premium on conversion of securities (TCGA 1992, s 133(2)) and cash received on compulsory acquisition of land (TCGA 1992, s 43(1)(a)).

Statute does not define the word 'small' in respect of these provisions. In *O'Rourke v Binks [1992] STC 703, CA*, the Special Commissioner held that shares to the value of £246,000 could be treated as 'small' for the purposes of s 122(2). This sum amounted to 15.58% of the acquisition cost of the original holding, but less than 5% of the value of the original holding immediately before reorganisation. The Court of Appeal reversed this decision saying that what is 'small' is a question of fact and degree and has to be considered in the light of the circumstances in any particular case. Judicial comment was made that the purpose of the legislation is to avoid the need for assessments in trivial cases, noting that this was not such a case.

The Revenue subsequently published their interpretation of the meaning of 'small'. In this the Revenue state that they will continue with their long-standing approach of accepting as 'small' 5% or less than the value of the shares/land, but will also accept as 'small' any receipt of £3,000 or less. A taxpayer does, however, have the right to argue that the particular circumstances of a case justify an amount in excess of these limits to be regarded as 'small' or, alternatively, an amount below these limits should not be so regarded.

Where there is a part disposal of land, this treatment is adopted and the consideration received is treated as reducing the base cost, in the same manner as in the foregoing, if the value of the consideration does not exceed the lower of £20,000 or one-fifth of the market value of the land-holding immediately prior to the part disposal (TCGA 1992, s 242(1)(a), (3)(a)). For land, it is not necessary to consider whether the amount received is 'small'.

Small self-administered pension schemes. There is a special regime for small self-administered pension schemes. Following consultation with interested bodies, the rules relating to such schemes have been revised and are now more restrictive than before. A small self-administered scheme is defined as one where:

(1) some or all of the income and other assets are invested otherwise than in insurance policies; and
(2) one of the members is connected with another member, or with a trustee of the scheme, or with a person who is an employer in relation to the scheme; and
(3) the scheme has less than 12 members (SI 1991/1614, reg 2(1)).

The connection required in (2) will be met if the two persons are husband and wife or the one is a relative of the other, or the other's spouse, or the husband or wife of a relative. 'Relative' for this purpose means brother, sister, ancestor or lineal descendent (reg 2(4)). Where the employer is a partnership, a member who is connected with a partner is treated as connected with the employer (reg 2(5)(a)). Where the employer is a company the member is treated as connected with the employer if he or a person connected with him has been a controlling director of the company during the preceding ten years (reg 2(5)(b)). The Revenue will also require a scheme with more than 12 members to be treated as a small self-administered scheme where some makeweight members have been included simply to bring the total membership up to 12 or more.

The principal attraction (usually to controlling directors) of a small self-administered scheme is the degree of permitted self-investment. SSA 1990 introduced restrictions to prohibit self-investment beyond 5% of a pension scheme's resources. Small self-administered schemes are exempt from the 5% limit provided: (a) there are less than 12 members; (b) all members are trustees; and (c) all members agree in writing to the self-investment (Occupational Pension Schemes (Investment of Scheme's Resources) Regulations 1992, SI 1992/246).

Social Fund. A fund out of which payments may be made in respect of (i) maternity expenses; (ii) funeral expenses; (iii) other needs in accordance with directions given by the Secretary of State; and (iv) expenses of heating incurred or likely to be incurred in cold weather (Social Security Contributions and Benefits Act 1992, s 138(1)). For awards by Social Fund officers, see ibid, s 139.

Social security benefits. These consist of (a) contributory benefits, eg sickness benefit, invalidity benefit and maternity benefit; (b) non-contributory benefits, eg attendance allowance, severe disablement allowance, and invalid care allowance; (c) benefit for industrial injuries; (d) income-related benefits, eg income support, family credit, disability working allowance, housing benefit; and (e) child benefit.

Society of Trust and Estate Practitioners. STEP was founded in 1991 and has 7,500 members, many of whom are also qualified as solicitors, barristers or accountants. Members are allowed to use the designation TEP. Website: www.step.org.uk

Special agent. An agent empowered to act as such in a particular matter, and not generally.

See GENERAL AGENT.

Stakeholder. A person instructed to hold a sum of money paid as a deposit on a contract for the purchase of property. Such sum is often paid to a person as a stakeholder as between the two parties, not as agent for the vendor.

Stakeholder pensions. In the Government's green paper 'Welfare Reform – Partnership in Pensions' issued in December 1998, it was suggested that there would be a separate tax regime for stakeholder pensions. During 1999, the DSS issued several consultation documents on the detailed aspects of stakeholder pensions. There was almost unanimous agreement from respondents that a separate tax regime would add unnecessary confusion to the existing tax regime for pension types. The changes to be introduced result in a single and simplified tax regime for all types of money purchase pensions, these are now called 'stakeholder pensions', a term that includes both occupational pensions and personal pension plans. Existing occupational money purchase schemes can opt to be approved under the new regime and subject to the same rules. The elements of a stakeholder pension scheme are as follows:

(a) Anyone who is not a member of an occupational pension scheme can pay up to £3,600 a year into a stakeholder pension regardless of their earnings. This means that individuals without earnings can contribute up to £3,600 a year. Several groups of individuals could fall into this category, eg carers, parents taking career breaks to bring up children, non-earning spouses etc.

(b) Contributions over £3,600 can be made based on earnings, using the age related percentage figures. This higher level of contribution can continue for up to five years after earnings have ceased, whether temporarily (eg career break, maternity leave) or permanently.

(c) All contributions are paid net of basic rate tax. The pension provider reclaims the basic rate tax from the Inland Revenue.

(d) A member can carry back a contribution made at any time up to 31 January after the tax year (but not later). This allows someone making contributions over £3,600 to maximise his/her contribution in any year where the actual earnings cannot be determined until after the end of the tax year.

(e) The existing personal pension carry forward rules ceased to apply with effect from 5 April 2001. The carry forward rules for retirement annuities remain.

(f) Up to 10% of the amount which is paid as a pension contribution can be used for life assurance. Tax relief for waiver of pension contributions insurance is simplified and can include other circumstances such as unemployment.

(g) Shares from an approved employee share scheme can be put into the pension, within the contribution limits, and attract tax relief.

(h) Individuals making contributions must be a resident in the UK or be undertaking Crown duties whilst serving abroad or have previously have been UK resident and are currently making contributions by reference to remuneration received whilst UK resident.

(i) An individual who is participating in an employer's pension scheme that has not opted for approval under the stakeholder regime is not able to make contributions under the stakeholder regime.

(j) Non-qualifying life policies held for the purposes of a stakeholder personal pension scheme are exempt from the tax regime applied to chargeable events.

(k) Instead of taking phased benefits from a scheme containing, say, 100 segments, stakeholder rules permit phased benefits from within a single arrangement. Stakeholder rules allow income draw-down from phased benefits to have a single review date.

(l) The maximum annual charge, which must cover all aspects of the management of the scheme and its funds, is 1% per annum. There are detailed rules for calculating this charge and these cover with-profit policies.

From 1 October 2001 an employer is required to provide access to a stakeholder pension for all employees unless he has fewer than five employees, except that an employer is not required to offer access to a stakeholder pension scheme if all relevant employees have the opportunity to join a personal pension to which the employer contributes at least 3% of the employees' basic pay and there are no charges or penalties if a member leaves the scheme.

Stamp duties. Stamp duties are one of the oldest taxes. They were originally introduced by Stamp Duty Act 1694 Will & Mary c 21. Strictly, they are taxes on documents and not on transactions or persons and are now governed by the Stamp Act 1891 and the Stamp Duties Management Act 1891 as amended by numerous Finance Acts and by various Revenue Acts. FA 1999 has significantly altered the structure of the stamp duties legislation in relation to sales and it also attempted to modernise some of the statutory language and procedure relating to penalties and appeals, for example. Stamp duties bring in a modest but not insignificant amount of revenue and they are relatively cheap to administer and collect. In the year ended 31 March 2000 stamp duties raised approximately £6.9 billion (at the pre-4.0% rate) which was more than the combined take from capital gains tax, inheritance tax and petroleum revenue tax.

As stated above, stamp duty is a tax on documents. There are a number of separate duties, under different heads of charge. The main stamp duty is a percentage charge of the price paid (*ad valorem*) on a conveyance or transfer on sale of various types of property by means of a document. The amount of the percentage varies according to the type of property being conveyed or transferred and the amount of the price paid. The threshold below which no stamp duty is payable on land and buildings and certain other property is currently £60,000. In addition, fixed £5 duties arise on certain documents not on sale, eg on declarations of trust.

FA 1990, ss 107 & 108 included provisions for the future abolition of all the stamp duty charges (including stamp duty reserve tax) on transactions in shares, from a date to be fixed by Treasury order. FA 1991, ss 110–114 included provisions to limit stamp duty to instruments embodying transactions concerning interests in land and buildings. However, the outcome of the General Election in May 1997 affected the implementation of these provisions: the Labour government indicated that it will retain stamp duty (and stamp duty reserve tax) on transactions in securities. In view of the significant changes and

further increase in rates introduced by FA 2000, abolition of stamp duty looks increasingly unlikely.

The introduction of an electronic system for holding and transferring title to securities ('CREST') in July 1996 has had a significant impact on the way in which stamp duty (and stamp duty reserve tax) are charged in respect of transactions involving changes in title or ownership of securities. Since CREST is a paperless system, there is no instrument of transfer on which stamp duty can be paid. Instead, stamp duty reserve tax is charged on agreements to transfer securities within CREST. In consequence, stamp duty reserve tax has become the principal tax on transactions in securities.

Stamp duty reserve tax. Stamp duty reserve tax is charged in respect of agreements to transfer chargeable securities for money or money's worth (FA 1986, ss 86–99). For unconditional agreements made before 1 July 1996 or agreements becoming unconditional before that date, the charge was deferred. A liability to tax was imposed after two months except where, within that period, an agreement to transfer securities to a purchaser or a nominee was completed by an instrument of transfer which, if chargeable with stamp duty or otherwise required to be stamped, was duly stamped. Where those conditions were fulfilled within six years of the charge to stamp duty reserve tax arising, there was provision for the repayment of the tax or the cancellation of the charge. There was also an immediate and unconditional charge in respect of agreements to transfer chargeable securities constituted by or transferable by means of certain renounceable instruments as soon as they were made to which the conditions for relief from the charge did not apply.

Under the paperless securities transfer system, CREST, which was introduced in July 1996, changes in title or ownership are made electronically. Accordingly, stamp duty is not paid on an instrument where a transfer is made within the CREST system. For this reason, the two-month period has been removed in relation to agreements made on or after 1 July 1996 or becoming unconditional on or after that date so that the charge to stamp duty reserve tax is now immediate in all cases (FA 1996, s 188). Where a transaction is completed by a duly stamped instrument within six years from the date on which the charge is imposed, there is, as before, a provision for the repayment of the tax or the cancellation of the charge. The provisions for repayment or cancellation do not apply in a number of cases.

In each case tax is imposed at the rate of 0.5% of the amount or value of the consideration rounded to the nearest penny. A higher rate charge of 1.5% is imposed in respect of certain transactions involving depositary receipts and clearance services, although it is possible for the operator of a clearance service to elect for a 0.5% charge on agreements to transfer chargeable securities within the system. The value of consideration other than money is the price it might reasonably be expected to fetch in the open market at the time the agreement is made (FA 1986, s 87(7)). The rates for stamp duty reserve tax are therefore the same as those for stamp duty on share transfers, but the tax base is broader. Stamp duty reserve tax applies to transactions which are not effected by means of an instrument of transfer and the tax is imposed irrespective of the nature of the consideration. It is for this reason that the introduction of CREST has had a significant impact on stamp duty reserve tax.

Liability for stamp duty reserve tax is imposed on the purchaser, but the tax is usually collected and paid by intermediaries in the securities market or, where transfers are effected on CREST, by the system operator, CRESTCo.

The tax applies whether or not the relevant transaction is made or effected in the UK and whether or not any of the parties are resident or situate in any part of the UK (FA 1986, s 86(4)). However, the Treasury may make regulations to exempt from the tax UK depositary interests in foreign securities to allow the operator of an electronic settlement service such as CREST to offer a settlement service for deals in foreign shares without incurring a tax liability (FA 1999, s 119).

As with stamp duty, the tax is under the care and management of the Commissioners of Inland Revenue. Unlike stamp duty, the tax is directly enforceable and may be recovered by the Commissioners. Appeals are heard in the first instance by the Special Commissioners, rather than upon a case stated to the High Court.

Starting rate. *See* RATE OF TAX.

Statement of affairs. A statement by a debtor in bankruptcy proceedings, listing his debtors, creditors, assets, etc (see the Insolvency Act 1986, s 288).

Statement of Recommended Practice. Statements of Recommended Practice (SORP) are statements issued with the intention of narrowing the areas of difference and variety in the accounting treatment of matters with which they deal and to enhance the usefulness of published accounting information. Since 1990, the policy of the Accounting Standards Board has been not to issue SORPs itself but to recognise bodies for the issue of SORPs, where the body agrees to abide by the ASB's code of practice in producing SORPs (ASB policy statement October 1990, revised June 1994). ASB states that SORPs are issued on subjects 'on which it is not considered appropriate to issue an accounting standard at the time'. There are currently 13 SORPs in issue:

Accounting for oil and gas exploration, development, production and decommissioning activities
Financial statements of authorised unit trust schemes
Advances
Segmental reporting
Contingent liabilities and commitments
Derivatives
Code of practice on local authority accounting in Great Britain
Accounting by registered social landlords
Accounting in higher education institutions
Accounting by charities
The financial statements of pension schemes
Financial statements of investment trust companies
Accounting for insurance business

Statements of Standard Accounting Practice. SSAPs were created by the councils of the six major accountancy bodies. When the Accounting Standards Committee was created in 1990, it formally adopted the 22 SSAPs then in issue, thereby giving them the status of accounting standards for the purpose of Companies Act 1985, Part VII. Each SSAP has continued in force, unless it has been replaced by a financial reporting standard (FRS), The statements of standard accounting practice currently in force are:

SSAP 2 – Disclosure of accounting policies

SSAP 4 – Accounting for government grants

SSAP 5 – Accounting for value added tax

SSAP 9 – Stocks and long-term contracts

SSAP 13 – Accounting for research and development

SSAP 15 – Accounting for deferred tax

SSAP 17 – Accounting for post balance sheet events

SSAP 19 – Accounting for investment properties

SSAP 20 – Foreign currency translation

SSAP 21 – Accounting for leases and hire purchase contracts

SSAP 24 – Accounting for pension costs

SSAP 25 – Segmental reporting

Status. The condition of a person in the eye of the law.

Status quo. The state in which any thing is already. Thus, when it is said that, provisionally, matters are to remain *in status quo*, it is meant that, for the present, matters are to remain as they are. Sometimes, however, the phrase is used retrospectively: and, if so, this will generally be indicated by the context; eg when, on a treaty of peace, matters are to *return* to the *status quo*, this means the *status quo ante bellum*, their state prior to the war.

Statute. An Act of Parliament made by the Queen in Parliament. It normally requires the consent of the Lords and Commons; but see the Parliament Act 1911, for the circumstances in which a Bill may become law without the consent of the Lords.

A *statute*, in the original sense of the word, means the legislation of a session; the various Acts of Parliament passed in it being so many *chapters* of the entire statute. Thus, by the Statute of Gloucester, the Statute of Merton, etc, is meant a body of legislation comprising various chapters on different subjects. But in reference to modern legislation the word *statute* denotes a *chapter* of legislation, or what is otherwise called an *Act of Parliament*.

Statutory declaration. A declaration made before a magistrate or commissioner for oaths in the form prescribed by the Statutory Declarations Act 1835, by which voluntary affidavits, in matters where no judicial inquiry is pending, are prohibited. Any person making a statutory declaration falsely is guilty of an offence under the Perjury Act 1911, s 5.

Statutory demand. A demand served by a petitioning creditor on a debtor in the prescribed form requiring him to pay the debt or to secure or compound for it to the creditor's satisfaction (see the Insolvency Act 1986, s 268(1)).

Statutory instrument. The most important form of delegated legislation including all Orders in Council and all statutory rules and orders which have to be laid before Parliament.

Statutory sick pay. Money payable by an employer to an employee who is incapable of work in relation to his contract of service (Social Security Contributions and Benefits Act 1992, ss 151–154).

Statutory interpretation. *See* INTERPRETATION OF STATUTE.

Statutory trust. A trust created by the operation of statute and not by a person's deed. For example, the effect of Administration of Estates Act 1925, s 47 is to create one or more statutory trusts whenever a person dies intestate. Under the 'statutory trusts' for issue, the property must be divided equally among the children who are alive at the death of the intestate, conditional on their attaining the age of 18 or marrying below that age.

See INTESTACY; STIRPES, DISTRIBUTION PER.

Stirpes, distribution per. A division of property among families according to stocks of descent. So, for example, if X has three children, A, B, and C, there are three stocks of descent. If X dies leaving one living child, A, but both B and C have died leaving children of their own, B leaving D and E, and C leaving F, G, and H, a distribution per stirpes takes D, E, F, G and H into consideration as 'representatives' of the deceased person, B or C respectively, who, had they survived, would themselves have taken property along with A. A, B and C would each have received a third of X's estate had they all survived X, being kin of X 'in equal degree' (all children of X); A, still alive, will receive one third, and under a distribution *per stirpes* D and E will together take the third that would have gone to B, and F, G, and H will together take the third that would have gone to C. This form of distribution is in contrast to distribution *per capita*, whereby descendants of equal degree take equally regardless of stocks of descent. Under such a distribution, all grandchildren, if they were to inherit at all, would all inherit an equal amount, regardless of the stocks of descent, for all are kin of equal degree to the deceased. For the present rules of succession on intestacy applying alike to real and personal property, see the Administration of Estates Act 1925, Part IV.

Stock. (1) With reference to the investment of money, the Oxford English Dictionary gives the origin of the current use of the term 'stock' as having been identified from 1710 as: 'Money, or a sum of money, invested by a person in a partnership or commercial company'. The term developed from the money advanced to a commercial enterprise to fund its activities to denote the moneys advanced to the Government, which constitute a part of the National Debt, on which a certain amount of interest is payable. The meaning of the word

'stock' has gradually changed and now usually refers to the principal of the loans themselves and, sometimes, of equity issued for the money invested. In this sense one speaks of the sale, purchase, and transfer of stock.

See STOCKBROKER; STOCK EXCHANGE.

(2) With reference to the stock in trade of an enterprise, the Oxford English Dictionary gives the origin of the current use of the term 'stock' as having been identified from 1762 as: 'The goods kept on sale by a dealer, shopkeeper, or pedlar'. The meaning of the word 'stock' has gradually changed and now refers not only to goods for sale, but also, materials kept for manufacture or otherwise for consumption in the business of the enterprise. The Accounting Standards Board has issued the following definition:

Stocks comprise the following categories:

(*a*) goods or other assets purchased for resale;

(*b*) consumable stores;

(*c*) raw materials and components purchased for incorporation into products for sale;

(*d*) products and services in intermediate stages of completion;

(*e*) long-term contract balances; and

(*f*) finished goods.

[SSAP 9 – Stocks and long-term contracts]

Stock certificate. A certificate showing that the stockholder is the owner of a specified amount of stock.

Stock dividend. When a person has an option to receive either a dividend or additional share capital, special rules treat the share capital so issued as giving rise to a charge to tax on the recipient (TA 1988, s 249). The payment, however, is not a distribution, although the recipient may be liable to the higher rate of tax. There is no liability to basic rate income tax. These rules also apply if the shareholder has shares which carry the right to receive bonus share capital and that right is conferred by the terms on which the shares were issued (or later varied if bonus share capital is then issued) (TA 1988, s 251(1)(a)).

Stock exchange. An association of stock-brokers and market makers in the city of London and elsewhere. The regulations of the Stock Exchange are, like the other usages of trade, recognised by courts of law as evidence of the course of dealing between the parties to a contract.

See STOCKBROKER.

Stockbroker. A person who, for a commission, negotiates for other parties the buying and selling of stocks and shares, according to the rules of the Stock Exchange.

See STOCK EXCHANGE.

Strict settlement. (1) This phrase was formerly used to denote a settlement whereby land was limited to a parent for life, and after his death to his first and other sons or children in tail, with a trust imposed 'to preserve contingent remainders', ie a trust to preserve contingent interests in remainder.

See ESTATE.

(2) Generally, a settlement in which land is limited to, or is held in trust for, persons by way of succession, ie whose interest takes one after another in succession, unless it is subject to 'an immediate binding trust for sale'. Its object is to keep lands in a particular family. Important alterations in the mode of creating strict settlements are contained in the Settled Land Act 1925. Under that Act a settlement of a legal estate in land *inter vivos* is to be effected (except as provided in the Act) by two deeds, ie a vesting deed declaring that the land is vested in the tenant for life or statutory owner for the legal estate the subject of the intended settlement, and a trust instrument declaring the trusts affecting the settled land.

See SETTLEMENT; SETTLED LAND; VESTING DEED; TRUST INSTRUMENT.

Structured settlement. A settlement whereby a successful plaintiff suing for damages for personal injury is awarded a lump sum and also an index-linked annuity from the defendant's insurers. See the Damages Act 1996.

Sub-division of shares. The division of shares of a certain nominal value into a larger number of shares of a smaller nominal values, eg the division of a £1 share into four 25p shares.

Sublease. A lease created by a lessee of land out of his leasehold interest. To create such a lease is to *sublease* or *sublet* the land, and the lessee creating the sublease is styled a *sublessor* and his lessee the *sublessee*.

See LEASE; UNDERLEASE.

Submission. A word especially used with reference to the submission of a matter in dispute to the judgment of an arbitrator or arbitrators.

Subscriber. (1) A person who signs the original memorandum of association and the articles of association of a company.

See MEMORANDUM OF ASSOCIATION; ARTICLES OF ASSOCIATION.

(2) A person who pays or agrees to pay a company in respect of shares or debentures offered to him by it.

Subsidiary company. (1) Companies Act 1985, s 736(1) defines a 'subsidiary' as:

A company is a subsidiary of another company, its 'holding company', if that other company

(*a*) holds a majority of the voting rights in it, or

(*b*) is a member of it and has the right to appoint or remove a majority of its board of directors, or

(*c*) is a member of it and controls alone, pursuant to an agreement with other shareholders or members, a majority of the voting rights in it,

or if it is a subsidiary of a company which is itself a subsidiary of the holding company.

(2) The Accounting Standards Board states:

'In principle, a subsidiary is an entity over which another entity (the investor) has control.' [FRS 2 – Accounting for subsidiary undertakings & FRS 9 – Associates and joint ventures]. ASB states this to be 'consistent with' Companies Act 1985, s 258 & Sch 10A.

Subsidiary undertaking. An undertaking is a subsidiary undertaking if another undertaking is treated as its parent.

[FRS 2 – Accounting for subsidiary undertakings]

See PARENT UNDERTAKING.

Succession. (1) Where a person succeeds to property previously enjoyed by another. It is either *singular* or *universal*. Singular succession is where the purchaser, donee, or legatee of a specific chattel, or other specific property, succeeds to the right of the vendor, donor, or testator. Universal succession is the succession to an indefinite series of rights, eg the succession by the trustee of a bankrupt to the estate and effects of the bankrupt, or by an executor or administrator to the estate of the deceased.

(2) For the rules of succession on intestacy *see* INTESTACY.

(3) When a trade which has been carried on by one person is transferred to another; such a transfer is called a succession and must be distinguished from the mere purchase of the assets used in the trade. In the case of a succession, there is a discontinuance by the old trader and a commencement by the new one, so that the profits since the last accounting date, which may be up to 23 months previously, are assessed to income tax on the old trader in the single year in which the succession occurs (see TA 1988, s 63) and the new trader is assessed to income tax under the opening years' provisions, which will commonly bring the first year's profits into charge twice, creating overlap profit relief for a later period (see TA 1988, s 61). In addition, there may be a clawback of capital allowances by means of a balancing charge (see CAA 1990, s 152) and there can be a loss of accumulated loss relief (see TA 1988, s 343). These affects can often be avoided if, instead of a succession, the transferee simply acquires the assets.

A succession to a trade must be distinguished from the purchase of the assets of a trade. Thus where a company which had a tramp shipping business bought a ship second-hand from another trader there was no succession to that person's trade, but only the purchase of a ship (*Watson Bros v Lothian (1902) 4 TC 441*). These are, however, questions of fact and it was important in that case that the purchaser acquired no list of customers along with the ship, that

the ship had no special route along which and only along which she used to ply her trade and that no goodwill came with the ship.

For there to be a succession, there has to be a 'very close identity' between the business in the former proprietorship and the business in the new proprietorship (per Rowlatt J in *Reynolds, Sons & Co Ltd v Ogston (1930) 15 TC 501 at 524*). A very close identity is, however, not the same as a complete identity. Thus a successor to a business with say 50 shops may choose to shut up some of them, make alterations in the goods that he sells, change his supplier or may cut out a particular class of customer or a particular area (per Sir Wilfrid Greene MR in *Laycock v Freeman, Hardy and Willis Ltd (1938) 22 TC 288 at 297*). The question whether such changes prevent there being a succession to the business is one of fact.

There can be no succession to a part of a trade. However, as Rowlatt J said, 'I do not think that it means that if what is succeeded to is not the same extent of trade or even does not include a particular line of customers, it necessarily follows that there cannot be a successor to a trade.' (*James Shipstone & Son Ltd v Morris (1929) 14 TC 413 at 421*).

Successor in title. Any person who will become entitled to the property in question after the present owner, ie any person who *succeeds* to the title of the property.

Sui juris. A phrase used to denote a person who is under no disability affecting his legal power to make conveyances of his property, to bind himself by contracts, and to sue and be sued; as opposed to persons wholly or partially under disability, eg infants, mentally disordered persons, prisoners, etc.

Supplemental deed. Recitals are often used when the deed in which they occur is effectual only by virtue of its complying with the terms of some other deed, to show that the terms have been duly complied with. But lengthy recitals of a previous instrument may be avoided by expressing the deed to be 'supplemental' to the previous instrument. Such a supplemental deed has to be read in conjunction with the deed to which it is expressed to be made supplemental in order to see that the terms of the latter deed have been duly complied with.

See RECITAL.

Supply. Value added tax is charged on a supply. Supply, in the enigmatic words of the parliamentary draftsman, 'includes all forms of supply' (VATA 1994, s 5(2)(a)). It is submitted that the term is no more than a generic description given to transfers in the possession or ownership of goods, the grant, assignment or surrender of rights in property and the provision of facilities or services. It thus includes transactions known by a myriad of names in everyday commercial life, eg sale, hire, loan, and so on. On this basis, 'a supply' is something that is supplied.

VAT is a general tax on consumption. Thus, that which is done must give rise to consumption, and this must involve either the provision of services to an identifiable consumer or the provision of a benefit capable of forming a cost component of another person's activity in the commercial chain. It follows that a trader is not regarded as making a supply of goods or services merely because he receives money, goods or services from another person.

It is necessary to identify the person making the supply (in order to determine who is liable to register or charge tax) and the person receiving the goods or services concerned (in order to determine who is entitled to an input tax credit, repayment or refund in respect of the tax charged). It is also necessary to identify the true legal description of that which has been supplied in order to determine whether it falls within the scope of tax and, if so, whether any tax is chargeable on it.

The true nature of a supply or, indeed, whether a supply has been made, is necessarily resolved by reference to the contract between the parties, or to the general law. The nature of a supply is determined at the time of supply and cannot be rewritten by reference to the unilateral act of one party or an agreement between both parties.

The tax consequences flowing from a transaction may be affected by some impropriety arising from the nature of the goods or services supplied or the manner in which they are supplied. In principle, a transaction does not cease to be a supply merely because it is void (eg the sale of a stolen car), it infringes a third party's rights (eg the sale of counterfeit perfume), the conditions for carrying it out lawfully have not been met (eg the unlawful operation of a game of chance); or the goods and services are used by the purchaser to carry on an unlawful activity (eg table rented to a drug dealer). However, no supply is made for VAT purposes if the goods or services are subject to an outright ban on the supplier and recipient alike.

Supra. Above. Often used to refer a reader to a previous part of a book.

Surrender (Lat *Sursum reditio*). The falling of a lesser estate into a greater.

(1) *Surrender in deed.* This takes place by the yielding up of an estate for life or years to the person who has the immediate reversion or remainder. To constitute a valid express surrender, it is essential that it should be made to, and accepted by, the owner (in his own right) of the reversion or remainder.

See REVERSION; REMAINDER.

(2) *Surrender by operation of law.* This phrase is properly applied to cases where the tenant for life or years has been a party to some act the validity of which he is by law afterwards estopped from disputing, and which would not be valid if this particular estate continued to exist; eg when a lessee for years accepts a new lease from his lessor, he is estopped from saying that his lessor had not the power to make the new lease, so that the acceptance of the new lease amounts in law to a surrender of the former one. The effect of a surrender by operation of law is expressly reserved by the Law of Property Act 1925, s 54(2).

See ESTOPPEL.

Surrender of share. The yielding up of shares to the company by a member. The articles of association may give power to the directors to accept a surrender of shares. This relieves them of going through the formality of forfeiture if the member is willing to surrender the shares.

See FORFEITURE OF SHARE.

Survivorship. A word used not merely of the *fact* of survivorship, but of the rights arising from it; ie of the right of the survivor or survivors of joint tenants to the estate held in joint tenancy, to the exclusion of the representatives of the deceased.
See JOINT TENANCY.

Syndicate. A group of underwriters associating themselves for business purposes, each syndicate being given a number. A list of the members of the syndicate is attached to the policy.
See 'NAMES'; LLOYD'S.

T

TEP. Member of the Society of Trust and Estates Practitioners.

TESSA. Tax Exempt Special Savings Account.

Table A. The regulations for the management of a company limited by shares.
See LIMITED COMPANY.

Table B. The form of memorandum of association of a private company limited by shares.
See LIMITED COMPANY; MEMORANDUM OF ASSOCIATION; PRIVATE LIMITED COMPANY.

Table C. The form of memorandum of association and articles of association of a company limited by guarantee, and not having a share capital.
See ARTICLES OF ASSOCIATION; COMPANY LIMITED BY GUARANTEE; MEMORANDUM OF ASSOCIATION.

Table D. The form of memorandum of association and articles of association of a company limited by guarantee and having a share capital.
See ARTICLES OF ASSOCIATION; COMPANY LIMITED BY GUARANTEE; MEMORANDUM OF ASSOCIATION.

Table E. The form of memorandum of association and articles of association of an unlimited company having a share capital.
See ARTICLES OF ASSOCIATION; MEMORANDUM OF ASSOCIATION; UNLIMITED COMPANY.

Table F. The form of memorandum of association of a public company.
See MEMORANDUM OF ASSOCIATION; PUBLIC COMPANY.

Tangible fixed assets. Assets that have physical substance and are held for use in the production or supply of goods or services, for rental to others, or for administrative purposes on a continuing basis in the reporting entity's activities. [FRS 11 – Impairment of fixed assets and goodwill]

Tangible property. Property which may be touched and is the object of sensation, corporeal property; this kind of property is opposed to intangible rights or incorporeal property, eg patents, copyrights, advowsons, rents, etc.

Taper relief. Taper relief is potentially available for any gain subjected to capital gains tax in fiscal year 1998/99 and subsequent years (TCGA 1992, s 2A). Except for gains made by a company chargeable to corporation tax, indexation allowance is calculated up to 5 April 1998 only. Taper relief is not available on gains that attract a charge to corporation tax; companies continue to apply indexation allowance up to the date of disposal. For non-business assets, a reduction of 5% of the gain is then made for each whole year after 5 April 1998 for which the asset has been held in excess of two years. The maximum reduction available is 40%. Where the disposal is of a business asset, taper relief is applied after the first whole year following 5 April 1998 for which the asset is held. Taper relief for a gain on the disposal of a business asset removes up to 75% of the gain from the charge to tax.

Tax Acts. The term 'the Tax Acts' is defined by Interpretation Act 1978, Sch 1 as: 'the Income Tax Acts and the Corporation Tax Acts'. These two elements are in turn, defined as: 'Income Tax Acts: all enactments relating to income tax, including any provisions of the Corporation Tax Acts which relate to income tax'; and 'Corporation Tax Acts: the enactments relating to the taxation of income and chargeable gains of companies and of company distributions (including provisions relating to income tax)'.

Tax avoidance. Legitimate arrangements designed to reduce or avoid the overall burden of tax. The UK does not have a general anti-avoidance clause in the Taxes Acts. Legislation to counter what is considered to be unacceptable tax avoidance is found within the various provisions for reliefs and also in TA 1988, ss 703–787.

See POWER TO ENJOY; TAX EVASION; TRANSACTIONS IN SECURITIES.

Tax credit. The tax credit given under the UK tax legislation to the recipient of a dividend from a UK company. The credit is given to acknowledge that the income out of which the dividend has been paid has already been charged to tax, rather than because any withholding tax has been deducted at source. The tax credit may discharge or reduce the recipient's liability to tax on the dividend. Non-taxpayers may or may not be able to recover the tax credit. [FRS 16 – Current tax]

Tax evasion. An act or arrangement designed to reduce or eliminate a tax charge by means of an illegal act, such as the failure to declare taxable income. Tax evasion may be the committing of a common law offence of cheating Her Majesty the Queen and her public revenue. 'The difference between tax avoidance and tax evasion is the thickness of a prison wall' – Dennis Healey, when Chancellor of the Exchequer.

Tax Exempt Special Savings Account. A TESSA is a cash account offered by a building society or an institution authorised under the Banking Act 1987 (or a relevant European institution) where interest and any bonus credited to the account is exempt from income tax (TA 1988, s 326A(1)). No TESSA can be opened after 5 April 1999 (TA 1988, s 326A(3)). However, existing TESSAs at that date are allowed to run the full five-year term and continue to enjoy tax relief until the account matures (TA 1988, s 326A(2)).

Tax Faculty. A faculty of the Institute of Chartered Accountants in England and Wales.

Tax haven. A territory that has a low rate of tax (or does not levy tax).

Whether or not a particular territory is a tax haven depends on the perspective of the person from whom the concept is to be viewed. The UK is a tax haven, offering attractively low rates of income tax and corporation tax, when viewed from the perspective of an individual or a company in Denmark. Sometimes, a territory will be a tax haven when viewed from the perspective of a particular tax charge. Hence, Belgium, although it has high rates of taxation compared to the UK, can be viewed as a tax haven by a UK individual who is intending to sell shares and thereby trigger a high capital gain, Belgium being a country that does not, in general, levy tax on capital gains made on foreign disposals when the proceeds are not remitted to Belgium.

More generally, certain territories have deliberately established low rates of taxation and/or deliberately established a regime that does not have certain types of taxation (typically, wealth tax, succession tax or capital gains tax), in order to attract business for its professional agents from those who wish to take advantage of the tax savings that may be obtained. Such countries include: Anguilla, Aruba, Bahamas, Barbados, Bermuda, British Virgin Islands, Cayman Islands, Costa Rica, Cyprus, Gibraltar, Guernsey, Hong Kong, Isle of Man, Jamaica, Jersey, Jordan, Kuwait, Liechtenstein, Macao, Malta, Mauritius, Monaco, Nevis, Norfolk Island, Oman, Panama, San Marino, Seychelles, Singapore, St Vincent & the Grenadines, Trinidad and Tobago, Turks & Caicos Islands, United Arab Emirates, Uruguay, Virgin Islands.

Tax presence. The obligation on an employer to operate the PAYE system arises if he has a sufficient tax presence in the UK. For this purpose a non-resident company carrying on business in the UK through a branch or agency has a sufficient presence. In *Clark v Oceanic Contractors Inc [1983] STC 35*, a branch was deemed to be in the UK by what is now TCGA 1992, s 276(7).

Where an employee works for a person based in the UK but the actual employer is based overseas (and so outside the PAYE regulations) the person for whom the employee is working can be made to apply the PAYE system on behalf of the employer. The same burden falls on the person for whom the work is done where someone other than the employer makes the payment and is also outside the UK (TA 1988, s 203C).

Taxable person. A person is a taxable person while he is, or required to be, registered for the purpose of VAT (VATA 1994, s 3(1)). A person is registered when his particulars are entered in the register of taxable persons maintained by the Commissioners (VATA 1994, s 3(3)). A person required to be registered is a person who, being liable to registration, has failed to register. He becomes a taxable person on the date from which he should have been registered. It follows that a person cannot escape his duties as a taxable person merely by disregarding the duty to register.

Taxable profit or loss. For the UK, the profit or loss for the period, determined in accordance with the rules in the Tax Acts. (The Accounting Standards Board has issued an alternative definition that attempts to define the concept by reference to the different principles in force in different jurisdictions: *see* FRS 16 – Current tax.)

Taxation, law of. The law providing for and governing the state's gathering of revenue for public purposes created by Act of Parliament (as opposed to Crown revenues deriving from ancient feudal rights, etc), by imposing obligations upon persons for the payment of sums of money. Taxes are generally classified as direct or indirect; a direct tax is one which is imposed on the person who is intended to bear the burden of paying it; an indirect tax is imposed for convenience on some other person, who is expected in the course of things to pass on the cost of paying it to those who should bear its burden. Income taxes imposed on individuals or companies are examples of direct taxes, excise taxes and customs duties of indirect taxes.

Taxation of costs. The settlement by a taxing master of the amount payable by a party in respect of costs in an action or suit. By the Civil Procedure Rules 1998, this is now called the 'assessment of costs' and is carried out by a 'costs judge' or 'costs officer'.

Taxing master. An officer appointed to tax costs, now called a 'costs judge'.
See TAXATION OF COSTS.

Ten-year charge. Inheritance tax is charged at an effective rate of 6% on the value of property in a discretionary trust (called 'relevant property') in excess of the IHT nil rate band (IHTA 1984, s 64). Where, immediately before a ten-year anniversary, all or any of the property comprised in a settlement is relevant property, tax is charged on the value of that relevant property at that time. The Revenue view is that the relevant property does not include undistributable income which has not been accumulated. It is first necessary to define the ten-year anniversary. Generally this means the tenth anniversary of the date on which the settlement commenced and subsequent ten-year anniversaries (IHTA 1984, s 61). The severity of this charge is mitigated where the property, although relevant property on the anniversary, has not been so throughout the period. This may be because it was not 'relevant' or because it was not comprised in the settlement at all. The mitigation takes the form of a reduction in the rate at which the tax is to be charged (IHTA 1984, s 66(2)).

Tenancy. The holding of land. All FREEHOLD owners of land under English law are tenants, in that the theory of land ownership holds that all land is held indirectly via a superior Lord to the Crown, or of the Crown directly. A LEASEHOLDer is a tenant of a freeholder from whom his or her land is leased, who is known as the landlord. Tenancy and tenant are now generally used only of leasehold tenants, save for the terms indicating the two modes of co-ownership (of any kind of property), viz TENANCY IN COMMON and JOINT TENANCY. Though strictly speaking the freeholder's status as tenant of the Crown remains the basis of land ownership, his holding is referred to as a TENURE, not a tenancy.

Tenancy, assured. A tenancy under which a dwelling-house is let to an individual as a separate dwelling (Housing Act 1988, s 1(1)).

Tenancy, assured shorthold. An assured tenancy
(*a*) which is a fixed term tenancy granted for a term certain of not less than six months; and
(*b*) in respect of which there is no power for the landlord to determine the tenancy at any time earlier than six months from the beginning of the tenancy (Housing Act 1988, s 20(1)).

Tenancy, long. A tenancy granted for a term of years certain exceeding 21 years, whether or not subsequently extended by act of the parties or by any enactment: Rent Act 1977 (Landlord and Tenant Act 1954, s 2(4)).

Tenancy, protected. A tenancy under which a dwelling-house (which may be a house or part of a house) is let as a separate dwelling (Rent Act 1977, s 1).

Tenancy, regulated. A tenancy which is a protected tenancy or a regulated one (Rent Act 1977, s 18(1)).

Tenancy, statutory. A tenancy arising after the termination of a protected tenancy of a dwelling-house (Rent Act 1977, s 2(1)).
See TENANCY, PROTECTED.

Tenancy in common. *See* COMMON, TENANCY IN.

Tenant. (1) One who holds or possesses land or tenements by any right, whether for life, years, at will or at sufferance, custody or otherwise; all lands being considered as held of the Crown or in the past of some superior lord.
(2) Especially, a tenant under a lease from year to year, or other fixed period. *See* TENANCY.
(3) The word is sometimes used in reference to interests in pure personalty, eg of a tenant for life of a fund, etc. *See* TRUST.

Tenant for life. A person who holds an estate for life. Under the Settled Land Act 1925 a tenant is given wide and unfettered powers of dealing with land.
See ESTATE; SETTLEMENT.

Tenant for years. One who holds a tenancy for a term of years.

Tenant from year to year. A tenancy from year to year is now fixed, by general usage, to signify a tenancy determinable at half a year's notice (or in an agricultural tenancy, one year's notice) on either side, ending with the current year of the tenancy. If the tenancy commences on one of the quarterly feast days the half-year may be computed from one of such feast days to another; otherwise, the half-year must consist of 182 days (see the Agricultural Holdings Act 1986).
See QUARTER DAYS.

Tenant right. The right of a tenant on the termination of his tenancy to compensation for unexhausted improvements effected on his holding. Governed by the Agricultural Holdings Act 1986. Also used to indicate the moneys so paid.

Tenants in common. *See* COMMON, TENANCY IN.

Term. The Accounting Standards Board gives the following definition of the term of a capital instrument:
The period from the date of issue of the capital instrument to the date at which it will expire, be redeemed, or be cancelled.
If either party has the option to require the instrument to be redeemed or cancelled and, under the terms of the instrument, it is uncertain whether such an option will be exercised, the term should be taken to end on the earliest date at which the instrument would be redeemed or cancelled on exercise of such an option.
If either party has the right to extend the period of an instrument, the term should not include the period of the extension if there is a genuine commercial possibility that the period will not be extended.
[FRS 4 – Capital instruments]

Testament. The declaration of a person's last will as to that which he would have to be done after his death. Strictly speaking, a testament is a disposition of *personal* property only.

See WILL.

Testate. Having made a will.

Testator. A man who makes a will.
See WILL.

Testatrix. A woman who makes a will.
See WILL.

Testatum. The witnessing part of a deed, beginning 'Now this Deed witnesseth'.

Testimonium clause. The final clause in a deed or will, commencing 'In witness, etc'.

Thin capitalisation. Broadly, a company's operations are financed from a combination of three sources:
(i)   funds raised by issuing equity,
(ii) funds raised by loans from participators and others,
(iii) bank borrowings.

A company that has a large amount of (ii) in comparison to (i) is regarded as having 'thin capitalisation'. The tax code operated by many countries then treats the interest paid on the loan stock as if it were a dividend, the thinly capitalised company, thus, not being able to deduct for tax purposes the interest that is paid. In the UK, thin capitalisation provisions are not applied generally. However, the Revenue have announced that they will use the provisions in FA 1993, s 136 to deny relief for currency exchange losses where there is a thinly capitalised UK company in an international group.

Third party. One who is a stranger to a legal proceeding or transaction between two other persons. A third party may, by leave of the Court or a Judge, be introduced into an action by a defendant claiming an indemnity or other remedy over against him. A third party to a contract or conveyance may acquire a benefit in fact from the making of the contract or conveyance, eg where A buys dinner at a restaurant for both himself and B, who though he is fed is a third party to the contract between A and the restaurant, but third parties generally have no legal rights or obligations under conveyances or contracts.

See PRIVITY OF CONTRACT; CONTRACT LAW.

Third party insurance. A policy of insurance which insures a person in respect of any liability which may be incurred by him in respect of damage or injury to any person not a party to the policy. Such insurance is compulsory in the case of users of motor vehicles (see the Road Traffic Act 1988, Part VI).

Time apportionment. FA 1965 introduced capital gains tax with effect from 6 April 1965. The legislation operates so as to exclude from the charge to capital gains tax any part of a gain that is treated as arising before 6 April 1965. For some assets, or where the taxpayer elects, this is achieved by valuing the asset at 6 April 1965 and calculating the gain as if the taxpayer had acquired the asset at that date for its then market value (subject, of course, to rebasing to 31 March 1982). Valuation is costly, time consuming and imprecise for many types of asset; hence, FA 1965 introduced a method of excluding part of the gain by apportioning the gain on a straight line basis over the length of the period the asset had been owned.

The gain is presumed to grow evenly from the date of acquisition or 6 April 1945 whichever is the later (TCGA 1992, Sch 2, para 16(6)). However, expenditure incurred before 6 April 1945 is taken into account in computing the gain. Where expenditure is incurred after the asset is acquired (but before 6 April 1965), the gain attributable to that expenditure is treated as accruing at an even rate from the date when the expenditure was first reflected in the value of the asset, and not from the date of acquisition. The total gain is allocated between the original acquisition expenditure and the subsequent expenditure according to the amounts of each (TCGA 1992, Sch 2, para 16(4)). Each element is then time apportioned as appropriate, but gains attributable to expenditure incurred after 5 April 1965 are not adjusted. However, the gain will be divided according to the value actually attributable to each and not the costs incurred if there is no expenditure on acquisition, or if that initial expenditure was disproportionately small compared with any item of subsequent expenditure, having regard to the value of the asset immediately before that subsequent expenditure (TCGA 1992, Sch 2, para 16(5)).

Time bargain. A contract for the sale of a certain amount of stock at a certain price on a future day, the seller not in general having such stock to sell at the time of the contract, but intending to purchase it before the time appointed for the execution of the contract.

Time of supply. For VAT purposes a supply of goods or services is treated as taking place on the occurrence of one of the following events (referred to as a 'basic tax point') (VATA 1994, s 26(2), (3)):
(1) As regards goods removed on approval, sale or return or similar terms before it is known whether a supply will take place—the time when it becomes certain that the supply has taken place or (if sooner) twelve months after removal.
(2) As regards other goods—the time when they are removed or (if not removed) the time when they are made available to the recipient of the supply.
(3) As regards services—the time when the services are performed.
The general principle given above is displaced by the following specific time of supply rules:
(1) The time when the trader issues a VAT invoice in respect of the supply.
(2) The time when the trader receives a payment in respect of the supply.
(3) As regards goods removed on approval, sale or return, or similar terms, the time of supply is the invoice date.
Special and specific rules to designate the time of supply are given for:
(1) A supply of goods which involves removing the goods from the UK to another EU member state.
(2) The compulsory purchase of interests in land.
(3) Freeholds granted for an undetermined future consideration.

(4) Goods sold under reservation of title.
(5) Services supplied by barristers and advocates.
(6) Supplies of warehoused goods.
(7) Coin-operated machines.

Time the essence of the contract. Where a contract specifies a time for its completion, or something to be done towards it, then, if time is of the essence of the contract, the non-performance by either party of the act in question by the time so specified will entitle the other party to regard the contract as broken. Whether time is or is not of the essence of the contract must, in the absence of express words, be gathered from the general character of the contract and the surrounding circumstances. By the Law of Property Act 1925, s 41, stipulations in a contract as to time, or otherwise, which according to rules of equity are not deemed to be or to have become of the essence of the contract, are also construed and have effect at law in accordance with the same rules.

Timing differences. A difference between profit (or loss) shown in the financial statements of an enterprise and the profit (or loss) on which income (or corporation) tax is charged, where the difference will be reversed in the later period of account. For example, in the UK, the depreciation charged against a fixed asset in the year of acquisition is commonly less than the capital allowance given for tax purposes. However, over the total life of the asset, the depreciation charged in the accounts is equal to the tax allowance given. Hence, the difference in any one period of account is a timing difference and not a permanent difference. A charge to (or credit of) deferred tax is provided in financial statements to reconcile timing differences.

In the current accounting standard on accounting for deferred tax, which was originally issued by the Accounting Standards Board in October 1978 and revised in 1985 and 1992, deferred tax is accounting for on a partial provision basis. In this context, the SSAP defines timing differences as:
Differences between profits or losses as

computed for tax purposes and results as stated in financial statements, which arise from the inclusion of items of income and expenditure in tax computations in periods different from those in which they are included in financial statements. Timing differences originate in one period and are capable of reversal in one or more subsequent periods.

A loss for tax purposes which is available to relieve future profits from tax constitutes a timing difference.

The revaluation of an asset (including an investment in an associated or subsidiary company) will create a timing difference when it is incorporated in the balance sheet, insofar as the profit or loss that would result from realisation at the revalued amount is taxable, unless disposal of the revalued asset and of any subsequent replacement assets would not result in a tax liability, after taking account of any expected rollover relief.

The retention of earnings overseas will create a timing difference only if:

(*a*) there is an intention or obligation to remit them; and

(*b*) remittance would result in a tax liability after taking account of any related double tax relief.

[SSAP 15 – Accounting for deferred tax]

In August 1999, the Accounting Standards Board exposed for comment the draft of a new accounting standard that requires provision to be made for deferred tax on timing differences, when the resulting deferred tax can be justified as representing an asset or liability in its own right. In this context, the exposure draft defines timing differences as:

Differences between an entity's taxable profits and its results as stated in the financial statements that arise from the inclusion of gains and losses in tax assessments in periods different from those in which they are recognised in financial statements. Timing differences originate in one period and are capable of reversal in one or more subsequent periods.

Timing differences arise when, for example:

- capital allowances for fixed assets are accelerated or decelerated, ie received before or after the depreciation of the

fixed assets is charged in the profit and loss account

- pension liabilities are accrued in the financial statements but are allowed for tax purposes only when paid or contributed at a later date

- interest charges or development costs are capitalised on the balance sheet but are treated as revenue expenditure and allowed as incurred for tax purposes

- intragroup profits in stock, unrealised at group level, are reversed on consolidation

- an asset is revalued in the financial statements but the revaluation gain becomes taxable only if and when the asset is sold

- a tax loss is not relieved against past or present tax profits but can be carried forward to reduce future tax profits

- the unremitted earnings of subsidiary and associated undertakings and joint ventures are recognised in the group results but will be subject to further taxation if and when remitted to the parent undertaking.

[FRED 19 – Deferred tax]

Title. Title to lands or goods. This means:

either (1) a party's right to the enjoyment of them;

or (2) the means whereby such right has accrued, and by which it is evidenced; or, as it is defined by Blackstone, the means whereby an owner has the just possession of his property.

When one speaks of a person having a *good title* to his property, one means that the evidence of his right is cogent and conclusive, or nearly so; and when one speaks of a *bad title*, one means that the evidence is weak and insufficient. A thirty years' title is, in general, sufficient in the case of sale of land, under the Law of Property Act 1925, s 44.

See PROPERTY.

Title deeds. Deeds evidencing a person's right or title to lands. Before Land Registration, whereby title to land is recorded at HM Land Registry, title deeds provided the standard proof of title to land, and the grants of land by deed was the basic transaction in 'unregistered' conveyancing. All titles to land must be registered when the land is transferred to new holders, whether by sale or by, for example, appointment of new trustees. Hence, the number of unregistered titles progressively diminishes.

See REGISTERED LAND.

The possession of the title deeds of land yet unregistered is of importance, as the land cannot be sold without them. Thus, what is called an 'equitable mortgage' is generally effected by a deposit of title deeds. Moreover, any mortgagee who negligently allows his mortgagor to retain the title deeds, and to raise money on a second mortgage of the land by fraudulently concealing the first mortgage, will have his security postponed to that of the second mortgagee. For the present rules relating to the priority of mortgagees, see the Law of Property Act 1925, s 97 *et seq.*

Total income. Total income means the total income of that person from all sources estimated in accordance with the provisions of the Income Tax Acts (TA 1988, s 835). Some allowances are given if the taxpayer's total income is below a specified sum and the allowance scaled down by reference to the amount by which total income is above the specified sum. Examples are the age allowances, working families' tax credit and disabled person's tax credit. The following items are included in total income:

(1) Income from each source according to the rule of each Schedule (TA 1988, s 1). Sums deductible in computing income, eg allowable expenses under Schedule A, are taken into account in computing the amount of income under that Case. If the figures show a loss, the amount to be included is nil.

(2) Income subject to deduction under the PAYE scheme is included at its gross amount.

(3) Income subject to deduction at basic rate at source must be grossed up to reflect that fact; the taxpayer is then given credit for the tax withheld. Grossing up is carried out by multiplying the figure by the fraction 100/(100–TAX) where TAX is the rate of tax applicable. This applies not only to annual payments within Schedule D, Case III but also foreign dividends under s 123.

(4) Bank interest and building society interest. Lower rate tax is usually deducted at source and so added back to calculate the income.

(5) Dividends under Schedule F together with the accompanying tax credit which is now geared to the new 10% Schedule F ordinary rate (TA 1988, s 20(1)).

(6) The taxpayer's share of partnership income.

(7) Income deemed to be his under the provisions of the Act, eg under a settlement.

(8) Income to which he is entitled as beneficiary under a trust.

(9) Income of an unadministered residuary estate in which he has a life interest in possession or an absolute interest.

(10) Any income of another which must be treated as his, eg under the anti-avoidance rules.

The following items are deducted in order to compute total income:

(1) Interest other than on a qualifying loan. Such interest payments can be 'deducted from or set against' his income for that year of assessment (TA 1988, s 353).

(2) Retirement annuity premiums and contributions to approved personal pension plans are to be 'deducted from or set off against' relevant earnings (TA 1988, ss 619 & 639).

(3) Loss relief: The taxpayer may claim relief from income tax on an amount of his income equal to the loss.

(4) Annuities and annual payments still payable under deduction of tax: when s 835 permits the deduction of these items, s 348 also allows the payer to withhold basic rate tax on making the payment. Without more this would mean that a person paying tax at 40%, who makes a payment of £100 gross under a covenant, would get a deduction of £40 and also withhold £22. In order to avoid a double deduction so far as concerns basic rate, s 3 directs that £100 is subject to basic rate tax as the payer's income even though it has been deducted in computing his total

income. The scope of these payments was greatly reduced by FA 1988. A similar but less complex regime applies to payments under Gift Aid and to covenanted donations to charity.

Total recognised gains and losses. The total of all gains and losses of the reporting entity that are recognised in a period and are attributable to shareholders. [FRS 3 – Reporting financial performance]

Trade. Trade is defined statutorily as including every trade, manufacture, adventure or concern in the nature of trade (TA 1988, ss 831 & 832; see *Johnston v Heath (1970) 46 TC 463*). Judicial definitions of trade have been given reluctantly. However, in *Erichsen v Last* Brett LJ said, 'Where a person habitually does and contracts to do a thing capable of producing profit and for the purpose of producing profit, he carries on a trade or business' (*(1881) 4 TC 422 at 425*). More recently Lord Reid said in *Ransom v Higgs [1974] STC 539* that the word 'is commonly used to denote operations of a commercial character by which the trader provides to customers for reward some kind of goods or services', and in the same case Lord Wilberforce said, 'Trade normally involves the exchange of goods or services for reward . . . there must be something which the trade offers to provide by way of business. Trade moreover presupposes a customer' (*[1974] 3 All ER 949 at 955*, per Lord Reid, and per Lord Wilberforce, *at 964*). Other judges have suggested that what amounts to a commercial deal is within Case I (Lord Radcliffe in *Edwards v Bairstow and Harrison (1955) 36 TC 207 at 230*), while others again have asked what the operation is if it is not trade, to which the answer that it is investment will be sufficient if that can be established. Hence an external Name at Lloyd's does not trade at all (*Koenigsberger v Mellor [1995] STC 547, CA*). The question whether there is a trade, as defined, is one of fact. This means that it is for the Commissioners not only to determine the primary facts, such as what transactions were carried out, when, by whom and with what purpose, but also to conclude that the transaction was or was not a trade as defined (*Jones v Leeming [1930] 15 TC 333, HL*).

Trade fixtures. Those FIXTURES installed in a premises for the purposes of business, including machinery and utensils of a chattel nature, eg saltpans, vats, etc, for soap-boiling; engines for working collieries; also buildings of a temporary nature erected by the tenant for the purpose of carrying on his business.

Trade mark. By the Trade Marks Act 1994, s 1, a trade mark is defined as:

'a sign capable of being represented graphically which is capable of distinguishing goods or services of one undertaking from those of other undertakings. A trade mark may, in particular, consist of words (including personal names), designs, letters, numerals or the shape of goods or their packaging.'

By section 2(1) ibid, 'A registered trade mark is a property right obtained by the registration of the trade mark under this Act and the proprietor of a registered trade mark has the rights and remedies provided by this Act.'

In general, marks, pictures, designs, and the overall packaging and presentation of goods may be used to distinguish the goods of one trader from another, and the use of these means is in the nature of a limited monopoly, for anyone using such marks, pictures, etc in a way likely to confuse customers so as to attract custom from the original user will be liable to damages and an injunction for 'passing off' his or her goods for those of the other. Trade Marks Acts, most recently the Trade Marks Act 1994, provide a statutory regime for the registration of trade marks and mechanisms of enforcement of rights to their use. Thus a registered trade mark is a personal property right (*see* REAL AND PERSONAL PROPERTY) in the nature of a monopoly, the general effect of which is to permit the owner or 'proprietor' exclusively to use the trade mark to distinguish his or her goods or services from others in the market place.

See INTELLECTUAL PROPERTY LAW.

Trade marks, register of. A register kept under the Trade Marks Act 1994, s 63.
See TRADE MARK.

Tradeable asset. If a tradeable asset is given to an employee, the employer is, generally, obliged to apply PAYE and NIC to the gift (TA 1988, s 203F; *DTE Financial Services Ltd v Wilson [1999] STC (SCD) 121*). An asset is tradeable if it can be sold or realised on a market—whether a recognised investment exchange or the London Bullion Market or on a market to be specified in PAYE regulations. In these cases the market value is taken to be the value of the asset (TA 1988, s 203F(2)). An asset is also tradeable if 'trading arrangements' exist in relation to it when the asset is provided. These are defined as arrangements for the purpose of enabling the person to whom the asset is provided to obtain an amount similar to the expense incurred in the provision of the asset (TA 1988, s 203H(2)(a)).

Trader. One engaged in commerce. Formerly there was a distinction between traders and non-traders under the bankruptcy laws, but this distinction has been abolished.

Trading certificate. A certificate issued by the Registrar of Companies enabling a public company to commence business (see Companies Act 1985, s 117). The customary term is misleading as the certificate is required before the company commences any business (and for the company to exercise its powers to borrow money), whether or not the business is a trade. The issue of the certificate is made in return for a directors' declaration.

See PUBLIC COMPANY; WINDING-UP.

Trading in financial assets and financial liabilities. Buying, selling, issuing or holding financial assets and financial liabilities in order to take advantage of short-term changes in market prices or rates or, in the case of financial institutions and financial institution groups, in order to facilitate customer transactions. Financial assets and financial liabilities bought, sold, issued or held in order to hedge the risks associated with another transaction or position are deemed to be trading in financial assets and financial liabilities only if that other transaction or position involves such trading. [FRS 13 – Derivatives and other financial instruments]

Trading loss. The trader must have been carrying on a trade and his allowable expenses must exceed his trading receipts. In addition the trade must be carried on on a commercial basis and with a view to the realisation of profit. The trade must have been conducted on a commercial basis for the whole of the year of assessment, although there may be a change in the trade, or a change in the persons running the trade (TA 1988, s 384; *Walls v Livesey [1995] STC (SCD) 12*; *Wannell v Rothwell [1996] STC 450* and *Delian Enterprises (A partnership) v Ellis [1999] STC (SCD) 103*. See also *Ensign Tankers Leasing Ltd v Stokes [1992] STC 226, HL* and *FA and AB Ltd v Lupton [1971] 3 All ER 948, 47 TC 580*).

Transactions in securities. TA 1988, ss 703–709 provide a code whereby the Revenue is empowered to issue a notice counteracting tax advantages gained in certain prescribed circumstances. The effect of the notice is to undo the transaction but only for tax purposes. Briefly, (*a*) the tax advantage must have been obtained as a result of a transaction in securities, and (*b*) it must fall within one of the five sets of circumstances set out in TA 1988, s 704. It is, however, open to the taxpayer to show that the transaction was carried out either for bona fide commercial reasons or in the ordinary course of making or managing investments and, in either event, not with the obtaining of a tax advantage as its main or one of its main objects.

One example is *IRC v Wiggins [1979] STC 244*. A company restored and sold picture frames. A frame was bought in 1955 for £50; ten years later, the picture in the frame was found to be The Holy Family, by Poussin and valued at £130,000. Rather than simply sell the painting and distribute the profits as dividend the company first sold all its other stock to one company after which another company bought the shares of the first company for £45,000. The courts held that the £45,000 represented the value of trading stock so that paragraph (D) applied, and the £45,000 could be treated as income of those who had sold their shares.

In order to be within ss 703–709, there must be a transaction in securities within one of five specified sets of circumstances. These are:

(A) The first concerns abnormally high dividends where in connection with the distribution of profits of a company or in connection with the sale or purchase of securities followed by the purchase or sale of the same or other securities, the person in question receives an abnormal amount by way of dividend. A dividend is regarded as abnormal if (*a*) it substantially exceeds a normal return on the consideration provided paid for securities, or (*b*) it is a dividend at a fixed rate and substantially exceeds the amount which the recipient would have received if the dividend had accrued from day to day and he had been entitled only to so much of the dividend as accrued while he held the securities. This special rule applies only if he sells or acquires a right to sell those or similar securities within six months.

(B) This concerns the drop in the value of securities as a result of the dividend and that in connection with the distribution of profits of a company or in connection with the sale or purchase of securities being a sale or purchase followed by purchase or sale of the same or other securities, the person in question becomes entitled to a deduction in computing profits or gains by reason of the fall in the value of securities resulting from the payment of a dividend thereon or from any other dealing with any assets of the company.

(C) This deals with the situation whereby another person receives consideration in consequence of a transaction whereby he does not pay or bear tax on it as his income.

(D) This deals with a receipt relating to a distribution of a closely controlled company where
'in connection with the distribution of profits of a company . . . the person in question so receives as is mentioned in paragraph (C) . . . such a consideration as is therein mentioned.'
This superb piece of legislation has given courts the most difficulty. *IRC v Wiggins* is an example of paragraph (D).

(E) This paragraph was added in 1966 and applies where there are two or more paragraph (D) companies and where the taxpayer receives non-taxable consideration in the form of share capital or a security issued by a paragraph (D) company and does so 'in connection with the transfer directly or indirectly of assets' of one paragraph (D) company to another such company, and the consideration is or represents the value of assets available for distribution by such a company.

TA 1988, s 703 does not apply if the taxpayer shows that the transaction was carried out for bona fide commercial reasons, or in the ordinary course of making or managing investments, and that no transaction had as its main object or one of its main objects to enable tax advantages to be obtained. It is perhaps interesting, in view of the decision of the House of Lords in *FA and AB Ltd v Lupton [1971] 47 TC 580* to note that this defence presupposes that a transaction whose main object was the obtaining of a tax advantage could be in the ordinary course of making investments or have bona fide commercial reasons.

Transfer of share. The conveyance of a member's share to another person. The shares of a member are transferable in the manner provided by the articles (see Companies Act 1985, s 182(1)(b)). The transfer is executed by the transferor and handed to the transferee with the share certificate. The transferee executes the transfer where this is necessary and sends it to the company for registration. The company then issues a new share certificate to the transferee.
See SHARE CERTIFICATE.

Transfer of value. A transfer of value is any disposition as a result of which the value of his estate immediately after the disposition is less than it would be but for the disposition (IHTA 1984, s 3(2)).

A transfer *inter vivos* (eg a gift) will be a transfer of value unless the transfer is exempt or potentially exempt. It is necessary to divide transfers of value into those which are immediately chargeable and those which are only potentially chargeable, which the Act chooses to call potentially exempt. Chargeable transfers enter the cumulative total of transfers made by the transferors at once and, if the total goes over the nil rate band, will give a charge to tax straight away. Potentially exempt transfers by contrast do not give rise to a charge straight away and do not enter the transferor's cumulative total of transfers unless and until the donor dies within a period of seven years from the date of the transfer, whereupon they become chargeable as lifetime transfers but at death rates, with reductions if the donor dies more than three years after the gift. Most types of gift are potentially exempt transfers.

A person's death is treated as a transfer of value, being the transfer of all the property to which he was beneficially entitled immediately before his death. The transfer on death is accumulated with *inter vivos* transfers whether originally chargeable or having become chargeable by reason of the loss of their potentially exempt status made up to seven years before.

Inheritance tax is charged on a chargeable transfer, which is defined as any transfer of value made by an individual other than an exempt transfer or a potentially exempt transfer (subject to commencement dates).

If it is shown that the transfer was not intended to confer any gratuitous benefit on any person and, either it was made in a transaction at arm's length between persons not connected with each other or was such as might be expected to be made in such a transaction, statute declares the reduction in the estate not to be a transfer of value (IHTA 1984, s 10).

See CHARGEABLE TRANSFER.

Transfer pricing. TA 1988, s 770 enables the Revenue to counteract the efforts of a trader with concerns in several countries who seeks to prevent profits arising in this country through the manipulation of prices. In such circumstances the Board may direct that face market value be taken (TA 1988, s 770(1) & (2)(d)). Although s 770 is framed in terms of sale and purchases its scope is widened to cover 'with the necessary adaptations . . . the letting and hiring of property, grants and transfers of rights,

interests or licences and the giving of business facilities of whatever kind' (TA 1988, s 773(3)). This is assumed to extend to the provision of loans. FA 1996 reinforces that assumption by providing that interest which is treated as arising under s 770 falls within the 1996 regime for loan relationships (FA 1996, s 100).

The issue of transfer pricing has become highly topical. The problem arises in various contexts. In connection with the sale of goods the problems mostly concern the method by which the goods are to be priced. In some situations there will be an actual market in which identical goods are dealt in at arm's length. Where this is not so another method must be sought. Sometimes a figure which will give a profit similar to that of the other companies in the same sector may be suitable and at others the yield on the capital involved may be employed. However, both these methods make a series of assumptions which may be quite misplaced and the more usual methods are either cost plus or resale price, the latter being more correctly described as price minus. Cost plus involves taking the cost of production and adding an appropriate percentage. This involves many problems in determining cost and the appropriate mark-up. It may, however, be useful where semi-finished goods are sold or when the subsidiary is in essence a subcontractor. The resale price method begins with the price at which the goods are sold on to an independent purchaser and then reduces that price by a percentage to reflect the vendor's profit. Here there are problems about the appropriate mark-up save where the goods are sold on very quickly with little risk to the person reselling and without having been subjected to any intermediate process.

Problems also arise in connection with royalty and trade-mark licence payments, with the allocation of research and development costs and of head office and other central administration costs. There are also many problems in connection with banking enterprises. However, one of the principal current problems is the effect of a loan by one company to another within the same group but usually, although not necessarily, in different jurisdictions. This is known as the thin capitalisation problem.

Translation. The process whereby financial data denominated in one currency are expressed in terms of another currency. It includes both the expression of individual transactions in terms of another currency and the expression of a complete set of financial statements prepared in one currency in terms of another currency. [SSAP 20 – Foreign currency translation]

Transmission of share. The vesting of a member's shares in another person by operation of law, ie on the death or bankruptcy of the member. On the death of a member his shares vest in his personal representatives. On the bankruptcy of a member they vest in his trustee in bankruptcy.

Treasury. The Lords Commissioners of the Treasury, being the department of State under whose control the royal revenue is administered.

Treaty shopping. This practice consists in a resident of a state which is not a party to the convention establishing an entity within a state which is party to the treaty in order to take advantage of its provisions. An OECD report concludes that the practice is consistent with treaty law but should be countered by express provisions in the treaties themselves or by the extension of domestic anti-avoidance legislation.

Tribunal. A body appointed to adjudicate or arbitrate on a disputed question or matter, as eg lands tribunal, rent tribunal (see the Tribunals and Inquiries Act 1971).

See LANDS TRIBUNAL.

True and fair view. Following the changes made by FA 1998, the profits of a trade, profession or vocation are required to be computed 'on an accounting basis which gives a true and fair view' (FA 1998, s 42(1)). Reference in the Taxes Acts to 'receipts and expenses' are now, by statute, required to be interpreted as 'items brought into account as credits or debits' and it is specifically provided that these may not have been 'actually received or expended' (FA 1998, s 46(1)). The specific statutory reference to 'a true and fair view' imports into statute the statements of the Accounting Standards Board (ASB), which since 1970 have been published as Statements of Standard Accounting Practice (SSAPs) and are now issued under the new name of Financial Reporting Standards (FRSs). SSAP 2 sets out the four fundamental concepts of accountancy. These, to an accountant, are the building blocks of all accounts. The four concepts are:

(1) *Prudence*: The principle that revenue is not to be anticipated and is only to be included when realised fits well with the *dicta* of many judicial decisions. But the requirement that provision be made for all known costs is not a concept which is so generally welcome to the Inland Revenue and is the area that gives rise to the greatest difficulty. The prudence concept is specifically stated by Disclosure of Accounting Policies SSAP 2, para 14(b) to prevail over the accruals concept.

(2) *Consistency*: Consistent accounting policies are to be adopted from one period to the next. This does not present much of a problem, given that it is fundamental to the determination of a proper annual measure of taxable profits.

(3) *Matching*: Revenue and expenses are to be accrued and, if related, are to be matched. Furthermore, they are to be taken to the profit and loss account in the accounting period to which they relate.

(4) *Going concern*: It is assumed that an enterprise will continue to operate for the foreseeable future; thus, for example, there is no requirement to provide for closure costs unless there is an immediate expectation of such an event. This is an approach that was approved in *Owen v Southern Railways of Peru (1956) 36 TC 602* and generally does not give rise to many tax problems.

In 2000 Parliament used the concept of 'normal accounting practice' to enact anti-avoidance leglisation (TA 1998, s 43A inserted by FA 2000, s 110). Certain companies have entered into an arrangement whereby the right to future rental income has been transferred and it has been argued that the amount received is assessable as a capital gain, not rental income. Statute counters this device by requiring a company to draw up its accounts for tax purposes in accordance with 'normal accounting practice' (TA 1998, s 43A(2)). This is stated to be the accounting practice that is applicable in the United Kingdom, whether or not the company is incorporated in the UK, thus the approach of the Accounting Standards Board in distinguishing revenue from capital is given statutory effect (TA 1998, s 43A(4)). The Treasury notes to Finance Bill 2000 state that the new legislation, which inserts TA 1998, s 43A, has been drafted on the assumption that the ASB will issue a Financial Reporting Standard on the basis of the provisions in the ASB discussion paper of December 1999, 'Leases: Implementation of the New Approach'. The way that the statutory provision has been drafted has the effect that, when Finance Bill 2000 was published it gave statutory effect to the 'normal accounting practice' in FRS 5 but a statement, at any time, by ASB that FRS5 has been superseded by a new statement would automatically cause the 'normal accounting practice' required by statute to be the practice in the new statement and the practice in FRS 5 would no longer be permitted.

Trust. The most significant continuing effect of equity is the law of trusts, a legal device essentially unknown outside England and Wales, the United States, Canada, Australia and other common law jurisdictions (save for Scotland, which derives its law from Roman civil law). Under a trust, there is a division in the title to property. The legal title to the property is held by a trustee, who holds it for the benefit of the beneficiary. Thus the trustee has all the legal powers to deal with the property as full owner, but must exercise those powers for the benefit of the beneficiary, whose right that the trustee acts for his benefit alone is enforced by the law of equity. As a result, in particular in the law of property, equity recognised a kind of indirect right in property, via the holding of another, the trustee. In consequence, equitable versions of the many different legal interests one might

have in land could be created, interests which would be recognised not at law but in equity. Thus one might have equitable rights as a co-owner, have an equitable mortgage in the land, or have an equitable easement, eg an equitable right of way, all of which will be enforced by equity against the legal owner of the land. The most important distinction between a legal interest in land and an equitable interest of the same kind was the relative frailty of equitable interests. If the legal owner of the land sold it, any subsequent purchaser would be bound by any legal interests in the land, whether he or she knew about them or not. Thus a buyer of a piece of land in which another had an easement of right of way would be bound to let the easement owner pass over his land. If the easement was equitable, however, a buyer of the land who was unaware of the easement and who could not discover its existence by diligently inspecting the title deed and the land, would take free of it, and the equitable easement owner's right would be extinguished.

A legal device by which the legal owner of property is required to exercise his rights and powers over the property for the benefit of another, called a beneficiary or *cestui que trust*, who is said to have the equitable title to the property in virtue of the fact that the beneficiary's interest in the property was enforced at EQUITY, not at common law. A trust is created by *self-declaration* when a legal owner of property declares that he holds the property on trust for a beneficiary or beneficiaries, or when a legal owner of property transfers property to another to hold on trust for a beneficiary or beneficiaries. In the latter case the trust is not established, or *constituted*, until the intended trustee acquires the legal title to the trust property. The original legal owner of the property who declares the trust is called the *settlor* and the legal owner of the property who holds it on trust is called the *trustee*. Where the trustee holds the legal title to the property to the order of the beneficiary, ie must do with the property as the beneficiary directs, including transferring the legal title to the property to the beneficiary absolutely, there is a *bare trust*. A trust may also arise by operation of law, whereby the law imposes a trust on property held by a legal owner; such a trust is called a constructive trust. The trust is a unique creation of English law involving a specific combination of property and obligations. With respect to property, the beneficiary's rights are *proprietary*, that is to say they bind the trust property itself; thus if the legal title to the property is transferred to a third party in breach of trust, the beneficiary may assert his equitable title to the property against the third party legal owner, except where the third party is a BONA FIDE PURCHASER for value of a legal interest in the trust property without notice that the property was transferred in breach of trust, eg if he buys the trust property from the trustee in good faith. The beneficiary's interest under the trust is also proprietary in the sense that the fate of his interest is tied to the fate of the property in cases of loss or theft. Where the trust property is lost or stolen through no fault of the trustee, the beneficiary's interest is similarly lost. Finally, if the trustee is made bankrupt, though he has legal title to the trust property, it does not form part of his estate in bankruptcy, but remains bound by the trust. As regards obligations, the trustee has the over-arching obligation to use his legal title to the trust property for the benefit of the beneficiary in accordance with the terms of the trust. He must distribute the trust property, ie pay its income and distribute its capital, in accordance with the trust terms. (The equitable interests under a trust are often arranged so as to give one beneficiary or group of beneficiaries an interest in the income of the trust fund, who may be called the income beneficiaries, and others an interest in the capital, the capital beneficiaries.) The trustee is obliged to keep the trust accounts, ie the record of transactions with the trust property, must keep the trust property separate from his own and never mix the two, and must invest the trust property, generally to maintain the value of the trust property while ensuring a reasonable return. A trust has no separate legal personality in the way a corporate body does (*see* COMPANY LAW); in carrying out transactions with the trust property, the trustee contracts in his own name, but in so far as he does so in compliance with the terms of the trust, he is entitled to an indemnity from the trust fund for any liabilities or costs thus incurred.

In order to create a trust a settlor's declaration must meet the 'three certainties'; the intention to create the trust, eg as expressed in the words of a will, must be clear or certain; the subject matter of the trust, ie the property, must be certain, eg declaring a trust of 'the bulk of my estate' is too vague; and finally, the identity of the *objects* of the trust, ie the beneficiaries of the trust, must be ascertainable.

The trustee is a fiduciary to the beneficiaries, and so must act in his dealings with the trust property only in the best interests of the beneficiaries, and in particular, never to favour his own interests. A trustee may not place himself in a position where his own interests conflict with those of his duty to serve the beneficiaries' best interests, and in particular is not allowed any remuneration for his services not authorised by the terms of the trust, by court order, or by statute, and in particular is not entitled to retain any incidental profits or payments which may come his way in the course of administering the trust.

The court has always maintained a supervisory jurisdiction over trusts, and trustees are entitled and encouraged to apply to the court for directions or advice wherever there is doubt about the propriety of any course of conduct they propose to undertake in the conduct of the trust.

See EQUITY; DECLARATION OF TRUST; CONSTRUCTIVE TRUST; RESULTING TRUST; PURPOSE TRUST.

Trust corporation. The Public Trustee or a corporation either appointed by the court in any particular case to be a trustee or entitled by rules made under the Public Trustee Act 1906, s 4(3) to act as custodian trustee (see the Trustee Act 1925, s 68).

Trust instrument. The Settled Land Act 1925 provides that all settlements of land created *inter vivos* must be effected by two deeds, ie a vesting deed and a trust instrument, otherwise the settlement will not operate to transfer or create a legal estate (s 4(1)). The trust instrument sets out the terms of the trust on which the person who for the time being is entitled to the actual enjoyment of the land must hold the fee simple which has been transferred to him by the vesting deed (see s 4(3) and Sch 1, Form No 3).

Trustee. A person to whom an estate is conveyed, devised or bequeathed in trust for another, called the *cestui que trust* or beneficiary. As to the powers of trustees, see generally the Trustee Act 1925, the Trusts of Land and Appointment of Trustees Act 1996, and the Trustee Act 2000.

Trustee, Public. *See* PUBLIC TRUSTEE; TRUST CORPORATION.

U

UITF. Urgent issues task force (of the Accounting Standards Board).

Uberrima fides. The most perfect frankness. This is essential to the validity of certain contracts between persons bearing a particular relationship to one another, eg guardian and ward, solicitor and client, insurer and insured.

Ultra vires. Beyond their powers; a phrase applied especially to directors of companies exceeding their legal powers under the articles of association (*see* ARTICLES OF ASSOCIATION) or the Acts of Parliament by which they are governed; though it is equally applicable to excess of authority of any kind.

Underlease. A lease by a lessee for years, for a period less than the residue of the term, as opposed to an *assignment* by which the entire residue is conveyed. A lessee who grants a sublease or underlease, called an *underlessor*, still remains liable on the covenants to the lessor, but the sub-lessee is not liable to the original lessor, whereas an *assignee* is so liable. As used in the Law of Property Act 1925 the term 'underlease', unless the context otherwise requires, includes a sub-term created out of a derivative leasehold interest. See s 190(4). And see the Law of Property Act 1925, s 146(5), whereby 'underlease' includes an agreement for an underlease where the underlessee has become entitled to have his underlease granted.

Undertaking. A body corporate, a partnership or an unincorporated association carrying on a trade or business with or without a view to profit. [FRS 2 – Accounting for subsidiary undertakings]

Underwriter. (1) A person who *underwrites* or subscribes his name to a policy of insurance, thereby undertaking to indemnify the assured against the losses referred to in the policy, to the extent mentioned in it. The word is used especially with reference to Names at Lloyds.

(2) Underwriters of shares in a company are persons who, for a commission, offer to take up any shares offered to but not taken up by the public.

See INSURANCE; LLOYD'S; UNDERWRITING AGREEMENT; UNDERWRITING COMMISSION.

Underwriting agreement. An agreement under which, before a company issues shares to the public, a person undertakes, in consideration of a commission, to take up the whole or a portion of such (if any) of the offered shares as may not be subscribed for by the public (see *Re Licensed Victuallers' Mutual Trading Association, ex parte Audain (1889) 42 Ch D 1*). A similar agreement may be made for underwriting debentures. Sometimes an underwriter enters into a sub-underwriting agreement with other persons in order to relieve him of some or all of his liability in exchange for a commission.

See UNDERWRITING COMMISSION.

Underwriting commission. A commission paid to a person who agrees to take up the whole or a portion of the shares or debentures of a company offered to the public but not subscribed for by them. For a company's entitlement to pay underwriting commission, see the Companies Act 1985, s 97.

See UNDERWRITING AGREEMENT.

Unfair Contract Terms Act 1977. An Act which limits the extent to which civil liability for breach of contract or for negligence or other breach of duty can be avoided by means of contract terms and otherwise. A person cannot by reference to any contract term or to a notice given to persons generally or to particular persons exclude or restrict his liability for death or personal injury resulting from negligence (Unfair Contract Terms Act 1977, s 2(1)). In the case of other loss or damage, a person cannot so exclude or restrict his liability for negligence except in so far as the term or notice satisfies the requirement of reasonableness: ibid, s 2(2). Where one of the parties to a contract deals as consumer or on the other's standard terms of business, the other cannot by reference to any contract term:

(*a*) when himself in breach of contract, exclude or restrict any liability of his in respect of the breach; or

(*b*) claim to be entitled:

   (i) to render a contractual performance substantially different from that which was reasonably expected of him, or

   (ii) in respect of the whole or any part of his contractual obligation, to render no performance at all,

except in so far as the contract term satisfies the requirement of reasonableness: ibid, s 3(1), (2).

As to whether a contract term satisfies the requirement of reasonableness, see ibid, Sch 2.

Other sections of the Act concern the liability arising from the sale or supply of goods (ibid, ss 5–7), and varieties of exemption clauses (ibid, s 11).

Unguaranteed residual value. That portion of the residual value of the leased asset (estimated at the inception of the lease), the realisation of which by the lessor is not assured or guaranteed solely by a party related to the lessor. [SSAP 21 – Accounting for leases and hire purchase contracts]

Uniform Laws on International Sales Act 1967 gives effect to international Conventions on (*a*) the application of the Uniform Law on the International Sale of Goods; and (*b*) the application of the Uniform Law on the Formation of such contracts. Its principal provisions are (i) the sphere of application (Chapter I); (ii) general provisions (Chapter II); (iii) obligations of the seller (Chapter III); (iv) obligations of the buyer (Chapter IV); and (v) provisions common to the obligations of the seller and of the buyer (Chapter V).

Unilateral. One-sided; a word used especially of a bond or contract by which one party only is bound.

See BOND; UNILATERAL CONTRACT.

Unilateral contract. A contract in which one party's performance of the contract also constitutes his acceptance of the other party's contractual offer. For example, where a person offers a reward of ten pounds for the return of his lost dog, a finder who returns the dog both accepts the offer, and so a contract between them is formed, *and* provides his performance under the contract, by doing so. Following the finder's return of the dog, the other party is contractually bound to pay the ten pound reward.

See CONTRACT.

Unincorporated association. An unincorporated association is subject to corporation tax, not income tax, on its taxable profits. When a capital gain is made on the sale of an asset that has been held by an unincorporated association, the entire gain (after indexation allowance) is subject to tax, without the benefit of the annual exempt amounts of the members and without taper relief. This was of great significance for the sale by Worthing Rugby Club of its grounds for a housing development (see *Frampton (Trustees of the Worthing Rugby Football Club) v IRC [1987] STC 273*).

In *Conservative and Unionist Central Office v Burrell [1982] STC 317, CA*, Lawton LJ defined an unincorporated association as meaning (*a*) two or more persons bound together for one or more common purposes, not being business purposes, by mutual undertakings, (*b*) each having mutual duties and obligations, (*c*) in an organisation which had rules which identified in whom control of it and its funds rested and on what terms, and (*d*) which can be joined or left at will.

In *Re Koeppler's Will Trusts [1985] 2 All ER 869 at 874*, Slade LJ gave a shorter definition, describing an unincorporated association as an association of persons bound together by identifiable rules and having an identifiable membership.

Unit trust. (1) An entity created by a trust deed designed to manage a portfolio of listed shares, or other investments. The distinguishing feature of a unit trust is that the trust issues units which can be purchased by individual (and corporate) investors. Thus, the small investor has access to a diversified portfolio of securities managed by professional fund managers. There is now a very large number of unit trusts available, enabling an investor to choose a trust with the investment profile that he selects. Thus, a unit trust can be chosen as a vehicle for investing in a part of the world where direct investment is costly, or otherwise inappropriate. Alternatively, a unit trust can be chosen to produce a high regular income, or conversely, minimal income, but managed on the basis of investing for capital growth. Legal ownership of investments in a unit trust is in the hands of the trustees, typically, a bank trust company, who have responsibility for supervising the managers appointed to select the underlying investment. The price of a unit in a unit trust is published, usually on a daily basis and many unit trusts can be traded on the London Stock Exchange. No tax is charged to the trustees of a unit trust on capital gains made on trust investments. Instead, the individual investor is charged to capital gains tax on the difference between the price at which he sells units in the unit trust and the price he paid for the purchase. Distributions by UK unit trust are treated as dividends and taxed accordingly. Supervision of a UK unit trust is by the Department of Trade and Industry. Most unit trusts are members of the Unit Trust Association. In the US, the equivalent to a unit trust is a mutual fund.

(2) An authorised unit trust is treated, in relation to income received by the trustees, as though it were a UK resident company, and as if the units were shares in the company (TA 1988, s 468(2)). Profits consist of income less expenses of management. Capital gains are not charged to tax (TCGA 1992, s 100(1)). Authorised unit trusts are also exempt from tax under Schedule D, Case I in respect of income from certain transactions in future or option contracts (TA 1988, s 468AA). Corporation tax is charged at a rate equal to the basic rate of income tax (TA 1988, s 468E(2)).

United Kingdom. United Kingdom means Great Britain and Northern Ireland (Interpretation Act 1978, s 1) plus, for income tax and corporation tax purposes, the territorial sea of the United Kingdom and every designated area designated under Continental Shelf Act 1964, s 1(7) (TA 1988, s 830). The Isle of Man and the Channel Islands are not in the United Kingdom. However, the Isle of Man (but not the Channel Islands) and the United Kingdom are treated as a single area for the purposes of value added tax only (see Isle of Man Act 1979, s 6).

Unjust enrichment. A cause of action developed at common law and equity whereby, roughly, a person who is unjustly enriched, either by receipt of value from the plaintiff in circumstances where he or she ought to return it, or by profiting from a wrong done to the plaintiff, is required to pay over the value of that enrichment to the plaintiff. The law of unjust enrichment, also sometimes called the law of restitution, was, until recently, confused in English law by operating via the implication to the defendant of a fictional promise or contract to pay or repay the value of the enrichment to the plaintiff, and much work yet needs to be done to reorganise and clarify the precise nature and scope of the law. The implied or fictional contract theory of unjust enrichment probably owed its origin to the importation of the Roman law term *quasi ex contractu*, roughly 'as if on a contract' to delimit the cause of action; because the defendant was held to be under an obligation to pay or repay value to the plaintiff as if he had a contractual obligation to do so, it was a short step to confining the circumstances where the cause of action could operate to circumstances where a real contract might actually have been made by the parties, and for a long time this hampered the provision of a satisfactory analysis of the law, which was generally taught as an adjunct to the law of contract under the rubric 'quasi-contract'. Partly because of this, there lingered a reliance upon the old common law form of action by which claims in respect of unjust enrichment could be brought to court, the action of assumpsit, and the particular counts of that action: money had and received, money paid, *quantum meruit*, and *quantum valebat*.

Under the modern analysis of this area of law, the cases of unjust enrichment are divided into essentially two classes; (1) unjust enrichment by subtraction from the plaintiff, ie those cases in which value has flowed from the plaintiff to the defendant in circumstances where it would be unjust for the defendant to retain the benefit; and (2) unjust enrichment by wrongdoing, where a defendant profits by doing wrong to the defendant and where in justice the defendant ought to be stripped of the profit and it be transferred to the plaintiff. The modern analysis is also devoted to explaining and making precise those 'unjust factors', ie facts of the case, which justify the claim that the defendant is *unjustly* enriched. A classic example of (1) is the case where A pays his gas bill a second time, forgetting that he had already paid it. The 'unjust factor' here is the plaintiff's mistake, ie it would be unjust for the defendant to retain the value of the second payment made by mistake. A classic example of (2) is the case of the bribed fiduciary. A fiduciary is required to be loyal to and act in the best interests of his principal, and where he takes a bribe to act otherwise, the principal is entitled to bring an action against the false fiduciary for the value of the bribe, the obvious factor rendering it unjust for the fiduciary to retain the money being his breach of loyalty. Further examples of cases falling under class (1) are payments made by the plaintiff to the defendant under a void contract, and payments made to a public authority in response to a demand which is *ultra vires* the authority.

The typical remedy in these cases is clearly a restitutionary one, whereby the defendant is made to pay over the value of a gain he received but is not entitled to retain. However the modern analysis of unjust enrichment may also provide the rationale for certain other legal responses to events, for example certain cases of subrogation; eg where an insurer under an INDEMNITY policy pays his insured upon the latter's being tortiously injured, the insurer is subrogated to the insured's rights to claim compensation from his tortfeasor; if subrogation did not occur in this circumstance, the insured might be doubly compensated for his injury, and so unjustly enriched.

Where a claim for restitution of value received is made, certain defences may be available to the innocent defendant, eg the gas company in the example above if it receives payment ignorant of the fact that it represents a second payment of the same amount owing. The most general defence is the defence of change of position. Where a defendant has innocently changed his position in reliance on the propriety of his receipt of value from the defendant, it may be unjust to demand that he make restitution of the entire amount received. For example, if a person receives a mistaken overpayment of interest by his bank which he thinks was correctly paid, and spends the windfall on a world cruise, an expenditure he would not have made but for the windfall he believed belonged to him, it would be unjust to require him to repay the entire amount of the overpayment, for that would put him in a worse financial position than he would have been in had he never received the payment at all, for he would not have spent for the world cruise at his previous level of wealth.

Unlimited company. A company not having any limit on the liability of its members (see Companies Act 1985, s 1(2)(c)). An unlimited company is exempt from the requirement of filing its accounts with the Registrar of Companies.

Urgent issues task force. A committee of the Accounting Standards Board that issues guidance on what it considers to be the generally accepted accounting treatment to be applied to new issues, as they arise. The Accounting Standards Board has stated that a UITF abstract should be regarded as part of the corpus of practises that form the basis for determining what constitutes a true and fair view and should be read in conjunction with accounting standards. If financial statements make significant departures from a UITF abstract, an auditor or reporting accountant should be in a position to justify that departure, although he is not required to report on departures, as long as adequate disclosure of the accounting policy has been made in the notes to the financial statements (see ASB 'Foreword to UITF abstracts' paras 13 & 5(b), issued February 1994). The following UITF abstracts are currently in issue:

UITF abstract 4 – Presentation of long-term debtors in current assets

UITF abstract 5 – Transfers from current assets to fixed assets

UITF abstract 6 – Accounting for post-retirement benefits other than pensions

UITF abstract 7 – True and fair view override disclosures

UITF abstract 9 – Accounting for operations in hyper-inflationary economies

UITF abstract 10 – Disclosure of directors' share options

UITF abstract 11 – Capital instruments: issuer call options

UITF abstract 12 – Lessee accounting for reverse premiums and similar incentives

UITF abstract 13 – Accounting for ESOP trusts

UITF abstract 14 – Disclosure of changes in accounting policy

UITF abstract 15 – Disclosure of substantial acquisitions

UITF abstract 17 – Employee share schemes

UITF abstract 18 – Pension costs following the 1997 tax changes in respect of dividend income

UITF abstract 19 – Tax on gains and losses on foreign currency borrowings that hedge an investment in a foreign enterprise

UITF abstract 20 – Year 2000 issues: accounting and disclosures

UITF abstract 21 – Accounting issues arising from the proposed introduction of the euro

UITF abstract 22 – The acquisition of a Lloyd's business

Useful economic life. The useful economic life of an intangible asset is the period over which the entity expects to derive economic benefit from that asset. The useful economic life of purchased goodwill is the period over which the value of the underlying business acquired is expected to exceed the values of its identifiable net assets. If purchased goodwill includes intangible assets that have not been recognised separately because they cannot be measured reliably, the useful economic lives of those intangible assets will have a bearing on that of the goodwill as a whole. [FRS 10 – Goodwill and intangible assets]

V

V. Versus.

VAT. Value added tax.

V-C. Vice-Chancellor.

VCT. Venture capital trust.

Vacant possession. Where a tenant has virtually abandoned the premises which he held, eg where the tenant of a house locked it up and quitted it, the court held that the landlord should treat it as a vacant possession. The term is normally used to describe premises which are for sale or have been sold without being subject to any lease or underlease.

Valorem, ad. *See* AD VALOREM.

Valuable consideration. A consideration for a grant, contract or other act which the law deems an equivalent for it, must consist of money or money's worth. A court will not, in general, enter into the question of the *adequacy* of a consideration which is *bona fide* intended as an equivalent. For the purposes of the Law of Property Act 1925 'valuable consideration' includes marriage, but does not include a nominal consideration in money. See s 205(1)(xxi).
See CONSIDERATION.

Value Added Tax. VAT is a broadly based tax on goods and services. Value added tax is charged on three classes of transaction that are specified separately in the legislation:
(a) Supplies of goods and services in the UK.
(b) The acquisition in the UK of goods and services from another EC member state.
(c) The importation into the UK of goods and services from a country which is not an EC member state.
VAT is charged on taxable supplies of goods and services made in the course of furtherance of business by traders known as 'taxable persons'. The VAT chargeable on taxable acquisitions is collected from the persons who acquire the goods concerned. Taxable persons account to HM Customs and Excise for the tax due on their acquisitions. A return, and accompanying payment, is normally required for each three-month period, but a taxable person can elect for either a one-month return period or a twelve-month return period if certain conditions are satisfied. To the extent that non-taxable persons are liable to VAT on their acquisitions, they make a declaration and pay the tax chargeable direct to HM Customs and Excise.

VAT is largely removed from business costs, and thereby confined to consumer expenditure, by providing taxable persons with a credit mechanism. Subject to a number of exceptions, taxable persons are entitled to recover the VAT they incur from HM Customs and Excise. This tax is known as 'input tax' and represents:
(a) Tax chargeable on goods and services supplied to them by other taxable persons.
(b) Tax accounted for to HM Customs and Excise on goods acquired from another EC member state.
(c) Tax paid to HM Customs and Excise on goods imported from a third country.

Value in use. The present value of the future cash flows obtainable as a result of an asset's continued use, including those resulting from the ultimate disposal of the asset.
[FRS 7 – Fair values in acquisition accounting, FRS 10 – Goodwill and intangible assets & FRS 11 – Impairment of fixed assets and goodwill]

VAT invoice. Any VAT registered taxable person (which includes any person who should be registered but has failed to register) is required to issue a VAT invoice, at the request of the purchaser when making any supply (VATA 1994, Sch 11, para 2(2)). VAT regulations, SI 1995/2518, regs 13–20 specify the information to be displayed on a VAT invoice, which is as follows:

(i) Where the supply is £100 or less:
  - your name, address and VAT registration number;
  - the time of supply;
  - a description which identifies the goods or services supplied; and
  - for each VAT rate applicable, the total amount payable including VAT and the VAT rate charged, shown in sterling.

(ii) Where the supply is over £100:
  - an identifying number;
  - your name, address and VAT registration number;
  - the time of supply;
  - date of issue (if different to the time of supply);
  - your customer's name (or trading name) and address;
  - the type of supply; and
  - a description which identifies the goods or services supplied.

(iii) For each description of supply:
  - the quantity of goods or extent of the services;
  - the charge made, excluding VAT;
  - the total charge made, excluding VAT;
  - the rate of any cash discount offered;
  - each rate of VAT charged and the amount of VAT charged at each rate and shown in sterling;
  - the total amount of VAT charged, shown in sterling; and
  - type of supply.

Variance. In costing the systems for budgetary control, the difference is recorded between the actual cost incurred (such as on the production of a particular batch) and the standard (or budgeted) cost. This difference is the 'variance'. A favourable variance is where actual cost is less than standard cost; an unfavourable variance is where actual cost exceeds standard cost.

Vendor. A seller. In sales of lands the party selling is almost always spoken of as 'the vendor'; but in sales of goods he is quite as frequently spoken of as 'the seller'.

Vendor's lien. The hold which an unpaid vendor of land has over the land for the payment of the purchase-money. This lien exists against the purchaser and his heirs, and against persons claiming by a voluntary conveyance from the purchaser; also against purchasers under him, with notice that the purchase-money due from such purchaser has not been paid. Now, to remain enforceable against subsequent purchasers of land, it must be registered as a 'general equitable charge' under s 2(4)(iii) of the Land Charges Act 1972.

As to the lien of an unpaid seller of goods see the Sale of Goods Act 1979, ss 41–43.

Venture capital trust. Although the aim of the enterprise investment scheme (EIS) is to encourage individuals to subscribe for shares in unquoted trading companies, it was recognised that there would be difficulties for individuals in finding suitable unquoted companies, in evaluating the investment opportunities, and in monitoring the progress of the companies after investments had been made, and that what was needed was a form of collective investment scheme managed by professional managers. FA 1995 sought to cater for this, by creating a new form of investment trust known as a venture capital trust. An individual who subscribes for shares in a venture capital trust will be entitled to income tax relief of 20% of the amount subscribed, up to a maximum subscription of £100,000 in any year. In addition, a chargeable gain can be deferred by subscription in a venture capital trust. In other words the tax advantages of subscribing for shares in a venture capital trust are the same as those available for subscriptions under the EIS, except that the period in which the subscription is to be made expires 12 months after the gain. As for investment in the EIS, VCT shares must be retained for three years in order for the relief to be granted and not withdrawn.

A venture capital trust is an investment company which, throughout its accounting period, meets the following conditions:
(1) Its income must be derived wholly or mainly from shares or securities.
(2) Its ordinary share capital (and each class, if more than one) must be quoted on the Stock Exchange.

(3) It must not retain, for any accounting period, more than 15% of the income it derives from shares or securities.

(4) At least 70% of its investments must be represented throughout its accounting period by 'qualifying holdings' of shares or securities.

(5) At least 50% by value of those 'qualifying holdings' must be represented by 'eligible shares', that is, ordinary shares carrying no present or future preferential rights to dividends or to assets on a winding-up, and no present or future preferential right to be redeemed.

Versus. Against. Smith *versus* Jones is the action or case of Smith against Jones. Usually abbreviated to 'v'. By convention, when speaking, a case is said to be [claimant] 'and' [defendant].

Vertical integration. The linking of two or more enterprises that operate at different levels in the supply chain. Thus, a car manufacturing company may have vertical integration by acquiring car dealerships, on the one hand, and a car component manufacturer on the other hand.
Contrast: HORIZONTAL INTEGRATION.

Vest. (1) To deliver to a person the full possession of land, and so to clothe him with the legal estate in it.

(2) To become a vested interest.

Vested in interest. A phrase used to indicate a present fixed right of future enjoyment, eg reversions, vested remainders, and other future interests which do not depend on a period or uncertain event.
See REVERSION.

Vested rights. In connection with accounting for retirement benefits, these are:
(*a*) for active members, benefits to which they would unconditionally be entitled on leaving the scheme;
(*b*) for deferred pensioners, their preserved benefits;
(*c*) for pensioners, pensions to which they are entitled.
Vested rights include where appropriate

the related benefits for spouses or other dependants.
[FRED 20 – Retirement benefits]

Vesting assent. In relation to settled land, the instrument whereby a personal representative, after the death of a tenant for life or statutory owner, or the survivor of two or more tenants for life or statutory owners, vests settled land in a person entitled as tenant for life or statutory owner (see the Settled Land Act 1925, s 117).
See SETTLED LAND.

Vesting declaration. A declaration made by the appointor in a deed of appointment of new trustees to the effect that the trust property is to vest in the persons who become or are the trustees. If the deed of appointment contains such a vesting declaration, the deed operates, without any conveyance or assignment, to vest in the persons named, as joint tenants and for the purposes of the trust, the estate, interest or right to which the declaration relates (see the Trustee Act 1925, s 40).
See JOINT TENANCY.

Vesting deed. All settlements of land created *inter vivos* must be effected by two different deeds, namely, a vesting deed and a trust instrument (*see* TRUST INSTRUMENT) (see the Settled Land Act 1925, s 4). The function of the vesting deed is to vest the legal fee simple in the person who for the time being is to have the actual enjoyment of the land, or, if he is a minor or otherwise incapable, then to vest it in some other person who is called a 'statutory owner'. For the contents of the vesting deed, see the Settled Land Act 1925, s 5 and for specimen forms, see ibid, Sch 1, Forms Nos 1 and 2.

Vesting order. An order of the Chancery Division of the High Court, vesting the legal estate in property (generally land) in any person specified in the order. This can be done, eg, under the Trustee Acts, when the trustees appointed are unwilling or unable to act in the execution of the trusts; or when for any reason it is desirable to appoint new trustees, and it is found impracticable or inconvenient to procure a conveyance to them in the ordinary way.

Vienna Convention. The Vienna Convention on the Law of Treaties 1969 requires that a tax treaty be interpreted in good faith in accordance with the ordinary meaning to be given to the terms of the treaty in their context and in the light of their object and purpose. In *Sportsman v IRC [1998] STC (SCD) 289*, the Special Commissioners have invoked the Vienna Convention concept of 'good faith', giving it its ordinary meaning and purpose and thus have held that the purpose of the treaty was not only to prevent double taxation but also to prevent illegitimate tax evasion. This was concluded despite the absence of the second phrase from the list of statutory purposes in TA 1988, s 788(3). They then held that the treaty should not be interpreted so as to allow a taxpayer to pay no tax in either country and so concluded that the taxpayer was not entitled to credit for tax which had not been paid in the other country; the taxpayer had argued that credit relief should be given on the basis that the tax was payable in the foreign country.

View to resale. If a company acquires a subsidiary with the intention of reselling the subsidiary within approximately one year of the date of acquisition, Financial Reporting Standard 2 – Accounting for subsidiary undertakings permits the consolidated financial statements of the group to be drawn up without consolidating the results of the subsidiary that is held with a view to resale. In order to qualify for this exclusion, the subsidiary should not previously have been consolidated in the accounts of the group and a purchaser for the subsidiary company should have been identified or is being actively sought.

Vocation. A vocation is analogous to a calling, a word of great signification meaning the way in which a man passes his life (per Denman J in *Partridge v Mallandaine (1886), 2 TC 179 at 180*). A dramatist (*Billam v Griffith (1941) 23 TC 757*), a racing tipster (*Graham v Arnott (1941) 24 TC 157*) and a jockey (*Wing v O'Connell [1927] IR 84*) have all been held to be carrying on a vocation but not a perennial gambler (*Graham v Green (1925) 9 TC 309*) nor a film producer (*Asher v London Film Productions Ltd [1944] 1 All ER 77*).

Void and voidable. A transaction is said to be *void* when it is a mere nullity and incapable of confirmation; whereas a *voidable* transaction is one which may be either avoided or confirmed by a matter arising *ex post facto*.

Thus, a transaction may be avoided on the ground of undue influence or fraudulent misrepresentation.

Voluntary arrangement. Under Insolvency Act 1986, s 1, the directors of a company that is, or is likely to become, insolvent, may make a proposal to the creditors of the company for a scheme of arrangement of its affairs, that would typically include an undertaking to pay a specified proportion of each debt on a specified timetable. Such a scheme of arrangement is referred to as a 'voluntary arrangement'. The company appoints a liquidator or administrator, who is then required to summon a meeting of the company and its creditors to consider the proposal for the voluntary arrangement (s 3). The chairman of the meeting is then obliged to report the result of the meeting to the court (s 4(5)). Any voluntary arrangement that is approved at such a meeting and reported to the court then binds every person who had been entitled to vote at the meeting (whether or not he was present) (s 5(2)(b)). If a winding-up had commenced, the court normally issues an order to stay the winding-up proceedings (or discharge any administration order) so that the voluntary arrangement can be implemented (s 5(3)).

Voluntary conveyance. A conveyance not founded on a valuable consideration. The Law of Property Act 1925, s 173 provides that every voluntary disposition of land made with intent to defraud a subsequent purchaser is void at the instance of that purchaser.

See VALUABLE CONSIDERATION.

Voluntary liquidation. *See* VOLUNTARY WINDING-UP.

Voluntary settlement. A settlement made without valuable consideration.

See SETTLEMENT; VALUABLE CONSIDERATION.

Voluntary winding-up. A winding-up in which a company and its members and creditors are left to settle their affairs without coming to the court.

A voluntary winding-up begins with the passing of a resolution that the company should be wound up.

Vote. The right of a shareholder in a company to express his decision for or against a proposed resolution. In so far as the articles of the company do not make other provision, in the case of a company originally having a share capital, every member has one vote in respect of each share or each £10 of stock held by him, and in any other case, every member shall have one vote (see the Companies Act 1985, s 370(1), (6)). Voting may be by a show of hands or on a poll.

Voting rights in an undertaking. Rights conferred on shareholders in respect of their shares or, in the case of an undertaking not having a share capital, on members, to vote at general meetings of the undertaking on all, or substantially all, matters. Schedule 10A deals with the attribution of voting rights in certain circumstances. [FRS 2 – Accounting for subsidiary undertakings]

W

Wages. Any money or salary paid or payable to any clerk or servant, labourer or workman. When an employer becomes bankrupt, a clerk or servant is entitled to be paid any sum owing to him, limited to a certain amount, in priority to the general creditors; and any labourer or workman is entitled to be paid any sum due not exceeding four months' wages, in priority to the general creditors.

See PREFERENTIAL DEBTS.

Waiver. The abandonment of a right by one party, so that afterwards he is estopped, ie stopped, from claiming it. Thus, it is said that a party waives a claim, or waives an objection, meaning that he does not put it forward. So, a person is said to *waive a tort* when he forgoes his right of treating a wrongful act as such; which he does, when he expressly, or by implication, adopts the act of the wrongdoer. Thus, if goods have been wrongfully taken and sold, and the owner thinks fit to receive the price or part of it, he adopts the transaction, and cannot afterwards treat it as wrong.

Waiver clause. A clause in a marine insurance policy stating that measures taken by the assured or the underwriters with the object of saving, protecting or recovering the subject-matter insured are not to be considered as a waiver or acceptance of abandonment or otherwise to prejudice the rights of either party.

Warehouse. In Part VII of the Merchant Shipping Act 1894 'unless the context otherwise requires includes all warehouses, buildings and premises in which goods, when landed from ships, may be lawfully placed' (see Merchant Shipping Act 1894, s 492).

Warrant. (1) In Financial Reporting Standard 4 – Capital instruments, the Accounting Standards Board defines 'warrant' by reference to the requirement on the issuer as:

An instrument that requires the issuer to issue shares (whether contingently or not) and contains no obligation for the issuer to transfer economic benefits. [FRS 4 – Capital instruments]

(2) In Financial Reporting Standard 14 – Earnings per share, the Accounting Standards Board defines 'warrants or options' by reference to the rights of the holder as:

Financial instruments that give the holder the right to purchase or subscribe for ordinary shares. [FRS 14 – Earnings per share]

Warrantor. A person who warrants, or gives a warranty.

See WARRANTY.

Warranty. A promise or covenant offered by a bargainor, to warrant or secure the bargainee against all men in the enjoyment of anything agreed on between them. The word is used especially with reference to any promise (express or implied by law, according to the circumstances) from a vendor to a purchaser, that the thing sold is the vendor's to sell and is good and fit for use, or at least for such use as the purchaser intends to make of it.

In marine insurance an *express* warranty is an agreement expressed in the policy, whereby the assured stipulates that certain facts are or shall be true, or that certain acts shall be done relative to the risk. It may relate to an existing or past fact, or be promissory and relate to the future; and the fact or act warranted need not be material to the risk. A formal expression is not necessary to give effect to a warranty. An *implied* warranty is such as necessarily results from the nature of the contract, eg that the ship is seaworthy (see the Marine Insurance Act 1906, ss 33–41).

In the sale of goods a warranty means an agreement with reference to goods which are the subject of a contract of sale, but collateral to the main purpose of such a contract, the breach of which gives rise to a claim for damages, but not a right to reject the goods and treat the contract as repudiated (Sale of Goods Act 1979, s 60(1)).

See SALE OF GOODS, CONTRACT FOR; CONTRACT LAW.

Wasting asset. No chargeable gain accrues on the disposal of tangible moveable property or an interest in such property, which is also a wasting asset (TCGA 1992, s 45(1)). A wasting asset is defined as an asset having a predictable life of 50 years or less (TCGA 1992, s 44). Plant and machinery is always assumed to have a life of less than 50 years (TCGA 1992, s 44(1)(c)). The Revenue consider that the definition of 'machinery' includes antique clocks and watches, as well as custom made vehicles such as racing cars, commercial vehicles and locomotives etc. However, the exemption for wasting chattels does not apply to assets in respect of which capital allowances were or could have been claimed, nor to commodities dealt with on a terminal market (TCGA 1992, s 45(2)–(4)).

Wear and tear allowance. A person letting domestic property is not able to claim capital allowances on furniture, etc, unless the letting qualifies as furnished holiday letting (see CAA 2001, s 35(2)). Instead, Revenue practice is to allow a deduction of a wear and tear allowance, being calculated as 10% of the rent receivable for the letting of the dwelling-house, after deducting water rates and any payments for services (Inland Revenue Extra Statutory Concession B47). The taxpayer can choose to deduct the actual cost of renewing furniture, furnishings and chattels, but not the cost of the original items; ie the taxpayer can choose a renewals allowance.

Westminster doctrine. The doctrine emerging from the *Westminster* case is that taxpayers and Revenue are bound by the legal results which the parties have achieved—even though this may be inconvenient for the Revenue. In the words of Lord Tomlin: 'Every man is entitled if he can to arrange his affairs so that the tax attaching under the appropriate Acts is less

than it otherwise would be. If he succeeds in ordering them so as to secure that result, then, however unappreciative the Commissioners of Inland Revenue or his fellow taxpayers may be of his ingenuity, he cannot be compelled to pay an increased tax' (*IRC v Duke of Westminster (1936), 19 TC 490*).

See INTERPRETATION OF STATUTE.

Whole life insurance. A type of life insurance policy which states that the sum insured shall be payable on the death of the person whose life is insured and not merely on the attainment by him of a specified age.

Wholly and exclusively. TA 1988, s 74(1)(a) prohibits the deduction of expenses not being money 'wholly and exclusively laid . . . for the purposes of the trade'. The word 'wholly' refers to the quantum of the money expended while the word 'exclusively' refers to the motive or object accompanying it. The question whether the expenditure was incurred exclusively for business purposes is one of fact and purpose. Following *Mallalieu v Drummond [1983] STC 665, HL* it has been held that the cost of modest lunches eaten by solicitors during office meetings was not deductible (*Watkis v Ashford Sparkes & Harward [1985] STC 451*) and rent for living accommodation provided with a public house is not deductible (*McLaren v Mumford [1996] STC 1134*).

The present position thus is that (*a*) expenditure incurred solely for a business purpose is deductible, (*b*) expenditure partly for a business purpose is not deductible, and that while for (*b*) the court will ignore a purely incidental purpose, which the court calls an effect, they will not ignore a merely subordinate non-business purpose, and for both (*a*) and (*b*) the test of purpose is applied subjectively but with a dash of common sense; evidence of the uppermost purposes in a person's mind is not to exclude common sense inferences as to other but unarticulated purposes.

This approach was endorsed, but glossed, by the House of Lords in *McKnight v Sheppard [1999] STC 669*. Here the taxpayer, S, was held to be entitled to deduct legal expenses incurred by him in resisting charges for breach of professional rules. If found guilty he could have been suspended from carrying on his profession or expelled altogether. The Commissioner found that the sole purpose was the preservation of his trade and that considerations of personal reputation were effects rather than purposes.

See DUALITY; DISSECTION.

Will. The legal declaration of a person's intention which he wishes to be performed after his death. It is revocable during the testator's life.

No will made by a person under the age of 18 is valid (Wills Act 1837, s 7). No will is valid unless

(*a*) it is in writing and signed by the testator, or by some other person in his presence and by his direction; and

(*b*) it appears that the testator intended by his signature to give effect to the will; and

(*c*) the signature is made or acknowledged by the testator in the presence of two or more witnesses present at the same time; and

(*d*) each witness either

(i) attests and signs the will, or

(ii) acknowledges his signature,

in the presence of the testator (but not necessarily in the presence of any other witness) but no form of attestation is necessary: ibid, s 9.

Every will executed in the above manner is valid without any other publication: ibid, s 13.

In general, a will is revoked by the testator's marriage: ibid, s 18(1). But where it appears from a will that at the time it was made the testator was expecting to be married to a particular person and that he intended that the will should not be revoked by marriage, the will is not revoked by marriage to that person: ibid, s 18(3).

The wills of living persons may be deposited and registered at the Principal Registry of the Family Division of the High Court (Administration of Justice Act 1982, ss 23–25).

There are special provisions as to international wills, and those of servicemen.

Winding-up. There are two categories of winding-up for a company:

(*a*) A members' voluntary winding-up.

(*b*) Compulsory liquidation.

Members can resolve to wind up their company at any time.

There are seven grounds for a compulsory winding-up under Insolvency Act 1986, s 122, these are:

1. The company in general meeting has resolved by special resolution to be wound up.

2. The company, being a PLC was not issued with s 117 Trading Certificate after 12 months from registration.

3. The company was formed prior to 22 December 1980 as a public company and has not re-registered under Companies Act 1985 (Companies Consolidation (Consequential Provisions) Act 1985, s 1).

4. Company does not commence its business within a year from its incorporation or suspends its business for a whole year.

5. The number of members is reduced below two (unless the company was registered since 1982 as a single member company).

6. The company is unable to pay its debts. This can be proved in one of four ways:

   (i) A statutory demand has been issued for a debt in excess of £750 (s 123(1)(a)).

   (ii) There is an unsatisfied judgment execution (s 123(1)(b)).

   (iii) The company is unable to pay its debts as they fall due (s 123(1)(e)): the 'commercial insolvency' test.

   (iv) The value of the company's assets is less than the amount of its liabilities, taking into account its contingent or prospective liabilities (s 123(2)): the balance sheet test.

7. The court is of the opinion that it is just and equitable that the company should be wound up. Three cases illustrate this:

   (i) *Re: German Date* – substratum of company gone (ie no longer possible to carry out main object).

   (ii) *Re: Yenidje Tobacco Co* – deadlock in management.

(iii) *Ebrahimi v Westbourne Galleries* – member of quasi partnership company excluded from management.

See INSOLVENT; WRONGFUL TRADING.

Winding-up, voluntary. *See* VOLUNTARY WINDING-UP.

Winding-up order. An order by the Court bringing to an end the activities of a company.

With costs. A phrase which, when used with reference to the result of an action, means that the successful party is entitled to recover his costs from his opponent.

Withholding tax. (1) It is common for a tax system to require the payer of interest, dividends or royalties to withhold from the payment a percentage which is then paid to the taxation authority having jurisdiction over the payer. Such 'withholding tax' is then a credit against any liability the recipient may have to pay tax in the payer country. Tax treaties typically allow repayment of all or part of the withholding tax on a payment of interest, etc, from an enterprise in one party to the treaty to an individual or enterprise in the other. Where withholding tax is not fully repaid, it is usual for the recipient to be able to reduce the tax liability imposed by the country where he is resident by reference to the withholding tax suffered and not repaid. For a person in the UK, such unilateral double taxation relief is provided by TA 1988, s 788(3) where there is a tax treaty in force and by TA 1988, s 790(1) where there is no tax treaty.

(2) The Accounting Standards Board defines 'withholding tax' as: 'Tax on dividends or other income that is deducted by the payer of the income and paid to the tax authorities wholly on behalf of the recipient.'

[FRS 16 – Current tax]

Without prejudice. Words used, particularly in a letter, to indicate that the document cannot be used as evidence in a court of law. A 'without prejudice' letter is typically used in two situations:

(i) as part of a negotiation that may lead to a legally binding contract, and

(ii) to make an offer to settle a dispute without going to court.

Woodlands. (1) No CGT charge arises on the disposal of trees or saleable underwood in respect of woodlands managed by the occupier on a commercial basis and with a view to the realisation of profits (TCGA 1992, s 250). On a disposal of any woodland, such part of acquisition cost—or the disposal consideration—as is attributable to the trees and underwood is disregarded for CGT. This exclusion prevents a taxpayer from buying land, cutting the timber and then claiming a loss for the decline in value due to the felling.

(2) A special inheritance tax relief is available in respect of growing timber if certain conditions are satisfied, the person liable so elects and the value is transferred on death (IHTA 1984, s 125). Tax may be deferred until the timber is disposed of or until the value is transferred on another death. In the former case the tax becomes due on the net proceeds or value. In the latter case no IHT will ever become due in respect of the first death. It does not apply to *inter vivos* transfers, nor to land outside the UK. The relief applies to the timber and not to the land. The effect of the relief is to reduce the overall inheritance tax due on the death; however, the relief is one of postponement not exemption.

(3) Schedule B taxed the occupation of woodlands in the UK managed on a commercial basis. The charge was on the rateable value, not the profits made. Schedule B was abolished with effect from 6 April 1988. Profits from the business of running commercial woodlands is now charged to income tax as the profits of a trade, charged under Schedule D, Case I.

Work in progress. Work that, at the balance sheet date, is in course of being undertaken, usually on a long term contract. The value of work in progress in a balance sheet is to be the lower of cost (including all relevant attributable costs) and the net realisable value of that work in progress. In considering the net realisable value, the assumption is made that the contract will be continued until its completion and that the sale will take place at the price determined in the contract. Exceptionally, where it is clear that the contract cannot be completed (for example, the potential purchaser has gone into liquidation), the actual consideration that it is expected to receive for the work in progress, if any, is then taken as the value of the work in progress at the balance sheet date, unless the cost to the enterprise is lower.

Working capital. The capital of an enterprise that is used in its regular trading. Working capital consists of stock, debtors, bank balances and cash. The 'available working capital' is the foregoing less liabilities that require to be settled in the short term.

Wrongful trading. During the course of a liquidation, the liquidator may make an application to the court where he considers that the directors have engaged in wrongful trading. The circumstances required for such an application are:

(*a*) the company has gone into insolvent liquidation,

(*b*) at some time before the commencement of the winding-up of the company, that person knew or ought to have concluded that there was no reasonable prospect that the company would avoid going into insolvent liquidation, and

(*c*) that person was a director of the company at that time (Insolvency Act 1986, s 214(2)).

In considering whether a particular director 'knew or ought to have concluded', the personal skills of the individual are taken into account. Hence, if the director is a qualified accountant, a higher standard of skill is required (see Insolvency Act 1986, s 214(4)).

Where a declaration of wrongful trading is made by the court against an individual director, the declaration will state the extent of the company's debts that are due to be paid by the named director.

See INSOLVENT; WINDING-UP.

Y

Yearly interest. It is sometimes necessary to distinguish yearly or annual interest from other interest, notably in the requirement to withhold tax at source on paying yearly interest to a non-resident (see also TA 1988, ss 15, 82, 338(3)(a) & 349(2)). Yearly interest, which presumably means the same as annual interest, is not defined in the statutes. The distinction between yearly and short interest depends on the intention of the parties (*Cairns v MacDiarmid [1983] STC 178 at 181, CA*). If a banker makes a loan to a customer to be repaid at the end of three months the interest payable is not annual (*Goslings and Sharpe v Blake (1889) 2 TC 450*). If on the other hand a mortgagor executes the usual form of mortgage, under which he becomes liable at law to pay the amount borrowed at the end of six months, the interest payable is nonetheless annual (*Re Craven's Mortgage, Davies v Craven [1907] 2 Ch 448*). A technical explanation for this distinction may be that in the bank loan the contract specifies that the repayment of capital with interest is to be on a fixed day and there is no law which, without a new contract by the parties, says that interest is payable thereafter as a matter of right (per Lord Esher in *Goslings and Sharpe v Blake, at 328, 454*). A simpler explanation is commercial reality. Mortgages are not usually repaid at the end of six months. Both parties envisage that the mortgage may well last longer than 12 months and thus the loan is in the nature of an investment as opposed to a short loan on moneys presently payable but held over (per Rowlatt J in *Garston Overseers v Carlisle (1915) 6 TC 659*).

In determining whether interest is yearly, the courts have regard to substance so that a three-month loan does not carry yearly interest merely because the rate is expressed in annual terms (*Goslings and Sharpe v Blake*). A loan of no fixed term carries yearly interest even though that interest is payable half yearly, quarterly or weekly (*Re Janes' Settlement, Wasmuth v Janes [1918] 2 Ch 54*). Following the same approach, interest may be yearly even though the principal is payable after less than a year or even on demand (*Corinthian Securities Ltd v Cato (1969) 46 TC 93*). Interest may be yearly even though the amount borrowed and the rate of interest both fluctuate (*IRC v Hay (1924) 8 TC 636*). It will also be yearly if the period of the loan is expressed and intended to be one year only (*Ward v Anglo-American Oil Co Ltd (1934) 19 TC 94*).

It is hard to see why, given the above approach, interest awarded on damages should be yearly (*Jefford v Gee [1970] 2 QB 130 at 149*) or why interest payable by a purchaser on an outstanding contract (*Bebb v Bunny (1854) 1 K & J 216*) should be yearly, at least in the absence of some positive intention on the part of the vendor to treat the outstanding amount as an investment rather than a nuisance. These are, however, examples of yearly interest.

It therefore appears that interest payable on loans or other sums which are expressed or intended to last 12 months or longer is yearly interest, while interest on loans both expressed and intended to last less than 12 months is not.

Since 1 November 1998, a trader has been permitted to charge interest at a statutory rate, when payment has been delayed on certain contracts for goods or services, even where interest is not specifically provided in the contract (The Late Payment Of Commercial Debts (Interest) Act 1988). The Revenue have stated:

'. . . that it is not (the intention of the Late Payment Act) nor will it normally be its effect, to provide interest of money over a long period. Accordingly we consider that interest payable under the Act will not constitute "yearly" interest, and that no obligation therefore arises to the payer to deduct tax from the payment under s 349(2). This same view extends to interest especially provided for under the terms of a contract for goods or services, where that contract is one to which the contract would have applied but for the prior contractual right to interest.'

However, the 'loan relationships' legislation applies, so that interest should be brought into account on an accruals basis if the matter is within corporation tax (see FA 1996, s 100(2) & (4)).

Yellow Book. 'Admission of securities to listings' issued by the Council of the London Stock Exchange, setting out the regulations that are required to be followed by a company with securities listed on the London Stock Market official list.

Z

Zero rate. *See* RATE OF TAX.

Zero rated preference share. A share issued by a company (typically with a very low nominal value) where the holder does not receive a dividend but on a specified redemption date the company will redeem the share on a payment that is higher than the price on issue, the final payment being calculated to reflect the income forgone during the period in which the share has been in issue. Many investment trusts now issue 'split investments'. The investor is, thus, able to choose between the purchase of a zero rated preference share in the investment trust and the purchase of an income producing share.

Zero rated supplies. A VAT registered business charges VAT at 0% on supplies specified in VATA 1994, Sch 8 as zero rated supplies. A zero rated supply differs from an exempt supply in that the VAT attributable to it is allowable for input tax credit (VATA 1994, s 26). VATA 1994, Sch 8 lists zero rated supplies in the following groups:

- Group 1 – food
- Group 2 – sewerage services and water
- Group 3 – books etc
- Group 4 – talking books and wireless sets
- Group 5 – buildings and civil engineering works
- Group 6 – protected buildings
- Group 7 – international services
- Group 8 – transport
- Group 9 – caravans and houseboats
- Group 10 – gold
- Group 11 – bank notes
- Group 12 – drugs, medicines, aids for the handicapped, etc
- Group 13 – imports, exports, etc
- Group 14 – tax-free shops
- Group 15 – charities, etc
- Group 16 – clothing and footwear